31 Days **MAY, 1935** 135

15 WEDNESDAY (135-230)

Scottish Quarter Day

was very enchanted by the gentleness & sagesse [illegible] fellow "What I have" when she came late to bed — we had talked & talked of the Incident at Max Gate & the Rudeness to her in his grief of Mr Kennington the Sculptor — whilst was not modelled by the great lady taking her to the Gate but she had forgotten this when she finally came to bed. Got up at 6-45 & lit her fire & took the ashes & cleaned my teeth & got her tea — I sat by the fire eating my bread-and-butter. She does so love these moments & does so hate it when I sit munching my bread & butter staring at the fire without [illegible]

so she comforted me and very affectionate one

to write a Romance about Owain Glyndwr — but during [illegible]

Ten Shillings [illegible] larder [illegible] told her [illegible] After [illegible] lot of [illegible] the morning [illegible] age [illegible] lapse cause [illegible] seeing [illegible]

Rotten [illegible] about Owain Glyndwr

Kavanagh

Petrushka and the Dancer
The Diaries of John Cowper Powys
1929 – 1939

Petrushka and the Dancer

THE DIARIES OF JOHN COWPER POWYS

1929-1939

Selected and edited by Morine Krissdóttir

Carcanet Press · Manchester
St. Martin's Press · New York
Alyscamps Press · Paris

FOR SALLY

First published in Great Britain in 1995 by
Carcanet Press Limited
402-406 Corn Exchange Buildings
Manchester M4 3BY
First published in the United States of America
by St. Martin's Press
Scholarly and Reference Division
175 Fifth Avenue
New York, N.Y. 10010
Published in France by Alyscamps Press,
35 rue de l'Espérance 75013 Paris

A CIP catalogue record for this book
is available from the British Library.
Library of Congress Cataloging-in-Publication data applied for
Carcanet ISBN 1 85754 096 4
St. Martin's ISBN 0 312 12770 7
Alyscamps ISBN 1 897722 982

Carcanet Press acknowledges financial assistance
from the Arts Council of England

Set in 11/12pt Bembo by XL Publishing Services, Nairn
Printed and bound in England by SRP Ltd, Exeter

CONTENTS

ILLUSTRATIONS

after p.148

Endpapers reproduce a diary entry for 15 May 1935, transcribed on p.187.

EDITOR'S NOTE

> Let none say that inventing is harder than cutting, or telling a tale than editing a tale [...]! For these latter activities are the Devil. [4 July 1931]

Almost every book Powys wrote was returned by the publisher with instructions to reduce it to a more manageable size. Although he did not enjoy cutting and editing his works, he did so: he wanted them published.

He intended the Diary for eventual publication, but realized that it also would have to be abridged. He hoped that he and Phyllis Playter, his companion of forty years, might edit it, but they never did. Sally and Francis Powys, who inherited the Diary, asked me to edit a selection of the first eleven years – from 1929 when it began, to 1939 when the war and deaths of loved ones gave it a 'sense of ending'. The resulting volume is based directly on the original manuscripts which are in the National Library of Wales, and from the microfilm of them. My reading of the originals was continually aided by typescripts made through many years by Sally Powys, who worked devotedly at them until her death in 1993.

The editing was governed by my publisher's request that I produce a single volume, without footnotes. This meant reducing the original material to one tenth of its extent. Within these limitations, my aim has been to make the Diary accessible and readable to a wide audience; to present John Cowper Powys, the man behind the writer, with his personal habits and attitudes, his eccentricities, self-contradictions, ecstasies and woes; to distil something of his quintessence.

Some bridging material was necessary. I have preceded each year with a summary of its most important interior and exterior events. As necessary, headnotes are used for further explanations of names and events, but these are simple aids, not exhaustive annotations.

Inevitably, in order to keep within the determined limits of space, whole pages of the original have been omitted and many days reduced to a few sentences. To keep ellipses to an acceptable number, each entry begins with a capital, whether or not something precedes it in the text. Each entry ends with a full stop regardless of whether the ending corresponds with that in the original. Otherwise the ellipses follow conventional style codes. Keeping the 'stories' intelligible while often being obliged to omit the links within or between them, and giving each theme or preoccupation the same proportionate weight and importance that Powys did, has provided the greatest challenge.

Powys's spelling is careless, his punctuation uncertain, his habit of capitalizing words liberal and inconsistent. He regularly uses '&' and 'and' in the same sentence. Each page is laced with exclamation marks, underlines, double and triple underlines – a habit of his which grew over the period the selection covers. Very recently I have had access to ten notebooks in Phyllis's handwriting which are partial transcriptions of the 1929 and 1930 diaries. In them she firmly inserts conventional punctuation, eliminates all but the most essential underlining and corrects his spelling. I have been much less ruthless: occasionally I have added a punctuation mark when required for clarity and I have silently corrected spelling errors, unless I felt they were deliberate. Aside from the effects of the above considerations of size and form, the *text* of the selections is as in the original.

To ease the pain of his ulcer, Powys began in the 1930s to write his diary while lying on his back, the journal supported by a piece of board against his drawn-up knees: a position that did not make his handwriting more legible or the spacing and order of his words more comprehensible. Thus a typical entry begins with one or more sentences above the date. It then proceeds downward, slanting steeply to the right. Powys then turned the page sideways and filled the blank area occasioned by the slant. He usually ended with a semi-circle of script at the bottom left-hand corner but occasionally fitted a final sentence sideways on the far right or in the middle of the page. By 1938 a new pattern emerged: he wrote discrete bits, circled, seemingly at random on the page. Although a knowledge of the rhythms of his days and a painfully developed editorial sixth-sense of the rhythms of his mind has been helpful, the true sequence of words or thoughts in the later diaries has sometimes been impossible to determine with certainty. Sample pages from the Diary reproduced on the endpapers illustrate some of the editorial problems presented by the manuscript.

Someone has said, 'No editor can be trusted not to spoil a diary.' Out of profound respect and a long acquaintanceship with Powys's art I have tried not to 'spoil' his Diary. Inevitably much is lost when a work is cut so severely, but something is also gained: the energy, the variety, the contradictions, the patterns are heightened and brought into relief by the concentration. The attempt in these selections has been to enable the reader to recognize and understand more fully the inner life of a master story-teller, who knew the magical art of transforming reality into myth; and to have a closer sense of his presence and essence.

ACKNOWLEDGEMENTS

The editor and publisher would like to thank the Estate of the late John Cowper Powys and Laurence Pollinger Ltd for permission to use quotations from the Diary. Thanks are also due to the National Library of Wales, owner of the Diary.

Many of the photographs are from my personal collection, given to me by the late Peter Powys Grey; I am grateful to Francis Powys and his family who contributed several rare photographs.

More informally, I should like to thank Philip Wyn Davies of the National Library of Wales who facilitated my use of the original manuscripts and arranged to have the microfilms made; Mary Swan of the University of Guelph Library who was most adept at finding the source of obscure references; Neil Curry and John Bligh who gave me assistance with Powys's idiosyncratic Greek; Robyn Marsack, a most civilized and supportive editor; Francis Powys who provided so much encouragement and practical help. Sally Powys is no longer alive to be thanked but to her I dedicate this book. To Professor J. Percy Smith I owe the most: he read each of my many versions of *Petrushka and the Dancer* with an editor's stern eye and a husband's patient, generous heart.

INTRODUCTION

FRIDAY 5 JULY 1935
I have been reading aloud [...] a thrilling Russian book [...] called *Semi-Precious Stones* where the fellow keeps a show-off Diary to be read if he is arrested. [...] This Diary of mine is just such an 'Apologia' when I am arrested by Death but it is also one of those things you are proud of doing just because it is difficult to do & it has always given me thrilling pride and pleasure when the T.T. reads it. She used, in her way, once to say that it was her favourite work!

John Cowper Powys was always showing off the semi-precious stones of his many selves. His novels, his stories, his books of popular philosophy, his poetry, his autobiography – all were written to arrest the reader with his brilliant, obsessive transformations of reality into myth; to dazzle with the glinting refracted light of his word-magic, the prison walls of death. But it is his Diary which is, above all, his Apologia; the alchemist's most difficult *werk*; the magician's fairy-tale written to enchant his captive elemental.

The Diary can be read on many levels: as an unforgivingly candid serial autobiography; or as a metaphor: the transmutation of chronic pain into art. It can be read purely for its skilful technical improvisations, or for the revealing information it gives about the processes of his novel writing. Perhaps most satisfyingly, it can be read as a romance, long drawn out, sad and amusing, touching and hurtful, of two 'half-human things' who struggle to cope with and escape from 'the world-trap'.

John was a forty-eight-year old itinerant lecturer when he met Phyllis Playter, then twenty-six. As fragile as she was, both physically and emotionally, Phyllis almost immediately became the foundation of his being and, in a sense, the real subject of the Diary. From 1923 until 1930 they lived together in New York City, but he was often travelling across America on his lecture tours and he made long summer visits to his family in England.

When he was away he would write the 'T.T.' (his 'Tao'; his 'Tiny Thin'), usually every day, a detailed account of his activities and thoughts, as well as of his love and longing for her. The letters gradually assumed the shape of an informal journal; and at Phyllis's urging, in June 1929, as he sailed from New York for Southampton, he wrote his first entry in a cheap black 'Standard Diary'.

What was the compulsion that drove Powys henceforth – for thirty-three years – meticulously to translate the activities of every day into prose, when so often he lamented that he had little time to write the novels which gained him a precarious living? Some answers emerge in the form and shape of the Diary itself, in his inclusions and exclusions, and in the silences between words. Some of the reasons have to do with his personal self, others with his creative self.

He was born in 1872 and lived until 1963. The first thirty years of his life were spent within the ordered tradition of a Victorian English, upper-middle-class society. He was the eldest of eleven children born to C.F. Powys, Vicar of Montacute, and to Mary Cowper Johnson. All the Powys progeny became formidable individualists in spite of, or perhaps because of, growing up within the stability and assured conventions of that world. John went to Sherborne, then to Corpus Christi. After Cambridge he began teaching, married, and had one son. Then, in 1904, he left custom and family in England to begin a life as free-lance lecturer and writer in America. It was a rootless, restless, unconventional existence, but it suited an important element in his complex nature. The last third of his life was spent in semi-reclusion in Wales with Phyllis his 'companion', their dog 'the Old', and the doll and the toys that were their surrogate children.

These life events were curiously mirrored in his own psychological, philosophical and artistic development. Powys grew up during a period when what he called the 'eternal two ways' of viewing the world diverged as never before: the conviction that the cosmos was a pluralistic multiverse of chance challenging the acceptance of an orderly interpenetrating universe. John Cowper swung wildly, and at times despairingly, from one world view to its opposite because he was aware that his own 'dualistic intelligence' reflected this split. One aspect of his personality demanded 'the Great Round of Containment' – the underlying unity of man with nature. The other revelled in the liberating explosion of the one into 'an immense plurality of separate universes'.

For Powys, an exterior multiverse of individual consciousnesses that do not connect had as its corollary an interior multiverse of one's own fragmented selves, swept along in an ever-changing stream of sensations, perceptions, cognitions, intuitions; in a flux of half-remembered, half-forgotten experiences. The function of a writer in such a world can only be, not to make sense of it, but, in William James's words, 'to turn up the gas quickly enough to see how the darkness looks'. The subject is the darkness; the technique is to create the illusion that for a fragment of time the darkness is made palpable. Brought up in a world that sometimes made him feel 'shut up in an unescapable prison', for Powys the vision of a multiverse was 'a startling delight', but it was not enough. He longed for a *coincidentia oppositorum*, a world that was 'neither an Absolute in whose identity all difference is lost, nor a stream of "states of consciousness" which is suspended [...] in a vacuum'; he sought a world in which the 'raindrops that fall in water' make <u>both</u> 'converging circles & <u>also</u> little Martello Towers'. This desire to bridge the gap had profound implications both for his personal life and his artistic life.

For example, although he was writing in the period of Joyce, Proust and Richardson, and was fully aware of their experimentation with new techniques that attempted to convey a multiverse, a world of outer and inner flux, Powys himself chose to experiment in other ways while retaining the traditional form of the novel. Similarly he chose to write his Diary in the 'day in the life' format of Pepys and Kilvert, even though by the time he began it, writers such as Barbellion and Nin had transformed the Diary into a *journal intime*, an unstructured, non-linear exploration of inner thoughts and feelings. It was a significant and presumably deliberate decision. Powys apparently felt no need for the soliloquy format of exploration of aspects of a fragmented self: by the time he published his first novel at forty-three (he began his Diary when he was fifty-six) he had an intimate acquaintance with the lineaments of his essential self, his psyche. He <u>knew</u> that he was a multiverse of selves always threatening to explode into chaos. He also knew that chaos could provide the cutting edge of creativity. But to satisfy the 'other' of his complicated personality, the other that longed for meaning and union, he learned, painfully, to keep these many selves in a complex juxtaposition by making them figures of mythology. His novels and his Diary are essentially fairy stories in which all the polyphonic fragments have roles in a pre-ordained plot. Powys's experiment was to retain the form and implode the contents.

Perhaps the main reason for Powys's writing faithfully a page a day for thirty-three years was that the very existence of each year's Diary, its shape and its demands, was a kind of reassurance. The 'thereness' of a bound book of blank pages organized so as to demand their filling conferred some sense of order on an outer life that was often chaotic and discontinuous, and to a wildly intense inner life that rushed and flooded like a river of stones. For Powys, the traditional diary format provided a container in which the self tending to dissolution could be supported, while allowing its creativity. So the consecutiveness of the day was emphasized, even when there are many indications that no regular pattern existed: the pattern on the page becomes the pattern of the day. For example: the first entry is usually the time, to the minute, that he gets up, as if by writing down a time he is reinforcing his sense of stable self in a serial world. The second entry is a brief weather report. Then comes an account of his day: his prayers, his chores, his first walk with the dog, breakfast, a Greek lesson followed by an afternoon of writing, his second walk, tea, bed. The entry invariably ends with a terse report of the ulcer pain suffered that day. He makes of the T.T.'s painful menstrual periods a pivotal pattern: the tense approach, two days of total domestic disorder, then the return to a semblance of normality – all within the ordered cycle of the moon. Another pattern established by 1932 is the administration of his enema every third day. The unusual circumstances which necessitate the enema explode the sense of mythic pattern. The gut is erratic but the enema is regular. Readers may find his emphasis on that enema repellent and tedious, but it gives to what is beyond his control a rhythmic beat that occurs, reassuringly, every three days.

After twenty-five years of circuit lecturing, by the late 1920s Powys longed for time and isolation in order to write without interruption his projected 'four long novels'. Later he was to find the necessary seclusion in Wales, but he found it first at Phudd Bottom, a rural retreat in Columbia County, up-state New York. The Diary begins at this period and may well have served initially to mediate the transition from his free-wheeling lecturing style to the constraints imposed upon him by the very different art of novel writing. The Diary, literary but not too literary, was both a release from those constraints and a vehicle for practising literary techniques.

For Powys, the earth-worshipper, the artist's creative role was first to see – directly, intensely, with a child-like innocence of perception – and then to record, iconically on the brain and in words on a page 'never-returning Miracles'. In a sense he used the Diary to rehearse the art of remembering minutiae. He made meticulous notes of the various stages of a sunrise, the look of pebbles under water, the colour of a bud just before it opens or of a frozen beech leaf, the particular sound of a wood-pigeon.

His creation of unforgettable scenes, such as the hero's ecstasy in the buttercupped pig field in *Wolf Solent*, depended in part on his ability to interleave highly detailed descriptions of the natural world with allusive mythological imagery; to conjoin the very taste, smell, sound – the total presentness – of the outer world of nature with the dream images of an inner cosmos.

> As his eyes fixed themselves upon the green hedge opposite him, he became aware, through the small children-made gap, of the amazing gold of the meadow beyond. Why the field was full to the very brim of golden buttercups! It was literally a floating sea of liquid, shining gold!
>
> […] Back and forth he walked, while the sun, fallen almost horizontal, made what he walked upon seem unearthly. Buttercup-petals clung to his legs, clung to the sides of his stick; buttercup-dust covered his boots. The plenitude of gold that surrounded him began to invade his mind with strange, far-drawn associations. The golden ornaments, tissue upon tissue, leaf upon leaf, covering the dead in the tomb of Agamemnon, the golden pilasters of the halls of Alcinoüs, the golden shower that ravished Danaë. […] The thing became a symbol, a mystery, an initiation.

He was acutely aware also of his 'tendency to live in my own self-created world' and the recording of everyday events served as a necessary anchor to and reminder of a world 'out there', of being alive 'in time'. 'Exiles from another planet' he called himself and the T.T. There are some very amusing passages in the Diary, most of them arising from the struggles of two totally impractical, reclusive, self-absorbed people to cope with the vagaries of living in a remote rural community. It was the urban, sophisticated Phyllis who made some attempt to involve herself in the community life of church socials and Christmas festivities. Powys stayed home and recorded her going: the Diary served as a way of distancing himself from the actual, even while giving him a reassuring link with it.

Observing the present human world was for John Cowper a spectator sport, safe at one remove. The real importance of the Diary for him, psychologically and creatively, was to re-engender an absent presence. He loved Columbia County but he invariably compares it with the England of his childhood: certain winds are 'full of English memories', Phudd hill looks like Montacute hill; the river reminds him of Weymouth Bay; 'the day is a wonderful Perfect Somerset Day'. In part this was a re-creating of an alien place in the image of a place beloved, with the past purged of hurt. But it was more than incontinent nostalgia; it was more than the mere use of a Diary to record reminiscences. Powys shared with his *compères* of the psychological novel a preoccupation, amounting to an obsession, with time – Bergson's *la durée* – 'the pure present being the invisible progress of the past gnawing into the future'. The Diary is sometimes tiresomely repetitive. But often the repetitiveness is intentional: he will return again and yet again to some small event, subtly transposing it, until the reader recognizes that this present event has become, is itself, a repetition of a past event. This iterative mode may defy the 'laws' of narration, but it is the essence of the mythopoeic imagination. He constantly telescopes past time into an immediate present: the 1934 Diary records the writing of the *Autobiography* which is both a re-living of the past and a recounting of the present, even as he is making the present Phudd into the image of the past and at the same time agonizing over the future – whether to move back to England. In Powys's 'self-created world' there is no distinction between presence and absence, now and then, reality and memory.

The science of neuropsychology has now demonstrated what Powys and others have long intuited: that the individual has an almost perfect record of his every experience indelibly etched in his nervous system and that these dormant 'memory traces' can be released by unusual states of excitation or disinhibition. The release of these memories is a re-collection, a re-possession of our fragmented selves scattered over past time. Powys went much further: he believed that 'the whole planetary experience of the human race is in our separate, solitary mind.' In one of his most important books of philosophy, *In Defence of Sensuality*, he calls for the breaking down of the boundaries between the real and the imaginary, the palings between the civilized 'self' and the 'other'. He demands the development of a new kind of ego – one that rejects its narrow concern with consciousness, one that does not exclude the outside world but incorporates it, one that 'steps sideways out of the human-consciousness groove into the backward consciousness of animal-vegetable life.' He calls this ego the 'ichthyosaurus-ego' and he believes that it can touch 'inherited memories' in the lowest layers of the conscious.

It was at Phudd Bottom that he seriously began to practise this 'new psychology'. He wrote: 'In this place [...] all my past began to be *Retrouvé – Le Temps Retrouvé*!' It was not, so far as we know, the involuntary forced reminiscence of an organic disfunction, but a considered mnemonic technique. The long daily walks recorded in the Diary were taken in part to assuage a strong physiological need for fast movement. But the walks also served to expose him to sights, sounds, weather conditions, smells of the present which would trigger in his mind sudden upsurges of childhood memories – and memories that went further back still: 'As I walked Eastward I got such an ecstasy for the wind was lovely, [...] with the infinite magic of the great voyages and the Isles of the Living & the Dead.' The walks were the point of contact, the time/place where past and present, psychic reality and external reality met; that 'potential space' which simultaneously joins and separates, contains and frees, the artist's selves in those rare moments of epiphany.

> Memory seems to retain, in great hushed vases and urns, at the bottom of its being, essences that have the power of redeeming all. [...] There is a dark store of race-memories hidden there, buried beneath our own life's casual impressions. Images, scenes, subtle and indescribable feelings, are stirred up [...] as the wind blows upon our face.

The role of the visionary artist is not merely to record an individual's stream of consciousness, but to dive into this most primitive level of consciousness to touch, to retrieve, memories that are part of one great Memory. To remember with the conscious mind what was knowledge before the coming of individual consciousness is the mythological equivalent of turning up 'the gas quickly enough to see how the darkness looks'. This doubling of consciousness is the visionary artist's technique of 'remembering back'. And out of this ritual mirroring came a tremendous burst of creative energy which allowed Powys to write four major novels, an autobiography and five books of popular philosophy, all between 1929 and 1939, the eleven years covered by this selection.

The Diary performed an important role for Powys, but what does it give us, his 'silent audience'? Whatever it gives he intended: the Diary was for publication; it was written for the 'unknown reader'. It gives that reader, whether familiar or not with Powys and his family and friends, an exceptionally vivid sense of this extraordinary man's physical, mental and emotional life. For those interested in the processes of creativity the Diary is of inestimable value in allowing us to trace in detail the mysterious transformations of inner and outer life into art. Somewhat surprisingly, in an author who deliberately adopted conventional literary forms, it reveals John Cowper as a master of experimental techniques. Finally, the Diary gives us what Powys best loved to give – a fairy tale. It could be called 'Petrushka and the Dancer'.

The fascination of John Cowper Powys, for those with the courage to follow him, lies in his ability to pass through boundaries as if boundaries did not exist. For him, there was no demarkation between the outer world and the inner, no gap of desire between the self and the not-self: the flower in the garden that he examines minutely is inseparable from the internal response it arouses. He clasps 'some extremely provocative embracing trees that I call the Lesbians', and the embracing trees embraced are, at the moment of enclosure, identical with his body.

He was many selves, but each self had a curiously unbordered transparency. The masks we all learn so painfully to wear he never acknowledged. He called himself 'an ice-covered stone'. He was, rather, a 'hard crystal' which has within it, shaped by unknown forces, writhing twisting lines and fissures that, without touching, are yet related so that the interior of the quartz is a world of silver and rainbow refractions: refractions that dazzle, bewilder, often frighten, those who look into him. This crystal world that is Powys is displayed in the Diary matter-of-factly, dispassionately – his self-centredness, his sadism, his sexual fantasies, his sicknesses, his shamanistic rituals, blandly poured out for the reader. In our world of carefully created borders, this antic eccentricity, this elliptical off-centredness, is either violently rejected or passionately accepted. There can be no neutral response to Powys.

He referred to himself as a 'super-Ritualist' and a large part of his day was governed by ritualistic practices: his 'long drawn out morning head dippings combined with long winded incantations and conjurations' took up hours. His bath becomes a ceremony; the lighting of a fire, however clumsily, an act of worship. Trees are kissed, stones are bowed before and head-tapped. He writes in the *Autobiography* that his 'dominant life-illusion' was that he 'would eventually become a magician'. The 'rigmaroles' and 'magicking' as he called these rituals, were part of an arduous self-imposed discipline much like that of a Tibetan yogi or a shaman. Particularly in the period covered by these selections, his daily life was an arduous, tortured, often humiliating apprenticeship. 'The god of Phudd keeps calling me to come and tap my forehead in Penance for a heathen Ash Wednesday upon that great stone.' He refuses the god's call and in the Diary he records his punishment for his 'hubris', for not understanding that, in the pre-lapsarian state of the stone, to call is to name: to command and to recognize are one action. In a fallen world of Babel we do not recognize our names; we do not come when called. He repents and goes to the stone – and learns his name. Powys gradually realized that to become a magician was to close the gap between commanding and recognizing the 'personhood' of all things, animate and inanimate, by giving them their proper names. An important part of his ritualistic day is to perform Adam's task of naming: the Prometheus stone, the Skaian gates, the Mabinogion swamp, Ashgard hill. Each name gives the inanimate a connection and an expansion: it is not a label but an invocation: names call. And each name becomes both an acknowledgement and a command: 'this Stone of Fal [...] this stone I myself have made into a Stone of Power'.

It was through ritual, he said, that 'inspiration flowed through him'. Just as one of the essential functions of his ritualism was the fuelling of his imagination, so also he needed sickness. Powys once said that he had learned from Dostoevsky 'how weakness and disease and suffering can become organs of vision'. Whether the intense transports Powys refers to as his 'ecstasies' were similar to Dostoevsky's epileptic auras is of little significance to the reader of the Diary. What is important is that his ecstasies were portals: openings to a visionary world where memory and reality coalesced and creative dream-time began.

But there is no doubt about the effect of his ulcers: here his disease and his creativity conjoined. His gut was his dark second brain. He had suffered from duodenal ulcers and the accompanying 'dyspepsia' since boyhood. After several severe bowel operations, he tried to control them with a diet which in turn required enemas. He knew that his long walks exacerbated them. Powys used his ulcers. He used them to escape tiresome social responsibilities, he used them to give himself time and space for his writing, he used them as emotional blackmail against the T.T. He was more often than not in severe pain with them and he used that to trigger and feed his imagination. The state of his gut becomes a signal for the state of his psychic life and his creativity.

As well as revealing the sources of inspiration that fuelled his writing, the Diary is invaluable as a record of novels-in-progress. The writing of *Weymouth Sands* (1934) can be followed from 1 February 1932 when he begins the first sentence with 'my father's Quill Pen' to its completion on 1 July 1933: 'I finished my book as the last carriages – cars I mean – damn them – drove off from our Grave-yard leaving old Uzener under six feet of earth.' We learn how he sets a novel in motion; how he chooses names of people and streets; his difficulty with plot; the pressures imposed on him by poverty, by people and events interfering with the amount of time he has to write; and, not least, how actively involved Phyllis was in the writing not only of this novel, but all his writings.

Powys did not, as some writers do, use the Diary consciously as a vehicle for working out ideas for his novels. How he <u>did</u> use it is most clearly illustrated by the entries made while he was writing *A Glastonbury Romance*, one of the great neglected novels of the twentieth century. *A Glastonbury Romance* (1932) is a 'modern' version of the Grail myth of the Fisher King, who is wounded and whose infirmity reacts upon his kingdom which is stricken by drought. He is cured by a virtuous knight who is rewarded by a vision of the Grail. During his trip to England in 1929, Powys toured the Somerset countryside in preparation for the novel he had vaguely in mind. He also made a 'sentimental journey' to Norfolk with his brother, Littleton, re-visiting places associated with their childhood. The memories regained by this visit eventually provided the material for the opening scene of the *Romance*: beginnings duplicated in a beginning. More mysteriously, perhaps, while in Norfolk his thoughts about fish and fishing and a visit to a mill pond appear to coalesce and the two central informing images of the novel – the pagan waters of Cybele and the Fish of Christ – come into existence. 'Went to Harrod's Mill Pool dark and deep with enormous fish swimming in it great dace and chub & trout – a mystic sight – the pool of Cybele.' On his return voyage to America he read Rhys's *The Arthurian Legend* nine times, and the episodes and imagery sank into 'the hushed vases of his mind' to be fished out when the need arose. But what startled him was his sense that a kind of 'equivalence', a vital echo, had set itself up between his outer actions and his thoughts about the Grail. Before leaving England he had bought gifts for the T.T. Now he 'suddenly realized that the silver tray I have bought is like the dish at Carbonek and the basin [...] a microcosm or an original of the Graal itself'.

The concentrated writing of this novel took place in the summer of 1931, and by this time Powys was fully aware that a complex dialogue was going on between his body, his mind and his characters:

> I got on well with my difficult chapter [...] for I come to Tossie Staples & the second I reach Tossie – all my mind becomes easy and relaxed & my style flowed like fresh milk! It looks as if my mood for the day depended on some psychic influence emanating from the particular character in my book who then dominates. Poor Mr Evans 'twas & his tormented mind, like one in Hell, that gave me that severe dyspepsia.

Then, as the book and the characters take on a life of their own, he becomes conscious that a synchronic correspondence which goes far beyond chance or mere simultaneity is operating between external events and his creative self. Further, he seems driven to tread out physically the pattern of the dance of the imagination. The Diary entries for this period are particularly vivid, so much so that the reader feels he too is forced to participate in a dramatic ceremony that is – beyond reason – necessary.

Powys began what became an obsessive ritual during this drought-stricken summer: transferring fish from shallow ponds to deep pools – an expiating reversal of his childhood mania for killing tadpoles by taking them from ponds to drying puddles. His ulcer flares up and he has a terrible struggle with constipation and an enema that doesn't work: 'Was it not odd that for the last few days in my book I have been writing of an enema & today this happened to me.' Then, as if freed mentally as well as physically of 'a cannon-ball stuck in my arse' he writes eagerly the scene where Sam, the Grail Knight, has a vision of the mystic fish, the Tench. 'My chapter is rushing along. It is writing me. I am not writing it.' He reads the chapter to the T.T. and when she says she does not like it, he begins revising it, all the while in great pain from his ulcer and exhausted by his efforts to save dying fish.

26 SEPTEMBER: After breakfast I rescued a lot of fish. [...] It was a curious coincidence that while I was at this job out of doors, on my couch I was writing about Ichthus the World-Fish.

29 SEPTEMBER: I caught the biggest Trout I have ever seen in this river & carried it to that deep pool. [...] Here it breathed. [...] O but my exhaustion and the feeling of my ulcer but <u>not</u> pain.

30 SEPTEMBER: I have finished my chapter. [...] And it is strange that this fish-catching should answer so well to Sam's vision of the <u>Sangreal</u>.

4 OCTOBER: She [...] wouldn't let me go to the fish till after breakfast. But about eleven I went to them & caught a lot & saw a very strange unforgettable sight. [...] I saw four fish in procession cross a strip of dry land from under the rock into the pool.

6 OCTOBER: I am writing very vast I mean fast and very happily. O it is such a relief to escape from Sam and the Grail! [...] I feel much less tired today in mind & body.

Perhaps for every great artist the creative act is both a sickness and a healing. Characteristically Powys does not distinguish between physical and psychic illness; between the curative power of creativity and the little white powders a Jungian friend supplies him with. There are no boundaries. He wrote: 'My Glastonbury Book is the expression of my natural & Normal life at Phudd Bottom.' In a curious and profound way, it was.

Powys said that the Diary was 'one of those things you are proud of doing just because it is difficult to do'. The techniques he employs in the Diary are more deliberate and complex than its seeming artlessness and haphazardness at first suggest. Even as one part of Powys plunged delightedly into chaos, anarchy, discontinuity, another part was imposing mythological patterns. He celebrates the disseminating formlessness of a flood, but, perhaps despite himself, his mind invariably relates it to some larger Flood which makes the barren soil fertile again. For example, in July 1933, after another long drought, the rain pours down on the wedding day of their young neighbour, Albert Krick. He writes an epithalamium: 'How their espousals are making it rain! [...] Just like the Terre-Gastee flooded when Sir Galahad sees the Grail.'

The apparent randomness of the Diary is one effect of the fluidity of a well-stocked mind, sometimes combined with his sense of fun. In the following passage, water reminds him of semen which suggests sea-men (Sisyphus was associated with river gods and with the marine divinity Melicertes, who is often represented as a child carried to shore by a dolphin), and from there his mind runs to pregnancy and then to the proverb of rats heading to shore after deserting a sinking ship. 'A terrific rush of water in the river – the Semen of Sisyphus. I saw another rat – very fat – maybe a pregnant mother [...]. We are in danger of being over-run. Well! it certainly shows this is not a Sinking Ship!'

Just as Powys employed a traditional format for his novels then let apparent formlessness reign, so he intentionally adopted a conventional mould for his Diary within which the sentence structure and pattern of thought in the entries appear to parallel this free fall into anarchy. In a fairly representative entry (8 October 1931), the stream of his thoughts flows from 'the most intense wicked pleasure perhaps that I have ever had because of the T.T.' to noting that the name of a plant Tear Thumb means 'not a crying tear but a rending Teat [sic]' to observing that the black and white bull 'I have always been so doubtful about' gets angry with 'the lesbian endeavours of several among the cows,' to remembering how he once was aroused watching a bull on Lodmoor, to wondering if wearing a black tie on his birthday is defying 'Fote', to speculating that a guardian angel 'changed the "a" to an "o" in order to save me from death,' to reading 'how eventually [Odysseus] shall die far from the sea'. Beneath the amorphous associations, the shifts, the slips, and the leaps, there is always in Powys an inner order that follows its own laws. This reverie on sexuality, homesickness and death, interwoven as it is with present events, past memories and mythic allusions, makes rigorous demands on a reader. Often the language of the Diary is as highly mannered and technically elaborate as skaldic verse. Some entries resemble kennings with a plurality of meanings: mythic shorthand, ambiguous but never irreconcilable. For a magician, words reverberate because they have their source and resource in the 'dark store of race-memories.' What he fished out of 'the deep vases' hardly mattered. Writing was poetic power: it was his formulation, *essomenoisin* (in later times), that gave the potential word-event reality and completion.

Once we have caught the drift of his mind, it is endlessly fascinating to trace the pattern of its swirls and eddies, then its free-flowing tide of association. For example, during the difficult spring of 1934, when he and Phyllis are trying to decide whether to leave America and move to England, they read aloud to each other Dickens's *Dombey and Son*. The ever-weeping Florence Dombey who has fled her home, and the kind Captain Carker's strangely sadistic refrain: 'He's drownded ain't he?' were likely the triggers for the following passage which condenses into one vibrant sustained metaphor their deep ambivalences toward this new life.

> She came to see where I was & when she beheld me so quietly seated on the porch she burst into a flood of passionate tears. Poor little T.T. she was piteously upset again and cried & cried. She leaned against the open china-cupboard with big tears streaming down her face & pitiful words issuing from the barrier of her teeth – a barrier that these days is like a dam that is drawn up! I much prefer her to be very angry & to scold than to cry like this. Is it not strange – that I the suppressed Sadist – feel so very sorry for this sad little Abject when her whole slight being melts as if it would melt away in these flowing tears. The snow melts these waters are released and the tears of this Elemental are released I shall never forget these wild disturbed days.

The words flood over us, almost drowning the reader in a sea of imagery, associations, impressions, information, emotions. But do we know much more about John Cowper Powys when we are tossed back onto the shore? His *Autobiography*, devastating as it is in its frankness and self-analysis, leaves out as much as it includes. While the Diary solves many minor and several major mysteries, in other ways it is maddeningly disappointing as a casebook for future biographers, particularly those of the minutiae school. A theme is taken up, then as suddenly dropped, a reference to a crucial family or personal event glanced at obliquely. We learn only a little about historical events or the social fabric of up-state New York or of rural Dorset or Wales in the 1930s. But the Diary does shed light on his complex relationship with his brothers and sisters, his reasons for moving from America to Dorset and then Wales, his precarious finances, his daily habits, what he reads, his friends, his physical health. And by the mid–1930s, it becomes increasingly more candid as John begins to unveil the darker terrors that fuel his creativity.

The Diary tells us as much about Phyllis – or rather, the T.T. –

as it does about John. She appears on every page, connected with every aspect of his day, his thoughts, his pain, his writing. Both in style and content, his portrait of her is one of the most complex characterizations in modern literature. As he obsessively discusses the T.T. – her mood-swings, her genius with gardens, her hysterics, her total inability to cope with running a house, her painful menstrual periods, her acute critical sense, her rages, her love of music and theatre, her child-likeness and thinness, her tantalizing sexual attractiveness to him – different slants of light fall on her and on their relationship. The Diary reveals their total incompatibility – his love of nature, walking, early risings, the cold; her love of cities, warmth, staying up late, music, theatre – which made their life together difficult and often intensely unhappy. Yet they were quite literally necessary to each other. In one of his first love letters to her, on 24 March 1921, he wrote: 'We are both weak, both half-mad, both enslaved by strange imaginations – but if we put our consciousness together and whatever in us takes the place of common human hearts we shall be living a sort of double life and that surely will make us strong enough to endure our lives.' Doubling: this is the vision of union – the see-er and the seen become one.

Phyllis was for him very literally the T.T., the Tao, the Tao – both the way to the Centre of his creative imagination, and the Centre Itself. One of the most important revelations to come out of the reading of the Diary is the force of John Cowper's determination to become a great story writer. This determination he connected with his desire to be a magician: through language he would become the see-er, the seer. He knew that to do this, he must learn how to pass through interpenetrating worlds, to use a source of power to break through into another realm, the 'realm of the Mothers'. To achieve this goal the magician Merlin had Nimue. Powys had Phyllis.

Powys called himself and the T.T. 'the Terminals'. The conductor between the two polarities that were Jack and Phyllis was their sexual attraction. It was as if, with sexuality acting as a 'conductor,' they formed a closed circuit of energy. Powys knew that if he could harness and control this current, it would give him the power to 'break through' to some new dimension. And, inevitably for the word-smith, to transform this power into a flow of language. As Powys puts it: 'One of my greatest thrills nearly equal to making love to her (& it is making love to her) is reading to her a new chapter.' To be a Merlin is to be entranced – given entrance into the Otherworld – by Nimue, the feminine Self, the Elemental 'Other'. This was the role John assigned Phyllis, the moment he met her: 'It is a kind of white magic you have thrown over me.'

But the Diary is a fairy-story, and like all masterly tales, it has many levels. Phyllis called Powys 'Petrushka' – her 'Inanimate Doll'. Stravinsky's ballet *Petrushka* is referred to specifically only three times, but the motif of the half-doll half-human grotesque is taken up by Powys and played upon endlessly in the Diary. This piece of dramatic theatre, which sets out to confuse the boundaries between dream and reality, has a simple enough plot. In the midst of a Russian square filled with people enjoying the Lenten Fair, stands a puppet booth. Suddenly the Showman-Magician flings open the curtains of the booth and in a *tour de passe-passe* charms into life his three puppets – Petrushka, the Ballerina and the Moor. Petrushka (always choreographed '*en dedans*' – turned in) struggles unsuccessfully against the expansive, extroverted Moor for the love of the beautiful Dancer. In the last scene the Moor kills Petrushka and he and the Dancer run off. The Magician reassures the crowd that the dead Petrushka is just a doll by shaking some stuffing out of him. The ballet ends with a macabre shriek as Petrushka appears as a tortured ghost over the top of the puppet booth in the now-deserted square.

In one of the most moving of the four scenes Petrushka is kicked into a cell by the Showman-Magician and cannot find his way out. Suddenly, through the door that he cannot find, comes the Ballerina. Intoxicated by love for her, and alternating between outbursts of joy and frenzied despair, he tries to impress her with a series of magnificent leaps. But the Ballerina says not a word. When she leaves, Petrushka keeps running at the prison wall until he partly breaks through one of the panels.

Much of Powys's Diary is a succession of 'show-off' leaps by 'Petrushka' to captivate this 'dancer' who can pass through the door he cannot find. The T.T. was his 'way to the centre', but she remained as elusive as the ballerina. There is only one way out of this impasse. In Powys's late novel *Porius*, the magician points out that there is a real *Annwn* – the Otherworld – and another made of sedge and sea-weed by enchantment. And that the trick, when you are a prisoner bound in heavy chains, is to pretend you are only in the *Annwn* of Illusion.

In the ballet *Petrushka* it is the elusive Dancer who flees into the life of the crowd; it is the 'man-doll' who cannot find his way out of his cell and is finally 'arrested by death'. But in an enchantment of reversal, a denial by reversal, the *Diary* becomes a fairy story written by a magician to entrance an elemental: it is Merlin who ensnares Nimue; it is Petrushka who captures the Dancer. 'I like it when the T.T. talks of being a Dancer. [...] Have I caught this lovely Elemental?'

Phyllis would likely have committed suicide had they not met. Powys took her 'out of the world trap' and put her instead in the Centre of the maze that was his imagination. Illusory or real, it was an *Annwn* she could not escape. Petrushka became the Showman-Magician and the Dancer became the Ghost.

> 5 NOVEMBER 1939: Betty arrived with those wonderful pictures of Petrushka like Paracelsus calling up a ghostly T.T. his Undine. [...] Oh oh oh I am so pleased to have this picture of the funny 'Terminals' – Petrushka & the Dancer!

What is real and what is illusion in this Diary the reader must decide. It is not always pleasant reading, but it is indeed an 'Apologia' and a masterpiece.

1929

The diaries of John Cowper Powys begin 1 June 1929, when he sails from New York for his customary summer visit to his many relatives and friends in England. John is fifty-six and at the height of his lecturing career in America. He has written five novels as well as articles, reviews, poetry, books of philosophy. His latest novel, Wolf Solent, *is selling well, and he has begun reading for and thinking about his next,* A Glastonbury Romance.

The first months of the 1929 Diary resemble the opening of one of his stories: we are introduced in rapid succession to his wife and son; to his sisters and his brothers; their wives, mistresses, husbands, children; to his friends; and to the 'indescribable intrigues and cross-currents of all these conflicting personalities'. In 1929 the father and mother of this 'Powys clan' are dead, but their influence is pervasive still. Omnipresent, too, are the childhood memories: the vicarage home at Montacute, the schooling at Sherborne, the holidays at Weymouth and Northwold.

Powys travels extensively this summer and we get a strong sense of the way in which every person, every experience, every landscape – past and present – is grist to Powys's creative mill. Much of what he does, thinks, reads, in these months is eventually transposed to 'the modern grail legend' A Glastonbury Romance.

At the end of August he returns to New York, where he lives with his companion, Phyllis Playter. He immediately resumes his onerous lecture tours but poor health and a desire to have the time and solitude to write 'long novels' evoke thoughts of retiring. By 1929 he has been on the lecture circuit – first in England and in Europe, then after 1905 in America – for more than thirty years. Weary, and plagued by his 'old enemy', a duodenal ulcer, John attempts to break his contract with his lecture agent, Lee Keedick. In September he and Phyllis spend a month in a farm cottage in the rural community of Hillsdale – 'up-state' some hundred miles north of New York City. John would like to live there permanently, but

Phyllis is dubious: the well-educated only daughter of a lawyer-entrepreneur, she delights in the cultural and intellectual amenities of big cities.

The remainder of the year is spent writing a book of popular philosophy and lecturing. In December a well-publicized debate is held with Bertrand Russell on 'modern marriage'. The private debate with Phyllis – whether to live in Hillsdale or in New York City – is, for Powys, of much more significance.

SATURDAY 1 JUNE New York seen from the boat at one (a.m.) was interesting – the buildings floating in air & in water with intermittent lights some preternaturally high up in the air. There was not one single hooting from the ship that I could hear but I saw the familiar search-light cross the Great Bear just as it does at the back door over the 3 ailanthus trees and it was queer to see the lights of the Battery at that hour.

THURSDAY 6 JUNE Five French Trawlers were visible this morning & as soon as I woke up still 200 miles from shore I noted that the sea had the peculiar smell of water that is near land – not exactly our smell of land, but of the sea near land.

John goes first to Folkestone, Kent, to visit his son Littleton (L.A.P.) an Anglican priest, and his wife, Margaret (M.), from whom he has been informally separated for many years. In mid-June he goes to London and then to East Chaldon, Dorset, where his brother Theodore – also a writer – lives with his wife Violet. The third writing brother – Llewelyn ('Lulu') – his wife, Alyse Gregory, and his mistress, Gamel Woolsey, live nearby, as do two sisters, Gertrude (a painter) and Philippa (a poet). Louis Wilkinson, a friend of the family, is visiting with his second wife Nan. John is trying to finish writing The Meaning of Culture.

SATURDAY 22 JUNE Walked with Lulu to meet Gamel. Saw her approaching afar off in the valley. Watched her afar off & observed when she stopped & sat down to rest – like two hawks watching a stock-dove. In the end we caught her up. Lulu held back like his own style in writing while I lifted up my voice & shouted & ran towards her [...].

MONDAY 24 JUNE Walked over High Chaldon with Theodore. Sat with him under the hedge and talked of his newly projected works which are many. He is in an entirely different mood from when I was here last. Friendly & humorous & even (in an odd sort of way) more candid; though he says he is never natural and that to be natural is the hardest of all things. [...] He showed me a lovely valley with elder-bushes and old thorn trees where he could hide from everyone.

WEDNESDAY 26 JUNE Had a thrilling talk with Lulu & Alyse at breakfast. Am writing this in their room while they go out to their shelters, of which Alyse's is the Life-Boat. Told them about the Durants. They both think <u>very</u> highly of the *Story of Philosophy*. […] Wrote to Frances while Lulu rested & then went a walk with him to a Withy Bed past a strange circle of very aged thorn trees & two nameless trees unknown to either of us. On the way home saw Louis & Nan far ahead going to the White Nore. […] Then Lulu took out of his pocket a whistle and blew loudly & Nan & Louis turned round and slowly came towards us. It was embarrassing walking slowly towards one another. At what moment to speak? And what words to utter?

SATURDAY 29 JUNE Theodore & Violet came with us to West Chaldon. Walked with Lulu & Alyse to the Fisherman's Cottage & dined with Louis & Nan. Gamel came in afterwards; argued with Louis or rather so it almost seemed. Louis launched an eloquent attack on Introverts and I spoke of the happiness of jelly fish. Endless <u>glow-worms</u> on the way back. When I went out to the Privy of the Fisherman's Cottage I felt many anti-social feelings.

SUNDAY 30 JUNE Lay long in bed listening to the lashing of the rain on the window also felt it on my face. I liked to hear it and I thought of the necessity of simplifying your pride to the very extremest limits. I liked to see the Horned Poppy on the looking-glass-stand. Had an exciting talk at breakfast about the dinner at the Fisherman's Cottage. Alyse said that it was a serious moment – that it was a <u>very</u> serious occasion of Louis uttering an eloquent Apologia as against all my doctrines. Worked all the morning and most of the afternoon. Louis and Nan arrived also Gamel and with Alyse & Lulu we all walked over to Gertrude's Sunday Tea. Philippa met us on Josephine looking like a Valkyrie. […] Nan suddenly said to Alyse – Why do you dislike Louis so? But Alyse took this with extraordinary calm, & appeared to reassure her that she didn't dislike him as much as that.

MONDAY 1 JULY Last night Lulu came to see me to bed and as he went down stairs he said 'some people love me – but others think —' He was <u>taking</u> <u>rather</u> <u>hard</u> all the indescribable intrigues and cross-currents of all these conflicting personalities. […] Worked till 4.30 p.m. Walked with Lulu & Alyse down to Ringstead where the cliff is low. Met Gamel. Lulu showed us way down to shore past the greatest bed of Honeysuckle I've ever seen. Sat down by the sea. Lulu bathed. Gamel hunted for fossils in the clay of the cliff. Walked for a little fast walk by myself along the shore. Lulu came running naked along the shore – turned to meet him & embraced him all dripping & drenched with sea-salt – watched him re-join Alyse & Gamel. Contemplated their three figures from a distance Lulu naked the two women clothed – like Epicurus with Leontion & Ternissa! Like Odysseus with Calypso & Nausicaa.

TUESDAY 2 JULY Philippa rode over on Josephine to breakfast. [...] She has got a new story ready about a Gipsy. Worked all the morning. [...] Walked with Lulu & Gamel thro' a wood that once belonged to the old family of the Trenchards. Here were Scotch Firs & Pink Campions & wonderful moss – also a little stone 17th century bridge under which ran a brook. Lulu made us all climb down into this stream's bed & sit under the bridge. I left them in this wood & went on alone up the hill to the stone circle where I prayed to the gods of Merlin on behalf of all, or nearly all, of the people of my life.

On 6 July he rejoins his wife and his son who are vacationing at a farm near their old Burpham (Sussex) home.

MONDAY 8 JULY After tea walked with them past Lower Burpham Farm a perfect little homestead in a deep cup of the green Downs with an old walled orchard & garden & a row of great elms, to the Beech Wood leading to Michelgrove. This place I well recall visiting in walks from Burpham in former times. It is a wonderful green Gothic Cathedral of inviolable quietness going up & down out of all memory. Owing to frosts the Beech leaves were yellowish-green but this was very beautiful & gave a strange Ruysdael-like effect. It is a hill, a wood, a park, a sacred grove opening into a great wide Elysian Field – a Manor entrance with no Manor. [...] Littleton & M. found lots of wild strawberries growing in the mossy earth on the overturned root of a fallen tree. They filled each other's mouths with these bright red fruits and then kissed each other like a mother-oread old & alert, & a son-faun, in intense happiness.

FRIDAY 12 JULY After tea there was a grand Fête Champêtre of the whole youthful population of Lee Farm. Chris Cox [...] played the accordion & all the children danced. Littleton started them on leap-frog & a thousand other devices. I was amazed at how happy & completely at ease he was fooling about with them all and letting the smallest infants pull him about and tumble him about. He came home from Findon Fair in radiant spirits having met gipsies & all manner of queer birds at the Fair. This is the life he likes.

SUNDAY 14 JULY Shall I finish my book in time??? All these days at Lee Farm I have been thinking more of those personages over whom the great god Kwang rules than ever before. I think this is due to the extreme content of these two in one another's affection & it being a little bit *à trois*! Never was there a more lovely quiet place. […] Went to Mass this morning. Found L. walking about in the dew of the hayfield in cassock & Biretta & Missal in his hand a tall thin black figure. […] Could have touched a white cow out of my bedroom window this morning as it ate grass under the wall of this house. A White Cow I could willingly worship but it is not quite so easy to worship Our Lord.

TUESDAY 16 JULY Visited the mail-box – in the wall – beyond the duck-pond & mailed a letter to Gertrude; then watched the building up of a huge rick from no less than five immense wagons of hay. This farm is very large and well-worked but Mr Stacey the great rich farmer says he only works it as a hobby having made his money in business. Mr Miles here is only his bailiff. Had a very happy breakfast with my son & heard him defend the art of dissimulation & diplomacy. But O deary I how surpassingly beautiful his face does become at times – his complexion like a sea-shell & his eyes glaucous & luminous. He has sometimes an angelic beauty. He said he felt a gentle diffused amorousness to girls. Was scolded roundly by M. as soon as we were alone – because I had been calling the daughter of Mrs Cox who waits on us 'Miss Kitty' instead of Katie which is what they call her! I had trusted in my innocence to please this young woman – but it evidently was not at all what M. wished. She said it was rude, vulgar & treating her like a bar-maid or a seaside 'summer-girl'.

WEDNESDAY 17 JULY Saw the sheep pass my window twice this morning in a cloud of dust & thro' the shadows of the ash-tree whose roots by the wooden palings I look at. Had lunch with M. & my son. […] His sweet-natured tact between two such eccentric and selfish devils as his mother & me is beautiful & touching to see. It appears that he waits on her at night like a nurse. What a saint he is! He is subtle and yet far more simple than anyone would guess from the gracious ease & lightness of his talk. He is very simple-minded. He told me he would like to be a farm-labourer – 'old Father Powys' – and sometimes be allowed to say Mass by the parson. I think he is very like Alyosha. Went to Evensong in the Evening & meditated on the changes in the Service introduced by these Anglicans. All the hymns are of a tender very childish character like Babies singing to a Baby. […] The grown-up masculine element in religion is entirely left out. It is 'except ye become as little children' with a Vengeance! Worked till Midnight over guttering Candles Counting Words. My son is a perfectly angelic character. How can a son of mine be like this?

John Cowper returns to Dorset 19 July. He stays again with Lulu and Alyse at their coastguard cottage on White Nose (also spelt Nore or Nothe) and is joined briefly by his wife and son who stay with Gertrude and Philippa at 'Chydyok,' the sisters' isolated cottage situated half way between East Chaldon and the sea. One day is spent in Dorchester (where he lived for a while as a child) to meet with the Nortons who are publishing The Meaning of Culture. *He begins to re-explore places that later figure prominently in his next book,* A Glastonbury Romance. *The 'T.' or the 'T.T.' is his diary name for Phyllis Playter.*

SUNDAY 21 JULY Sat under a shed with the Nortons working at my MS on Fordington Great Field in view of Max Gate & Maiden Castle near those tumuli which I used as a child to call 'the Humps'. […] I recall how when I first went as a youth to see Hardy here I made a vow to write a good book – & here was I bringing my publisher to read my MS under a hawthorn hedge and a shed with thistles & nettles.

THURSDAY 25 JULY My son came here to lunch and I walked back with him to Chydyok, Lulu & Alyse far ahead. We found a White Harebell – beautiful beyond words. He caught 3 sick butterflies – two marble-whites and one Lulworth Skipper – & let them go after freeing them with a grass from some deadly little parasites. They flew away cured. I liked to see him do this. Had tea all together at Chydyok in the kitchen. Lulu & M. talked happily about the first things you could remember. My son rode on Josephine. Walked back at night alone. One glow-worm, one star, and the noise of the sea. It was dark. I thought of standing on stars with the T.T.

FRIDAY 26 JULY Set out early for Glastonbury. [...] Took the train from Weymouth thro' Dorchester for Poole. To our astonishment M. & L. suddenly entered our carriage at Wool! Lulu said my son looked nice (like a sailor in sailor's garb) like a young battered priest with lavender in his coat and sea-gulls' feathers in his hat. M. gazed searchingly at Gamel! Took the L.M.S. railway thro' Sturminster, Blandford, Stalbridge. Had milk at Evercreech. Then saw the Tor from the Train. Walked slowly up the town. An angel like a Tax-gatherer took us to our lodging very nice and the tower – The Tower the Tower the Tower the Tower.

SATURDAY 27 JULY When last night we were in the middle of the Ruins of the Abbey Gamel was vexed with Lulu & Alyse for debouching thro' the space where the lost old walls were. She said she felt distinctly pushed back by these walls. She said she was compelled to go out where the gates were by an invisible force. We saw where King Arthur's tomb was. This morning we went by train to Wells and spent long hours in Wells Cathedral. [...] The steps were wonderful, enchanted, leading to some vast Royal presence. We sat by the moat round the Bishops palace near the drawbridge where there were ducks & little tiny ducks. [...] We had salmon for lunch & beer & cider and drove to Wookey Hole Cave. The stalactites – the boat of Charon – the old bell-shaped stalactite and the thin one – the underground river – the Witch turned into stone. Noted the scenery between Glaston & Wells. Found the Holy Graal Well. [...] Then we sat in a field below the Tor and I lost my spectacles.

SUNDAY 28 JULY Went alone to that field where I found my spectacles – a good omen for my book. I knelt and said Tower help me Tower help me. [...] Went by bus to Ilchester. Here we got out & saw Judge Jeffreys' hall and Roger Bacon's House and we leant over the bridge of the Yeo and saw red waterlilies and enormous chub & Gamel thought it was the river of the Lady of Shallot for on our way in the bus we had seen Cadbury or Camelot.

TUESDAY 30 JULY At this moment Lulu & Alyse & Gamel are busy downstairs cooking Haddock because it is my favourite fish – but I have got that curious sensation of being swollen in my hands & legs & swollen in my head too which I get when I long to walk fast and for a certain distance! I must not allow this sensation to spoil my happiness; but it is hard not to! Alyse is extraordinary in her thoughtfulness for everyone – & if ever Lulu shows any tendency to practise 'mental bullying' towards me Gamel always says 'Mr Powys shouldn't do so & so.' On Monday night Lulu read us his novel [*Apples Be Ripe*]. It is like a water-colour. It is gentle. It is like his most childlike moods. [...] Alyse has just stretched a rug over Gamel as she lies on the sofa. She is to sleep here tonight.

WEDNESDAY 31 JULY After lunch we walked in a terrific wind to meet Gamel at the Obelisk. They hunted for flints as they always do. I begged them to desist from this tiresome antiquarian pursuit. The wind was so high that it made Gamel feel funny almost faint & so Alyse took her home to White Nose. Lulu & I walked down to 'Scratchy' Bottom a great level expanse half a mile wide. He climbed down the cliff to the shore. I was a coward and was afraid to follow him. I had to adjust my mind to enjoying the wild sea & Lulu's figure down there & the glaucous sea-cabbages & samphire – all blue-green & very beautiful – with the awareness of being a Coward. [...] Down in Scratchy Bottom we saw a pregnant lizard with a scorched tail.

In August, John and his school-master brother Littleton make the long drive to Northwold, where as children the two had spent idyllic vacations with their Norfolk relatives. On the way they pass through the many places which figured so largely in their childhood and later in John's novels.

THURSDAY 1 AUGUST Walked with Lulu & Alyse to meet Littleton in his car. [...] It seemed very strange setting off in the car with them left behind at the gate of the White Nore. Past Dorchester got a glimpse of Rothesay House. Past Poundbury & Charminster (the site of *Ducdame*). [...] Stopped at a gate to look at the Cerne Giant with erect cod-piece. Littleton had shown it to Aunt Etta and it had made her blush – being old fashioned. But the Giant looked like a monstrous Quetzalcoatl or Baal. I think it is Punic. Past the place L. & I had walked as boys when I beat him because I tumbled down.

FRIDAY 2 AUGUST Resolved to work hard and steadily at my book on Glastonbury to repay the gods for all the happiness I have – which is entirely owing to my having by Chance found the T. Luck – luck – luck – luck – luck – luck – all luck! Found the T. – does that mean the Tao, O casual eavesdroppers upon this Diary? Does it mean that? […] Started via the Bristol Road to nearly the Corton Downs which end with Cadbury Camp which is the same as Camelot. Saw a signpost for Milborne Port. Came thro' Wincanton in Somerset. […] Past two lovely young girls with very thin legs driving cattle. L.C.P. greeted them very gently. Past the village of Mere. Saw Shaftesbury in the distance. Came within a few miles of Stalbridge. Here was I, going direct from my father's birthplace to my mother's, or near it. […] Reached Stonehenge. I prayed to the actual stones of Stonehenge. I said – 'O Stonehenge help me to write such a book on Glastonbury as has never been writ of any place.' I drank rain water out of a hollow in the stone of Sacrifice. I knelt on the edge of the altar-stone. I invoked Merlin and my Three Great Spirits of the Earth. I carried water in the palm of my hand for the handle of my stick.

SATURDAY 3 AUGUST Reached Brandon Heath, crossed the heath & came to Northwold entering by the drive through the field. The large Cedar is still there but the Lime has been cut down. Walked to the little River and the boat house. The pond is dried up – the lily-pond in the rose-garden is filled up with earth. Tapped the ground with my forehead where the Arbour stood to propitiate the ghosts of some worms that one Sunday in dark secret intense passion when all were in church I cut to pieces with a knife. Three times I tapped the ground – & what old Littleton thought I cannot tell; he was smelling the Phloxes as I did too presently for it is of this place I always think when I smell Phloxes. […] After tea we went by a long Drove to Dye's Hole – here was a dark silent youth fishing alone. Long grassy Droves over this fen-like land – poplars willows alders dark woods in the distance over rough fields full of tall weeds it is wild far off country – far more remote than Wessex.

SUNDAY 4 AUGUST Went to Morning Service at ten – no sermon – the 19th Psalm – tried to work and adjust the engines of my mind to find some sort of a secondary place in my secret mythology for the God of my parents' grand-parents but found it rather difficult but in a certain way easier and less of a committal, than that crucified God of my son. […] Then went to Harrod's Mill Pool dark and deep with enormous fish swimming in it great dace and chub & trout – a mystic sight – the pool of Cybele.

At Northwold he feels the 'pricking' that is the first indication of another ulcer. John was related, on his mother's side, to the poets John Donne and William Cowper.

TUESDAY 6 AUGUST I did feel a faint pricking when I woke up – but it will pass off. […] But I could not shirk that walk towards Oxboro' Ferry where once with Grandfather, Father, & Uncle Cowper we all went fishing. I recall that Uncle Cowper refused, he alone, to 'put on worms'. […] I thought a great deal of the Tao (the T.T.) while I waited for Mrs Royal to bring the cup of tea at 7.30 a.m. & so I listened to the wind in the great trees – no other sound audible. I am in Grandfather & Grandmother's room – Littleton in Aunt Dora's. How the wind does sound in the poplars and the big cedar-tree!

THURSDAY 8 AUGUST It may be right to kill to live. I actually heard the Dace cry out as well as the sound of its neck breaking. It is certainly wrong to kill for pleasure. I cannot rid my memory very easily, though I can do so, of the sound of the breaking of the neck of the fish; which is L.'s way with them. Personally I would sooner drown in the thin air – which is their death. It struck me as discordant (to put it gently) to hear this sound in the soughing of the reeds and the splash of the swallows. L. gets the most intense pleasure out of it. He does throw back the little ones – but there it is! – it is wrong; & I am ashamed of supporting it by sharing these thin morsels with the voracious cats. […] Spent the whole of this day in the boat. L. sacrificed his fishing for the most heavenly drift down the river I've ever had – nearly to Oxboro' Ferry. Loosestrife, Willow herb, water buttercups, yellow water-lilies. Clear water and green weeds – perfect – had lunch in the boat.

FRIDAY 9 AUGUST Met Aunt Etta at Brandon & took her back to Northwold. […] I behaved badly with old Littleton while Aunt Etta was talking to the madwoman. I defended Uncle Cecil to whom reference arose and told old Littleton that I advocated Free Love and was a champion of it. This was of course untrue;

but his peculiar tone in speaking of Uncle Cecil annoyed me. Poor 'Rackety Rector of Rickinghall'. But it was malicious to burst out for it is not 'complacency' as Lulu says that is Littleton's fault. I don't quite know what it is but he is so grave & anxious and serious & concerned – not complacent at all! He then drove me with Aunt Etta to Yaxham where I saw Aunt Dora's grave also those of my grandfather & grandmother and Uncle Cowper, Hamilton's father. [...] Drove to Norwich. Julia waited upon us at dinner in Aunt Etta's house. After dinner we walked across (in the Close) to visit Katie Donne who is going with her daughter Mary to East Chaldon. [...] Katie Donne is a cousin of Mrs Siddons whose name was Kemble. Aunt Etta gives me all the whiskey I want which I am glad of for I still have that pricking.

SATURDAY 10 AUGUST Above us at this second as we finish breakfast is Cowper's picture & on the side-board his tea-caddy & in the spare-room his washing-basin. Julia brought me my morning tea in Aunt Dora's presentation silver tea-pot given her by the Lady Mayoress of Norwich & the Labour Leader of Norwich the famous Sheriff, Miss Clarkson. I am now fiercely pleading that the Cowper MSS especially his *Odyssey* should be given or sold to Olney Museum. [...] Saw the tomb of Sir Thomas Browne. L. translated the Latin. Saw the tombs of my great, great, and great, great, great grandfathers – John Pattesons both, Lord Mayors of Norwich.

During the remainder of August Powys moves around constantly – to Suffolk to visit Frances Gregg (the first wife of Louis Wilkinson), whom John had once deeply loved; to London to visit Dorothy Richardson, his architect brother Bertie (A.R.P.) and Bertie's second wife Faith; back to Kent 12 August for a further visit with his wife and son; finally to London again where – to his surprise – he finds Llewelyn, Alyse and Gamel. Gamel has come to London to abort Lulu's child – a child Llewelyn desperately wants. John then goes to stay with his youngest sister Lucy and her husband Hounsell and daughter Mary before leaving for America on 21 August.

MONDAY 12 AUGUST Went to Theodore's favourite German bookseller in Red Lion St and signed a lot of my books. He is publishing a book of Lawrence's which is very rough & crude & violent and angry and plebeian and obscene. It is the miner's son revolting. He has married his 'Lady Chatterley' who is a German lady – a Von something. [...] It was the smallest shop I have ever been in. Then I went to the British Museum & in excuse of reading the inscription which said Demeter of the school of Scopas, found in the Temenos of the Infernal Deities along with Hermes, Persephone & Pluto Epimachos, I was able to kneel on both knees and pray to her – the earth-mother. She is the most beautiful work of art in the whole world – but she is a real goddess – & was actually this very piece of marble worshipped in old days. [...] I sat long & long before this figure. I prayed for the T.T. and also for a certain power of motionless contemplation.

TUESDAY 13 AUGUST Woke up in the same room I had before with 'the Soul's Awakening' over the Mantelpiece. [...] Wrote to Frances telling her that out of all of her attack on my book I would promise to remember to try & make ordinary people exciting and not pile up too many exciting people – this was the best of her onslaughts and it tallies with many words of the T.T. How can it not then be in some way justified? This malleability hid a certain old surging up of maliciousness responding to her maliciousness! Went on the Downs with L. & M. [...] In the evening L. read from Lucas' life of Lamb and the talk of Coleridge and Hazlitt brought back many old literary ambitions.

SATURDAY 17 AUGUST Took the elements from my son with two black veiled Anglican Nuns but what I thought of, as the Graal was lifted & I tasted the wafer & wine in my mouth, was Demeter, my mother, & the T.T. But I associated these with the childish beauty of my son & with a marked ancestral look about his eye-sockets & forehead & nose that made me think of my father & of his father – a regular Welsh prince look going back to the service of the great Cymric Demeter – the goddess Ceridwen whose Cauldron gave immortality like the Eleusinian Mysteries of that Temenos of the 'Infernal Deities' including Persephone – not infernal in the Xtian sense but sub-terrestrial and Chthonian! His vestments made me think of old Byzantine pictures and of some of Veronese's of the Doges. In the morning light & candles the foliated leaves of a grey pillar-capital looked lovely & very mediaeval.

SUNDAY 18 AUGUST Last night when I got out at Charing X I saw Bertie coming down the platform with a woman's figure by his side. I thought – can that be Faith? It was Alyse. I knew at once that something was very wrong & she soon told me hurriedly and nervously that Gamel had to have an operation at once because of her heart being weak and her lungs being bad and having night sweats. 'Lulu is here too,' she said. [...] I slept at Faith's. The others are all at Bertie's house where they have it all to themselves. After breakfast went round and found Lulu very nervous. Saw Gamel in bed. [...] Lulu is very agitated – more upset than I have ever seen him in my life by anything. [...] [Gamel] is not nervous. She only is calm and resolute.

MONDAY 19 AUGUST Last night I forgot to say I treated Bertie & Faith to dinner in a café in (Faith is a great friend of Havelock Ellis) Shepherds Bush. Between them they drank a whole bottle of Sauterne. Their talk to each other when excited was very quaint and pretty. [...] After I kissed Lulu & Gamel au revoir Alyse & Faith came with me to London to choose a tray. [...] Alyse went back to get their lunch & then to take Gamel to the Hospital.

TUESDAY 20 AUGUST Lucy & Mary met me last night. Sat up late talking to Lucy & Hounsell thought Hounsell steadily nicer – all right if you steer him a bit: he is very proud of them both. Before supper walked with Lucy & Mary on the Little Down. Mary found a grasshopper. What a lovely place for a little girl. The river and grasses smelt lovely at night & were very calm at dawn. Walked this morning along the road through the meadows to the bridge over the main river Test; here there is a Mill and a great rushing mill-wheel far bigger than Hounsell's on the smaller stream which is only a tributary of the river. Walked by the banks & saw yellow Loosestrife and blue Skullcap & when I went a little stroll by myself & turned & looked I saw Lucy & Mary's frocks reflected among the reeds in the river – also an apple-tree. When I returned to them Mary showed me a strange phenomenon that she called a Water-Convolvulus. It was a tiny water-whirlpool a little very rapid whirlpool with a long wavering stalk, as it were, going down into the depths – a very queer thing to see & very lovely in the green-black deep water. Then a strange event happened. I struck the turning Mill-Wheel with the handle of my stick holding it by the end. I said 'Give my stick your power, oh great-splashing Wheel of Fate.' But lo! my stick was whirled out of my hand – & carried round the wheel. Lucy burst into tears – Oh the bad omen! Oh the bad omen! I frantically rushed down the stream thro' the reeds prepared to wade to get it if I could only see it. No sight of it! Mary said it has got stuck down below the wheel! Sadly I turned & steeled my heart & tried to comfort Lucy who was very agitated. Suddenly Mary saw some children about a thousand yards away – far down the stream. She said 'perhaps they will find it.' She & I ran back but I felt hardly any hope. But a long way down there was a narrow wooden bridge over the fast river. As we came near the children ran to meet us; and lo & behold! one of them – a little boy beautiful as an angel – had leant down and caught it as it swept past – for another one, a little baby, had seen it floating down. I gave the boy who had saved it a kiss and a pound. It seemed like a miracle. […] Suddenly I felt that I was glad to leave England for to be in the Room where is my home.

THURSDAY 22 AUGUST Saw the lights of Cherbourg and the cliffs of France. This night just before going to sleep the Purser came in with a telegram. […] It said 'Operation successful – love – Lulu' […] The sea was calm today, but grey and formidable and 'wasteful' with deep under-waves going all directions & little waves above them. […] Thought of this mass of grey waters and wondered if it had really & truly any godlike consciousness. Read about Stonehenge – also about Glaston and about the Graal. Made up my mind to write freely, exactly as I please; exactly as I please. That pricking is really better. It is the sea. Saw the sun go down till it was like an island, a fiery island – a hill of fire, like Glastonbury Tor. Then it became a straight golden barge or raft before it sank. Made up my mind that my book on Glastonbury should be really mythological and yet modern. This is later Thursday night and I have just been looking at the Moon about a yard above the horizon – I missed its rising – but it is almost as red or at least as yellow as the sun when it sank. It looks like the same orb re-risen only with a fragment lost from some battle under the sea where it was bitten off by the World-Snake. I have found out how to dance a peculiar dance with a certain stamping of my feet that gives me a very curious feeling of being a real magician and of the earth being porous and of floating in immense space while I hold the T.T. […] & neither the attacks of Frances such as I went thro' on that night of falling stars nor the 'mischief' of High Chaldon (and this last I can think of without a trace of malice being roused) can interfere with my mythology – now I've got the T.T. the Tao! the Tao! the Tao!

FRIDAY 23 AUGUST Read Rhys' Arthurian Legend all day and meditated on 'Mythology' – thinking not only of Glastonbury but of Stonehenge – and not only of Stonehenge but of heathen nature-worship in reality – the sea – the sun – the moon. [...] All day long have thought of the T.T. in connection with all my English memories.

SATURDAY 24 AUGUST The sea calm is a sea of glass and sometimes a dark blue and sometimes grey. [...] I keep thinking of my Glastonbury book. I begin to get an idea of what I would like it to be. The difference between contemplating to worship and enjoy, and contemplating to discover & understand. I still feel a bit troubled by dyspepsia following upon the 'pricking' caused at first by that attempt to reach Oxboro' Ferry with old Littleton when we met the ex-policeman carrying five dead wood-pigeons. [...] Saw the Moon rise, shapeless, very curious, very yellow and heavy, like a molten projectile. Prayed to it about the T.T. Saw a large rainbow and several solitary birds with brown backs and white bodies. Tried to practise that contemplation which I associate with the Demeter!

SUNDAY 25 AUGUST All day I have been reading Rhys' Arthurian Legend until I now have got on the track of the mythological Graal far older than the Holy Graal. I have learnt about the Birds of Rhiannon, and about yr Echwy∂ and about the Castle of Carbonek and about the Cauldron of the Head of Hades (Pwyll) and about Bran and the Graal and about Yspy∂aden the father of Olwen – and the Mwys of Gwydno Garan-hir – and about Avallach the Unknown – and about Gwyn son of Nud and about Gwlâd yr Hâv (*Aestiva regio*) and about 'Bendigeitvran' and about Ur∂awl Ben who is said (by himself) to be 'gorlassar' a dark blue livid colour.

> 'On the Echwy∂ evil has fallen
> From the dread of a savage knight
> Will there ever be another Urien?'

Rex 'semi-mortuus' the god of beginning & ending; of death and of the sea.

MONDAY 26 AUGUST Saw one unique sight that I have never seen before; an enormous stretch of this yellow sea-weed – like the tail of the sea-serpent or the poison of the Cauldron of Ceridwen racking on the calm sea which today for the 1st time this voyage has approached that wine-dark purple look; this yellow tinted sea weed stretched in a straight long line cut in half by the ship. In this straight line it must have floated a thousand miles from the Sargasso sea! Saw some porpoises in the evening sea raising splashes of foam that broke the dark-blue livid 'gorlassar' mirror of this level plain of waters. [...] Read the Arthur book for the ninth time.

TUESDAY 27 AUGUST Last night out of my porthole thro' which I stuck my head for a long while I saw the moon not only yellow but orange, no red! On deck early this morning before breakfast after a night wonderfully free from pricking – it is the salt – I saw the sea & sky as never before in my life & as never before in my life I prayed to the sky. The sky was very pale whitish-blue but covered with every kind of feathery filmy tenuous tendril-like clouds, clouds that were hardly clouds so delicately veined & like frost-marks on a window they were. But I had never seen the sea as it was. It was like an oily pearl dissolved – a moonstone dissolved – not one ordinary ripple only the cut of the ship's bow dividing it into long smooth oily waves. It reflected the sky. It was a sea of glass – 'de voirre' like the sea round Glastonbury. I have just now seen the spouting of three whales. This miraculous sea is like the sea leading to Echwyð – the land of evening – such a sea has the peculiarity of leading anyone to Paradise. Such a sea is one of the great Mother's uncoverings.

I have suddenly realized that the silver tray I have bought is like the dish at Carbonek and the basin I have bought for Olwen is like the Cauldron of Gwydno Garan-hir – which is a microcosm or an original of the Graal itself.

He returns to New York 27 August, to 4 Patchin Place – 'the Room' in which he has lived with Phyllis Playter (the T.T.) since 1923. On 12 September he and Phyllis and their doll, Olwen, travel to rural Hillsdale, Columbia County, for a month's holiday.

MONDAY 2 SEPTEMBER Crowds and crowds & crowds all very hot & perspiring. Was struck by the difference between New York and Dorset. But was thankful to be back in the Room. The T.T. had gone mad for a little while thinking about the End of the world.

WEDNESDAY 4 SEPTEMBER I went to the bank to put into it Mr S[chuster]'s enormous and most welcome cheque. The sun seems quickly to get slanting in this extraordinary heat. It is slanting with concentrated golden burning rays by 3 or 4 o'clock. It has a blood-red look. It looks dripping with red blood that it has sucked out of living things – the great fiery world-eye! All the people in the streets look indecent. They all seem undressed because of the heat. [...] It is mysterious to me how these streets can look cheerful when everything about them is so hideous!

THURSDAY 12 SEPTEMBER Lay listening to the wind in the trees. P. said it was like the falling down of hay or cut grass. It was beautiful and unusual. I lit the stove like Wolf and made P. a cup of tea – but spilled a few drops on the dressing-table cover to the dismay of Olwen who is puzzled as to where she is. I have had my greatest thrills over all this from going to the Well across the road to get water. There is an apple-tree there like the one we used to climb in the orchard at Montacute.

SUNDAY 15 SEPTEMBER This morning when I got the water I gave the brown Cow with a crumpled horn a drink out of the pail. It drank while I held the pail & caressed it. Of all animals I worship the Cow. And my deepest Religious ritual is for 'the Mothers' – Cybele and Gaia and Demeter and Our Lady and Ceridwen the Welsh Demeter; & another one too! Walked with the T. along our dry River bed to the road that goes by curves towards the hill with the long high hedge. Here to our delight we found a stream of running water – Alders were growing beside it & fish in it – I think little trout. The last Alders I saw were at Alder Dyke by the Wissey with old Littleton.

MONDAY 16 SEPTEMBER Woke up & meditated on the accidental shapes of trees outside and the fall of sunlight upon objects in the room. It required some effort of will for me not to think too much about how & why I ever started this ulcer or whatever it is that worries me so.

SATURDAY 21 SEPTEMBER Heavy white frost so that all the ground was phantasmal in the sense of being unusual, but not ghostly, because there is such an association of activity and power about white frost – hoar-frost – yes, it is quite otherwise when it comes to black frost – that bites in the darkness like an old cold corpse god -'Mortuus Deus'.

FRIDAY 27 SEPTEMBER Last night I read a lot of Malory aloud and it got more & more exciting. We have come to the Sangraal at last. [...] P. said that I am less alert & alive in the country.

SATURDAY 5 OCTOBER Dreamed a dream that P. & I were on a light-house island and I wanted her to walk with me on the water which was dark blue and it seemed easy to make her walk on this blue water if I held her hand and I held it tight all the time. [...] I got up to 'pump ship' while it was still dark – but there was a deeply bloody stain in the East. But the Morning Star was there & over my head – over the Hill was Jupiter very large. I felt hypnotised by the power of the earth to stay & I stayed. I had my coat. And I saw all the processes of the dawn. Tawny brown clouds – then light brown clouds – then gold in the east – then rose coloured clouds everywhere – then daffodil sky. Then a very curious phenomenon. A Dull sky like a mid-day without sun; without character – a neutral day – the sky fallow, waiting. And, at this, the earth too lost its hypnotic power. Until this, the earth was dark, insubstantial dark, deep, full of liquid hollows, mystic, more important than the two silver planets or the gold sky, dark, living, full of indrawn spirit. But now all was neutral & flat. O how slow the dawn was! I climbed the Hill, led by the hamadryad Birch tree & then higher up led by the five nakeds – five Birch trees – and as I kissed them at that second the Sun rose; pure white burning fire. We got dead leaves to cover the plants. We locked up the house and came to New York [...].

Powys would like to move to Hillsdale but Phyllis prefers New York. He resumes his lecture tours, despite another ulcer. G. Arnold Shaw was his first lecture-manager, one of his early publishers, and a friend.

SUNDAY 6 OCTOBER Arnold came and we had tea. He is penniless but he is a real gentleman; gentle and low voiced and ready to talk of any other matter than his ruin. [...] Why has he to go thro' this abominable misery – with fearful possibilities looming on every side and fear of his wits breaking down? Why has he? And what is this that I should be so selfish as to still get my happiness from what I like – these vivid green final autumn

Ailanthus leaves and the morning sun – and this Sun-Beam on the wall of the Room that is an elf called Trivia and these cups of china, of Limoges, cups [for] my Lipton yellow label tea – and P. being so particularly nice and so very beautiful & Olwen in a good temper. Why should I have all this pure luck and Arnold – a good man – be so persecuted by God? I cannot forgive God for this.

TUESDAY 8 OCTOBER P. [...] gave me a complete Blake which I have now been reading, especially the Prophetic Books and have found out that his Mythology is much more definite and clear and what I can understand and get something from than I have hitherto thought. [...] Had a very happy and a very important conversation with P. about her thoughts as she walked alone thro' Union Square. Her health has been benefited by the month at Hillsdale but she is glad to be back in the Room. Set out at 2.15 by Taxi to the Grand Central. Took the 3 o'clock for Cincinnati.

FRIDAY 11 OCTOBER Read *Le Temps Retrouvé* to the end of it all the way back in a Pullman seat with the awfullest people. Most Pullman-seat people are awful. Nice people hardly ever use 'em. On arrival at Patchin Place found a fire in 10th St – in which two artists of coloured glass were burnt to death going down the staircase instead of going on the roof. [...] Does any memory hovering over this city record these things? Found Mrs Bertelle doing the Room so walked out with P. via Waverley Place to Washington Square where we talked about emeralds and went soon and bought four emeralds and then we thought of the rolls at the French Pastry shop and we bought one roll and two Croissants and so returned with four emeralds and two Croissants and one roll.

SATURDAY 12 OCTOBER P. ate the croissants, I ate the roll. One emerald got lost on the bed but was found again. [...] I often meditate on the gravity with which ladies take the little ordinary events like shopping & getting the laundry ready & the questions of wood, ice, kindling etc etc – whereas to me there seems a sort of empty space & remoteness between these little things & the real issues of life making these things a half-real amusing & very pleasant game of which one is very conscious but in a detached way as something undertaken in order to make life more real and exciting; but in reality all a pretence, a game;

not more than half-real!

WEDNESDAY 16 OCTOBER Spent the morning writing on my back and struggling with sleep – sometimes yielding deliberately to it. Struggling against the delicious temptation to reach peace & to escape worry & to get away from responsibility – struggling against this most sweet of all sensations of men, beasts and birds (I know not about fish). What a thing! That if the secret of life is the struggle of the spirit against inert matter, the most delicious moments for individual spirits should be when they yield themselves up to inertness. The moment of death must be like this. O Death is this your trick and is no sleep we ever struggle against so delicious to yield to as the last one and is this the reason of that ineffable look of happiness they talk of on dead faces? But life might answer I suppose that the more conscious you are the more you can enjoy the unfathomable feeling of sleeping and dying.

SUNDAY 20 OCTOBER I went out before breakfast to get milk – the silence was lovely. I talked to old Mr Ycre at his Bakery. [...] Last night we read *The Sound and the Fury* and P. interpreted it. She liked it where it wasn't too obscure and so did I. In the silence of this morning I heard at 8 a.m. the one single bell of St Joseph's. It was the one sound & it was so mellow and rounded – like a great rain drop on a cabbage leaf after a stormy night. So far no visitor has come and we have had one of our very happiest after-breakfast conversations. I get such immense satisfaction from seeing the crimson & green squares of the Patchwork Quilt when I put it in the window when I take the covers off the bed.

SUNDAY 27 OCTOBER Left Detroit at 8.35 – the train stopped so that passengers could see Niagara. My automatic cave-man's maliciousness to anything that the tribe likes always leaps up at show-places. But I got a certain degree of comfort from imagining myself & the T.T. clinging tight to each other & being whirled down to annihilation where the current was smoothest round a wide bend of the fall. Canada looks just like America except for a few more brick houses and a few different advertisements. Albert Edward Johnson met me at the Syracuse station.

MONDAY 28 OCTOBER Am staying with Prof. & Mrs Eaton,

she being a sister of Morse Lovett and a champion too of Sacco-Vanzetti. O how I understand, O how I like & prefer, my sad, funny, dilapidated shell-shocked neurotic fellow-countryman, Mr Albert Johnson, to these thoroughly good philanthropic clever well-meaning kind people!

WEDNESDAY 30 OCTOBER Have just been for a walk with Professor Eaton & he described to me his hunting for De Quincey letters at Abbotsford and in the Lake Country. He is a typical professor and a very scholarly man – he is a fine gentleman & a scholar. I have a low taste sometimes & today the evil maliciousness takes me of wanting to talk with almost any voluble vulgarian of the roughest bluntest brutallest lewdest sort. And yet I really do <u>know with my reason</u> that this man, of my own age, is working hard, teaching & writing and has very nice 'upstanding' sons & daughters – & yet I feel embarrassed and awkward with him […].

FRIDAY 1 NOVEMBER Visited Mr Schuster and found him as urbane and as soothing to mind as always. I never visit him but I come away with all my nerves pruned like those of a bird. I mean preened I suppose.

SATURDAY 2 NOVEMBER Had no time for anything but writing endless letters. I must have written twenty letters in these last three days – and none of them of the least interest, except as proving how craftily I can tell lies or rather how I can simulate so much more emotion or affection than I feel. I would dread to say how little I feel!

MONDAY 4 NOVEMBER When I got up this morning I pulled the blinds very wide apart & the left window was open below. This made me see that there were polypodium ferns in the front room window-box formerly belonging to our lovely and unique & beautiful & rare and lost Miss Rowe. These ferns did please me so. Ferns are like moss & lichen. They are not like flowers. […] They <u>look</u> like the earth <u>smells</u> when you kneel down and press your face into it.

TUESDAY 5 NOVEMBER Saw the new moon over ramshackle litter in Brooklyn also a great cart full of red apples. […] P. says it is like asceticism living in a city; like enjoying rare beautiful things in a hair-shirt.

Wishing to spend more time writing and less lecturing, Powys tries to break his conract with his lecture agent, Lee Keedick. He is advised in this by his American publisher and friend, Max Schuster of Simon & Schuster. The 'ichthyosaurus-ego' book is In Defence of Sensuality, *published in 1930. A debate with Bertrand Russell is arranged for December.*

WEDNESDAY 6 NOVEMBER Wrote my 'ichthyosaurus-ego' book all the morning and in the afternoon had my Grand Interview with Mr Keedick. He was ready to relinquish the 10 per cent on my books (a monstrous transaction) – in return for my renewing the contract with the 50/50 partnership entirely unchanged. But when this contract was produced I was aghast to learn the words 'option to continue' had a totally different meaning to his mind than they had to mine. O what a fool I was not to get a lawyer when this shrewd 'dirt farmer' thus intended to get me to sign myself his slave forever! I then walked to the Plaza Hotel & hated that part of this city as I always do & I walked in Central Park and hated that Mock-Park made of Rock & Rubbish and villainous Pools. I threw an ichthyosaurus forked-tongue defiance at all the energies of New York – including Mr Keedick. Yes I defied it all & I felt able to do so, drawing magnetic power out of the universe.

FRIDAY 8 NOVEMBER Mr Keedick's famous 'epoch making' letter arrives by Registered Post 'I Exercise my Right Option.' Thus is the Declaration of War starkly made. Now it will be our turn to cross the Rubicon. This is an important moment in our life as far as outward circumstances go – of no importance at all before the eyes of the gods. [...] Well; let us see what happens! Even if I am left 'eyeless in Gaza at the Mill – with slaves – ' I think I shall still be thrilled with happiness because of the T.T. & because of such a line as that one of Milton! P. went to see Dr Thomas about Mrs Woolsey (a Henry James story) for the fortune of Gamel is connected with it. Mr Koneck came to ask me to debate with Bertrand Russell on Marriage. Shall I or shan't I?

SATURDAY 9 NOVEMBER Wrote my feeble ichthyosaurus-murmur out of the aboriginal mud. Is this rambling essay worthy to be called philosophy? I can't help it if it isn't. It expresses

1929 feebly but honestly the particular point I have now reached in dealing with the universe. In this sense it has some undoubted interest. I get satisfaction from writing it but there are so many interruptions that I never write it long enough at a time to get inspired. Thus it resembles that 'priming' of the Pump with just a quarter of a bucket of water and working the handle before the real well is drawn on! But after all I do work the pump and the 'priming' water does come from an honest rain-water Butt even if not from the Well; & the pear-tree still has its pear against the sky & anyone who reads this book will be led to the Pump & can pump the real water for themselves. [...] Mr Evans one of the Prison Warders of Michigan Prison came to tea and we had a thrilling conversation. A Welsh man on both sides. [...] Mr Evans is a monk. He can be cruel. He is very lecherous; he can be sensitively sympathetic. He smells of Prison-life but he is a mystic & a virtuoso; an ascetic. He is a strange saint.

THURSDAY 14 NOVEMBER We went to see the famous Spanish Dancer La Argentina. P. had longed for this & looked forward to it. She loves the light, the airy, the Watteau-ish, the exquisitely disciplined technique of such dancing – but my heavy rustic scrutiny spoilt it for her [...].

SUNDAY 17 NOVEMBER I had my weekly Bath. It took from 7.30 to 9.30. It seemed to over-lap with getting the breakfast – so that was a pity – but it was a very thorough & very ritualistic bath. [...] I have just now taken over to Mrs Woolsey a dinner on a plate even as mother might have told me to take a dinner to old Jane Geard, erect, elegant, indrawn, proud. I shut her window, turned on her electric light, and set the dinner on a chair. She looked like Flora MacDonald in Exile after Bonny Prince Charlie was dead. Her hair stuck out. Her night shirt clung to her skeleton. But she remained a dignified lady worthy to be descended from General Beauregard!

MONDAY 18 NOVEMBER A bad disturbed night because we kept waking up thinking it was time to get up. Finally when we did get up at 6.45, it was very nice in the Room – a wild wet wind blowing thousands of raindrops which splashed down the window-pane & through this rain came a lovely pallid faintly blue dawn-light. The fire was fiery red & P. wouldn't think of spoiling it by putting coal on. We had the tall candle lit & two purple night-lights on the chimneypiece by one of which I shaved. And aye! but we had one of our loveliest & happiest breakfasts – most elegant with exquisite dry toast & very good tea & coffee. Then I set out & walked to the subway & went to Providence Rhode Island by train. The country was all wet yellow bent-grass, & couch-grass & stones & reeds & willows in swamps. I would not think of [Hillsdale] because when P. thinks of it she thinks of too great efforts in an undefended exposure, but I practised that static contemplation which I vowed to learn the trick of when I was in the British Museum & worshipped Demeter. Static contemplation makes a person totally independent of such things as [Hillsdale] whether it happens or does not happen. It can use & exploit <u>any</u> surrounding – except I suppose the very worst – when it just has to escape.

TUESDAY 19 NOVEMBER Visited Mr Schuster and met Mr Leigh the Manager. [...] He said I was well known to be the most under-paid lecturer of the platform. Various methods were discussed, none of them very satisfactory, for bringing Mr Keedick to book. Things look pretty bad. Mr Leigh said that Keedick's last letter was 'very clever' & probably advised by a lawyer. [...] All this has left a most unpleasant feeling in my mind. I feel as if I were already under suspicion for not being normal, <u>for being a toad</u>, by the Police. The mere rumour of lawyers & the law fills me with distaste & I recall my father's hatred of them. But Mr Schuster <u>has no such feeling</u> & retained his noble presence & all his suavity & grandioseness. Went to Brooklyn to lecture. The metaphor of 'the stone'; for I dared to be more wantonly fanciful than usual – P. was there. If she is ever there I lecture only for her. This time she felt sleepy & the explanation may be that my magnetic grappling-hook worked badly because of Mr Keedick. Had rather an agitating tea for she said that it might be better not to leave Keedick. I heard this discourse as if when you thought the day was Saturday it turned out to be Monday after all.

SATURDAY 23 NOVEMBER Reached New York by Sleeper at 8.30 & reached the Room at nine. The room looked especially nice because of the two new Bureaus of white bare wood & because of the new Chinese Box placed on one of these – the one in the alcove; & because P. had got the bed made & the coffee & tea 'most ready'. [...] I listened to P. tell of all her adventures about going to Wall St with Mrs Woolsey & about her talks about Japan with the Midget and then we read our letters & I heard of P's last Suicide – for she collects these as if they were beautiful dark butterflies. I longed for some wretched person to whom I might pour out some drops of my overbrimming cup of happiness. After lunch at Childs I persuaded P. to walk with me & we walked all round Washington Square, which we had not done for a very long time & looked at the sparrows roosting in the plane tree & at a gilded chair in a shop and we bought Theodore's *Fables* at the shop & this will be, we can see, our favourite of all.

SUNDAY 24 NOVEMBER P. & I ought to be a Monk & a Nun allowed by some especial Dispensation to live together. Today she uttered those words that alas! I know so well upon her lips – 'Would we were both Dead!' & all because of this crisis in our days & Mr Keedick & 'the Option' & the danger of Novelty in our life – new pleasures new troubles. Everything new is too much for her.

TUESDAY 26 NOVEMBER Our letters this morning are full of overpowering matters – burdens & tasks and appeals. Our life is getting to be overwhelming. Too many people hold tight to us & our raft sways & we bail the water out & the sea mounts up & the sky is full of whirling clouds. There are still little tiny plants growing under the rim of our threshold stone.

TUESDAY 3 DECEMBER I talked to Schuster over the 'Phone about the Contract. Then it came over me that it was necessary for me to go & see Keedick so as to keep a door of reconciliation open for any emergency. This I did, wearily & sadly, but without nervousness. But I found it very hard to look the chap in the face because his countenance is like that of an old School Bully at Sherborne. […] I looked shiftily down at my cigarettes on the Table. But I said what I had come to say & intended to say. […] I had a thrill of happiness in Washington Square however before tea when I thought of living in the country and only lecturing for 3 months.

WEDNESDAY 4 DECEMBER P. actually went to the Library for me […] & brought back Ibsen instead of the Sacred Books of China. What wretches, what frivolous fools to change their lecture-subject from Chinese wisdom to Ibsen's tiresome Norwegian or Icelandic opinions! O how silly, how abysmally shallow all opinions are! To have 'opinions' is to belong to the lower order of intelligence – to 'philosophy' or 'morality' rather than to the wisdom of life. But I got up so early that instead of visiting the Tree or Rachel's grave I read Ibsen before breakfast. The pompous old Horn of Conceited Maliciousness is bad for the stomach always – but before breakfast! After breakfast I opened a letter from Weinberger the Lawyer I had gone to about Keedick and he had sent me a bill for $50 for half an hour's talk. This robbery does stick in my gullet. Fifty dollars for half an hour's talk! Well! I suppose its all right. I get $50 for an hour's talk very often!

FRIDAY 6 DECEMBER We had lunch at Childs and I had to have my evening dress on. It was odd sitting in Childs in my father's evening dress what he used to dine at Montacute House in. Then I went to the Studio of Fox Movie & Talkie Film and in that atmosphere of greenish malign grotesquerie & gross crudity & peculiar brutality of a boyish sort I had to make an imaginary speech & gesticulate like a Mandarin in favour of Marriage. [...] We had the statement from Mr Glass and it was only $200 when we expected it to be $1200.

MONDAY 9 DECEMBER O what a horrid rush it was for I had to start by 8.45 to catch the train for Utica. I read Russell's book on Marriage to which I have to reply in the debate on friday. It is amusing but very academic & schoolmasterish very austere and devoid of all mystical sap [...] – a vein not exactly priggish but depressingly superior. All the pastures of New York State were covered with grey glacial ice. I saw a sled crossing one ploughed field as if it had been a pond. I was driven 30 miles from Utica and I liked the look of the country. These younger professors in American universities are a pathetic and touching type – very sincerely absorbed with their work in their brains but it is not yet in the marrow of their bones.

WEDNESDAY 11 DECEMBER I have been reading Keyserling on Marriage. [...] Mrs Bertelle came & did the room while I lay in bed. I did not mind an occasional word with her – whereas all the other people who have come lately except Marian tho' good friends have stayed much too long. I am a lonely malicious inhuman degenerate selfish 'ichthyosaurus-ego' & I wish people gone – the moment the first glow of exchanging news & ideas is over & that happens so terribly soon & then when that warm pleasant gossip begins I slowly freeze like a log in a black frost.

FRIDAY 13 DECEMBER I woke up very early, my head full of the Debate – thinking of arguments to support Marriage. [...] I left at two & made my way to the Commodore Hotel where I lectured on Hardy to the oddest old-fashioned quaint parochial small-town set of ladies you ever saw. [...] I had to wait till such a quaint one talked of certain plays now performing & as I stayed & sat there & waited for my turn in that awful place for all these grand hotels are deplorable & devastating to anyone's spirits I thought how necessary it is to learn the art of transporting yourself in mind to a place different from the place where you are. I transport myself now with incredible ease – it's a kind of magic that I possess – actually to Stonehenge. I think I might be visible there to the rooks of a wet lonely winter evening; but probably not to even them. [...] We all liked Mr Russell very much but thought nothing of his arguments! He kept the topic down to a humorous level. It was not really exciting.

SUNDAY 22 DECEMBER Have been reading Unamuno all day and also *Don Quixote* with a view to my lecture tonight. P. has cooked a wonderful lunch but oh she does hate cooking so she does hate it hate it hate it. But she makes herself do it & my will is as weak as water or like the will of a great old Bull or Ox with a little girl who pulls & tugs at the rope tied to a ring in its nose. She stops to pick flowers in the ditch & jerks the rope without remembering that there is an Old Bull at the end of it and the animal waits till she has picked what she wants with its fiery breath against her pinafore. We keep talking & talking about the future & the Contract. It is hard to know what to do for the best. It is now twilight in the room. The fire is red. On the top of the red coals dances a lavender flame. P is just finishing washing-up [behind the yellow screen]. O it is wicked that Such should have to do such. Never have I noted such deep quiet in New York as this Sunday has. There is no quiet like it. And aye! this grey twilight as I sit over these red coals. How odd that it is more important to me what is going on behind this yellow Screen than what is going on behind the Ultimate Screen of the Universe at which I shall bark like a dog this very night.

MONDAY 23 DECEMBER Woke up at ten and had breakfast at noon – the latest I have ever had breakfast. [...] Then I went to the bank and got cash. On the way, as I came down University Place from the bank I saw a black horse pulling a cart of Xmas trees. O how wicked it is to kill these young trees! They lay in the cart like young calves newly massacred only instead of their heads their roots had been cut off by the most evil of all the spawn of the earth except insects. As this black horse passed, slipping & heaving & struggling, I caught its eye. These things are unpardonable. But I was too great a Coward to follow it & call the Police or call the Prevention of Cruelty. Besides – it just could pull. It was only that slipperiness was awful to it, worse than to be arrested by the Police to me. So in my cowardice and soft hypocritical self-indulgence what must I need do but go and kneel down then & there on the sidewalk & pray – 'O let this horse reach its Stable!' but of course I ought to have acted not prayed. What was the good of prayer? Then I went to Wanamaker's and bought a gun for Peter. I hope he will shoot the kind of people who let horses pull Xmas trees on slippery roads.

1930

1930 is a year of transition for Powys. After one last gruelling tour, he and Phyllis move to Hillsdale. The shift from 'the Room' in central New York City to an unmodernized house in a rural community is not without its difficulties. From the beginning it is obvious that Phyllis is temperamentally unsuited to the demands of housekeeping and visitors. John's ulcer and accompanying 'dyspepsia' is a constant worry for them and they try various cures.

Another concern that takes up a significant amount of their time and thought in the latter part of the year is the Gamel-Lulu-Alyse ménage à trois. *Llewelyn is still enamoured of Gamel Woolsey and determined to have a child by her, but Gamel has met Gerald Brenan and in June accepts his proposal of marriage. In August a distraught Lulu and Alyse sail for America. Despite, or because of, the twelve years difference in age and their dissimilar temperaments, John and Llewelyn have an especially intimate relationship: to go to John when he is troubled is a natural response for Llewelyn.*

In 1930 at least there are no money worries. Wolf Solent *is selling well, as is* The Meaning of Culture. *John makes characteristically generous gifts of money to his wife and son, as well as to various relatives and friends in America who are beginning to feel the bite of the Great Depression.*

In spite of the problems connected with the move, his health and family problems, he writes steadily, completing his 'Ichthyosaurus book' In Defence of Sensuality*; a short story,* The Owl, the Duck, and – Miss Rowe! Miss Rowe!*; and he begins seriously the writing of* A Glastonbury Romance.

On 5 January, John begins his last 'mean jump' – a forty-four day lecture tour through many states. He is plagued by 'dyspepsia' caused by the constant travelling, irregular hours and meals. When mocking himself, he calls himself 'Mr Powg'.

MONDAY 6 JANUARY This is the most hateful of all towns in the world except Chicago and Detroit and Atlanta Georgia for if they are the 3 worst here they then must be the 3 worst in the world. [...] O how I wish I need never in all my life see Pittsburg again.

FRIDAY 10 JANUARY I had breakfast on the train and looked at the landscape of Iowa. [...] I wrote to the T.T. a love letter from the Sheldon-Munn Hotel. [...] But my dyspepsia took me just as I began lecturing at 4 o'clock and went on all thro' a wretched dinner they gave me in a grand Memorial Place like a smart Mausoleum. Then I met two chinese a man & a woman & we liked each other & they said I was like a Chinaman & he said he was a Confucian and I said I was a Taoist [...].

SATURDAY 11 JANUARY All day long I travelled in a snow-mist out of which great Farm-buildings kept emerging [...]. I lay in a trance and gazed at my green book & two grey books all about Percival & Merlin and the secrets of the Graal. And I meditated about my philosophy of eating & drinking and ravishing half of God & forgetting the other half of God.

SUNDAY 12 JANUARY I think of that youth propping up that drugged man or drunk or sick man first against a stationary motor-car then against a door & I heard the thud of his falling – just as I heard a dace utter a little cry when L.C.P. unhooked it. What sounds there are that enter or do not enter the ear of God. I thought of my cowardness & shrinking & all pride went out of me and rolled itself into a little ball like an external soul and stayed in the air outside of me. And I knew that I had the soft fussy egotistic coward soul of that Archdeacon to whom Lulu always compares me. But perhaps even the Archdeacon would have gone up to those two figures last night – but Mr Powg retired into his comfortable Hotel and only once more peeped out [...].

WEDNESDAY 15 JANUARY I am in Racine – the cold lake with a red light streaming over the ice. I am afraid this room is too high up. Dizzy to me are all heights & dizzy & *very* hostile to me all whiteness except the girl's body I love. I don't like the idea of the Beatific Vision being whiteness. I like it to be green or sometimes blue. In Milwaukee. Dyspepsia bad & a long, long lunch. A wild reckless lecture on Dostoievsky.

WEDNESDAY 29 JANUARY I have got a letter from the T.T. that does redeem all sorrows. O how well she refutes the unctuous clap-trap of Krishnamurti about Sorrow! But O dear I have left behind in my hotel room Chretien de Troyes' Graal Book – O ass! ass! ass! How could I do that? Took the day-train to Des Moines. [...] I have had to pay *six dollars* for my room. I shall never dare to put six dollars down in my expenses! I *had* to go out & get some air but I have got dyspepsia but these empty ugly streets lighted entirely by ads and by closed shops and the sort of people who go about at seven o'clock in Des Moines. Why is it called Des Moines? And I had an outburst of a sort of hysterical hatred of this country & I said aloud 'I defy America!'

SATURDAY 1 FEBRUARY Had dyspepsia in the night & had a terrible dream of a great line of *colossal horses* all wounded & drooping and *half dead* being dragged forward in the Streets of America – of some, of *any* American city – being compelled by harness that was machinery to go forward on their bloody way. And I saw a little tall thin man who was a little great actor (I can't think who 'twere) who stood hushed and still with horror & disgust and pity at this sight – and I woke up [...].

TUESDAY 4 FEBRUARY Not left alone for one second. Mr Gottlieb – God love him! – the Jewish bookseller and Mr Van de Veer, a nervous tall Dutch man & another all came uninvited to talk to me at breakfast. [...] They took me (after half the town had paid me visits) to lunch in an awful little sham mill-wheel house by a sham river where they kept two real Swans. Think of it, Swans! surrounded by those unspeakable freak Erections called Homes built by the same Realtor – O Lord! O Lord! I had to stand at a reception like a drill swaying and twisting with my hands on my stomach. Finally I begged leave to sit down. I must have contorted my countenance for they apologized & well they might. I see advertisements of a great whale (dead) brought in a truck to be exhibited. They took just that sort of gloating interest in Mr Powg! O damn! O damn!

WEDNESDAY 5 FEBRUARY Woke up in the berth at Atlanta – such a nice coloured porter. Have had such a queer time here in Atlanta. O the agitations! My money is at an end. Have wired Glass for to wire me $150 (I hope it's enough) to Fort Worth. […] It is a disgrace having to go so far as Texas for only one lecture of $150. I shall make about $25, the same as a lecture at the Finch school, by 4 days travel!

MONDAY 10 FEBRUARY I have had a bad night & yet strangely enough I did not mind […] for even while I suffer this discomfort which I refuse to dignify by the name of 'pain', that most tragic of all words in our speech except the word '*love*', I had an under-current of some queer nameless secret satisfaction. Who can explain this? […] Once on this accursed tour my stomach was so upset that I dreamt of nothing else but going to look for places where I could 'shit' in peace. I also have the T.T. wherever I go in my skull, on the ledge, and in the little round crystal of my soul but once I dreamed that when the bodily T.T. was there & I wanted to slip off for that purpose I cried quite crossly to her like I never do in real life – 'Go away!' There spoke that old lonely deep animal, old mangy-wolf, old beast or wounded snake, or some savage constipated panther like my father when my mother was dying; & he cried out 'Can't I even have my breakfast in Peace?' This constant feeling in my stomach isolates me from the world. […] But always in the crystal, in the Monad, in what of Jack says 'I am I' there ensconced & installed is the T.T. Why she was there even when I said 'go away' when my bowels felt so horrid. For wherever I go she goes & so it shall be until the 1st Cause destroys us both. As long as either of us is alive – the other is alive. […] Cousin Alice said 'your father is more selfish than your mother but if he dies she will live long but if she dies he wont live long.' This proved just true. He got dumb, then helpless and then died.

WEDNESDAY 12 FEBRUARY Yesterday about noon I again crossed the Mississippi on a ferry. […] I got out & stood at the edge of the flowing water carrying so many dead trees along. I thought for the 1st time in my life that something in the landscape of America had really become sacred to me – independent of all I hated so bitterly. Think how I've seen this river on this very Tour at Minneapolis, at St. Louis, in Iowa, & now here – the careless father of rivers; the longest of all rivers. I

1930 recall how when once caught, imprisoned, restless, in too early bondage in England I dreamed of being saved by America – of taking ship for America. This was long before there was any chance of such a thing. I have been reading Maritain's clever & illuminating attack on Rousseau. I know well what he is talking about – who better? For I myself am Rousseau – a Jean-Jacques, though, who in another avatar has grown roots & learnt a few more ways of bending to the four winds! Arrived at Augusta.

SATURDAY 15 FEBRUARY This day I suffered serious dyspepsia. Had a dinner before and a reception after the lecture – shook hands with 50 young ladies, swaying & crouching like a sick Poke Weed in a shower. The lecture, the one at Sweet Briar, was on Hardy. The old man who once said to me, 'Your fate is in the lap of the gods, Powys.'

Powys returns to New York the evening of 15 February, glad to be back with the T.T. and their doll Olwen. Phyllis and his principal American publishers, Simon & Schuster, urge him to try to find a cure for his ulcer. He continues to lecture and debate, but looks forward increasingly to the move to the country. Marian, the only sister to emigrate to America, is a lace-maker and has her own lace shop in New York. She and John are particularly close. Peter, her son, was born in 1921.

FRIDAY 21 FEBRUARY I had a dream about little Peter in which I thought he was my son – not my Littleton but another son.

TUESDAY 25 FEBRUARY At breakfast the T.T. decided that I should tell Keedick I must have a year's total rest. Mr Simon came. Olwen admires Mr Simon. She liked to see this handsome tall young man. [...] He made us go to Dr Schreiber his young doctor. But first we went to Doctor Thomas who gave me those pink tablets to take instead of Dr Einhorn's white powder. We took a taxi to Dr Schreiber's. Oh, how the T.T. hated him, but I did not. I was pleased to hear about the great Jejune operation 'over the whole ulcer-area'. I like names for my case and to be told what is what. [...] Went to the office and waited an hour talking to Glass. Then I announced my decision to have a year's rest. Keedick apparently accepted this. We shall see. Had a lovely tea and talked about our Decision. Then I read to the T.T. from my Ichthyosaurus book. All this talk about jejun[um] operations

& about not lecturing for a year has made my Dyspepsia go away today. Is that not strange? Am reading about that blundering well-meaning noble Cosmic-Comic ass Victor Hugo.

THURSDAY 27 FEBRUARY Set off for the Town Hall. In the middle of my lecture when I mentioned Cowper's madness they laughed. [...] I got angry with them for laughing & I stopped & scolded them harshly & bitterly. [...] Had my boots shined twice once the boots then the over-shoes, purely for selfish propitiation & a special sympathy with two men there one dark & sullen, one old & whimsical. There are at least 50 there in Union Square. The unemployment here is very bad. Tea was rather interrupted by sending Marian $50 Special Delivery. Then I went to lecture at the Hamilton Grange church and it was 149th Street and such a scene. I sat between a Banker & Manufacturer and a Y.M.C.A. Holy Terror. I spoke on the Purpose of Life & tried to undermine the bluff of these rogues.

FRIDAY 28 FEBRUARY I think sometimes with such a thrill of the white postbox by the grave yard in Hillsdale. O may she be happy there. O may she be happy there! How I did snatch at that place! How I do turn to what I want – in spite of my stern conscience!

SUNDAY 2 MARCH The debate on Reality or Unreality, the Rationality or Unrationality of the world, with Dr Harry Woton, an ex-Rabbi radical leader, a great Talmudist & Cabalist was perhaps to me the pleasantest & most congenial & most enjoyable debate I have ever had. [...] We had a lovely tea although the T.T. was terrible exhausted & wanted something more sustaining than bread & butter. We had boiled eggs – which of all things she & Olwen despise! [...] I am still reading Balzac. I am always fascinated by his world-creations, are they real are they unreal are they even <u>interesting</u>? Well! What arrests & fascinates me in Balzac is <u>the idea of his undertaking</u>. Just the torrent of his energy, just its tide and every detail of that Coffee-drinking. The contact with Balzac makes me think of when I first wanted to be a novelist. This was a certain walk at Cambridge, near Trumpington Mill, near Queens' College.

SUNDAY 9 MARCH We set out by train to Glen Head. On the way we read together *The Embezzlers*. A Russian Modern book

1930 humorous & non-committal fantastic & yet real. [...] The T.T. adores it. Since Radiguet she has not liked any author so well! Schuster met us & we walked up to his house. I asked leave to have an Enema & the old gentleman brought me a kettle of boiling water from the kitchen. They waited dinner for me. We were alone; we five. It was perfectly harmonious. The old gentleman kept the fire going. We had music all one day especially Grieg & Mendelssohn. [...] It was the 1st day of Spring! Spring was in the yellow stalks of the weeping willows! Spring was in Mr Schuster's rapid steps & eloquent talk about the Inner Sanctum Classics. It was the Pervigilium Veneris of the year. Both of us enjoyed it very much. They are an interesting family. We got back early. The T.T. stood very long in her dressing gown by the window after I was in bed. She had that wild bird craving to fly over the roofs. It was the Spring which makes un-mated girls restless and mated girls want to follow the wind or the voice of Adonis 'whose annual wound in Lebanon allured the Syrian damsels to lament his fate'.

MONDAY 10 MARCH Before she slept the T.T. recovered from her wild desire to float over the roofs of far cities. I was glad when she came back to me! I wrote endless letters all day long, letters of proclamation to all the world that I was going to give up lecturing. [...] Went up at 5 o'clock to the Inner Sanctum and had a long interview with Mr Shimkin his lawyer about my Income Tax. This also Schuster is taking off my back. He is also going to pay for the typing of my book – the Ichthyosaurus book which perhaps not very wisely I named to him as a *Defence of Sensuality*.

WEDNESDAY 12 MARCH Helen Morgan came to tea – & gave the T.T. a wrist-watch so prettily. I got a thrill from watching her caress the T.T.'s hand & white arm sheathed like an Arum Lily stalk by her new sleeves – calyx-like. I was enchanted by hearing these refined & aristocratic young girls play & rally and tease and float on the waves of their nervous interest in each other.

THURSDAY 20 MARCH Got up at 6.30 thinking of my book which I am finishing. Wrote my book all the morning. [...] She feels so terribly exhausted these mornings when I wake her up so early. I suppose I ought not to do it. I am driven on [by] my selfishness and my morning galvanic energy. Its like the sleeping Beauty and a furious Robot of mechanic jerks. […] I went to lunch with Marian up town & walked with her to her Bank down the Avenue. She is Adamant in her heroic strength. I am no engine I can tell you by her side. I am a leaning tree held up by an iron bar as she takes my arm and I gaze in wonder at her Babylonian profile; set to defy the Desert with all its jackals & vultures. […] Orage came to tea. He rubbed his hands in ecstasy at the T.T.'s thin bread and butter. […] He excited our affection – as a Saint might do when you want to protect & soothe him from the stress of his own austerity. His humility was weird & appealing. He answered questions like one taking off his clothes till you shuddered at his self-inflicted stripes.

FRIDAY 28 MARCH We had a letter from Lulu and a letter from Alyse. Both too sympathetic about my dyspepsia. This makes me feel a malingering fool. […] I set off at six-fifteen to the Pennsylvania station to lecture at New Brunswick. Was met by a regular Budding Grove of young girls who sat opposite me behind the stage and afterwards took me to the station. I felt weak and tired & prickings vexed me in my side but not bad ones. […] When I returned the T.T. had the floor strewed with old MSS of mine. I neither want to look at these – nor to destroy them. I want to pension them comfortably off, these past selves and never see them again.

WEDNESDAY 2 APRIL Went out to Marian's. […] Peter in bed with one of his colds. He looked beautiful. He was good. He was playing chess by himself. Marian took me over her empty house next door. I thought how easily it might have been my house but aye! this place so pretty is not the real country. I have no chance here of a cow drinking out of my pail or of being able to see fish in a stream under alders. But the T.T. is so tired. Did I do right in snatching at Hillsdale? The other morning the T.T. woke up crying for Paris!

THURSDAY 3 APRIL Wrote my ichthyosaurus book. I have put the most secret things of my secretest life into this book. It is much truer than superficial readers will ever know and it is much nearer the secret of life than they will guess. It is really a very serious book and it is really a new philosophy. It is roughly, feebly, stupidly, awkwardly expressed but it is the beginning of a very deep idea by the use of which many people long after we are all dead will be able to steer their lives and get certain secret thrills of happiness – else perhaps quite unknown to them.

FRIDAY 11 APRIL The T.T. didn't come to bed till three o'clock. I got up at 5.30 two and a half hours after she came to bed. [...] But she stayed asleep – beautiful as a Giorgione picture – till the right moment & then to my amazement jumped up & out of bed in a second. And it was a funny breakfast because she did not open the paper or even look for the theatre page. She is worried over this packing. She began work at once. I caught sight of her lifting up her head – up & down – like a weed in a whirl pool – in a minor desperation over the locking of one of the trunks. This job, I, the Wise & the Great One, easily performed with the method of entirely disregarding The Key! From this we learn thus sometimes the secret of the world is best discovered by disregarding the Key!

On 12 April they move to Hillsdale. They are met by their friends, Gladys and Arthur Ficke, who helped them find and buy the cottage. Other neighbours, particularly the Kricks and their nephew Albert, make them feel welcome. 'Excelsior' is wood shavings used for packing.

SUNDAY 13 APRIL I made toast at the parlour stove very successfully. I dared to announce to the T.T. that this was the happiest day of my life. Was not that a daring of Fate? [...] Mr & Mrs Krick called on us with their nephew very nice and friendly. I do like them the best by far of all our neighbours.

WEDNESDAY 16 APRIL It is very cold and quite grey today and a north wind with a feel of snow in it. We had a happy breakfast and were enjoying our cigarettes. We began breakfast at 7.30 and this was 8 o'clock when lo! there appeared Mr Steuerwald in his great truck with all our goods! What a scene. The incredibly philanthropical Mr Krick (may he live long in this land) came striding across his meadow to assist. And one by one all the things were brought in save the couch & the wicker chairs which were left on the lawn. Mr S. is of Herculean proportions. I detected a funny chuckling smile on his face as he drove away like a keeper of a Zoo who has just given straw to absurd new beasts from far away. We then went over to the Krick farm and inspected their Silo & a thousand gleaming eyed tiny chicks.

How can little fowls be so nice? It looked like the Creation. Evolution be damned! [...] My couch & the chairs I unpacked & lo! it has begun, the creation of a girl building her nest like a bird putting its head on one side.

THURSDAY 17 APRIL A lovely letter from Alyse who is our most exciting correspondent, and the German edition of *Wolf Solent* in 3 vols. The T.T. did so enjoy going through each volume very thoroughly. All the people were become German; plurismus, pantheismus and magnetismus. The poems sounded splendid. The dialect has been evaded. The German tongue makes the book much longer, but they have divided it beautifully and very skilfully.

SATURDAY 19 APRIL Last night I recited to the T.T. all the melancholy grave stoical elegant classical poems of Tennyson – 'Lawn Tennyson' as that Smart Aleck James Joyce loves to call him and as I saw the head of the T.T. against that picture I was profoundly content with my lot. [...] The new wood brought round by Harold Albright yesterday must have been so wet that it wouldn't burn quick as usual – and I had forgot the sticks. So I had to use excelsior. This strewed itself about and I had to blow too. [...] At last we got both the fires under weigh & I went with her letters. But O woe betide I put more wood on the kitchen stove at the wrong moment. This was the last straw & the T.T. collapsed on the Linoleum. In vain I referred to a possible happy future in Europe. She returned to the Bed & shut the door. Even after she came out all was still askew, for the coffee refused to boil. After breakfast things recovered a little. I took her out with Lulu's brown shawl on and showed her the Periwinkles out & told her we were the only people for miles round that had Easter flowers in their garden. But unluckily at this moment the bedroom curtains were ready to be put up. This meant half an hour's misery. The T.T. is a very good carpenter but she does not exactly whistle at her work.

SUNDAY 20 APRIL I have begun my Glastonbury Book. May I be inspired by all the spirits of all hills; and of all stones upon all hill-sides and upon all plains raised up above sea-level. Went alone to the Fishes & saw five little ones. Went to the Nymphs Grotto, & sat above the water-fall in the twilight. Had a thrill coming back thro' the field & by the stream. The T.T. ran to meet me.

1930 MONDAY 21 APRIL Easter morning there was the half moon upside down and this morning there seemed to be the Great Bear upside down. I think in those cold strange hours before Dawn the very silence and in-drawnness of the earth acts as a singularly powerful gravitation – and a sort of profane cosmic vertigo is the result wherein the moon and the Constellations seem upside down. I am now wearing my father's flannel shirt [...]. I like the feeling of wearing his shirt. The neck is very large and the arms are very short. Neither of these peculiarities would be natural to him. Someone has been meddling with my father's shirt! Either Time itself or some accursed law of physics or mathematics has been interfering with my father's shirt. [...] That Discovery made by the T.T. about the Draught made all the difference. The Stove lit easily. Why this discovery will ease my whole life. What a Clever Girl!

THURSDAY 24 APRIL All day I read Homer in the Murray translation with the Greek opposite. I mean all the morning, I mean the *Odyssey*, and I got just to Circe & Moly 'μωλυ' & didn't turn the page because it then comes to the other side of the stream of Ocean & the willows & poplars of Persephone & the land of the Cimmerians. This I would not enter without the T.T. who told me how she were writing the story of Cimmeria when I first saw her alone. [...] She had a terrible reaction against this place. I had to adjust my mind to the idea of not living here very much or very long or hardly at all if she was to be really happy as I want her to be.

THURSDAY 1 MAY I saw a Heron & so did she only farther away. I took her to the river. [...] But with my pharisee fuss, a priggish, finicky, un-ease of conscience – I must needs make the T.T. cry over the Water Mint down there; by implying that she couldn't transplant it so 'twould be as happy – of course she could. She is herself a Water Mint & I have transplanted her – who am I then to make her cry? [...] I walked by the road to Harlemville and got bread. The fresh green of the Willows by the river is like a child's paints.

SATURDAY 3 MAY Looked very closely at the new leaves and the small blossom-buds on the apple-trees & pear-tree. Even the old apple tree with the stirrup on it and with breasts like Demeter is putting out leaves & blossom buds. [...] I began a rather feeble Essay on Dorothy Richardson. The T.T. will improve it later on.

SUNDAY 25 MAY Worked at Glastonbury all morning. Had a very late lunch at four o'clock & the T.T. felt grievous sad at so much of her time gone with tedious labour. Went twice up the hill to get earth for her to plant with. [...] Once she said that all this smart gardening with swell tools was hateful. How much better to leave Nature as it is & just admire it & let it alone. It is the cult of The Seedlings that drives her on. The Seedlings are the only things really weaker than herself that she has ever found to practise her little-girl protective instinct upon. The Seedlings dominate her life & our life at this time.

MONDAY 26 MAY [A] funny & agitating conversation about the Modicum & how for Ten Years the T.T. has had no rest from her labours no rest from the Dragon's Maw at one end and looking after her parents at the other – no iced coffee, no bathroom no tea on a silver tray, no sea of Marmora no balcony, no croissants & coffee in a little French Pension at Chartres. O Deary I! Ailinon! Ailinon!

SUNDAY 1 JUNE Corrected the Galley proofs of *Defence of Sensuality*. [...] The T.T. worked in Garden very late – we had a very happy tea – yes this has been from dawn to night one of my happiest days. The T.T. spoke very eloquently on the problem of whether it was better to have a child or to refrain from having a child. Her conclusion, after all was thought of, was against it.

Marian and her son Peter (eight years old) are among their first visitors. 'Pump-ship' is Powys's euphemism for urinating.

WEDNESDAY 4 JUNE I had a most serious quarrel with Peter before breakfast. He thought it was an amusing game to tease his uncle by spying on him while he went distracted to & fro hunting for a hiding-place wherein to pump-ship. At last I was seized with fury welling up from the very bottom of my soul (shall I ever recover from the shock of this feeling?) and I bore him kicking hitting out savagely and even biting into his mother's room where I denounced his conduct (myself weeping & trembling with agitation). He spied on me! He spied on me when I was pump-shipping! I kept crying out in a sobbing voice.

'I hate him! I hate him,' screamed my antagonist with still louder sobs. It was a very disturbing scene. The T.T. came flying from the kitchen & kissed away her angry mate's fiery tears while Marian soothed her outraged son. I went alone then (as ever is my wont when grievously upset) to a certain Hickory Tree in the field by the wood going to the village & I kissed the soul of this Tree & trembling still I cried to it 'O help me to forgive Peter! O help me to forgive Peter!' And I got just enough magic from this Tree (the Tree of Knowledge of Good & Evil) to forgive him but only if I did not see a certain expression in his face like that of a demonic Puck. This event has caused Pricking in my side.

THURSDAY 5 JUNE Last night I went to deep sleep before the T.T. came. I saw moon-light on the floor. There really was a certain amount of air blowing thro'; & Falada our horse looks out of the same little window there as Olwen who is the T.T.'s younger sister & her confidant over the agitations of living with a man. The T.T. always turns & glances at Olwen on those occasions when masculine stupidity or pride or roughness seems so awful to feminine elegance and love of dainty and even palatial Elegance! [...] Marian's devotion to Peter is an infatuation. It always makes me tremble & shiver with dread these desperate and passionate loves of mothers for only sons. [...] One feels that if a mother & son are absorbed in each other like two lovers it doesn't matter what the outside world feels.

WEDNESDAY 11 JUNE Worked on all the morning and far on into the afternoon in fact till dinner at 3.30 p.m. on my Book. Wrote better & quicker – am yet still in Northwold & with the image of Old Littleton before me. He my faithful, he my constant, he my prop & upstay when I was weak & irritable & bad; he dominates this early part of my Book.

SATURDAY 14 JUNE Worked a little on my book & was getting on very well with it when lo! Arthur & Gladys in their car very kindly offering to transport us to Hudson. We agreed; as I wanted to see of our neighbours & noble Protectors a little more; having been (perhaps) a trifle surly of late, not uncivil. [...] The T.T. spoke at tea which we had on our return very early (for us) on <u>her fear of life</u>. But later she spoke with the sagesse & gentlelesse of the youngest of the angels. O I do pray that a time will arrive when really & truly she will be constantly happy. The T.T. finds this world a very difficult place. She must have come from some quiet Cimmerian land where the sun always shines through mother of pearl.

MONDAY 16 JUNE The party last night teased her in retrospect – though really it all went well – but she felt it did not – she feels things that are often beyond my grosser wits. But this I know that they do not set themselves to find out what she is really like. She speaks & no one listens. […] The T.T. is such a psychic clairvoyant Elemental that she becomes what people think her – or at least she feels as if she became what people think her.

MONDAY 23 JUNE Last night the T.T. spoke at length after tea upon the matter of guests. Resolved was she to have none out here save our two families & I in this give her my Absolute Support. It fell to my lot to write therefore to old James putting him off […]. Then she went on and revealed that she had not yet been happy here (save at rare moments) but had been shocked by moods of irritable misery & sudden angers. Something very deep she thought some bruise some hurt some disappointment caused this & is yet causing it. My having snatched at this little house & spent two thousand when that two thousand might easily have kept us both for a whole year in Europe. Deep longing for old things, 'Great, good places,' or drifting imperceptibly up & down wide staircases, wide terraces, wide balconies, free from all Care! But she admitted that […] she did with part of her nature desire an established Refuge of her very own but this desire has lately been over-passed by the desire to wander free as air through the Gothic North. […] But again, the T.T. did say that it may partly be the newness of the experience that was so hard. […] We went to Bed at the same time about Eleven and as Lulu always says, 'I was happy.'

TUESDAY 24 JUNE The T.T. and I have been reading Einstein's speech on how space swallows up Time and Ether & Matter & is the same as Fields of Magnetism or is influenced by such Fields of Magnetism – all gibberish to me – but yet not devoid of some queer interest (probably wrongly interpreted) for the imagination. […] The T.T. said yesterday that it was a trying experience for a girl to live with a man – & that girls who had

had experience of love ought to be considered lucky to be alone in the world if only they had enough money to escape jobs. But the T.T. also let pass the Barrier of her Teeth words of a quite opposite import indicating that it was unthinkable to her not to have her Dragon, her Snake, her Centaur, her Magician, her hulking Numbskull alive at her bed & board. Thus doth wind & tide whirl up in Contrary Ways the surface of the Ocean – aye! what an experienced Odysseus a companion of one of these sensitive & delicate beings has to be! [...] My contribution to all this is that it is necessary to mix a certain extreme goodness with a certain very definite badness to concoct the Druidic philtre that brings them into peaceful calmness. But even Merlin mixed this philtre wrong on the last occasion – or maybe he knew better & didn't but let all the world think he did – the final magic!

They begin to modernize and redecorate the cottage, which he names Phudd Bottom. Electric lights and a fridge are installed; more efficient stoves bought for heating the house. A handyman, Mr Scutt, paints, papers, builds shelves. They find a gardener. A neighbour, Hattie Steitz, does the washing and occasionally provides meals for their guests.

FRIDAY 27 JUNE We now have light. Like some celestial visitors men from the Red Car climbed the Black Post and our Roof & at last, first in the Kitchen, then in the Pantry – light! light! No more Lamps with their smell & their wicks!

SATURDAY 28 JUNE I ought to confess to you, dear far off reader whoever you are that very late last night when it was nearly dark after taking the Garbage up hill, I left the pail & scrambled up, sans any stick using my hands like a Gorilla with satisfaction – but overcoming a certain degree of natural fear – to the top of the mount [...] and I found the great heap of White Stones & I knelt & prayed for inspiration for my Stonehenge passage in my Book. O 'twas a thing clambering down in the dark like an elephant. This morning Mr Scutt came about the papering, an unctuous nervous religious vicious amorous emotional hypocritical pious excitable eccentric kind sly lame simple man sorrowing for death of his only son & with tears telling us of it. And the Frigidaire men came and started the Frigidaire. And the T.T. says it is what she values most of all she possesses. Mr Krick mended our gate for [us] before breakfast today. I had to help driving the cows back.

THURSDAY 3 JULY Woke up at 6.45 was woken up, in fact, by Mr Scutt. He did so pathetically desire to surprise the T.T. by having the kitchen re-painted ere she woke up. He didn't know how few things can Surprise this little Missey before she has had her first sip of coffee. [...] Mr Scutt calls me 'Pop', 'Pap', 'Dad' & 'Uncle Jack'. He lusts after the T.T. with all a good Religious man's intense desire – but I like him very much. He is so like a kind benevolent Goblin. And after all the T.T. can always Scream. He calls the T.T. dearie. [...] Perhaps now he is so enamoured of the T.T. I shall get help from him (for it is all Give & Take in this world) about having the Privy cleaned out.

FRIDAY 4 JULY I wrote a bad poem on the Convolvulus & the T.T. is now composing a poem of her own on this – for she did not like mine. She is right. O she is poetical thro' & thro' and her feeling for poetry is always right where I get so tied up with the rhymes & get all heavy & rhetorical. Rhymes & Metres are hard to me for I lack music & all those delicate 'dying falls' that our favourite Paul Verlaine uses so well. I ought not to struggle with poems for I get into a mood of dogged obstinacy & I get a funny beating of a nerve in the pit of my stomach.

SATURDAY 5 JULY Last night was peculiar because just as we got back from our walk & were getting under the railing there were Arthur & Gladys asking [us] to supper no not supper but to 'come up'. The T.T. said yes & so I said yes at first. Then it seemed to me so Awful to lose my tea which the T.T. had promised to give me just before she came hurrying across the field near our river to unhook me from the Barbed Wire where I was stuck like a Ram that I said No. This No following on her yes made the T.T. feel – it is all a great imaginative & subtle Circle – very upset & we went to bed in great agitation.

SUNDAY 6 JULY Woke up early – very happily – and there was Maggie the Heifer eating our flowers. Went over to Mrs Krick after having been outrun by this little-girl Cow to the amazement of the T.T. who saw me run & Maggie run. We have had an extremely happy day. The T.T. has been in a mood so good that it is almost awe inspiring. She has had literally a saintly expression in her face today. What a subtle girl she is! – what varieties of moods she has. [...] Tonight when I made love to the T.T., it was like making love to a little Saint Thérèse.

1930

WEDNESDAY 9 JULY Woke at 6 got up at 7. Found Mr Scutt nearly finishing papering Attic with a pretty paper. [...] I have written hard & fast today & excitingly too dealing with Glastonbury. The T.T. has felt sick o' the stomach all day owing to the Paint. She has felt the sort of sickness which she would feel were she Pregnant. Fancy, if she were, how nervous & alarmed I would be! No; no too great a risk.

John has several close literary friends in America, including the novelist Theodore Dreiser and the poet Edgar Lee Masters. Llewelyn's friends, the poet Edna St Vincent Millay and her husband Eugen Boissevain, live nearby. John is reading his sister Katie's book, The Blackthorn Winter *(1930). Phyllis's menstrual period invariably begins with twenty-four hours of vomiting and severe pain.*

THURSDAY 10 JULY I wrote all day in Attic. Suddenly about noon I heard voices & I recognised the voice of Edna talking to the T.T. I went down after a little delay during which I felt exactly like my Father in his study when Dick Ponsonby was talking loudly on the lawn. Presently they all came up to the Attic & the T.T. brought up glasses of Gin. Loud and fast waxed 'the Fun of the Fair'. Edna looked Pretty & was nice to us both. The T.T. likes Mr Boissevain very much & thinks he has many of the attributes of a 'True Aristocrat'. And yet she feels that there must be Social Circles more Formal where more attention would be given to various Watteau-like Nuances and Monsieur-de-Charlus, St Simon, Proustian Divagations – than can be bestowed by the Hell-for-Leather-Bantering-Persiflage of our kind & high-spirited allies out here. [...] I felt Nervous Prostration after so much agitation & had to drink whiskey alone in Pantry.

FRIDAY 11 JULY For the first time since we have been here in this little Hillsdale house on the road the T.T. has on's own accord expressed pleasure & real spontaneous enjoyment. It is the Attic that has done this, it is sleeping in the Attic. She has looked particularly beautiful sleeping there as if it was meant for her. She is like a fairy Princess in a little room in a real Castle. Olwen & Falada also are happy there. So with the Attic I have at last got my Family more or less into Control.

SUNDAY 13 JULY Woke up in the night twice – once to find

the T.T. hitting me with her little clenched hands! She does not recall what dream she had. [...] Finished Katie's powerful & poetical story – & meditated what formidable egoism in it prevented me from feeling like crying.

MONDAY 14 JULY   Last night, just as we went to bed the T.T. Felt Sick! Ailinon! Ailinon! [...] She ought to go to Hospital when as sick as this. O woe is me – she is gone way when she is so sick & I be left alone. [...] I get my wretched meals which are no meals without her & Dyspepsia grips me sharp like a clawing Demon. I get hypochondriacal and afraid, with her sick upstairs – Aye! [...] 'Tis like her having temporarily & *pro-tem* 'died on me' as Dreiser always says.

SATURDAY 19 JULY   We had breakfast in the New Dining Room & although I upset the little Hot Water Jug & said it was so tipply we were very happy. O it was a perfect breakfast – to me anyway – and maybe to the T.T. I sat by the fullest Window Box & I did get such a thrill – in spite of the Heat – by seeing White Geraniums and Blue Lobelias & red & pink Geraniums all so near to one another in the cool green leaves of Geraniums. [...] O she did say such lovely things & did look so very lovely herself. She is now nervously rushing about ere MR MASTERS comes.

THURSDAY 24 JULY   This night we went up to Arthur's after dinner and the T.T. stood about embarrassed in the garden while I played a poetical game of Catch as Catch can with Arthur in his study choosing poets from Prof. I.A. Richards' list.[...] I have now taken two brown trout – they have red spots on their sides and faint black streaks almost like Perch discernible on their backs – to the Grotto. O what a good thing! Yes I have saved two. Cool they lie.

WEDNESDAY 30 JULY   On Tuesday night July 29th while we were smoking cigarettes after lapping up chicken-soup & plucking red currants off their strings ready for Jam we made the great Decision that we would stay out here this Winter [...]. The T.T. was so tired by scrubbing the kitchen linoleum floor that she was nearly dead. But O how she revived under this great Decision! No, she didn't revive.

THURSDAY 31 JULY   Got up late; for she was tired. So worn

out, her face swollen with tiredness. After breakfast I read the Stonehenge chapter. She is pleased with my book! […] I have now caught almost all the tiny fish, the water-flies, the big tadpoles & I found a dead Dragon-fly grub. The fierce dragon of these places – a creature I have not seen since we had our Aquarium at Dorchester. Aye! how I recalled as I carried pail to grotto walking from the Stinsford brooks there where Hardy's heart now lies! & also walking back from Foulden Bridge at Northwold. In this place, I tell 'ee all my past began to be Retrouvé – Le Temps Retrouvé!

Warwick Powys is a distant cousin living in New Mexico. They invite him to stay in the hope he will act as a general handyman/housekeeper. He sleeps at Phudd and has his meals at the Steitz'. Phyllis goes to her parents' home, 'Wildacre,' Kansas, for three weeks.

FRIDAY 1 AUGUST Cousin Warwick is coming today. She was asleep – Worn out – Worn out – Worn out. But she woke up when Mr Scutt came bringing Mr Chick Moore to act as Gardener. […] The presence of two men on the side of the garden & the hearthstone hearing & seeing all had the same effect on my nerves that New York street-criers have when I am hesitating where to go next. It's a psychological peculiarity of mine. If I am fussed up about her I cannot bear any interruptions. So it happened that when she said I'd brought dirt into the bath room mad waves of wrath against her burst out from the Pit of my Stomach. It was a wonder that I didn't Shout at the top of my Lungs. But all I did was to hiss like a Cobra halfway up our Attic stairs. 'I'll soon be afraid of such a Shrew as you be – so I will!' I could see then exactly what a hare looks like when it is very angry. But O how awful the next hour was! Because I wanted to be forgiven by the T.T. 'I forgive you. You forgive me.' But she would not […].

SATURDAY 2 AUGUST This morning has been a very strange one. The T.T. likes reverences and admires Warwick but her nerves are done-in, raffled – ruffled – ragged – raw & her face – her dear eyelids – swollen as if she had been crying, crying, crying, for a month. She must go home to her mother. I must, I must carry this through. […] Having sent off the Fatal Telegram, *Alea jacta est*! The die is cast. The T.T. feels a sort of relief. But she is very sad at leaving her Ogre – but this sadness is better than that absolutely nervous and physical exhaustion wherein she becomes indifferent to all & dead to all.

TUESDAY 5 AUGUST I have to write *The Owl, the Duck and Miss Rowe Miss Rowe* for Olwen, Falada & the T.T. Olwen looks so very sad today & Falada looks like the Blind Horse. [...] I thought of how my philosophy had twice broken down in all these agitations but thought I'll make it stronger. I won't, I won't give it up. But I will add to it those feelings that come when it has broken down! The luggage of the T.T. is now on the Porch.

THURSDAY 7 AUGUST This morning I walked by the road to the village with Warwick. O it is very hard to be always nice. [...] As we returned from Mrs Steitz, suddenly as if by two gods in a chariot, overtaken were we by Edna & Boissevain. They tried to carry us past our house but I seized the wheel & stopped them near our door. Edna in her bathing dress, sat on the knees of Warwick & Mr Powg. We took them in. Warwick sang his songs & Edna learnt them & repeated them with tears in eyes. She sang also one of her own called Mariposa – 'Suffer me to take thy hand.' Then in Warwick's coat they went away. Thunder thunder thunder & terrific lightning & rain. They left in this storm. The blind horse keeps crying out tho' it is safe with the other. Warwick is singing wildly he is wild with excitement – Edna having sat on his knee and sung his song and now a wild storm rages and the rain falls in torrents.

SUNDAY 10 AUGUST O I have got so to detest the visit to the Steitz house. I stare at those terrible pictures & at the hanging plants and I think will the T.T. come back safe? [...] The effort of coping with Warwick has reduced my humanity to its limit. Civil to him I must remain, & kind to him; but the strain is such that the outside world must be prepared to find me as stony as Theodore in the drawing room of Max Gate. I tell them all I am writing and so I will write in spite of all. Yes, in spite of all. [...] I become a slave to Warwick just because he is a sort of liberated slave – sulky as a child if he is not allowed what he wants. I allow him everything he wants except that I will not go out to see people.

WEDNESDAY 13 AUGUST LULU'S Birthday. I love watering the T.T. seedlings & the two beds & the boxes. I water so long –

1930 I water from 7.30 to 9.30. I water all the evening. It is an escape. [...] I water even if sky is grey. I only don't do it when it rains. But I get the fish out when it rains. I carried a pail of them at night to Grotto. [...] O they must have been glad. I have had a contest in my mind over this. I like to put they fish where I can see 'em going in in clear water but they like it best to be put in where I can't see 'em because of green weed. I have overcome my tendency. I put they fish in weed part as they tell me. I obey the wishes of every organism I am with. I am a cold fish-medicine-man. I am the holy man of the fish – & all organisms are the same to me. All are like fish in shallow water longing for Grotto but wanting to get there in darkness & hide in weeds & not be watched going in by inquisitive staring Saviours! I do so depend on the T.T. All my philosophy came in Being since I met her.

Llewelyn and Alyse arrive in America. Llewelyn goes to John and Alyse to her parents. The luckless Warwick is sent back to New Mexico. John meets Phyllis in New York and they return to Phudd Bottom on 26 August. Lulu and Alyse stay with them until 2 September when they go to Edna Millay's.

THURSDAY 14 AUGUST Have had a cable that Lulu & Alyse are at sea coming to New York. They cabled to leave the key of our room with Mrs Keenan. Do they know about Mr Van Wageningen? I cannot think they do. But they are probably fighting for their own hand in that sad desperation in which most mortals are. It will be wonderful to me to see the rugged face of my Lulu. [...] But he will scold me about Warwick. We are different there. I don't scold people. I have the heart of a Stone – but I am a benevolent Stone. Everyone is 'up against it'. All organisms, as the T.T. once said, keep crying 'I. I. I. I. I!' And here am I – tho' a Stone – doing just the same! What is this Diary but that? Only this Diary is of two Egos – two 'I's' – for the T.T. is my other I – my alter-ego – & I do put my stone-angles & stone-surfaces into the stream for the T.T. to use as stepping-stones.

SATURDAY 23 AUGUST This has been a day of unbelievable agitations. Lulu's mind is so occupied with tragedy or babyishness or both together that it is hard for him to do anything or take any part in anything. He touches me to heart & also excites my

Sadism. He is *hors de combat* – aye but it is sad to see the great Master of sun & sense & The Only Reality so hit by the Dart of Aphrodite. He has drunk the Philtre & all the while with Iseult of the White Hands he keeps thinking of the Dark Iseult of Ireland [...]. That is the tragic & noble side of it, dignified & Romantic – the old ancient dart of the Terrible Cyprian. But again Lulu acts and has acted like a Baby. He wants to be the lamb, suckled by both cow & sheep. [...] He got a wire that Alyse was not coming on this day. W. had ordered Mr S. to take us to station to meet her train. Then we got wire from her that she was not coming – and got a letter from the T.T. saying that she herself would get rid of Warwick alone. Warwick got a letter saying that they were glad he had got such a nice job with his cousin & they would send him his things. But luckily Mr Jackson said in another letter; if by chance you do want to return you can return as before! I decide that if the T.T. was to be spared this agitation it was up to me to take the initiative and Kill the Chicken myself. I said to Masters You behold an Executioner. I am going to 'Kill the chicken.' So I suddenly decided that all three of us should go into New York together. Lulu to Alyse & I to Hotel & to train with Warwick. We found train at station just starting for New York but we missed it. [...] But as we sat waiting 3 hours for next train and Warwick was ordering tea at Hotel, suddenly there was Alyse. She had come because Lulu had threatened to go in to Patchin Place if she didn't & she thought 'twas bad for Lulu's health to be in Patchin Place. Why the devil they made us turn out Mr Van Wageningen our Perfect Tenant if they have no intention of using our room is a puzzle to me but they are both too agitated to think of anything.

SUNDAY 24 AUGUST Had journey last night to New York with Warwick who talked 'sans cesse' & I listened with a sort of strange intensity. Warwick composed poem to Olwen. A touching poem. Her first love-letter. Had supper at Child's in Union Sq. – got room with bath for W. at Hotel – got lower berth for W. on special train to Buffalo which cost me six dollars extra. [...] He went off at 10.30.

MONDAY 25 AUGUST Set off to Station. Waited by the Announcer of Trains. At last with a great stir he wrote Track 36 in chalk and shouted out 'South Western Limited!' That was a phrase not unknown to I! I went to opening & there nearly last of all came the T.T. There she was & that wispy voice gave me old Thrill. More lovely than I'd ever known her was she: & unbelievably gentle to the Ogre. [...] Then we got to Room at 2 o'clock. O the cool darkness! O the lovely London smell like an old Library! O the peace & quiet & hidden seclusion. Here I had my T.T. [...] The happiness – aye! the happiness. Tho' there was no Western Wind blowing or small rain falling, all was beyond what I can tell you, you Reader of this!

TUESDAY 26 AUGUST [I]t's possible to take hold of a great happiness like this so full of deep & liquid Peace & spread it out or sprinkle it out like Celestial Oil & Milk over hard hard days to come. This is a great secret. And I have learnt it. I learnt it from Tiresias who learnt it from Chiron the Centaur.

WEDNESDAY 27 AUGUST Lulu & Alyse were up and out for a walk when I came down. [...] We had a prolonged breakfast – Lulu silent & absorbed in the Poison in's veins.

FRIDAY 29 AUGUST [W]hen the T.T. first woke up she said that life was too much for her & she seriously, quietly, and in reasonable cold blood wished she were dead. I wonder how many Ogres & Dragons & Magicians & Centaurs have beautiful girls who wish they were dead?

SUNDAY 31 AUGUST At tea we four were alone. I felt ashamed secretly in my heart in the presence of these three I love so well. [...] I felt very humble & I wanted to talk in a whisper and stop my hard swoopings & pouncings and my crude insensitive dartings down. I felt I had a sort of electric force where they had gentle lovely tender ironical human nuances. I felt like a Neanderthal Man – taken captive by three human beings & full of awe & respect & shame in their presence.

TUESDAY 2 SEPTEMBER Lulu talked of Suicide [...]. The T.T. told him what it was really like. [...] Went with Lulu to get the Mail. There was one from Gamel. [...] We sat down in a cool grove under a festoon of purple grape which, against his head, looked like a Titian picture. He read his letter which he regarded as a Rejection; but I (taught by the T.T.) regarded it as a wise calm action of common sense for all concerned. We stayed for a long time talking about 'love' in this Grove of Ceres &

about fate and free will and about Edna St Vincent's entrance for the 2nd time in his biography. [...] Ficke came and took Lulu & Alyse off to live with Edna at Steepletop. They left their biggest bag behind. The T.T. felt a calm peace at being alone.

WEDNESDAY 3 SEPTEMBER I am slowly very slowly getting on with my Glastonbury Book which is pure effortless pleasure. But I feel very sleepy & tired & sickish. [...] This comes from my bowels. I am an invalid in some way that is hard to follow. It is hot. It is hard to be thrilled when one is feeling slightly sickish – but I can do this, hard tho' it is. I can do this (and not once or twice either) by getting secret strength from the top garden apple tree. This morning all the misty rainy distance was like that French Painter Corot. You could see hands of nymphs raised out of the dew. It is lovely to see the T.T. so happy, & she does like her garden. Can we stay all the winter? Would that be wrong?

THURSDAY 4 SEPTEMBER Woke up at dawn hearing a large brown horse gallop up & down. Did not go to it. Mr Curtis says better leave well alone over strays lest become Responsible for Keep. So it is; & who knows not that doctrine as well as I? [...] Tried that Pail on the Nail Enema & got all fussed up & mixed up & had to have recourse to my old Squirting one but I was so agitated that I forgot my usual arranging even with that! I wonder I didn't confuse my head with my tail. However! I got on somehow. Then I fetched the Mail – & lo! & behold. There came Ten Copies of *Defence of Sensuality*. The T.T. opened this parcel at once and at once began reading – when she came to a passage about loneliness she was pleased & her dear face lit up [...]. I could write for her alone and some remote, very remote posterity – or at least I rather think I could.

FRIDAY 5 SEPTEMBER [S]he said at breakfast today that she got more satisfaction in her Life Illusion by helping to write Six Massive Books that we project than by 'travelling about Europe'. But I nevertheless see her now so thin so worn so white so haggard – with her mouth like that Passport photo – & I wonder what is really right to do? Of course while her father lives she is handicapped from leaving this country. But then again, is it right for me to let her give up Patchin Place & concentrate on facing the winter out here?

FRIDAY 12 SEPTEMBER This was a day devoted to work on

my Glastonbury Book. I do want to get some Communist Propaganda into my book; for at heart & at brain I am a Communist. Only in my selfishness (for life is short and I dearly like an easy life) am I a possessor of Private Property! [...] Now I have just composed a letter to Mr Keedick. On Saturday morning it will be posted – agreeing to debate with Chesterton. I walked to the High Barn which is now my favourite walk. But no mountains were visible. It was extremely hot – this thrice accursed American summer weather came back. [...] Hot weather makes me hate every form of matter & every form of organic being. [...] I am not well. I am sick – and black flies take me for Carrion.

The nicknames they give each other are 'the Inmates,' 'the Terminals'. Phyllis's nicknames for John are Jack, the Ogre, 'the Man,' the Dragon. She often calls him Petrushka – the Russian folk equivalent of Punch. Petrushka is a puppet, brought to life by a Magician, who falls in love with a Dancer.

SUNDAY 21 SEPTEMBER To my complete amazement after breakfast & washing up what did she do but retire to the attic for a very long while – for 3 hours! – & then at last she came down when 'twas nearly tea time & lo! & behold she had been

WRITING

This is really the 1st time she has done this since we came here a year ago. I was so proud of her & so very glad. She is writing about the two Inmates of an Asylum – one is mad about making the world happy & the other is mad in thinking the other to be a Puppet; in fact to be the puppet Petrushka.

MONDAY 22 SEPTEMBER I did all my rounds. Do you know what they are – fill up all water-pails – fill up oil thing – light stove & electric – fill up White Kettle with hot water. Take garbage up hill; pick apples, golden Hesperidian apples, what the Dragon guards but not into the house any more! Walk round orchard visiting the two wounded trees & touching gingerly at the back the Bewick-Tree which is terrifying to me. Walk up Top Garden to the apple tree there which is the one that gives me strength to endure and which I hug the trunk of, pressing my stomach on it which helps my ulcer or dyspepsia as well.

WEDNESDAY 24 SEPTEMBER This morning Mr Wickam

brought her a big bouquet of the most lovely Dahlias, so cool so wet so full of watery sap. I love best the whitish pink ones with yellow calix. Pink and yellow are colours which when together thrill me with a strange delight. Why should that be? Early memory do you think of yellow sea weed & pink shells? [...] Yesterday at tea after I had returned from seeing the Mountains from the high hill above the other hill the T.T. spoke with unbelievable eloquence about the absence of an aura in this coldly and neutrally & indifferently lovely land. She said Indians and Dutch were not enough. O she does so pine for the Gothic North! I must take her there one day. Yes I must one day take her where she will be really happy. [...] I really must not in my passion for this place, this cold place, doom her to renounce her Moyen Age. The trees are beginning to look autumnal.

THURSDAY 2 OCTOBER There arose the Accursed Question of Mr Keedick & the Debate with Chesterton. The T.T. & I got angry over it. I was greatly to blame – she says I don't even have the Courage of my own Cowardice but am cowardly over suggestions and yet not committed but really obstinate in my own grovelling tactics! Alas! 'tis but too true. We wasted at least an hour of this 2nd Oct. on this thrice accursed matter. In the end it'll be that I will follow my own method – it'll at least spare the T.T. the responsibility of any change! But what cowardice is mine. Think of being so afraid of anyone – & as I am – so afraid of Everyone!

They buy a black cocker spaniel which they call variously Peter, the Black, the Old and – eventually – the Very Old. Accident-prone, nervous, untrained, he is none the less well-loved and is to play a large role in their lives. Llewelyn and Alyse, both still tortured by his passion for Gamel, return to Phudd in late November. John's ulcer flares up.

MONDAY 6 OCTOBER At breakfast had a very exciting talk about the real secret cause of my prejudice against Gamel. [...] At breakfast too the T.T. & I spoke of our attitude to each other. She mentioned the sea & the shore & I mentioned the twig in the crystal. But no matter for these mentionings! The T.T. is the T. T. & I am (like Capaneus in Dante) what I am.

SATURDAY 18 OCTOBER We took P[eter] for a walk across the Big Field – the T.T. in her Red Dressing Gown. She ran all flushed & her fine hair tossed wild holding up her red gown while P. ran after her. It was a happy walk. Read *Esmond*. And at tea the T.T. told me the story of *War & Peace*.

SATURDAY 25 OCTOBER How strange and mysterious a Being [...] the T.T. is! Who can read the ebb & flow of the Ocean or predict its storms & calms, its wild weather, its curious weather. [...] And who am I to have – wicked as I am & as I have been – to have the luck to live with so wild, beautiful, exciting, absorbing, perilous & strange an Identity as this is. O let me make her happy, O let me make her happy. But it is going to be difficult – for hard, O bitter hard does she take this being alive on the earth & she is so terribly a Half-Born & so sensitive to everything to 'Everything'.

MONDAY 10 NOVEMBER Had a terrifying dream that I entered a hostile community-dwelling; & white excrement ran out of my feet! For this I was disgraced & a Scaffold, resembling an enormous red Fireman's ladder, was set up to execute me with the word

PUNISHMENT

writ on it in vast letters.

SATURDAY 22 NOVEMBER [W]e walked across the field to where the accident to Peter occurred. [...] He goes by scent and sound and never by sight. In sight he is worse than stupid, he is an idiot. [...] At lunch today the T.T. discoursed on why she has not been happy in this house. [...] And she said the cause was because of the responsibility – the stoves etc. etc. etc. & all the rest which never allowed her to feel free. I said, 'when I bought this house I made the greatest mistake of my life' and then she laughed and said, 'No – earlier!'

FRIDAY 5 DECEMBER I have never seen – nor has the T.T. ever seen – such a classic instance of the arrow of Eros – sticking in his throat as he goes like a wounded Centaur or a wounded lion or an injured & outraged child of the gods – or just like Lulu not having what LULU wants! Such a pitiful trouble comes into his eyes. O such a pitiful trouble. As for myself – I am on Alyse's side – but that is because I am for some mysterious and to me quite inexplicable reason, queerly prejudiced against this gentle, passive, dreamy, mediaeval, lovely incalculable young girl. [...]

After tea Lulu was again very sleepy until I talked of Gamel & until the T.T. suggested his living first with one & then with the other.

SATURDAY 6 DECEMBER Lulu and I walked to the Two Rocks past the Yellow House. He scolded me very severely sawing the air with his hand as he does, about my gushing & over effusive manner with the Lower Classes. We disputed fiercely about Dorothy Richardson whom he holds in contempt.

FRIDAY 12 DECEMBER I took up the T.T.'s hot water. Bitter-sad was she. Her eyes like those of a mad person. I came down in a mental turmoil from the sight of those eyes. But coffee can work a miracle. After breakfast she was herself again – the little T.T. – & that mad strange pitiless Being had been Exorcised. It was the Sink & L. & A. coming & having to go to Kricks & having to take the Black & it was <u>Mr</u> <u>Everything</u> who is always waiting to pounce. Mr Krick our Guardian Angel – the noblest of men – has 'fixed' the sink. [...] The T.T. is happier today O how I do praise the gods for this! How I do thank & praise them. Alas! I had scarce writ those words when things got worse than ever – the sink got right but the stove got wrong & the T.T. is terribly upset – & at this juncture who should appear but the unluck bearing Gladys! I got rid of her as best I could amid echoing Barks from Black. O what can I do? What can I do? Things are getting serious.

FRIDAY 19 DECEMBER <u>Got</u> <u>up</u>. I never can make my fucking pen write this first word 'got up' – at the Last Day it'll be the same – 'Got up' to hear myself condemned to a million years of Purgatory for cutting worms in bits; for going with a young girl of twelve to that 'Madame's' house near the station at Brighton when she said 'you like them young'; for marrying Bertie to Dorothy; for deciding to return to America to lecture simply & solely in order to go to the Living 'Peep-Show' in Philadelphia – for striking out for my own hand over this little Phudd Bottom house, instead of thinking what way will be most harmonious in the long run to the T.T. – for not daring to openly join the Communist Party & take the risks of being imprisoned & beaten up – for not devoting my life to try & be Saint. Well enough of this. 'Got up' & lit the stove & put coal on the fires & took the little Black Worm out for his walk. [...] A letter from the T.T.'s father warning us of possible Bank failure. Where would we be if this really occurred? [...] This evening the T.T. said that I was only lively at breakfast and at tea. At other times amiable but far-off. I totally deny and reject this accusation.

SUNDAY 28 DECEMBER She talked at breakfast very very imaginatively & eloquently about Manuscripts as opposed to Print & how they were a world in themselves. We came to the conclusion that all my writings belonged to the Manuscript Class – but not those of Llewelyn or of Theodore.

MONDAY 29 DECEMBER I took the Black for his two walks. He likes it best in the fields. [...] She went tonight to the Village Entertainment while I wrote to her parents. [...] She went with the Kricks to this entertainment and she described it to me very vividly very imaginatively. O how she will write when she does once begin. It is awful to me to think that I am stopping her from writing. I have written a lot of my book today.

WEDNESDAY 31 DECEMBER Mr Simmonds has come to finish up the storm-windows. O how nice & snug & safe, O how buttressed in & cosy they make this little house to be. [...] Our tea was happy all four. The T.T. cooked a Leg of Lamb for late dinner at 8. I had cold Spring Rooster to eat, the one I had seen being killed. The one she had heard crowing. We talked quietly & happily. We sat up till twelve. [...] But Alyse had brought Gamel's letter & showed us – sad news for Lulu. But we said you must show it to him. There was moonlight outside. Lulu read Ballads to us. No sooner had the T.T. come to bed than I embraced her to the limit; this was my beginning of 1931. And Lulu when they were in the kitchen put his head like a child upon my knee & asked my blessing which I gave him.

1931

The seclusion of Phudd gives John what he has always longed for: 'real time to write in, hours and hours of time.' The trips to Somerset and Norfolk in 1929, his extensive reading in Welsh mythology and Christian grail legends, are transformed in this year into the huge and complex Glastonbury Romance. *The forty-six characters and myriad events of this novel mingle in his mind with his everyday life at Hillsdale. There is Sam Dekker, the twentieth-century Christian grail knight whose quest forces him to abandon his love, Nell Zoyland, and whose reward is a vision of the Fisher-King. Geard is an itinerant preacher determined to make Glastonbury the centre of a 'religious revival'. He is another quester, but his quest is 'other' – for the pagan cauldron of re-birth and for re-union with Cybele, the earth-mother. There is the rich industrialist, Philip Crow, owner of Wookey Hole; there is Owen Evans, the tortured sadist whose obsession is to watch someone being killed. The novel ends with a great flood that drowns Geard and restores Sam to joyous life. In the drought-stricken summer of Columbia County, Powys walks the Black, prays his prayers, and re-enacts the myth of the wasteland with his exhausting rescue of dying fish. He is himself often startled by the synchronicity of real and imagined events. And as always, intermixed with his creative preoccupations are the memories of his childhood and of childhood places – of Montacute, Dorchester, Sherborne, Weymouth, Northwold.*

The intensity of the writing awakens his ulcer and he tries to cure it with a special diet, 'vegetable pills', and bed rest. He becomes accustomed to using a board to write on while lying on his couch, and this is his regular writing position for the rest of his life.

Despite a decreasing income, at the end of January they hire Magda Hagen as their live-in housekeeper. This gives Phyllis the freedom from 'boring routine' that she craves but the venture is not a success. His deep love of Phudd and Columbia County is obvious; she is becoming increasingly unhappy.

1931 THURSDAY 1 JANUARY Woke up at 9 o'clock – very exhausted by being so happy before I went to sleep. The head of the T.T. on the pillow did so make me 'fond of her'. This head on the pillow belongs to me. It is a head of mine. My head. [...] Now it is after breakfast, late (11.45 or 12 noon even) and Alyse has told Lulu about Gamel's letter & he has shaken his fist at the sky crying out 'But she belongs to me! She is mine. He is taking mine!' Alyse says that his mouth gets twisted awry like Katie's in this frenzy.

SATURDAY 3 JANUARY I have given up all attempt to do any work while Lulu is here. But I think a lot of what I am writing at this moment namely Mr Geard at Mark's Court with the Marquis & his daughter. Mr Geard must think of the secret of real life beyond this spectacular world. He must think of the Graal as a symbol of this secret life beyond life. He must think of Christ as a majestic God; not a Tortured Crucified Sacrifice. And this Christ Himself is less mysterious than the Graal.

MONDAY 5 JANUARY A LETTER from GERTRUDE arrived for me from East Chaldon speaking of Peace Versus Passion as her Ideal but also of Gamel having a house in Dorset. This has greatly cheered Lulu who has now set out to Philmont to meet Alyse. [...] I watched him go behind the willows & past the school. I thought to myself this place is just as good as East Chaldon for seeing people far off – as memorial Events in a Platonic landscape – & I thought There goes He, my Lulu walking there past that little school, & I thought there in that house under Phudd is my True love the T.T. & I thought how softly bluish grey making you long to eat them, ravish them, plunge your hand into them, are the distant hills, the sun being so misty. A letter has come from Dorothy Richardson yes! from Miriam Henderson herself. The T.T. has taken down our Christmas Tree for Twelfth Night & all the air of this room is fragrant with hemlock.

MONDAY 12 JANUARY A heavy snow storm & I took the mail with difficulty and took the Black with difficulty round by Witch's bridge. O how deep & snow white – on every pine & birch & willow & blade – masses of soft white elemental Substance the flesh of God the Son, white as wool, as ivory, whiter than milk, white as light itself & heavy & soft & silent on all. The T.T. was in a wonderful happy mood. She said after breakfast, 'O it is so nice! no one coming – no one being able to come!' Then suddenly Miss McNeill came – gallantly marching on foot covered with snow like a robust virgin Cow.

FRIDAY 16 JANUARY I must tell you to prove how deeply I […] sympathize with Nell Zoyland when Sam Dekker decided to stop making love to her in order to be a Saint, that the T.T. yesterday say to me 'Something is Matter'. I say no she say yes – 'no,' yes, 'no,' yes, & then I have to confess I was sad because of Nell Zoyland. Thus I have really assumed the Creator's job & without any wicked Sadism but just like God for merely artistic reasons I've made Nell sad.

TUESDAY 20 JANUARY First sun & then it was snowing and then it was shining. Took the Black over bridge and by river & up hill. The yellow stalks were shining gold and on each were many diamonds of melting ice. I counted 4 on an upright grass on its stalk and 5 on a horizontal grass bent down by age. Thus I noted & came into relation with 9 drops of glittering water doomed to die. […] I climbed that bank to high railings and there were bright red berries of rose bushes – hips or haws against the snow. I looked at these as I listened to the sound of the river. They were drops of blood. I thought of that passage in Malory when Sir Percival (I think it's he) stares in a Trance at blood-drops on the snow. I noted also how the ice hung like sea-weed of a faint coral colour to the dead seeds of the Ash Trees.

FRIDAY 23 JANUARY First day of […] Magda Hagen. But the T.T. did not dare to ask for her Bacon! She wants someone to manage the Housekeeper! I fear she will suffer some odd feelings alas! […] I lay exhausted in bed & contemplated the <u>Blueness</u> between those blue curtains of spare room O how lovely the <u>Blueness</u> was – the great American Mystery that queer <u>Blueness</u>. I never recall it in my own land. At tea, to which she came down in her black velvet & her lace the T.T. spoke of Lulu & his love affair. She defended Romantic Love & when I said it did change into <u>something</u> <u>else</u> when the lovers lived together O how the T.T. did open her beautiful eyes & make such a quaint face of protest! At such times her eyes (<u>my</u> <u>world</u> of tides & currents & ebbs & flows are they!) get as blue as that Blueness in window. How is that? It must be the white part of them – like snow – when that blue comes, but thus lifting her eyebrows at my saying that Romantic love changed O how blue they looked. But she is surely right! I was talking about what I had read in the books about PASSION, of which I have never known anything.

SATURDAY 24 JANUARY I did not feel ulcer when I woke up – to my astonishment – could it have not really got started again? I am absurdly hypochondriacal maybe but no – alas! – after breakfast I did feel it & I knew it was there, but I have no dyspepsia – & as long as that evil acid doesn't pour out over ulcer to make him seethe & foam & bubble like an angry sea-anemone all will be well again. He will subside & retire & cease to cry 'here I am!' I have no dyspepsia because of the perfect dinners I have been having recently of Mashed Potatoes and Spinach & Olive Oil. Today when I took Black by Chicken path & the Three Willows, the sun was all pale & misty & there was a lovely greenish tint in the northern sky. The ice-snow was all glittering like the tiny little scales of a great Leper-Dragon.

TUESDAY 27 JANUARY We had a very wild night full of mysterious occurrences. I remained on my side turned to the wall in dead stillness and the T.T. could not sleep and woke up early and there were noises & steps & voices the barking of many dogs – others beyond our well-known Rover – and Ferdinand singing in the road and wild sad disconsolate Raccoons crying out at dawn. [...] Had a wonderful long letter from Dorothy Richardson in which she said she had torn up many pages full of 'masculine resentment' & bitterness against their trials.

WEDNESDAY 28 JANUARY I had a very hard job over my book today having to write an 'Inset' for Persephone & an 'Inset' for Sam. [...] After tea we worked together on my book putting in the Insets. The T.T. composed whole passages. [...] She is so happy because of Mrs H. She said I look forward to tomorrow. She never has said that before [...].

THURSDAY JANUARY 29 She dresses for tea always now. It is nice. I greatly like it though naturally I miss what she can do in making the tea-table look so lovely. But when I see her so happy (and I tell you she does radiate a delicious vibration of a little girl being very happy) of course I think that such a thing is more precious than any tea-table & I don't only think so, I see that loveliness that used to be on the tea-things now upon her face [...].

MONDAY 2 FEBRUARY The T.T. took Black in the afternoon. This is ever a distress to me. It causes twinges in my vitals. There I lie & tremble lest she return in Hysterics & full of misery – & I so longing to do it myself. But today I used self-control & held my nerves in check & all she said was that she wouldn't bear it another winter.

They had installed a pump in October 1930, to provide running water in the house. The problems they have with this become a recurring motif.

TUESDAY 3 FEBRUARY This is the Coldest Day. The Faucets were empty. No Water. Took Black the round by Mail & nearly to White Tree. [...] No water. Aye & when I said it was exciting to try the Old Pump in Orchard the T.T. was terribly upset. I could not shave nor put my head in water. Only a little hot from kettle & a lump of snow that I brought in to clean my teeth. Cold Coffee too. Dog barking. All agitation. Then did the wise heroic Nausicaa-Phyllis set out to Kricks & telephoned to Mr Rumery. Meanwhile I got two buckets of water from Kricks. The T.T. got hot water & undid some harm that with my excited 'priming' earlier I had done to orchard pump. Then Krick's car broke down & he borrowed our kettle. Then Rumery came & Lo! he saved us! He brought a great Machine Torch like the clever city labourers in Subway. With this flame-shooting machine he warmed the pipes of the Pump in the Cellar. He watched the Hand in the Index Clock on Pump. It pointed at Zero. Were the pipes frozen? Still at Zero it pointed. Then it wavered where he applied his Torch. Triumph & glorious relief! It moved; it moved! Then Water! water! we were saved.

WEDNESDAY 11 FEBRUARY Took Black via Mail where I posted endless letters. [...] When I reached the red bridge the ridge was receding in mystical mists one behind another & I said to the Black – you & I – dog & man are crossing a Bridge before a misty Range of Hills over which sun-rays advance & recede & these hills go on receding forever as Dog & Man with the Leash follow the Road. All my life in sideway thoughts have I followed the road to that far off sun-touched misty range! O how I do like Hillsdale & Columbia County. O T.T. forgive me. I cannot let it go without saying how I like it. Phudd in place of the T.T.'s Watteau-ish 'Small Measure.'

1931 SUNDAY 15 FEBRUARY Had to get up at 5.15 owing to 3 Vegetable Pills & I hated this & I hated the Dragon's Excrement like that of a Sick Wyvern, that it compelled me to void making me a laughing stock of disgust. These are the times when I long for a 'Toilet' as it's called in America, at the end of a Corridor & reserved entirely for myself! [...] I have now begun at last my great Pageant chapter. May the gods aid me. I have read a lot of Osbert Sitwell's Granada story.

MONDAY 16 FEBRUARY Tried to practice being a God & not taking off my fur cap to the Earth my Mother – but couldn't achieve this. Like Faust before the Earth Spirit I had to go down & kneel & kiss the Sod. The God kisses the Sod. The Sod answers the God with a very ancient Silence! [...] But when I crossed the Bridge of Lulu [...] I thought this splashing murmuring water these dark sepia-green-black Rocks below our little house are as romantic to me (& more too) as those Alhambra rivers spoken of by Osbert Sitwell. Thus I cry my Cymric War-cry – 'a Powys! a Powys!' & defy these bastard Normans who must have travels to historic spots in order to get their thrills. This river (nameless) this Hickory tree, this tall Cypress so dark & as Sitwell would say 'like a flame of green' (not really at all) and above all the God of Phudd's great Stone on the slope behind house – these are enough for a Druid maker of Triads – to the deuce with these Troubadours – have I not the blood of Taliessin in my veins? Have I not Ridden on a Stag?

WEDNESDAY 18 FEBRUARY Today the god of Phudd keeps calling me to come & tap my forehead in Penance for a heathen Ash Wednesday upon that great Stone, but I have defied the god of Phudd today; telling him that I too am a god! I shall however not hesitate to Compromise with him as is the way of my English blood & I shall no doubt tap my forehead for him before many days are over: but it shall be when I please and not when he pleases!

THURSDAY 19 FEBRUARY A morning of wailing & calamity. This comes of defying the god of Phudd! But I shall go on I shall go on I shall go on go on defying him as long as I choose. But Calamity has descended! I read Ajax & his lamentations. His very name Aias, he says, is the same as 'Ai-ai! ai ai' & he defies all the Gods. Ajax defying the Gods, Ajax defying the gods, Ajax defying the gods. [...] O calamity is upon us & the gods are hostile to me. Let me think! Did I defy them all – no! not the rain all except the god of the rain – but did I not make Wolf hate him & throw him away? Mukalog, the god of the rain? So I have no one on my side of the Immortals. O the unhappy little T.T. how cruelly are you being tormented by this kakodemon this whoreson Nausea [...]. She keeps crying out & she does fix on me such heart-breaking reproachful looks like an animal or a child as if I could do something if I only would. O damn! [...] She is very ill with these Nerves in the Stomach. At this very moment the Doctor is in the Attic with her. She is very bad. It is still Thursday. I can hear the Doctor talking to her. Can he do anything for her? Can he make her sleep?

FRIDAY 20 FEBRUARY This has been perhaps the Most AGITATING time I recall since the New Relations at 4 Patchin Place except perhaps – when we had that breakfast at Childs when the T.T. tried to get a job there as a Waitress & that noble present of $100 (for such it seemed to be, though he called it advance on lectures) from William Durant saved us. Which is the most agitating – Poverty or Sickness? In my time I have known plenty of the latter but relatively nothing of the former – no – really nothing.

Phyllis goes to her parents from 25 February to 4 April. John is left with Magda Hagen to manage the house and animals in winter.

TUESDAY 3 MARCH Got up at 7 just too late to see the Sun rise. Saw it thro' lilac out of parlour. But Calamity on Calamity. Last night I took 3 pills, as Reginald Hunter would say 'of my vegetable variety' and all the while was getting the matters attended to, what in Columbia County & elsewhere we call 'Chores,' & keeping an eye on the Bath Room watching when Mrs H. would use it & shut the door. Finally I had just used the Toilet (for the 1st time for three days) when the Water Stopped. Luckily kettles had been filled but O deary I! I cannot tell you what a struggle to be philosophical! God! could Marcus Aurelius have managed it with all the water on the Palatine Hill stopped? Could he & if he had just used the only Palatial Latrine? [...] The Pump is now going Continuously! Something is very Wrong. 'You are taking my water' cried the old lady when I used an inch for shaving & sponging my eyes; letting my teeth go. We Are Saved. Mr Rumery has come & started the water all right by priming it for a very long while. […] Just before they went they thought they heard a Leak in the pipes somewhere but he went off disregarding that item. 'Call me up again if anything wrong.' 'So I will Mr, So I surely will!' Well, *tout s'arrange* we must struggle on. Cheerio O! All righty! Carry on! Right Ho! but O deary I! How I miss the Missy!

WEDNESDAY 4 MARCH I seemed to hear Pumb going. There! see my Welsh trick of 'b' for 'p' – bumphet! & I thought it's off sans Cesse! it'll work itself into Fever-heat & get red-hot & set Cellar on fire & I'll hear flames. I thought what I'd do. Climb out of south window drop from roof run round to front door – thro' smoke & fire enter there – a Fireman of noble descent – a Knight of Festoon. Carry Mamma Magda in strong arms out into Road! God! I notice in these considerations that I forgot my MSS. […] Did chores. Shook down too much Red but got it up again, the fire, got it up all well. Took letters. Took Black. Tail up a Good Hunting Dog down by River all snow once more – looked at rushing waves of river & thought of how in John Blanch's mathematic schoolroom at Sherborne I used to shut my eyes & call up the waves on beach outside Penn House. Thought of how Blanch slew himself in Honeycomb woods slashing his Throat & crying God Save the Queen so that far off labourers in field heard 'un.

SATURDAY 7 MARCH I find I do not write half as much now the T.T. is gone away – not half as much. There are so many little things to be done. I felt weary & sad & therefore at eight o'clock I went to bed. And I dreamed I was to act in a Pageant and had not prepared my Part.

SUNDAY 8 MARCH A wild, wild night. I woke up to hear terrific wind. I feared the chimney would be blown down. […] This is the longest storm that ever I knew. I have seen this day no sign of man or beast – no living thing save one little dead bird. This East wind is bitter. I have written to Theodore because he likes to hear from you when you are sad but not when you are happy.

WEDNESDAY 11 MARCH I must make my book better. I must gather it together and make it more dramatic & exciting. I must make it mount up. I must get suspended excitement over the plot. I must gather it more tightly. Had Red Cabbage for lunch. Went to Krick's and got eggs & butter. There was a tradesman there selling them something from Chatham. I was struck by the jokes – all the time – how the necessity for perpetual joking takes the place of intelligence.

WEDNESDAY 18 MARCH A terrific rush of water in the river – the semen of Sisyphus. I saw another rat – very fat – maybe a pregnant mother, clamber out of the String-box. Yes, I expect it was to be a rat-nest. We are in danger of being over-run. Well! it certainly shows this is not a Sinking Ship!

WEDNESDAY 1 APRIL Stove Out this morning, Out, Out, Out. Took Mail, got oil, cut wood with axe. [...] I did not light Stove till after breakfast and then it got so hot that I went up to Attic to see if all was right up there. Those boards are a little darkened by the winter's perpetual fires. They are tinderwood! I believe I see the T.T.'s Bleeding Hearts coming up. I certainly see the Polyanthus little crinkled primrose leaves. It is so hard not to count the days but I don't want to do it!

SUNDAY 5 APRIL You can believe that as soon as it was at all decent after tea & a little talk I coaxed her to say goodnight to Magdalena & come up to the Attic where I had so often told my self stories of how it would be. It surpassed all my stories to have she again. I was happy as Lulu always says. [...] But at breakfast she was very very sad. And the cause of it was that Magdalena was there & we were not alone in the house.

FRIDAY 17 APRIL Visited the 3 Ashes. Mister & Madame & Missy. Missy growing up in Madame's arms. I kissed the rough shoulder of Mister which is in Russia the salutation of Serf to Master. [...] Came back by New Bridge & saw at Calamity Place the long-beaked Rattling bird & I found out what it was! It was the Female King Fisher for I saw the Male too – a much Bluer bird. (The other morning I saw the real Blue Bird in the Willows.) I have been just writing about the Fisher King Le Roi Pescheur, King Pelles or Pellam or Pelleur. [...] I was irritable – what the T.T. calls CROSS & I scolded the T.T. at breakfast when she refused to tell Magdalena to hurry up with the Coffee & when she had to go herself to obtain a little pot of strawberry jam. O I did scold her. But she defended herself very well recalling Jones' shop in Kansas City & how she dared not to call the floor-walker. I explained that I would be bottling up furious physical anger & wanting to dig my chin into the person but she said she only felt a humble desire to remain imperceptible.

SUNDAY APRIL 26 I am profoundly happy this Spring for it is such a relief to see the countenance of the T.T. relaxed easy girlish blushing & smiling & pouting & wilful like a real young girl again & no more haggard & strained like a Cooking Slave – whereas Magdalena really likes cooking.

MONDAY 27 APRIL I have had slight Pricking all day, in fact ever since that unfortunate day when I got so agitated by Magdalena tell[ing] me to take off my shoes & when I had to go to Mail after breakfast about her confounded Money Order. It is these agitations of the mind that always start my Pricking. [...] I believe Ulcer is really healing up. But all yesterday I was conscious of it – even during that heavenly walk. Took Black to three Ashes – Missy was groaning. I touched her I stroked her slender hips & I told Monsieur to think what to do & I told Madame it was the West Wind. We have finished the coal. We must now get wood from Mr Albright. [...] This night occurred an agitating & awful event for the T.T. a Rat caught in Frigidaire with its Head & Eyes staring at the T.T.

TUESDAY 28 APRIL When I announced to the T.T. in Attic about the Milk she collapsed covering her dear head in the covers of the bed so that only a few pretty chestnut curls could be seen. How often have I been hit by the beauty of the T.T. in a moment of her collapse!

SATURDAY 2 MAY Woke up to enchantment; as I do always these heavenly Spring days cold or wet or fine! Pricking is gone. Pricking is gone. But the T.T. had a complicated Bad Dream including a grown up Dorothy Reed the little girl she used to play those Corinthian Games with in Boston; Games that stimulate my fancy – it is Petrushka's Temptation to think of them! [...] Her heaven would be to live for six months in a comfortable Hotel – well warmed – & so One Day – you note this my dear Reader unknown! – one day she shall!

SUNDAY 3 MAY Woke up very late to find Magdalena

hovering over a Rat stuck half way out of a hole in Bath Room. I could easily have jabbed or clubbed it to Death or even chopped off its head [...] but Magdalena felt Pity & withheld me which was only too too easy. The T.T. scolded me & explained it was tooth & claw & that she could have strangled it with her hands with gloves on. She went to Krick's to telephone for Clough for Water had stopped & he came & said it was want of Air in Pump not Sand! A new tale forsooth!

MONDAY 4 MAY Last night the Aged White Cat the Grandmama of All sans teeth & half one eye very thin from Age but wonderfully philosophical. A profoundly wise Cat. Mr & Mrs Krick brought it last night & Mrs Krick showed it the holes which the T.T. uncovered so that the Enemy might make a Sortie, evil to itself, lucky for us. We both slept in Spare room with Black & the T.T. heard great noise & struggling at first but no squeaks. This morning I got up at 7.30 & found the Old White Cat happily seated on Horse Hair Sofa. It could not speak. It purred.

THURSDAY MAY 7 The T.T. has frequently referred to that path by the stream under elms & willows. She likes terraces, avenues 'Addison Walks', Monks' Walks, Park-like & lawn-like walks where her stockings are not torn. I shall cease calling this path the chicken-path. I shall henceforth name it the Willow path or Willow Terrace or even the Terrace Walk in honour of the T.T.'s liking it so well.

MONDAY 11 MAY Last night the Fuse went wrong so we have had no Toast. There is nothing like an absence of Toast (compulsory) to make you appreciate Toast. I now feel that Toast is the most desirable of all forms of human food. Took Black to Ashes via Alders. It was very cold. It was very cold.

On 14 May, Schuster and his associates, Fadiman and Rosenburg, visit Phudd and take back with them the partially completed Glastonbury. *John goes to New York on 25 May for five days for further discussions with Simon & Schuster and to see Marian. Phyllis now has Mr Shaver to help her in the garden.*

SATURDAY 16 MAY Just before I went to bed last night she talked so humorously & with such subtle Henry James penetration about our 3 visitors. She spoke of the learned assurance of Mr Fadiman but of his having a Nordic point of view which he could use to detect ripples of nuance hidden from the others – & also his Nordic fancies – Romance & Faery and Grail Celtique. She spoke of a terrible & even Harsh Determination to get his Will displayed by Mr Schuster below his superficial velvet glove. She spoke of the childishness of Mr Rosenberg but of a massive physical sympathy for women which he has. As she spoke of these things her face was so varied that it was like watching a great actress [...]. She has a wonderful genius for recreating these essences which she has also such a genius for detecting.

SATURDAY 23 MAY Last night the T.T. said that in September we would be alone. I think I shall resist this and strongly oppose this & try to keep Magda for it is impossible not to see how well & happy the T.T. is! [...] Now I hear the sound of the Mowing Machine – Mr Shaver cutting the grass. How that sound carries your mind back! Back to Shirley Vicarage to Yaxham Rectory to Rothesay House Dorchester and to Montacute. The T.T. spoke eloquently about the difference between Nordic & Jewish Publishers & of the loss of Dignity in dealing with the latter but – perhaps because of some drop of Jewish Blood in my own veins – I do not altogether share her feeling. But I understand it & it may be when I am five or ten years older I shall understand her words sharingly but at present I am so thrilled to have my long Amateur Manuscripts published at all!

TUESDAY 26 MAY Took Peter to school. I read to him last night the *Deerslayer*. I was very glad to read for the first time in my life a work of Cooper. I liked it very much. I shall read more. He has the same mania I have for getting the exact geography of events. In many respects I have the same technique as this excellent 'Up-State' author of old days. Had lunch with Marian at the Perfect Childs the Spanish one. Then finished the XII chapter of my Book & wrote the Dramatis Personae and took these to tea at Inner Sanctum with Schuster & Fadiman and Rosenberg and Shimkin. It was a very friendly meeting & a pleasant one. They were thrilled with the photos taken by the T.T.

SATURDAY MAY 30 In the train yesterday I had serious dyspepsia but today it is quite gone. [...] I caught the T.T. just now in Attic & courted her even as the Black does Olwen. The T.T. when I court her becomes thirteen years old.

MONDAY 1 JUNE I sat on the little chair under the Apple Tree that noble aged tree & watched with wonder how far advanced the T.T. is with the making of her garden. This is the first time in my life I have seen a Garden being made except Old Littleton's at Sherborne. I am daily more deeply impressed by what a Gardener I have captured in the T.T. who would have thought it. She is so frail. But she works & works. That top garden of hers is beginning to look like a real garden. Marian's both at Sneeden's & Palisades had gardens before & besides she is a Sorceress with Plants – a Witch – a Fairy-godmother – a Hecate of Gardens! And Old Littleton is a heavy man with a heel to plant. But the T.T. is an Elemental – & I watch her with wonder. In her brown suit & brown cape she looked like a living fragment of the earth; the youngest daughter of Demeter kneeling & digging in the rainy wind.

SATURDAY 13 JUNE I spent whole morning reading chapter XXV to the T.T. But she says (& quite right too) that I must not let Mr Evans & Cordelia really overhear any words about Murder in the Sheep-fold. I am very shy myself of murder. I do not like very much bringing it into my books. But the T.T. is a great authority on murder; just as she is upon Suicide [...].

SATURDAY 27 JUNE I had Farina again for tho' the Spinach yesterday did me good I distrust heartily – yes heartily – all other vegetables. Farina is a good meal much nicer by God! than Ghandi's Dates. I think nothing of Dates. But this Farina regime is doing me good. [...] I have had a very important letter from Schuster & Fadiman. They want to cut out nearly – O I don't know how much including certain characters such as Red Robinson & Lily & Louie & the Robber Band. [...] I fear I shall have to agree. If I write books so unwieldy I suppose this is the consequence.

SUNDAY 28 JUNE Meditated long & long on the Schuster-Fadiman letter [...]. Personally I would prefer to cut out Lady Rachel & Edward Athling. I don't know that I mind very very much cutting out Red; but I don't like cutting out Lily & Louie and 'de-emphasizing' as Mr F. calls it, Emma & Tilly

Crow. We shall see! I wonder what the T.T. will say! Not a little I wouldn't wonder! [...] There are wild roses and wild strawberries everywhere on the hills. As to cutting my book my point of view is not that of an artist at all. I write for delight & cut for Ducats.

THURSDAY 2 JULY Was happy in Lulu's sense last night. [...] Another cause of my diffused happiness is the BOTANY BOOK flowers of New York State in two volumes which the T.T. got for me at Damber & Pine's. I have already discovered by means of it, *Hieracum venosum* a hawkweed growing in the wood with leaves marked like a Snake's Skin and I think I have discovered also the name of the great wrinkled-leaved Green Rank Plant in the Spinney that the T.T. thought was Skunk Cabbage, from these wonderful Pictures. Woke up thinking of this Botany Book & like it more and more. It is for my birthday it cost $15. I think we shall get the Rousseau Head for the Niche in the Bookshelf [...].

SATURDAY 4 JULY O so profoundly exhausted. The T.T. too is harassed today – dreading her sickness O so much & also dreading the appearance of Catharine & Creighton who will blow their Trumpets & force the drawbridge to drop & the portcullis to rise tomorrow. This fills the T.T. with terror for all people frighten her save Mr & Mrs Krick & Mr John Powys & this is really true. [...] Let none say that inventing is harder than cutting, or telling a tale than editing a tale, or 'creating' a world than improving or revising a world! For these latter activities are the Devil. [...] How sweetly the T.T has helped me with my revising & counting words. O how kind & good! & I liked how she did laugh at me over the fuss I make. It makes it all easy; it makes everything easy.

TUESDAY 7 JULY Have found out that the sulphur yellow Potentilla on hill above Alders is not *Potentilla anserina* but *Potentilla erecta*. [...] The T.T.has been *hors de combat* all day long but she is better & life for all the Dolls begins again.

WEDNESDAY 22 JULY How I did sit like a Baby on the Privy (with Mrs H. in the kitchen) crying for the T.T. I went out for her & she comforted me just as if I was a Baby on the horse-hair sofa & then what must this sweet little Being do – this little

Dorrit – 'what I have' – but put arms round neck last night & take all the blame because tea isn't always exactly ready when the Ogre wants it & Magdalena is taking her evening stroll in the Garden 'in the cool of the evening' like God in Eden. Of course it is absolutely all right – we are both alike – we are too afraid of hurting Magda's feelings to dare to assert ourselves. We are Inmates with a nice but dominating Keeper! The T.T. has put a circle round Sept. 1st in her Diary. And yet – how well I know what it will be like when the burden of the Kitchen once more descends on her! But next time I swear I, the Man his Wone Self, will go to the Agencies in New York & choose a servant – an English Servant. You'll see. This I resolve on Wednesday the Twenty Second of July! This morning – for I took three Pills last night – my stiff & obdurate Bowels worked all right & dung hard as Owl Pellets or Ichthyosaurus turds were driven out of my throbbing bum-gut. Then full of incredible lightness & joy I went with bare thin legs, like Don Quixote, to tap stone above our house not asking for anything but expressing gratitude to the gods of Phudd and of Columbia County. [...] And I saw by the rain washed flint-grey road way the great mossy lichen covered stones by the wayside & I saw a great clump of purple Star-Thistle with glaucous stalks which I used to call Knapweed but this is an error. Seeing this plant and seeing the river I did feel such a wave of intense happiness and I did like Columbia County & Phudd Bottom so very, very, very, much. [...] Boissevain & Edna drove by in full evening dress. They said a Grand Dinner. It must be at Arthur's. They brought a pot of Thyme & a very small forget-me-not. Their appearance saddened the T.T. For she saw herself as they saw her.

THURSDAY 23 JULY Belle the blind horse got caught in Burchfield Garden & Minn (Albert said) stamped in the river to show her the way out. [...] Mr Shaver brought his family out. We both love the Grandmother. So Perfect in her Print Dress. She made me think of my Mother's Mother – a certain look with her mouth open. Magdalena's Beckonings & Summonings to me to leave my calm Retreat & obey the Potsdam Orders of the Day filled me with Fury thinly disguised in bowings & scrapings. But the T.T. behaved beautifully – like a living branch torn from my soul & doing exactly what I wanted done – hustled me back to my chair & asked them all in & was Perfect to the Perfect Old Lady & also put down all that was nice in garden to

1931 Mr Shaver. Sometimes the T.T. seems to be the very Projection of my soul acting as I want to act but cannot.

FRIDAY 24 JULY I worked hard at the last chapter of my book which I do want to make good but it is very hard. So far I have made Mr Geard aware that he is going to die. Does this take the spirit & the heart out of the narrative? I am puzzled about it! But somehow I feel as if Mr Geard did really know he was going to die but I may of course have just plunged idly & irresponsibly into this situation & then used all my talents to thicken it up! I wish I knew whether it was irresponsible or whether it was an inspiration. I do not know.

SUNDAY 26 JULY I must tell you that Mrs H. (I formerly called her Magdalena) is beginning to get on both our nerves to a point that is barely endurable.

MONDAY 27 JULY Took Black on string to have him all ready for the T.T. for have I yet told you that on Saturday the Black Bit & went on biting till Blood came the long slender fingers of the T.T.? [...] The T.T. took Black from my hand where I lay in the chair under apple tree. I saw her going along behind willows wearing the same dress – only she forgot to pin it tight round her waist today – that she wore when she was Bitten. Then 1st came back the Black. Then her figure came & I saw her fall down on the grass the other side of bridge. I went to her & she cried & moaned saying I only want to die I only want to die. I have never been happy & I never can be happy. I only one thing want, O, I only want one thing! to be Dead. I put all this down to my not taking the Black for his 3 walks a day & to the acute irritation which the Presence of Magda [...] causes her.

WEDNESDAY 29 JULY The fatal Day of our Row – final & concluding with the Old Lady. And it was really all my fault. The tea-pot appeared the very second the T.T. had started to take the Black. It is another very Hot Day & all our three sets of Nerves are exasperated. I met the T.T. on the Bridge & there looking down at the water flowing over the pebbles I cunningly & indirectly with that deep Meanness which lies in my Coward Nature; & with that dangerous Black Magician Craft – steering things without any overt gesture, simply by the Devilish power of my Sub Conscious Nature – and getting what I want without striving direct for it – which must be a trick inherited from my Powys ancestors – from Sir Thomas who got hold of Lilford Hall doubtless in this way from the old 'Elms' family & also got the Seven Bishops Acquitted altho' he had been appointed by King James to get them Condemned – I began to murmur about a Tea Cosy. O dear I shall always think of this Tea Cosy when I stand on that bridge. Thus the second the T.T. entered the room she said 'Is that water hot?' 'Feel it!' went the Potsdam Whip. I won't feel it! 'Feel it!' I won't. 'You must.' I won't. Then in my Devilish Mocking way I said 'It is Burning Hot' & a smile of victory – like that of Kaiser Wilhelm the First when he was Encamped outside Paris (& all the Watteau Dancers had to Feel It) – crossed the Old Lady's expressive face & forward-thrust chin! Of course – Magdalena now says in righteous self-approval – 'She Throw me Out – and I Go!' – & of course 'Mr Powg' – alias Sir Thomas the Crafty – by his excessive propitiations & an exaggerated Testimonial evokes the impression that he is the mild one & the T.T. the one of blood & iron whereas it is my cold Stone-like heart that is really sending the Old Lady away using the T.T.'s passionate nerves as my Weapon & Shield. [...] The T.T. is now helping her to pack and tying up parcels & all. She has telephoned for Mr Steuerwald. I am not hardening my heart because a Stone needs not to harden its heart. But in my cunning detachment I do see how this sudden indignant self-righteous departure will save all three of us from many exhausting moments [....].

THURSDAY 30 JULY   Cooler, cooler. O it was The Inmates once more alone so wonderful when the T.T. got tea & we had the Toast as she makes it once again & the tea so hot & all so nice. Aye! how we did hug & embrace & dance!

Despite the usual summer visitors, John writes two articles as well as writing the final chapters of Glastonbury. *At the same time he is cutting the first part of the novel by one third, as the publishers request. Arnold Shaw and his wife and two children arrive unexpectedly. They acquire a white cat they call Mees.*

SUNDAY 9 AUGUST   Wrote the beginning of my last chapter but one, about Mr Evans. This is for me by far the hardest of all the chapters & for a deep & subtle reason for I have to describe his sadistic feelings convincingly and yet I am resolved to describe no feeling that would excite my own vice. [...] It is of *this* difficulty that I thought when I took Black up the over-Alders hill. I thought how can I take Mr Evans & his Sadism & handle it so that there would be no vibration of Sadistic pleasure sent out in the world. Thus I should resemble *not* Thomas Burke who sends out deliberate vibrations of Sadism & does it for his own pleasure but Dostoievsky, my great Daimonic Spiritual master with whom it is always remorse and grand Shakespearean terror; beautiful & inspired.

MONDAY 10 AUGUST She came *late* to bed. She had been looking at her early fragments of writing writ in Patchin Place. [...] At breakfast she spoke of these writings & she read to me the beginning of the Stuffed Owl & the beginning of Mrs Tell Fair's Companion. Both are *very* good. Long convoluted Henry James sentences, subtle & flowing – about the spring rain falling in vain upon the sterile sea & about the soul of the owl slowly faintly returning unto it. Delicate filmy diaphanous writing much fainter & more aquarelle than Henry James. O how tantalizing it is that she does not finish anything. How to be blamed, how to be blamed, I am for not forcing her to write when she has such a delicate & flowing style.

WEDNESDAY 12 AUGUST Last night Arnold slept at Steitz but Hattie slept in the Study & A. & P. in the Spare-Room. The children had made such a Row before going to sleep. The T.T. had cooked them a Steak for supper. Arnold did enjoy this so, and we had talked of our old lecturing days: near *30 years* ago Arnold & I came to America together to seek our Fortune on the *Ivernia*. [...] No sooner had she woken up than the T.T., finding it was *Raining*, felt that they would not be able to go and her Despair took her. She told me of her biting her arm in hysterical madness yesterday. It came on her now again. [...] I was stupidly meanly brutally angry & brought out all the old blundering & ponderous chat – so irrelevant to her outraged Nerves – about 'my oldest Friend'. 'I will send them away at once!' I cried & in such an angry strain & went on & spoke of how nice I had been to Mrs Ortt – the oldest friend of the T.T. O with what shame I recall all this scene & what if Hattie *heard it* all all – *All*. I recall how in our dreadful quarrel in whispers & on our knees by the bed the T.T. veered between an *insane* Being mad with blind angry frenzy & a tender exquisite sweet hurt Identity craving for pity & tenderness. The two extremes of what a girl-child is made up, contended in her nature. I was tightly mean & angry & wild too.

FRIDAY 21 AUGUST When I looked up, there was a thin erect quiet little man spectacled small grizzled moustache, grey suit, straw hat. It was the Mythological Mr RADEK whose name I have seen so long on Trespass Boards – the Owner of the Grotto & its Nymph! I told him that the T.T. liked his house her favourite 'Fir Tree' House so well & he said for 7000 Dollars it was hers with 160 acres & for less too if money was Cash! But what do you think, O unknown Reader of this Diary of Two Persons' lives? The T.T. said she preferred to stay at Phudd where she was beginning to get her Garden into shape. Imagine what my feelings of joy were at this! I got on well with my difficult chapter – called the 'Harrying of Annwn' from Taliessin's poem for I came to Tossie Staples & the second I reach Tossie – all my mind became easy & relaxed & my style flowed like fresh milk! It looks as if my mood for the day depended on some psychic influence emanating from the particular character in my book who then dominates. Poor Mr Evans 'twas, & his tormented mind, like one in Hell, that gave me that severe Dyspepsia.

TUESDAY 1 SEPTEMBER I continued working at my article and wrote on about Joyce & Proust and read it to the T.T. who advised several very excellent alterations. […] At lunch and at tea the T.T. spoke very strongly in favour of my not cutting my Book at all and just issuing an ultimatum – take it or leave it – all or nothing. Her arguments were very convincing. I must think. I must Beware. O the Pain again is upon me. It is against my miserly & money loving nature to refuse to cut it. I have a lot of common sense not revealed to all.

MONDAY 7 SEPTEMBER Last night had loathsome dream of Insects which I had to use all my Lethean machinery to get rid of. Do you know what my theory about Insects is – that where they become horrible is always where the person has practised self-abuse & been a great & vicious onanist. Anyway I feel sure that in some mysterious way Insect loathing is connected with sexual excess. When Dostoievsky makes Ivan Karamazov describe the motives of Sadists in cruelty to children & asks why do they do it? the writer makes Ivan answer because of the Insect there. As if there were an actual Insect – the Lust-Insect living like a vicious Grub of Greed & craving, inside the Penis itself, driving you! Was this on the feminine side of it the famous Gad-Fly that drove the World-Heifer Io along as a punishment for the amours of Zeus?

THURSDAY 10 SEPTEMBER Thought of the letter received from A.R.P. yesterday about Lulu's being so sad. The T.T. takes G.'s side & finds my simple prejudice hard to understand. I think it pure 'anti-feminine,' inherited from my father & rage that a male animal should be so rattled. [...] The T.T. had her dinner by herself in the dining room. This strikes me as rather sad – unless she read *Barnaby Rudge*. Wrote a very hard part of my chapter & this possibly was the cause combined with the heat that I have Dyspepsia again curse it all! [...] Thunder & Rain came suddenly & the Black & I sheltered under the Three Ashes. I did not make love to the Missy but touched her standing between her parents the Black at my feet.

SATURDAY 12 SEPTEMBER Last night I took & this morning 3 Pills my constipation was acute. It was as if through my bum-gut I was giving birth to a Cannon-Ball. [...] I could not make it go out nor could I draw it back. I sat on the stool & tried to read Stanley Lee on the Art of Balance! But I thought I must use my wits. So I struggled into the kitchen & got the kettle & heated water & soap. Then, at first, my enema would not work; I thought 'It is broken' – O what will I do? with this cannon-ball hurting so & stuck fast. But at last it became workable & I began to use it but the water I squeezed into my lowest bowel hit against the cannon ball & came out again & drenched all in soapy water. But it did loosen things up a bit so when I sat down again & strained fiercely & furiously at last it did come out. O what a heavenly relief. My bottom now feels terribly sore but all is well. [...] Was it not odd that for the last few days in my book I have been writing of an enema & today this happened to me!

MONDAY 14 SEPTEMBER Wrote all day a very difficult part of my chapter on Sam & his extremely questionable Sanctity. I had decided that he must for all our sakes have a Vision of the Sangreal but it's the devil of a job to work it in. And Sam has got so damnably real a person to me anyway. [...] Without my consent his mind is growing under stress of events; when I told him to keep as he was; & have assumed all along that he would never change! But here is the bugger changing and doing it every moment my attention wanders!

THURSDAY 17 SEPTEMBER I wrote the beginning of my Article on Licentiousness in Modern Life for St Louis University, referring to Cabell, Anderson, Huxley and Hemingway; but when the T.T. read it she denounced it as twaddle; but I cannot persuade her to suggest to me how to improve it – & for myself it beats me to invent or discover any philosophic generalization to include such different writers as these – all of them lively & readable but none with any deeply stirring or original thought. We came near to quarrelling over it for criticism without definite suggestions is liable to excite anger in my heart. However I continued my chapter & tried to banish this annoyance. No pain, no pain, no pain. My chapter is rushing me along. It is writing me. I am not writing it.

FRIDAY 25 SEPTEMBER Got up at 6.50 a.m. The sun was rising as I was dressing in the Attic. Got kindling & when the T.T. came down she lit the Fire. I took Black [the dog] & White [the cat] to Tony Stone & we were pursued by Sis [the cow] in a Rampage with her forehead covered with Burs & her eyes wild & feverish. She butted at the White who was up a small tree. She stretched out her tongue like a dragon breathing fire & smoke at me. The Black fled for home by a wide Circuitous Route. It was so early that I was far ahead of the T.T. & I went with my animals like Zarathustra with Eagle & Serpent to the open space a sort of hay field beyond Top Garden. [...] I sat on a fallen stone wall at the end of the T.T.'s Estate. I saw the smoke rising up tall & straight – for it was windless – from our parlour chimney.

SATURDAY 26 SEPTEMBER After breakfast I rescued a lot of fish. Two largish ones & hundreds of little ones & there are endless others. It is a Burden this fish-rescuing. [...] I exhausted myself – & at once became conscious of my side not exactly pricking & certainly no Pain at all or dyspepsia but a faint awareness that I was an ulcerous man. [...] It was a curious Co-incidence that while I was at this job out of doors, on my couch I was writing about Ichthus the World-Fish. This chapter about

Sam and the Holy Grail is the hardest in the book. O I do pray it will pass muster with her my Perfect Critic. [...] Full Moon. White cloud like a fish came towards it to swallow it. The T.T. had on her Chinese Silk dress tonight.

WEDNESDAY 30 SEPTEMBER She showed me a lovely picture of herself at fourteen in Breton dress on bridge in Compière. Aye! but what straight innocent eyes! what a clear brow, what a darling little smiling mouth! I see her exactly like that – & so she is yes! I hold this little fourteen year old being in my arms! [...] I have finished my chapter about poor old Sam. I have come to grow quite attached to Sam & to know him very well. And it is strange that this fish-catching should answer so well to Sam's vision of the Sangreal.

THURSDAY 1 OCTOBER Took Black to Perdita Stone & kissed it. The only daughter I shall ever have! A stone – & the proper daughter for a stone to have!

SUNDAY 4 OCTOBER She said I had acted funny of late. I said I felt exhausted in mind and body. She insisted on taking the Black & wouldn't let me go to the fish till after breakfast. But about eleven I went to them & caught a lot & saw a very strange unforgettable sight seen by few living men I wot! I saw four fish in procession cross a strip of dry land from under the rock into the pool. One of these in my foolish blundering with the net I drove back over this strip of dry land under the rock again – I hope not to its death – but what a fool I am. [...] My brain feels very very tired. I feel I want all decks cleared and everything very large & calm & quiet before me so as to finish my book.

TUESDAY 6 OCTOBER Brilliant red now is the Sumach on Stein's Hill & also near our own garden – what a garnet-red and ruby-red and wine-red all mixed together the Sumach is. Why then do I not do justice to the Sumach – I'll tell you why – because I have no old memory connected with Sumach. [...] I am now at page 1823 so I shall certainly pass by a good deal 2000 pages & so clearly can I recall writing the first pages at Easter – last Easter a year ago. I am writing very vast I mean fast and very happily. O it is such a relief to escape from Sam & the Grail!

SATURDAY 17 OCTOBER I went down in the middle of the

night & found the T.T. asleep on couch. I had come down before & had tried to console her but she was inconsolable. [...] This inert lethargy of misery frightens me for I feel so helpless. I feel very anxious to soothe her but I cannot think of the magic clue. I like it far far far better when she beats me up.

TUESDAY 20 OCTOBER She found it hard to break up her Sea of Marmora dreams & thus we were still fasting when Mrs Krick turned up – and we venerate her beyond all neighbours so we had to ask her to stay & we pretended that breakfast was over. Then old McNeill in his cart drove up to get the shingles we had kept for his fire-wood and old Mrs McNeill her face half-paralysed came in & rocked up & down in the T.T.'s green chair talking to Mrs Krick of her dead face. When they went I got such praise from the T.T that it was like a fresh Swan's egg sweet & delicate as hedge-sparrow egg & as blue too was this heavenly praise & O how quick she got our meal & the Black how he <u>did</u> jump! But twice today he has done Number One in the dining-room. The T.T has scolded him – but she has been <u>very</u> good today under many trials. If you who read this are interested in the moods of <u>very</u> beautiful girls please note that with all these agitations & a lady selling Vanilla and writing a cheque of 150 dollars for Scutt & her Dreer plants come & Gladys bringing a Picture in Water Colours of Phudd Bottom she has been very good & gentle & wise and competent today though she had to go twice to the Mail and the things still not washed up.

SATURDAY 24 OCTOBER Mr Shaver came and planted things for the T.T. Then I gave him his cheque of ten dollars for two days & a half's work & we went with him into Philmont to his house & to the mail with some plants for Marian by Special Delivery. His house was very nice & his mamma & invalid sister very well attired & flowers on a nice table – a very nice house except for upholstery which one had to try and avoid. [...] We called on Mr & Mrs McNeill on the way back & found only the old people for Maud was driving. I like Mr McNeill <u>very</u> much he has hollow eye-sockets & a high forehead & a white mustache. I talked with him of the expense of digging graves & buying coffins which Mr McNeill held was monstrously expensive & with this, as we sat looking out on Mr Alf Curtis' milk cows I cordially agreed. The old lady sat on a sofa-bed. The house was a little forlorn & bare, but it was a comfort to me to see no horrible upholstery.

FRIDAY 30 OCTOBER Lay frog-wise thinking how I would worship-defy the God of Phudd and remain in close 'Worship-Defy' of the First Cause. My Glastonbury Book is the expression of my natural & normal life at Phudd Bottom.

Phyllis goes again to her parents from 1 to 21 November.

SUNDAY 1 NOVEMBER She stayed up again till Four & I also till 1.45. But she counted all the words. [...] We had a happy breakfast in spite of her going. And after breakfast instead of planting her Bulbs she read the last chapter of my Book & told me I must change it & introduce Cybele to whom I have always prayed for it to be good & the Towers of all cults coming & going – Never or Always. Think of her having this Inspiration at the day of her going away! And she did up all 3 volumes of my book for the Mail so well tied up & there they were – tied with string by her on this All Saints Day [...] – begun Easter Day a year & a half ago!

SATURDAY 14 NOVEMBER Today is chiefly to be noted by the sharp & villainous way my ulcer has hurt. It has been grumbling all day & in the afternoon it got rampageous – to the point where I have to put fingers down throat. This I did by bridge & returned home feeling pretty bad; yes sharp was the hurting, & twisting & bending was I and humming little tunes of woe to myself [...]. O I shall go to bed and stay there a long long time when the T.T. comes home. [...] Sent the Cybele Pages, that end of Glastonbury invented by the T.T. & due entirely to her original genius to Mr Fadiman.

SUNDAY 15 NOVEMBER Lay listening to Rain & pretending to be the T.T.! This I do when I am such a Nympholept that I want to enjoy my little maid's lovely limbs in a kind of Absolute Ecstasy!

MONDAY 16 NOVEMBER This slight hurting is not – I say not – worthy of name of pain. How will you get on my well-fixed & happy Worm? Very much better than most people these days & yet you whimper to your Diary so that the T.T. shall know about it indirectly & you will get that satisfaction & yet not have told her exactly.

SUNDAY 22 NOVEMBER Warm as September, a perfect day, a

lovely day, a wonderful day. The wonderful miracle is that her coming seems to have stopped that hurting in ulcer Completely.

MONDAY 23 NOVEMBER I visited the Perdita Stone & had to kiss it nine times for the Black pissed on it ere I could stop him for I generally make a detour to prevent this but my mind was occupied & I forgot. [...] She brought my beautiful pyjamas which I hope to wear when I seduce my Cimmerian Elemental. I seduce her all over again very often! That is because she is always a little girl & needs to be seduced again & again.

SUNDAY 29 NOVEMBER The birthday of the T.T. She came late to bed having had a hot bath & tidied up the house. Lay holding her & thinking for a long time before I got up, till way after I heard Mr Curtis whose father the Colonel is dotty in mind & 'may have to be taken away,' says Mr Krick, stop at the door with milk. [...] She was pleased & surprised to find the Love-Sonnet I had writ for her & had hidden away – on her plate at breakfast. [...] It is so hushed and still & quiet & isolated and escaped from all the world, today here! Took Black to Perdita. A warm, wild, still, silent, black-bastion, jagged, white, torn by bolt-levin, god-walking Sky with vast rolling black clouds. The T.T. made me change to red shirt black trousers evening waistcoat chess blazer evening tie. After our Tea Supper we are going to play chess like they of the *Mabinogion*.

THURSDAY 3 DECEMBER Mr Rumery came in & talked of the Depression & utters ideas that resemble those of Oswald Spengler on present events. [...] Took Black up Phudd & I can tell you this was an effort! I have not been there for so long. I went the steep way, past the 5 Nakeds who I embraced & past where the T.T. slept when we first went up there in September so long ago and I prayed to the dead Indians in the highest heap of stones and also in the first I came to and also in two heaps in the Avenue of the Dead up there. But as I went away three more ghosts of dead Indians – dark swaying slender bodies cried come to me – come to us! come to us! But I would not.

FRIDAY 4 DECEMBER Lay enjoying the T.T. with incredibly wicked joy & thinking how lovely she was & how lucky I was & how exciting the crows were & the rain & the silence & an owl too but that may possibly have been Albert imitating an owl –

one has to look out for Tricks in such affairs as the sound of owls! Miss McNeill came after tea. I had read aloud from *Unclay* – Theodore's new book. It is a lovely book in my opinion save for a few passages of his usual sadism which is a revelation not of the soul of any actual person but of the soul of the imagination of Theodore. How strange that this fact should be totally unknown save in Phudd Bottom. But I put *Unclay* at the top of all his works. There are more generalizations in it of a mingled wisdom & fantasy like a mixture of Schopenhauer & Robin Goodfellow. But the T.T. & I enjoy reading him aloud as much as any book but not for the story – I can tell you that! The Dog is now barking with ringing resounding echoing barks – the only revenge I can take upon this hideous & overwhelming sound – is like all writers simply to record it – to set it down in malice. [...] I note the exact way raindrops fall in water; making Converging Circles & also little Martello Towers.

SUNDAY 6 DECEMBER Dreiser & Helen came last night about 8.p.m. [...] The T.T. gave them a nice supper with an Omelette & Coffee & Cake & even Soup. [...] He most eloquently described his air-plane flight across the whole of America and he spoke long & very excitingly about Russia. [...] We had a very happy tea. I had mine on the table by the couch. We were so impressed by Dreiser's countenance at once so formidable & like a tormented Titan – in fact like Hercules among the Dead as he appears in the *Odyssey*. The T.T. was very happy with them. She talked at ease and they hung upon her words. I was hit by Dreiser's gentleness.

MONDAY 7 DECEMBER [Dreiser] spoke of death – & said he desired to die. He is different from the Powys family in this. He has a vein of deep Cosmic unhappiness. He has not got our kind of selfishness or our enjoyment of simple sensations or our power of forgetting the sorrows of the world or our earthy rooted English content in merely being alive.

TUESDAY 8 DECEMBER The wind howled. She said that wind always frightened her. She said 'at home' winds were dangerous. This wind was a Valkyrie Hyperborean wind – it is a Norse wind – a Runic wind – a Varangian wind – & this little frail super-sophisticated Byzantine Paleologue shivered under it. The toast burnt & we had so little the remains of the famous Half

Loaf which I got from Krick's for Dreiser when I ought to have got a whole one. The T.T. impatiently threw two pieces of burnt toast into the garbage but after breakfast she got one piece out & I had it with honey.

FRIDAY 11 DECEMBER I had last night only faintly watched the T.T. as she spoke of her life in Girard at Craig's Hotel & her work for Manuel emerge from her Sadness which I know was simply caused by a longing for 'something nice' when who should turn up but Albert to offer to take her with them all to a Movy in Hudson. This he did & she went. Something in her going must have left me in my nerves completely deserted for I got very nasty suffering in Pit of Stomach. She came [home] when I had been to bed but I came down in my hurting & begged for help & comfort. She made Malted Milk. [...] She came to bed then & it was like sleeping with the loveliest Nymph that has ever been made – a little Elf-child of incredible slenderness & exquisite docility. [...] Yea! I was 'happy' in Lulu's sense of the word! [...] At breakfast Daddy Scutt came. He has got that $460 safe into the T.T.'s Postal Order Account in New York. So if I died suddenly by accident or by Peritonitis the T.T. would have something safe!

TUESDAY 15 DECEMBER The T.T. at breakfast most eloquently defended O'Neill the Dramatist who I said was over-rated. [...] She said the Theatre deals in Passions. It is not the same thing as Literature. [...] My point of view in Drama as it is in Art is a literary & bookish one – but the T.T. has [...] a love of the technique of the Theatre. I must try to yield to her view. I am going to read aloud the whole of *Mourning Becomes Electra* to her. She even defends the title & says it is not clever or tricky or an affectation but instinctive & deep & inevitable. Certainly it is exciting to read as a story which is a great thing to me.

FRIDAY 18 DECEMBER Mr Krick and Albert brought the V I C T R I O L A and carried it into the 'Proper Place' after uncrating it with two hammers and a short iron bar. The T.T. played Mendelssohn's Spring Song on a Harp and also the Overture to the Opera *Raymond* [...]. Then we made up our minds that she should make it play the beginning of *Petrushka* which she has bought ready for its arrival for 12 dollars – no I think 8. [...] The T.T. was transported. I watched her pleasure with intense satisfaction. She sat on horse-hair little chair with back to Attic steps entranced. […] [T]he T.T. said she was happy. This is a very very very rare thing.

THURSDAY 31 DECEMBER Miss McNeill came and then Mrs Krick came & they talked of the way 'Jenny' had died after 'doing Stunts' upstairs – and they talked of diseases like they had been Two of the Witches in *Macbeth* – a young Witch & an older Witch – & the T.T. sitting on the floor listening awe-struck. […] I took Black at 4.10 and again I went a completely new way. I went by the Mees Stone & straight up right thro' that wood opposite to the rails at the top which look out into field. Here I sat down on a fallen tree & looked at Phudd through the trees & thought it looked like Montacute Hill & I thought of my father & mother there buried and in their graves and I thought how their characters abide in my mind – their power & individualism lasts still and will last as long as long as any of their children live. I found the house so charmingly lit up by the T.T. with at least nine candles if not more. She does make things so nice! Last night she looked so lovely and magical in yellow dress & brown velvet waistcoat. What will she wear tonight? She has come down and it is a lovely dress. She does look so beautiful. I tapped head on the Phudd Stone & fell down as I came back.

1932

Except for the occasional trip to New York, in 1932 John stays at Phudd Bottom, writing and nursing his ulcer. In January he and Phyllis correct the galley proofs of A Glastonbury Romance. *In February he begins* Weymouth Sands, *but, finding this novel difficult to launch, puts it aside when Simon & Schuster ask him to write* A Philosophy of Solitude. *This he completes in October.*

He makes a second start on Weymouth *in August and a third in September, but he decides that it 'must have been begun from the outside' 'instead of some inner* entelecheia'. *Despite trying several different approaches and introducing new characters, it is not until November that suddenly he sees the way ahead.*

The solitude of Phudd is broken by visits from old friends and the increasing number of local people who begin as employees and become their new friends. His walks with the Black give him the opportunity to work through various problems connected with his current writing and to carry out his 'ritualistic rigmaroles', as he calls his prayers and head-tappings. He continues to give special names to fields, rocks, trees.

His regular diet now consists of milk, raw eggs, bread-and-butter, and tea: a regime which he appears to think is the only way to control the ulcer pain. By 1932 the enema is a regular routine: after several mishaps it is Phyllis who administers it.

Phyllis enjoys her record player (the 'Victriola') and the occasional village entertainment but her constant exhaustion and recurring 'sadness' worry John. They continue to improve the house and the garden, but they also begin to talk of a possible move.

1932 SATURDAY 2 JANUARY Last night we went to dinner at the Krick's. [...] I asked endless questions of old days on these Dutch Farms. Mr Krick told of going to church with Oxen and saying Gee! for turn left & Haw! for turn right or the other way round. And about corn husked by lantern-light in barns & dances & feasts. Then they showed us incredibly wonderful Quilts. One of these, lo! the T.T. must fain copy & she has actually made one patch of it already. The second she came home she began working on it! But as she worked [...] she said I had not entertained them enough with picturesque tales of my early experiences by land and sea. She said we never had the power of being animated & amusing simultaneously – either she talked in a manner American or I talked in a wild fantastical Powysian way but never did we entertain our hosts in rhythmic concert harmoniously. This is a subtle point [...].

On 5 January John goes to New York for three days, primarily to see his publishers, Simon & Schuster, in 'the Inner Sanctum', but also to see sister Marian and friends. The seriousness of the Great Depression becomes apparent.

THURSDAY 7 JANUARY Went to lunch with Lola who is working for relief of the starving. Describes the situation as pretty awful. Lucky indeed are all of us who have enough to eat! Gave Lola $5 for herself. [...] Went to Inner Sanctum. They took me round & introduced me to all their staff even to the Coloured Man in the doing up parcels room. [...] Gave a speech to their travelling men on my book. [...] Begged Marian for another tea tho' theirs was over. Listened to her reading to Peter out of Henty. [...] It was pretty to see Peter lying on the floor listening to Henty's tale & then (when he got tired for he had been playing football & his legs were bleeding from kicks and he was very tired) lying in Marian's lap like a little lion in a lioness's embrace.

FRIDAY 8 JANUARY Yesterday at the shop where there is a head of a person unknown reduced to a small size by a tribe of head-hunters I bought a silver milk jug for Marian & today I bought another little one for the T.T. Also bought strawberries 15 cents; pound of mushrooms 25 cents; both reduced by depression. [...] I went to the Brevoort Hotel where in Basement are those French Barbers of Monsieur Henri that I have known for a quarter of a Century ever since I used to live at the Brevoort when in town before I lived with Marian on 12th Street. O what a thrilling welcome I got from them all – & I had my hair cut to the Skull as short as possible. [...] I gave to a beggar (of this great mass of people who are on the edge of starvation) about 40 cents. That was my sole gift to the Unemployed. 40 Cents to a beggar of the old Régime! It is surprising how it is possible to go on enjoying yourself when you are within 100 miles of such frightful destitution. We Bourgeois people are however used to this Pathos of Difference for I can well remember the destitute & homeless sleeping on the Thames Embankment in old days. Then the War seemed to absorb this unemployed element substituting another terror & another shame.

SUNDAY 10 JANUARY I meditated on my luck not to be half starved & cold and on the streets. Cold and hunger are pretty bad things I warrant but I have never known what they are but I feel them near me in this depression. I hear their growls and I begin to be compelled to guess at what they are like. The Dead Indians and the God of Phudd told me to tap my head on their stone. But in spite of their commands and in spite of [...] my knowledge – not fancy – after seeing Lola – but knowledge that many animals are exactly as greedy as myself and as dependent on food as myself and as egoistic as myself and probably more sensitive – I refused to tap head on stone & I refuse to stop my deliberate cultivation of a particular mood of profane ecstasy in the enjoyment of certain especial sensations out of which I choose to create my habitual consciousness of continuity.

Albert Krick becomes their handyman, Miss McNeill their cleaning woman and Mr Shaver their gardener. The proofs of Glastonbury *arrive on 16 January.*

TUESDAY 12 JANUARY All yesterday in spite of visits from Miss McNeill in morning & a long visit from 'Little Albert' in evening I have [been] working at a Short Story to be sold for the Unemployed. Shall I be able to write it? It is a peculiarly hard task for me to write a short story.

WEDNESDAY 13 JANUARY O how eloquently last night she spoke of what rôle she would like to play as a Dancer. I like it when the T.T. talks of being a Dancer. She always talks of it so excitingly. Have I caught this lovely Elemental (who could write mysteriously well or dance in wild ecstasy) & captured it to my Vestal Hearth & Cinders & all my great thundering Enchiridion Cult? Have I done this thing?

THURSDAY 14 JANUARY Yesterday when I lay with my back to a stone fence on the top of the One-Tree Hill above the Fir Tree House I had an ecstasy of pleasure at the deep deep deep beautiful lonely wildness of Columbia County. O how I do like my life here how I do like it. And it is given to me by the T.T. who sacrifices her Watteau sophistication in the City & her Theatres, Concerts & shops. [...] We all sat on the wall & the T.T. took photos of the Black & of Albert & of Miss McNeill. Albert took one of the T.T. & me & Black.

SUNDAY 17 JANUARY An ice-cold film hard & slippery and very cold covered every stone & even the wooden steps. [...] I heard the Indian Tombs on top of Phudd telling me this layer or film of ice lay on them & begging me to climb up the Mount & salute them. This I was too lazy to do. I notice how if you are to be happy in this world you have forever to be hardening your heart. My heart also – that other stone – hath a film of slippery eyes [*sic*] on it. I too O dead Indians am an ice-covered Stone. I took Black to Stump but not to Perdita – her appeal also I refused. O how icy-cold blew the East wind over Massachusetts. A chilly & wicked puritan wind – a witch-persecuting wind! Yes – a sinister day.

MONDAY 18 JANUARY I meditated on the fact that I had the spirit to write that Short Story about Quilts that the T.T. said would not do (for the Unemployed) but not the virtue or the spirit to Revise it and make it do! What a weak luxurious easy Worm I am – living this snug, smug, sleek, comfortable, delicious, perfect life – & too lazy even to revise a short story to earn a hundred dollars for food for the half-starved. [...] After breakfast the T.T. went to Kricks & burst out in a brave breathless Defence of Dreiser & his revolutionary ideas.

TUESDAY 19 JANUARY Worked at Revising my Proofs. The T.T. & I worked at this together and O dear me! how nervous & agitated we get! The Black is always having to run under couch at the sound of our raised voices just as he always comes running out into dining-room or kitchen or wherever we are if he hears the sound of caresses and of love-making.

WEDNESDAY 20 JANUARY Tapped Phudd Stone praying for the T.T. to be strong & happy & well & long-lived! – & happy after my Death. It is an interesting moment when a person first of all writes down in black & white the words 'after my death' or 'my death' & feels an odd sensation but not at all a seriously disagreeable sensation! [...] And after breakfast what must this very clever girl do but discover that in my book I had made the absolutely New Moon be visible at ten o'clock at night so we had terrific alterations & argued & struggled & struggled over it so as to get rid of the word Crescent. Just think how Old Littleton & Llewelyn would have scolded if I had made a new Moon be seen at ten o'clock. But so totally unscientific & in certain ways inobservant am I that I simply was ignorant of this great fact in astronomy. [...] Took the Black late over Field. [...] The Black deserted me thinking it is too late, too dark, O my friend! He does not know anything about the relation established between a dog & its Master – 'Who is a Master?' thinks the Black.

THURSDAY 21 JANUARY The T.T. has decided to get rid of that Chicken-House out there. I said goodbye to it & tapped head on it uttering the words *Moriturus te saluto*! which however really means 'I about to die salute thee'! so it is the other way round but every Person & every Object in this planet is in a position to say to every other – one way round or the other way round. [...] Albert & Miss McNeill talked Shakespearean Talk about the death of old Mrs Beaver of the Workhouse whose husband was drowned in this river – drowned as he was on his way to kill her below Wohn Orchard. As a rule Albert said Grand Dad Coon drove him away from the old woman with a club.

FRIDAY 22 JANUARY Never Never Never never was any girl so ballad-like in her feeling for the death of old women. When she heard of our former inhabitant of the Burchfield house – the one who made that wonderful quilt of many thousands of little squares – she cried & cried because the old woman got what she wanted so intensely & was buried in her Blue Dress or will be tomorrow. Albert is digging her grave in the Wohn Burying Ground. Think of the peculiarity of this country when Albert plays Sexton! I shall go to her Funeral which according to Nonconformist custom will be in the Private House of the Undertaker! Think of your funeral being in the house of the sleek Mr Drayton the carpenter-undertaker of Montacute who nailed up my sister Nelly's coffin in the Spare-room while I tried to distract my mother's mind in the drawing-room.

SATURDAY 23 JANUARY Americans regard their Dead as an exciting Show. The great plush cover like a vast Devilish Candy Box is left half open so all can get a good view of the Show. The case is lined with white satin. It is the most unpoetical and most ghastly way of dealing with death that is conceivable.

SUNDAY 24 JANUARY I did the chores & took the Black to the lower Bull Rush Bed over the rough Battlefield & held my serpent stick given by Lulu & heard the waterfall of the Grotto & called out to the Nymph 'Guard Lulu & Alyse & Gamel!' I called out – leaving to this Naiad the problem as to how to work this out [...].

WEDNESDAY 27 JANUARY The Indians of Hill & the God of Phudd commanded me to come to the Phudd Stone & tap my head. But I refused. I too am a Magician! I said. So they set themselves to show their Power & I set myself to show my Power. Today has been a struggled day but I would not do it till they fancied they had done their worst. [...] I gave myself a good Enema after my fashion with the squeezing tube and I squeezed it sixty times. The spirits of the Indians were making a grand coup, a great rally against me however – & all went Wrong. It would not work!! but it worked enough to thrust an Iron Ball and Iron Wedge of scoriac excrement into my lower gut which gave me that particular extreme Discomfort – do you know it my Refined Reader? You see, living on nothing but milk & eggs my bowels for months & months have totally given up working – which is one of the Minor Limits of Petty Misery! 10 times I tried again hurrying backwards & forwards & getting more hot water. Then I gave up the struggle & sitting on the Close-Stool in the Bathroom resigned myself to awaiting events. But I still said in my heart to the Indians of Phudd – I too am a Magician! & finally the T.T. was asked by me to get the Doctor. She bravely went to Kricks & told Mrs Krick all & she telephoned to Dr Nichols.

THURSDAY 28 JANUARY It was only when a lovely wave of indescribable comfort & peace, relief & joy and melting magical happiness came thro' me that I went up yesterday and tapped Phudd Stone when the Doctor was gone and simply thanked these Powers. But I obstinately repeated as I tapped my head – I also am a Magician! I also am a Magician!

SATURDAY 30 JANUARY Went to bed at 8.45 & the T.T. came at One Fifteen. But O the Paradise when I held her in my Second Favourite night gown. It is a terrible mistake for anyone to Renounce such ecstasies unless by so doing they get, here, in this world, real over-powering Beatific Visions. Never I say never have I known such fulfilment of all my deepest 'wicked' desires since I looked at those old editions of Punch in the Sherborne Library on Sunday Afternoons hunting for those little angel figures they sometimes drew there – so like the T.T. with sylph-like limbs & little oval faces – just like hers! […] Had an ENEMA with the help of the T.T.

SUNDAY 31 JANUARY O how cold how cold how ice-cold how deadly bitter cold the North wind is today. […] The T.T. insisted upon a change where the actual Figure of Christ appears to Sam or rather appears although Sam does not see Him. It was Dickensian & Bombastic the T.T. said & she was satisfied with my change which no one now could call Dickensian. I brought into this paragraph some of the bitter cold that went thro' my skull as I looked for possible Traps on the Bank where Fritz & John once were setting traps! […] The T.T. went to sleep on the horse hair sofa in her struggle with my Book – over the back of the sofa Page Proofs hung over her body page proofs were stretched & on the floor by her side lay page proofs! Heroically she had struggled. How lovely and sweet she looked asleep in her grey sweater. Well – she finished the *Glastonbury* Proofs and made me make Tossie stick to her dialect in the end.

MONDAY 1 FEBRUARY Last night as we burnt incense & our crooked smoke rose to the gods of our hearth the Mees was very inquisitive & the Black grave & very interested because Olwen & Falada came down to be present at this Rite which took place at midnight. The T.T. made me change the death of Mr Geard to 'Bloody Johnny, lost in the dark. The bed is deep. Where is Megan's head?' – which is an incredible improvement. What I owe to her over this Book! Her imagination & her inspired critical penetration have both been lavished on't & her long long nights as well! Well! it is now gone & the T.T. says she feels as if it <u>were</u> <u>dead</u>. […] I shall (Today) begin *Weymouth* with my father's Quill Pen.

THURSDAY 4 FEBRUARY The T.T. was very discouraged about her Vicious & Opium-like habit of staying up to 3.30 night after night. She feels so wretched in the morning that she is in misery. What <u>can</u> be done? […] I began today Reading the Guide Books about Weymouth sent me by Lulu. Slowly very slowly various basic ideas for my Weymouth Book are gathering in my mind.

FRIDAY 5 FEBRUARY I did the chores thro' 10 inches of Virgin Snow. And then hearing a sound I found the Kind Albert with a vast snow-spade clearing our steps. I took the Black the Round in my Seven League Boots & O it was heavy walking. He ran straight for home along Willow Path & that enabled me to brush the snow off my Stone Daughter Perdita & her round Toy Stone laid by her by the T.T. […] But a worse mania took me then & what must I needs do but clamber laboriously up to the Rail & hunt about digging stick into snow drift to find the Tony Stone. I could not find it! So my Stone 'Son' has had to remain under the snow! But I was thoroughly exhausted – deeply exhausted – & this made me profoundly hypochondriacal for it made me <u>feel</u> my ulcer. Now if there is one thing that makes me hypochondriacal in a curious silence of inward brooding it is when <u>after</u> <u>having</u> <u>been</u> <u>very</u> <u>well</u> <u>&</u> <u>strong</u> I suddenly grow aware of ulcer […].

TUESDAY 9TH FEBRUARY All yesterday – The Eve of Shrove Tuesday – I had exciting inspirations over my Weymouth Book. And I believe it was due to the New Moon which I saw from the Willow Path & prayed to it, lifting up my hands & kneeling on a patch of grass from which the snow had melted. […] Yesterday we received a cheque from <u>W.W.</u> <u>Norton</u> with the sum of $685.81 on the Culture book from last <u>March</u> <u>to</u> <u>August</u>. This was an immense relief to our finances. The T.T. sent off Orders & cheques to her two Theatres for Performances of Chevalier & Escradwallon [*sic*]the Dancer.

WEDNESDAY 10 FEBRUARY I am working slowly at my

Weymouth Book beginning by making a list of the houses where the people live and inventing names for all these houses rather than giving them street numbers & after that inventing names for the characters themselves – characters that emerge out of Limbo, out of airy nothing, to receive these names and lo & behold! as I name them and name their houses they begin to gather to themselves a faint reality! I have also got in my mind two underlying Themes for my book; one of an extremely Platonic and Mystical character & one of a very simple, childishly simple Melodramatic nature. These Guide Books sent me by Lulu about Weymouth & Portland are very useful especially the Maps. Only I would like a vast number of photographs of many streets! The T.T. has already begun to help me with these names. We had both our lists on the wall [...]. The Kricks came at seven and the dinner of roasted Lamb was a terrific success.

Phyllis goes to New York for two days and sees the flamenco dancer Vincente Escurdo.

SUNDAY 14 FEBRUARY O I was so glad to have her safe again. During tea & afterwards last night when she recovered she described The Spanish Dancer [...] dancing the Gipsy Dance called 'Farruca' like an Obsession & a spirit-dance among other spirits but all from within. [...] O how eloquently (& like the most beautiful of dancers herself) in every gesture she did describe that Spaniard, that Gipsy, & his two companions. [...] The T.T. has been so very nice to me since her agitation before breakfast when she allowed to pass the barrier of her teeth the wish that we could sell this house at once! [...] But eventually I shall take her Across, 'twould be wicked not to when she is made up of the very clay of passionate feeling for old-world sophisticated art & life and traditions. She is pining for 'Europe' & I do know it! All this morning and afternoon since she has shown me her Colonial Prints from Macy – & given me Hardy's *Well-Beloved* about Portland – she has been helping me find a Christian name for Skald, the hero of my new Book. At last she has found it for me by looking up 'Jorum' she stumbled on 'Jobbernol' & from there to the name I intend to use Jobber. Jobber Scald: Scald the Jobber. The Jobber has a good sound and has in it all the moods & subtleties I need – rich in Mythological Suggestion of *Gleichnis* such as homely popular tang of pubs and the backchat of wharfs – such as something affectionate & yet formidable – a very hard note to strike – I think I've got it exactly in the Jobber – *Skald the Jobber*! So today, St. Valentine's Day, I am really going to begin my Weymouth Book – that is to say carry on that first sentence I wrote on my Father's Birthday with his Quill Pen.

MONDAY 15 FEBRUARY Took the Black. It is an icy cold day with a black frost very hard. [...] When I returned my acid drops began & simultaneously the little T.T. coming down [...] had a paroxysm of piteous crying to see *Kitchen so cold* & she lifted up voice & said for these Last Two Years I have not had enough to eat. O I feel (she wept) like a child left without its mother! Lost in this Hillsdale where I am so helpless & the house is so big & cold – & my mother will never, never come! Hearing these words I mentally resolved really to *End it all* & take her away from here. This Resolution as I took upon myself to Scramble the Eggs – made me so grave – & made me look so *Different* – that in a flash she had recovered & came to me at stove & begged me not to do any[thing] Drastic. While you are *unruffled* children do cry but, when they see you *really* different, in a second they recover!

TUESDAY 16 FEBRUARY After breakfast which the T.T. got without one Collapse & came down in such good time, she spoke of Modern Novels & how she would like to write four massive long not too personal Stories. [...] Very slowly and with a curious sort of lazy difficulty, taking advantage of every sort of interruption, I carefully & punctiliously went on with the 1st 2 or 3 pages of my Weymouth Book. I think it is that at the start I have to depend on my Invention alone in a Void whereas when once the characters assert themselves they do all with a sort of rush of their own. Thro' my skull like a wind, blows a sort of neutral inspiration and this is, as it were, a gale to their sails, trimmed in various kinds of riggings as they are, with hulls & masts & keels all different, but each ship manned by its own spirit, & getting out of control & plunging thro' the shoals & gulfs & waves on its own initiative. But in this early stage I have to invent all in a void, & an incredible lethargy & laziness possesses me.

WEDNESDAY 17 FEBRUARY *Cold is awful*. I don't like to think of what the poor people & street-walkers in the City suffer from this cold on the top of hunger. Damn these tricks of God & Society! What a good thing that such a drastic change as the Soviet system exists in the world. [...] There was a very exciting letter from Schuster about good prospects for my Cybele book of Glastonbury. He had been himself – the Great Baghdad Merchant – on the road 'about' or as he said 'out in the field.'

THURSDAY 18 FEBRUARY I waited by the not very warm stove for it needs the Fire Elemental to deal with the stoves for I am in no sense a Being of Fire. I am of Earth & Air (or Wind) & the T.T. is of Air & Fire. Neither of us are Water – in spite of my interest in the River & in the Fish! [...] I worked at my Weymouth opening, re-writing & re-writing – going over & over & altering every word. At four I took the Black to the Clum Meadow past Arthur's Lane & there was the dead horse still. They had just left it there. Very likely they dragged it there! I told the Black that one day he & one day I would be exactly as that Dead Horse. But he jumped up, shook ears, & caracoled on. O the bitter bitter cold as I walked back & the old hurting too.

SATURDAY 20 FEBRUARY I have gone on slowly & with laborious polishing & correcting for rhythm & lilt working at the start of my Weymouth book as I never do when I am really launched. Good Lord! I work like the good Flaubert in his house at Rouen or wherever it was! Faintly we heard Young Albert Krick hammering – but otherwise we have seen no body – not did we yesterday nor the day before nor before that save Miss McNeill. How heavenly to me is this seeing nobody but the T.T. [...] She spoke of inviting Edna & Boissevain to tea but I do not show myself very keen nor must it be confessed have they as yet shown themselves very keen to come!

WEDNESDAY 24 FEBRUARY Worked on at the Secret Platonic Essence of High House, Greenhill, Weymouth. I want this Book to be more Subtle than *Glastonbury*! [...] Miss Margaret Gilman wants to come & the T.T.'s cousin Lewis Lukes from Canada wants to come. The T.T. cries out that she wants no Visitors & wants never again to pay a Visit! [...] I meditated all the way back as I watched the snow clinging to the seeds of tall dead flowers upon the great Demeter Secret learnt in British Museum 3 years next summer about Static Contemplation. Learnt then but O so hard to practise. It's an art of divesting the mind of all thought, and sinking down or out and away through any material objects but keeping these (any) objective things in mind & working outwards centrifugally upon these casual little material objects, not getting tied up & numb in a Tight inward knot – but forgetting all worry all future all past in a sensation of Being; but not of any sort of Over-Soul or Religion or Unity or Brahma or God – entirely lonely & separate – a hard little Crystal!

FRIDAY 26 FEBRUARY Mr Steuerwald brought some oil before breakfast & some more after. He came in with little Dick who loves to see our toy animals. I gave him a cheque for $11.85 but O how sad how bitter-sad is this poor good-natured man's plight. It is pitiful to talk to him about his affairs. He cannot cope with business or get business & he is such a nice man. It's a shame. This morn I took the Black the Round & greeted the Perdita Stone, the Half-Gate, the Flotsam, the Jetsam, the Bowsprit, the Gate, the Stump, the John's Stone, the Other Unknown Stone, the Unknown Stone, the Noble Wreck, the Other Noble Wreck, the Apple Tree, the Saddle Stone, the other Apple tree, the Thorn Bush, the Broken Stone and the Sea Coal!

MONDAY 29 FEBRUARY My philosophy teaches me that within certain limits the mind can do anything in making over a person's character. My own character has changed for instance from being a touchy nervous jumpy personage into being a calm humorous strong quiet personage with nerves of iron!

The first copies of the American edition of A Glastonbury Romance *arrive on 4 March. Margaret Gilman, a teacher at Bryn Mawr and a friend of John's cousin, Father Hamilton Cowper Johnson, visits Phudd Bottom 4-6 March. Frances is Frances Gregg, whom John had met and fallen in love with in 1912. The relationship was always difficult but until her death he wrote to her regularly, sending her money to supplement her attempts to make a living by writing. Maurice Browne, a theatrical producer, is another friend of his early years in America.*

SUNDAY 6 MARCH [The T.T.] says it is entirely personal but that M.G. is too much a teacher for her & that her mind has been deformed by the academic world. She says she is a nice person & possibly all right for Hamilton but not all right for her but spoilt by being a professional academic competent! [...] But M.G. is not only too academic & even tolerant in an academic way & not with the passion of Heretic! she is also too moral and ethical. Whenever these things appear the T.T. gets as hostile & agitated as when Nietzsche hears a strain of *Parsifal*! [...] I feel towards her myself as if she were a relation – exactly as if she were Marian Patteson or Marian Upcher or Marian Hoare or Marian Staniforth! Indeed to speak the truth I feel as if she were Aunt Annie who – *absit omen*! – married Uncle Cecil, the 'Rackety Rector of Rickinghall'. But of course all these relations were academic & all (except Uncle Cecil) decidedly ethical! So I am used to her type & feel an understanding quiet sympathy with it whereas the Elemental with whom I live excites my amorous propensities & wickedness & rouses my romantic interest. In fact I am like the Scholar-Gipsy who lives with a real Gipsy!

MONDAY 7 MARCH The T.T. actually expressed a wild desire that Frances had come in – that Arch 'Betrayer' of Constructive Virtue! Thus might Iseult of Brittany cry out for the presence of Iseult of Cornwall when some Athletic Collegiate Britomart came by on her quest after the Fisher King or the Questing Beast armed with the Spear of Purity & the Shield of Faith! What a wavering of the wild Figures on the blown Tapestry of Phudd Castle! [...] I have just laid down on my couch on a Lady Bird & killed it – Ailinon! Woe! Woe! I took the Black the Round posting the T.T.'s letter to 'my mother' – that letter for which every night she sits up, so late, endangering her peace of nerves the next day! But of course I agree it must be done for her parents have few interests outside her letters. But O if only it need not be done at Midnight! [...] Yesterday when M.G. went our life was in rags & tatters – all day the T.T. tried to sew it together. [...] We see so few – so few – that we grow too much self-absorbed – too easily upset!

TUESDAY 8 MARCH Have worked quite hard at this difficult First Chapter of my Weymouth book. [...] I want to have a very definite King Lear effect with the Captain & Mrs Cobbold & Mrs Lily. I want to make Daisy Lily a very nice young girl of seventeen – an ideal young girl – the loveliest young girl ever described in a novel. But how retiring & shy & silent therefore! I must make her nice by dipping pen in Silence!

THURSDAY 10 MARCH A letter from poor old Hamilton full

of fears about M.G. as if she were his Only Child & one from M.G. herself – a very nice one – in which she says that *War & Peace* is 1143 pages long so that *Glastonbury* is some thirty pages longer than *War & Peace*! Frances has sent me another MS about the wild sea & cliffs & winds of Tintagel where she is now & a Dwarf & an idiot servant called by the good name of Yewly & all with a crowd of children enlarged out of her real ones, Oliver & Betty. It is better than her last by a lot!

SATURDAY 12 MARCH At Breakfast she spoke most eloquently on the subject of Frances and her idea is that F. has remained at the Pre-Raphaelite Epoch & has not let herself grow with the times. She said that I too had something of the Maurice Browne Epoch in my nature but had deliberately changed my nature & from being a Cardinal of 'Spiritual Insincerity' as Lulu says, have become a Hermit & practise my games on the First Cause & on Stones & Posts! Yes, it is true. I have deliberately allowed what I inherit from my Father and Mother to overcome a certain theatricality & over-relish for dramatic Gestures. Thus I have, with growth of a more refined taste, & also – above all be it noted – having found my Little Ballad Girl who Satisfies all my abnormal Wickedness – completely re-created myself & by degrees, in my worship of the Chthonian Demeter of the British Museum & my life with the T.T., I am changing my Life-Illusion into something quieter, more earthy, more patient, more primeval, more simple. To this end my use of Homer as my Breviary is very beneficial!

SUNDAY 13 MARCH At tea the T.T. talked eloquently but with a certain intense troubled sadness of what she missed in this place and indeed in all America. She missed Heightening.

MONDAY 14 MARCH Took Black the Round. I was teased by the Mees trying to get out & go with us. I was teased by the Black's slow ways of advance & his persistent pissing at every post & stone but I struggled against these teasings & clutched my Serpent Stick & I looked at the ridge as I stood by the graveyard praying for the Dead there & especially for Willy Gearing a dead child. Rise from the Dead, led by Willy I said. [...] And I saw this array of risen spirits go trailing over the Stein Hill. Thus each day I have a word with the Dead. Standing near Perdita Stone I stared long & long at the Ridge and the Six Branch Tree & I heard Crows and chickens & far-off the noise of a Train – an American Train's peculiar noise like a great far-off Mammoth muttering to itself. [...] I had thought as I came from the Round home by the Windmill fence how it was really true that I had a trick of isolating objects like grey posts and a sloping field of tawny grass as in a Picture not necessarily by Salvator Rosa! And how I was not as sensitive to the background of human life 'heightened' as the T.T. says she always is, but how a group of objects on the earth as long as I clutch my serpent stick & am alone is enough.

TUESDAY 15 MARCH I was late last night, didn't come till midnight because I was occupied with expurgating *Glastonbury* for Mr Gollancz, the English Publisher, & I was shocked to discover that he regarded that passage about the 'worm-snake' in Mr Evan's obsessed soul as a description of his Penis. I do pray readers of the American Edition won't make the same mistake. I have writ to Mr Fadiman to ask if I had not better make the same change substituting 'Lemur of the Mind' for 'worm-snake' in the second printing of the American edition. Mr G. also wants Bugger me Black! written like this – hee! hee! hee! '—— me black!' So I was late but I finished it, counting the letters so as to save expense in the change. I don't mind such expurgations one bit. I am proud of my cleverness in making 'em. I have nothing in me of that new Puritanism which has so austere a Conscience over the '39 Articles' of stern aesthetic probity. I am an unscrupulous Time-Server over Art because I am a writer of a kind that is not aesthetic so much as – what dare I say? – Prophetic or Inspired sounds too presumptuous! Over things of art I am very careless and very philosophical – with the Philosophy of detachment!

SATURDAY 19 MARCH The T.T. in the morning looked at the sky thro' the window of the Spare-Room and she said to me 'here is a Spring Sky – those are not simply grey clouds – it is the sky which is grey and it is the peculiar grey of a spring day.' I accepted her divination; though I would never myself have known the difference between a sky of low-hung grey clouds & this Spring sky of hers which is not clouds at all! [...] And the Black and I both noticed the Smell of a Skunk, but I did not know this! To me, for I am an obtuse smeller, it was lovely & delicious smell! I came & told the T.T. that I had smelled the

1932 Dung of a Herd of Elephants, mad with the Spring urge. The Black had an ecstasy. And he smelt of Skunk when we got back.

On 17 March John has a bad fall on ice. He leaves for New York on 4 April to give three lectures 'on the subject ostensibly of Enjoyment of Literature but really on my Book!' He stays with Marian & Peter, is interviewed by reporters, meets his many friends and sees the executives of S.& S. Keedick accepts these lectures 'as my farewell'.

SATURDAY 20 MARCH The mail contained the great window card, a strange looking image of the author of *Glastonbury*, which I was deeply and profoundly proud of. She came late late late to bed I expect was Two or Three because she swore she did not know what the time was! And in the Night she had the Worst Dream she has ever had in her life. She dreamed that we both cheerfully decided that I must die. And I said it was easy if I willed it so – thus was I like Mr Geard! But she suddenly got a Panic Terror that she had seen me for the last time & that *Glastonbury* was my last book. She was in the Subway – some men were talking about some body they had found & they said 'He had for long been trying to kill himself; he was in anguish he asked & commanded us to shoot him to kill him.' [...] This dream is partly due to her remorse because she advised me to lecture to help Schuster start Glastonbury & partly to my own telepathic thoughts so dreading my visit to New York & so dreading that this crashing fall & the queer sensation in my back behind my left shoulder-blade means that I am in real danger! [...] I read aloud to her *Sanctuary* by Faulkner. O how I do dislike these Southerners!

FRIDAY 25 MARCH The T.T. that lovely Being enjoyed the Play & the Assembly of our County People with infinite zest. O what a Novel, what a Chapter more than any Horse Fair did she tell me of. How Albert acted so Natural. How Carl acted so Rhetorical & School-for-Oratory. How Mr Renwick's Chauffeur looked, how Mrs Uzener spoke of her Family & how they all treated Hattie Steitz so humorously and tenderly & how well she acted but O the tragedy below it all of her growing blind & how grand Miss Knuckle-Bone of the Curtis House looked! How the T.T. visited the McNeill's. Old man so worried with fear of losing his Old Wife. Miss McNeill so cold & calm & not worried; & her sister so haggard from raising children. I could hear from the Attic all the cars rolling home as after a Montacute House party we would often hear the carriages come past the Vicarage. I came down to greet the T.T. on her return & aye! but she looked so beautiful in Russian cap & blue chinese silk shawl!

SUNDAY 27 MARCH I took Black an extra Easter morning walk. [...] There was water held in the Stone Chalice or Grail of 'The Stone of Fal' & into this I dipped my fingers & crossed myself & also put a drop into my mouth. [...] Now a thin filmy lovely haze covers all the sky & mitigated suffused sunshine – very springlike – is over all & there is a delicious sense of mud abroad & the grass blades by the edge of our river-bridge, for there is a patch of grass at water's edge there, are growing green. [...] I tapped the earth with my head & prayed to Demeter the Mother of all Gods! In the Manger in the Barn I pretended to be Faust & held a little bottle in my hand till I heard – that is to say pretended to hear – the Easter Bells. But sublimely indifferent to all these rites & pious practices of mine [a hawk] hovered high up above my head. I looked up fascinated & hypnotized till I actually shared his grand egoistic loneliness & defiance of all – the huge Hawk Of Phudd!

TUESDAY 29 MARCH Waded thro' one perpetual Drift along road between Graveyard & Spinney, my serpent stick sinking within a foot of its handle at each step! Took Garbage. Got oil. [...] As I was shaving – lo! Mr Curtis' car being pulled by his white horses; Mr Stein, helping, carried our milk to door, & the young man 'help' was aiding also. I hid for alarm of all this. Then was ashamed & opened kitchen door & it seemed as if all these gallant fighters against the snow contemplated the effeminate & useless Mr Powg with amused contempt standing at his kitchen door. [...] All the time after breakfast the T.T. played *Iberia* by Albéniz on the Victriola. She explained to me the theme of the old very old Spanish folk-lore ballad-tune & she discoursed most eloquently on how she liked modern composers who like T.S. Eliot in poetry use the old ballad refrain & intellectualize them. But I found it hard to catch the tune. [...] The T.T. went to the Kricks where she learned that a boy had arrived yesterday at their house in the snow so exhausted that Mrs Krick took him in for the Night. Would we have had the grace to do this? O I hope so! How awful if we had let him go on his way & he had died!

Quite possible. Like those two Tramps at Montacute to whom Gertrude refused food and money and both were found dead of starvation in Tintinhull Great Field the next day. Gertrude could not bear to have it referred to – even now she cannot.

MONDAY 4 APRIL This lovely little Being does look so white & haggard. It hits me to the heart. She is much more in need of care than I am. The winter has been too long for her & all these late nights & it being too cold for her to be out and the Stoves – & the man & the dog & the cat to care for. O I do wish I could take her away to the Sea for a week! [...] It did touch me so to see the way the T.T. had got all my clothes ready for me to put on. I dressed in the Attic. I called her to sew on a button. I said my real word to her there in the Attic. [...] I caught the 2.47 train.

WEDNESDAY 6 APRIL Miss Dorothy Dricas came to Interview & asked O O O so many searching questions! I said I lived absolutely alone & with no one in the house. I also implied & more than implied, that my lady in England was no more of this world! Marian said that to Mr Driscoll I had denied my American wife and to Miss Dricas I had denied my English wife! You can imagine how Marian said it! [...] I had been until then worried only by wondering whether to go & see Keedick. Marian most strenuously & even commandingly & contemptuously tells me not to. [...] Went to lunch in the Inner Sanctum. [...] They showed me a Chicago Tribune saying *Glastonbury* was one of that week's best sellers in Chicago. [...] I stayed till four o'clock at the Sanctum having a long talk with one of their authors called Dr Potter who lives in the Adirondacks and also at Nyack in a community under the care of an astonishing Magician – of that Thaktrad Yogi Cult a Secret Phallic Order under ambiguous Repute with the best Oriental Phallic Library anywhere in the Land.

FRIDAY 8 APRIL Marian has decided to give classes in Lace to make a little cash. She is in low water. Mending even is failing. [...] James Abell came at 12 o'clock we spent three hours together partly diversified by the appearance of Mr St John Interviewer for the Associated Press which the Schuster office was very pleased to have got. [...] Took Marian in Taxi all the way to Labor Temple. There I met [...] many familiar Jewish faces going back to the days of Mr Gould & Arnold: Arnold himself & Hattie & Edith, Schuster & Simon, Will Durant. [...] I made so much of Dorothy Richardson that Mr Simon & Schuster looked at each other and said 'We must have a Conference of the Sanctum about this.' If it does result in their publishing 'Pilgrimage' it will have made my Lectures of this crowded week well worth all.

SUNDAY 10 APRIL The kitchen stove is out. The Black is feeling sick. The T.T. is overworked. What can be done? What can?

SATURDAY 16 APRIL Everywhere now in every direction even on hillsides the earth is soft for several inches deep & at each step you sink in. The green patch beyond the Spinney that I call grass & the T.T. calls Rye is very pretty to see & I like to see the grave-yard from the other side of it. Growth & death together. But you cannot see the spirits of the dead. [...] I felt dead-exhausted – because of the various little extras – seeing to people & things – due to the illness of the T.T. But she is better now & I shall soon pick up my energy again. [...] I went on with my Book which is easier work for me than writing letters. I am never in the morning too exhausted to enjoy writing. Writing my book – like lecturing – seems to put magnetic energy into me. It is my best cure. It is the passivity of life. It is becoming a reed – a writing Reed.

WEDNESDAY 20 APRIL I must do something Drastic. It's no good any more telling her to be good. I must always come raging down at 12.30 or one or I must on my own authority get a Servant. [...] It is my rôle to look after this Little Infantile Fixation if she won't do it herself. [...] Miss McNeill came to pay us a Call in a new green Dollar Dress & White hat. She looked Pathetic. We were the only place she could go this lonely hard-worked maid this spring day. [...] Took Black past 3 Ashes to the Stone of Fal & up hill & back by the Wood but foolishly I had my Rubbers on which prevented the earth-magic from passing up my feet into my bones. I will leave off Rubbers now Spring has come!

THURSDAY 21 APRIL Mr Shaver cut off some of the gamboge-yellow sprouts from the old Willow by the river-path

1932 & planted them in a row between the grass outside the Barn & the Road. He then raked away several Wheelbarrow loads of Dead Leaves. This taking Dead Leaves from a lawn in a Wheel Barrow by a nice Gardener like this good & quiet man, so gentle & abstracted – what memories of quiet Spring mornings it brings back! [...] Mr Krick came to move the 'Toilet'. This was a revolutionary event of primal importance.

SATURDAY 30 APRIL O how the T.T. does loathe & hate & abominate & suffer from Visitors. She says she would sooner be Sick than have them. I must make an unforgetting Note of this in my mind.

SUNDAY 8 MAY Mr Masters came. [...] The T.T. got a small chicken from the Krick's & cooked it for mid-day dinner. It was a Perfect Day warm sun no wind all wet soft greyish though sunlit & peaceful and the air full of the sound of birds & water and even Sunday cars did not spoil it. There was the T.T. shut in cooking & doing house-work. O deary I! What a pity. As for Mr Masters & myself we sat on two chairs on the lawn by the barn. [...] Mr Masters told of his literary difficulties with Publishers. How he gets on I can't think save when I look at his chin!

WEDNESDAY 11 MAY I took Black to the sunrise-river reaching its shingly bank by the East end of the Spinney where the Flood (O sacred Flood!) has left such lovely rubble & torn out the posts & the barbed wire. Glittering like silver was the river! O it was so exciting. That molten silver glitter is to me the ecstasy of the Beatific Vision like Dante describes at the end of the Paradiso. And the pebbles & shingles by the river give me the old feeling of the Beach at Weymouth opposite Brunswick Terrace where when L.C.P. & T.F.P. were at Northwold I was so very happy, rapturously happy with my mother & the 'little ones' who then were Bertie & Lulu & Marian! [...] I read the whole of Chapter Three to her this afternoon. It took three hours from two to five. She lay on the Horse-hair sofa & was not overbowed by it but seemed impressed by it. It is 200 pages long! She said it was a Record in Invention & in being a Difficult Technical achievement. She also said she really began to feel sideways in it the Presence of the Sea.

A two-day visit from Richard Simon results in John writing for Simon &

Schuster A Philosophy of Solitude, *which he begins on 31 May. They meet a psychoanalyst, Dr Frink, who becomes a particular friend of Phyllis.*

SUNDAY 15 MAY The T.T. found getting breakfast a cruel effort. The poor wildly-distracted Elemental thus saddled with laborious human toil of kitchen did come like a wild Being distracted into Bathroom when I was there beating her head with her clenched fists pitiful for to see & hear. After this meal she sat with the visitors and me on the grass in North Garden. […] [Simon] said that after consultation with Durant & Dreiser he would tell me how I was to write a book of my ideas on 'First & Last Things'. All this maddened the T.T. who uttered an eloquent Defence of Authors. *Apologia de Auctoribus, contra Tyrannos*! […] The Mees had Five Kittens last night.

WEDNESDAY 18 MAY From 12 to 5 – five hours – is generally now, day by day, my time for writing. It is not a good time because it is a low-ebb time & a somnolent time & I often about two feel terribly sleepy. I have more inspiration when I write after tea. But it may be that when anyone is sleepy as they write a certain realistic solidity & convincingness is the result for when your brain is very alert there is a tendency to philosophize too much & digress from solidity and reality!

THURSDAY 19 MAY Dr Frink came & had lunch with us in the front parlour & looked at our book of Death Masks with interest. Then he took the T.T. to the Auction Room on the road beyond Hudson of Mr Sibelas. And he bought a wonderful table for the T.T. for fifteen dollars from a weird & monstrous Jew Peddler called Reuben. They visited the shop of Mr Travers the dealer in Hudson & came home a roundabout way through lovely scenery which simply thrilled the T.T. with the smell of lilacs & beautiful little houses. […] The T.T. was enchanted. It was the aura she craved.

WEDNESDAY 25 MAY Had a long talk with the T.T. about my *Philosophy of Solitude*. I made a Synopsis to send Schuster – but the T.T. 'went up in the Air' over the whole Project. She feels I ought to be a Novelist alone. But I say that if S. & S. support me with Royalties as a Novelist – in return I ought to give them a gambling chance with a little Pamphlet of 'Ideas on Living' such as they seem to crave as a 'hit or miss' little Speculation!

1932

SUNDAY 12 JUNE The T.T. came running across the road to the gate to meet me. Something had struck her mind about us as a queer pair of Terminals being pathetically out of it among clever & competent ones. She was weeping.

THURSDAY 30 JUNE Had a very serious talk about my ulcer which has hurt me so of late & the T.T. said I ought really to go to Johns Hopkins. But I said instead of this I would start going to bed for the whole time from Breakfast till 4.30 when I go my walk & I would go a much shorter walk. This I did and I found I wrote well in bed. [...] I have been happy today for the T.T. is in good spirits having so far for some unknown reason – not the Grand Reason of going to have a child called Perdita – escaped the coming of her Sickness. [...] As I lay in bed with the T.T. bringing up bread & butter I felt such profane & egoistic delight in being alive and in so lovely a place & writing a philosophy of Solitude – a lovely, lonely place. O if I could only write a good book for forlorn spirits to be helped by!

MONDAY 4 JULY The T.T. scolded me for leaving the rag – wet – with which I had dried the Black – on the horse-hair chair in Spare Room. She said that little chair had belonged to some careful woman; & now was outraged by these hulking things. I will not hang my wet socks on it any more. At breakfast the T.T. was inspired by a rush of fierce eloquence – first directed at the limitations of the Powys Family – their primordial lack of civilization & appreciation of the refinement of art; & their tyrannical rules of Simplicity and their Welsh Princes' pride and Bardic primeval ways – then directed at my Victorian Security of 2 or 3 generations according to which I think in old stale grooves of doling out Shillings to the Starving Children. There is a shiver of direct understanding with Privation from real experience that is worth – so cried the T.T. like an Elemental Sybil – all the doled out money in the world. [...] Then the T.T. helped me with an ENEMA.

TUESDAY 12 JULY In the afternoon of this day the T.T. came up to the Attic with a wild look saying to me 'Armour thyself!' & poured forth a flood of indignant eloquence against the whole idea of my writing this little wretched *Philosophy of Solitude*. [...] It struck her that all the wiser & more self-respecting Public would be made to regard me as a Charlatan and not an honest hardworking Craftsman of Fiction if I kept bringing out these hurried little Tracts for the Times. If you really are to turn from novels to writing a massive philosophy it would be different the T.T. said but these little books – these little Cults for funny ones – these 'Pigeon Roost' sermons.

TUESDAY 26 JULY Worked away steadily at the VIIth chapter of my wretched philosophy which the T.T. thinks so ill of. But I am led on by perpetual hope that suddenly a wonderful inspiration may seize me that will please her. [...] At tea the T.T. spoke of her life. She said her longing for Death was really for an after-life of happiness – of all those extras of rest and contemplation that she misses so. I have been deeply touched & hit by her words. O why did I bring her here. The moment Mr Playter no longer lives I shall take her away. I know she could be happy in a foreign Inn in some old town. We shall see. I have been very stupid if not very selfish.

SUNDAY 7 AUGUST After breakfast wrote steadily at Philosophy. Then wrote an important letter to Schuster acknowledging the receipt of a Statement indicating that *Glastonbury* is a Failure. Only 4000 copies sold. And $500 dollars to pay for its typing & in Nov. to receive only Seven hundred & eighty dollars – when three thousand was what we hoped for. This is a Serious Blow to which I must adjust myself when I had been secretly hoping for I know not what terrific Kudos including the Noble Prize & being knighted by my Sovereign & receiving the acclamation of Europe & seeing the book translated into all languages – & best of all sold at the entrance to the Ruins in Glastonbury itself! Well I must resign myself to its being a failure.

They have many summer visitors, including the Jungian psychiatrist Dr Mabel Pearson who supplies him with his 'powders' for ulcer pain. On 29 August, Phyllis goes to visit her parents. While she is away the kitten Toby is run over. Phyllis returns 20 September and John makes a third start on Weymouth.

MONDAY 8 AUGUST Called Mabel just in time for breakfast. She told us about James Joyce whom she had doctored & seen several times. She told us of his daughter Lucia. Last night I read aloud from 'Work in Progress' out of *transition* – but no one liked

1932 it but the reader & he perhaps only for curious & heretical reasons because of a certain cold sardonic 'history-cosmic' exultation and this orgy of infantile reactions to gibble-gabble words all mixed-up. She told us a little of Dr Jung also. [...] Then Dr Mabel drove off in a black hat of the T.T. & by mistake leaving her rubbers on the porch.

SATURDAY 20 AUGUST Up at 7.15. Down at 7.30. There was Mr Shaver cutting the grass so long & thick & heavy with a lovely grey dew – drenched with it. [...] He said things were going up at the Factory. 5 days work & the men taking turns. O the Depression is beginning to lift. This Factory is a sign. The real beginning of the end of the Depression was the Conversion of War Bonds in England. Whatever that means! [...] In this country they mow the grass & pile it up into these round hay-cocks & then next day they carry it away. They do not 'make hay'. That must be why their barns burn down so. [...] I gave myself an ENEMA practically alone in preparation for when I am alone altogether.

WEDNESDAY 24 AUGUST Mr Krick came in his Spectacles looking so particularly nice to see the 'Produce' Market News of Prices in our *Times*. [...] Mr Johnson brought the Mail. [...] Arthur talked of spending the winter in Jamaica & Edna of spending it in Algeria. So it looks as if – unless we die – there would be loneliness – unless we die! For who can tell? Boissevain liked the idea of my praising Walking in my book. I felt a little uneasy & remorseful because I told Arthur that in my book I attacked his Bare Thighs & he replied that I never saw him without caressing them with my hand – which is the truth – for I have a great attraction to all mortal Thighs of beautiful persons whether masculine or feminine. [...] The day was very hot with a South Wind and I felt a sudden Nostalgia for my native land.

SUNDAY 28 AUGUST At breakfast she spoke most eloquently about my Weymouth book & how I ought to put in more of my original feelings & make Magnus Muir my new character really more like myself than Wolf or John & [...] Weymouth and the whole circumference of the book being the feeling of Magnus Muir but the other characters left as they are only cut & condensed and shortened & the whole thing given a romantic 'Tempest'-like 'aquarelle' kind of atmosphere – enchanted &

transported out of all dullness but the characters real tho' not too stolid but volatile and like figures in a crystal which were the thoughts of Magnus.

THURSDAY 1 SEPTEMBER Yesterday during Eclipse when a strange Cimmerian light like an under-ocean landscape covered all, the cows led by Maggie & Sis (all except Peggie) left the shelter of the trees where as usual of an afternoon they were resting & advanced in a line into our orchard. A big woodchuck played with the fowls – they pecked at it. It heeded not but continued its own gambles. But the cats as if conscious of something queer crouched side by side on the kitchen steps just outside the door. [...] I wrote several paragraphs – well! one or two – of my book on Solitude actually during the Eclipse. This ought to make this book lucky, eh? For in my horoscope the Moon is predominant – exactly in the position, so Ralph Shirley said, that it is in the horoscope of W.B. Yeats.

THURSDAY 8 SEPTEMBER First Day after Toby's Death. Visited Toby's grave with the Black & stopped him from pissing on it. [...] As my Father – who often resembled a great old Cat – when my sister died took all his sons walking walking walking leaving my mother alone in house – so did the Mees go off to hunt & forget that her first-born was dead. I keep going over and over in mind every detail of yesterday.

FRIDAY 9 SEPTEMBER I can't get his Clock Tower look out of my head or those two paws held so bravely under his chin while all his body was crushed & his white leg bent under him. Mr Curtis our great Mr Curtis is in hospital at Poughkeepsie with a blood-poisoned arm from a splinter which he took out with his pocket-knife. [...] I have just had an ENEMA. I have just been out to [Toby's] grave. The moon shines on it. I tell him it was my fault.

MONDAY 12 SEPTEMBER I mailed my *Philosophy of Solitude* to Simon & Schuster telling Postman to insure it for $100. [...] I pray they will like this Philosophy. O I do so wish the T.T. could have liked it better. But she has a soul for Watteau loveliness that comes & goes in the world 'in small measure or not at all' rather than for my stern and rocky Inanimates. And yet she is an 'Elemental' herself; but to be an Elemental is not at all the same as being what in my proud & stern book I call an Elementalist.

SUNDAY 25 SEPTEMBER After breakfast I read the whole of my brother Theodore's *Two Thieves*, only expurgating the cruel scenes. It is very Allegorical and divides – like Schopenhauer – all wickedness by a vast gulf from all goodness – leaving the goodness somewhat feeble, pallid, helpless. As against this I hold the view that by a certain Compromise life can still be active and positive with the evil kept in its place. But this allegorizing gives a good point to T.F.P.'s writing! And is in its way effective.

MONDAY 10 OCTOBER After breakfast she read aloud from her own Translation on Fontenelle. [...] The T.T. then discoursed on a Book for me to write after the Weymouth Book – on Poetry; giving the essence of what my family possess in their unique prejudices. [...] She now says – since the little lyric poems now leave us cold – why not be on our metal to start a new wave of new poetry. Taking the pioneering of T.S. Eliot of Joyce of Dorothy Richardson & really dispensing with obvious sermonising & meaning, of obvious philosophy – compose a thing like a Symphony of Music – full of echoes, tags, fragments, breaking it up – queer parodies of ancient very old things – inspired parody – giving indirectly the subtle values of thought without the weight of actual dullness of thought – using the strange old Mythology of the *Mabinogion* – why not? – & changing quick from one form of poetry to another – lyric to blank verse – & so on – what an idea! Will I really ever be able to try what the T.T. thus suggests? We shall see. Those frogs in the Mabinogion Swamp, before this, have croaked Write it! Do it! Write it! you fool! We shall see. What things come into her head.

SATURDAY 22 OCTOBER At breakfast the T.T. got Perfect Toast for me. How this is the nicest taste – to my ideas – in all the world. It is a sensual rapture to enjoy it. Afterwards she played Spring & Heart's Wounds by Grieg. [...] Her face is the most sensitive & mobile thing I know; like a poplar leaf. Music transforms it.

SATURDAY 5 NOVEMBER I have not yet decided what do about my Weymouth Book which must have been begun from outside; from the names of houses & streets & people; and from Lodmoor & Chesil Beach; instead of from some inner *Entelecheia*.

SUNDAY 6 NOVEMBER I have been trying to think about my

Weymouth Book – but I find it nigh impossible to think in the void. How do authors manage it? I can only think when I'm lecturing or talking to the T.T. I am not a thinker. I am a reed through which thoughts come! [...] She however – thank the Lord! – is able to think. She thinks all the time: Sans Cesse. And now she has thought out a wonderful idea for my book – about making Sylvan Cobbold into a revivalistic preacher with a little idiot or sub-normal girl-friend & he to be Put Away & I thought as I talked to her – about a Punch & Judy group too! Now we shall be able to go ahead with Magnus & his Curly Wix of the Wishing Well.

MONDAY 14 NOVEMBER I found the T.T. playing on the Victriola Schubert's *Symphony* & I listened with pleasure while lying with my eyes shut – which I call my Yoga practise [...]. But the T.T. has got used to seeing me lie like this like a Stone Effigy & has ceased to regard it as a reproach or a playing the Martyr which is a great Comfort. Yes I get great comfort by her not being teased by my practising this very simple Art of Solitude!

WEDNESDAY 16 NOVEMBER The T.T. still has this Sadness. I tried to talk about it comparing it to her old unhappiness. But she was unable to stand my too rough and boisterous way of handling this deep matter. But O I don't feel like such a rushing wind. I tried to tell her that I feel like a flood of water round an Island lapping it & gathering round it & hugging it but even so – water that cannot become land! Deep, deep were my own thoughts. She has given me all! This place which suits me so, this country which suits me so, all her ways & above all her own lovely form – a Paradise to hold – & all the little things she does for me, such as this Perfect Toast twice a day. Such as my socks so wonderfully mended; such as this lavender sweater of her own which she lets me wear though it is so vexing to her how many things I put on till I be bundled up more like a Beast than a man – and here I live by her side & yet she is so very Sad & all seems without Interest to her. Ailinon! Ailinon!

THURSDAY 8 DECEMBER Took Black via the Mail to Prometheus Stone. [...] I feared to jump across just as I did so long ago with Father & old Littleton at Preston Brook near Weymouth where L. always jumped at a particular place and I

1932 always feared it at the last tho' many times I ran to the edge to jump. So I feared at the Prometheus Stone but the old Black wanting to show off pushed past me & jumped – but missed his objective. [...] So leaning on my stick I stretched out & got him by the collar & swung him back. He was pleased; & not ashamed! He gambolled off – like Ares, after a rebuff – 'glorying in his strength'. [...] At tea I asked the T.T. what it was that made her read those pitiful sad events in the paper – & she said it was not just gaping stupid morbid curiosity – but a feeling that when such sorrow was in the air someone ought to recognise it & share it. [...] Dreiser looked at her once and in his rough formidable way noticed this – for it is what he feels himself.

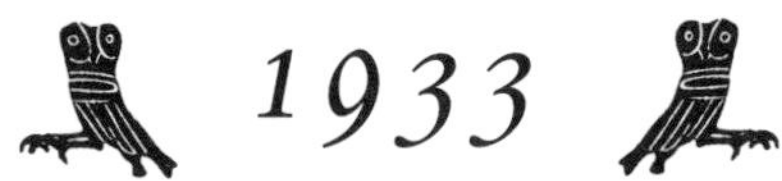

1933

1933 seems to be a relatively uneventful year but circumstances are pushing them towards leaving America. The death of Phyllis's father, the knowledge that they are living beyond their means at Phudd, the severe illness of Llewelyn in August, John's desire to go to Wales and to write a novel about the magician Merlin – are countered by their ever-deeper involvement with the life of the community (the neighbours are gradually becoming characters in a book) and Phyllis's desire to stay where she is now fairly comfortable.

A continuing characteristic of the diary is the careful noting of the changing seasons and weather patterns. Columbia County is very cold and snowy in winter; in summer the heat and drought are often oppressive.

Two more traditions are established: feeding the birds and having a 'lesson' after breakfast. The latter consists of readings from Homer, the New Testament and one other classic. John reads and rereads the Odyssey, *and increasingly the diaries reveal through names, phrases, allusions, patterns of speech, his growing knowledge and love of Homer.*

His ulcer continues 'rampageous'. He spends two weeks in bed in January after Phyllis returns from Kansas; this calms it but it continues to flare up periodically.

John hurriedly finishes Weymouth Sands *in July for autumn publication in order to provide a much-needed source of income. However, Simon & Schuster do not like* Weymouth Sands *and demand revisions. It is not published until February, 1934. In England, Gollancz turns down* A Glastonbury Romance, *but John Lane accepts both it and* Weymouth Sands. *He writes a preface to the English edition of* Solitude, *published by Cape in October, and begins to write his* Autobiography *in August: this famous work was conceived initially as a way of earning money.*

1933 *Phyllis leaves for her parents' home on 4 January, and stays until after her father's death. During her absence, John can do little except nurse his ulcer, feed the birds and keep the stoves going. Hattie Steitz comes in every day to do the housework. When Phyllis returns on 20 January John takes his ulcer to bed, leaving her to cope with the winter chores.* A Philosophy of Solitude *comes out in early February.*

MONDAY 9 JANUARY Attended the stoves which were all right. When I took the ashes out at the back I found a strong wind blowing from the South-East & ricochetting against Phudd. Opened Kitchen door & let out the Mees & prayed to the earth & to the divine Ether. Then I put on the Patchin Place kettle & boiled water on the gas. Then I gave myself an Enema [...] but it was too dark to read the *Anatomy of Melancholy* as is my wont & in which I have now reached well on in Volume Two, always reading it on the Close-Stool. Took the garbage with the Black. It began to snow. I took up to the garbage place later some extra bits of bread for the Tits, but fearful of the snow they were in hiding somewhere. Then I took the Mail. [...] Then I read the *Odyssey* about Telemachus & Athene sailing in a ship to sandy Pylos. Hattie came so bravely in spite of the storm of heavy snow – half a foot deep it is now! When I told her about my book coming out on Jan 19th! she said I was lucky, when so many could not get their books published. This remark was a good jerk for me back into the humility I am always talking about. The vanity of authors is simply boundless. Of course she is right; I am lucky, & that's the truth! Hattie is always so kind to me – why should I exact from her the last subtleties of praise?

THURSDAY 19 JANUARY I have broken a little plate and that cracked Dresden cup. O I hope the T.T. will not be upset by this or by the Mees having done No. 2 & No. 1 on her Precious Rug & by the cushion rug being wet & by two or three of her plants being quite dead! I know not why they died.

FRIDAY 20 JANUARY I did not feel equal to shave even think of that! & the T.T. coming too! Shall I be able to wash up? O & I have forgotten to tell Mr Curtis to bring cream for her & extra milk! But I did remember to ask Albert to get some nice chops for her & a lettuce & bread & beef to boil for the Black. [...] Took Black to Mabinogion Swamp and the Lesbian Trees. Tore my blue Corduroy Trowsers terrible – so that I walked home like a bottom-ragged Pantaloon. […] She Came! She came! She have coom back! O it was a happy evening. She got tea & then she told me all the chief things – & how like Alyosha after Fr Zosima's death she went out & wept with joy & then again even after she got to Albany she had another ecstasy feeling him at her side & all right. She says her mother will some day come and see us and will also some day go with us to England.

MONDAY 23 JANUARY A Bad – a very bad night – one of the Worst. Discomfort from one till three a.m. Two glasses of Malted Milk – no good – then a plate of bread-and-butter not much better. […] Then when she came at last she brought me a hot water Bottle. This I pressed to pit of stomach & this with the comfort of her dear form lying there with her thin little waist & her back to me & my arm round her brought indescribable peace – & I slept like a Top. […] Last night the T.T. spoke about 'Perdita' by the shores of Lethe; & twice the door flew open! But the T.T. herself – says the old Man of Phudd – is the only child allowed here. But seeing her father die so very hard has made her feel deeply as if nothing were important save life itself as different from death. Yes she has returned changed spiritually in a singular way. […] But I will not even consider – in this point Petrushka's deepest Selfishness or Egoism is Adamantine – even so much as a thought of a little Perdita! My only daughter is a Stone – the daughter of a Stone – & my only little girl is the T.T.!

TUESDAY 24 JANUARY I cannot believe she could get on as bravely as she is doing. It amazes me. We spoke of this bawdy light Georgia Book called *God's Little Acre* that the Viking Press Editor is worrying me to praise – all about easy lads & girls 'having' each other sans any fuss at all save beating each others buttocks. […] But there's no sadism & no vice & no malice in this little, easy-going, rough & tumble work. I don't quite know what I'll say about it! Then we had the Lesson – O how I did enjoy it! […] Now I must revise my chapter. She is fairly satisfied with my revisions so far about Gipsy May – but she does not care for the knife in her pocket. 'Your fault is not a cold heart but facile writing' – & she spoke of a tension that does not require any violence. […] I am still keeping drastically to my regime of staying in Bed.

THURSDAY 2 FEBRUARY We have spoken yesterday & today

of our own Money Affairs which are threatening to cause us serious Worry & anxiety – unless this *Solitude* sells well. We have got our ten copies & I do like the look of it. […] The T.T. in her long walk had the idea of writing an autobiography not to be published till after death. It awes me to think of such a work.

FRIDAY 3 FEBRUARY She spoke as she dressed very strongly about her new growing Inferiority Complex due to living with the Great Petrushka. […] I watched the T.T. from Attic carrying two pails of ashes followed by the Black & the Mees. Worked all day at my chapter. It is an attempt to begin making things move & get the characters together. In this way it is a very important crisis in this book. […] After tea, during which I discoursed on my epochs of inferiority & shame & on the numberless persons who have outraged my life-illusion; till at last I was really 'liked' by the T.T., we read the syllabus of *Anthony Adverse* & I envied it and longed to write a vast Historical Novel.

Marian's shop in New York is burgled. She comes to visit them briefly. They are very short of money, having sent more than they could afford to James Hanley, a relative stranger, later a good friend. During the Depression many of the small American banks went bankrupt. Despite warnings that the Philmont bank might close, Phyllis transfers all her money from post office to bank.

THURSDAY 23 FEBRUARY Before bedtime Marian opened her red chest of old lace & did so enchant the T.T. with its contents like a witch-queen beguiling a young princess with treasures. She consoled herself under the calamity of the burglary by what Bertrand Russell says about moral courage in a world like this. […] While we were having breakfast at eight o'clock in dining room Albert came. Marian does not at all like the entrance of the working class arrived on some business. She said that Mr Delaney our Ideal Cleaner who always stays so long talking politics ought to come to the kitchen door. However, the T.T. tactfully let Albert in – but not in the dining room & he waited in parlour tho' I addressed a word to him now & then. […] Then the T.T. when he had gone, told of the respect and awe she felt for Marian's extraordinary & remarkable character.

SATURDAY 25 FEBRUARY Got a great thrill from watching two Crows flying among the tops of the Pine-trees to the right of the Sloping Field, where they rose one above another & I got the feeling of these great flapping birds themselves & also that sense of tree-tops against a space which I used to get from the fir-trees in Montacute House Drive from Spare Room window – the way such branches lie on the air and are like green boats in a purple sea of space; and mingled with this I got that feeling Wordsworth so well describes in *The Excursion* of a great bird flying lonely, with its cry accompanying it thro' the empty hollowness between tall hills. Saw faint, faint, faint, the last pale dying tint of red in the last dead flower of the last stock after all this winter frost & snow. I now must set to work and revise my chapter for the 2nd time under the criticism of the T.T. [...] After an eloquent description of all she felt about Marian – when I referred to Alyse being so good at looking after Lulu's health – the T.T. with more than usual intensity launched into a scornful attack on the Powys Family for making so much of the quiet virtues of devotion of a neutral kind and always saying 'Out you go!' to any person of spirit and of independent original character. It was a surprise to me this desperate judgment but there may be something in it for I recall well what my father was in this very peculiarity.

WEDNESDAY 1 MARCH I struggled up thro' snow-drift – weary as I was – to un-snow – there's a word like T.F.P.'s 'Un-clay' – my son Tony – a stone – but the T.T. says both our Stone children Perdita & Tony like best (as she does) with 'the Covers' – to lie in peace so!

FRIDAY 3 MARCH It is still snowing a little & looks very grey – not 'doleful' as Mr Schuster says the book-sellers are – but very grey. [...] I heard faint sounds of the little Elemental on the move in Parlour & ere long – at 10.30 a.m. for I was not down till 8 a.m. this morning & she did not come to bed till Three a.m. being occupied with the worst Psychological effort she has ever made to get her Post Office Affairs in order so as to draw out for our Necessity – *Anangki* – in these 'doleful' times, & since we have just sent off all my New York current account to James Hanley (for the birth of his lady's child) all she has, in the way of her own savings. [...] She wondered to see me snuff up the fragrance of the coffee & the tea & I was amused – *Emeidiasa* – to see her so puzzled. Of course it was really my automatic ritual in her absence – when I snuff at the coffee saying 'This is

1933 the Flesh of the T.T.' & at the Tea saying, 'This is the hair of the T.T.!' How was she to know about such ways of the old Dotard when left alone?

MONDAY 6 MARCH So dazed & rapt in paradisal imaginings of her garden full of masses of Regal Lilies was the T.T. that she forgot to attend to the Parlour Stove & left its door open & the draught open. It went Out soon after I came down. Did things. Took Black hurriedly to Prometheus. Noted the glittering reflection of the very Sun in water, not those separate water-spouts of fire – but a sun-path like that I used to see at Weymouth from Penn House which my Father called the road of the Fairy 'Sprightly'. How characteristic of him to call this fancy-being of his by just that name! On my return all the Five Cows were at the railing clamouring for Apples. I went into Cellar & gave Sis two, the fierce Blackie two & gentle Maggie one and I threw one to Peggie – poor little 'Ev' alone got none. [...] Mrs Krick came to get Malted Milk for her Old Man & she said he was very low & thought he was dying & talked about the Lot in the Cemetery & the Tombstone. Today, therefore, after a hurried but happy breakfast – which she ate & drank in her out of door things – she went off at once to visit old Krick & [...] & also to do the complicated business of taking $400 from Postal Savings & putting it into the Amalgamated Bank. Thus the T.T. upholds her principles, & is too public-spirited to rush so basely to clutch her cash [...]. She puts into Bank when all the world is taking out of Bank!

TUESDAY 14 MARCH I have an idea I am getting on pretty well with this Portland & Chesil Beach chapter. I divide myself into at least three characters if not more! I pray & hope I have got somehow the real feeling of the Sea – but I can't tell – I have so many things on my hands at once!

Vivisection was for Powys man's 'most vicious cruelty.' In Weymouth Sands, *Dr Brush does experiments on dogs in Hell's Museum; in a later novel,* Morwyn, *John consigns these 'sadists' to hell. He writes now his first article on the subject.*

WEDNESDAY 15 MARCH Armies of grey chilly damp ghosts go up & down over the sleety thawing landscape & they hover about the hills & they go drifting over the valleys – grey cold thawing ghosts! All the fields are white with snow again & it had only just melted away. […] I went up to Attic. There finished my 35 page Essay on Vivisection. Where to send it? That is the rub. Then I wrote about the encounter of Magnus & Skald on Chesil. Then we both went together to visit old Krick who was a bit more cheerful. Then I took Black to Fountain. Wild & dark ridges & banks & racks & ramparts of menacing clouds swept the sky and a wild early spring – & – winter-lost-on-the-moors – with retreating-armies & alarums – & longings for firelight.

THURSDAY 16 MARCH Went to Attic & worked. The T.T. wore her brown velvet & the Black's Leash round her hips. I liked well to see this. Here is my 'Pet Animal' that I have! When did I first utter those words? The very first day when I met the little Being. And now it has come true.

SATURDAY 18 MARCH I saw a Jay on the Hickory calling to its mate up in Phudd – & its whole body worked up & down – rose & fell – yes it rose half its own height in a terrific spasm as it uttered its call to its dear companion. I also saw on the extremest top of the Apple tree by the Well a Starling looking like a little upright dash Torpedo of Spring-joy all alone & ecstatic & it made its funny whistling noise. I saw the twig it stood on & its wedge-like or shuttle-like form outlined against the faraway Ridge of hills. The Sun was breaking through the spring-clouds & a great streaming misty ray fell from it sloping down from the heavens like an old Italian picture of some apotheosis of a saint but what it fell on was the form of this solitary Starling. […] Read my chapter. She said it will have to be Revised a lot. Too much <u>Rodomontade</u>! My ulcer. O my ulcer has started being <u>troublesome</u> – damn! blast! <u>fuck</u>!

MONDAY 20 MARCH All day we have worked at the book. The T.T. helping me <u>all</u> <u>the</u> <u>while</u>. She ought to have her name on this book but I am far too selfish to let her have it there! But this book – O Unknown Reader – is owing a great deal to her. […] She helped me all day with my chapter about the Storm & the Wreck. With incredible skill revising & correcting my innumerable lapses & rough debouchings into unconvincing Melodrama. […] Ulcer awake.

WEDNESDAY 22 MARCH The Tits follow me from what I

give them up hill to what I give them under Lilac. I have never in all my life got to know birds any at all as well as I have come to know these Tits – their various notes, & every mark on their plumage. [...] After breakfast the T.T. said how when she thinks of any person she cares for – her Father for example – it is always of the 'sideway thrust' of the pitifulness of their existence that she thinks but when they are dead she can think of them with happiness – as now of her Father. What a worshipper of Death the little T.T. is! Into the next world she throws all that she finds desirable. To hover imperceptibly when dead & see without being seen is her ideal. I had villainous discomfort in Ulcer as I came back from my walk & took two powders before breakfast. After breakfast we had a heavenly Lesson. Hera plotting in Heaven to make the Trojans break their '*pistia horkia*' their faithful oaths. The Lord and the Gadarene Swine & the steep cliff. [...] I was called down to see who do you suppose? Our well-loved & long-hoped for Perfect Gardener – Mr Shaver. His son was with him out of work such a particularly refined man & an authority on birds. He said that my tits are Chickadees.

WEDNESDAY 5 APRIL We went to bed together after reading my chapter from 10 to midnight. Thank the Lord she liked it save for little things & save that she is terribly doubtful about the whole business of Dr Brush & Hell's Museum & Vivisection. She advises me to let the vivisection be entirely in the Mind of Magnus. But O I do so want to give it a deadly blow. And if it is all in the mind of someone will that do? She thinks it will do it better than to risk mistakes of fact & maybe she is right.

MONDAY 10 APRIL A Perfect Day. Warm & Sunny The First Real & True Spring Day. Bad news of the Philmont Bank. They now have had some rebuff from the authorities in Washington & no one knows when they will open. It is a blow.

WEDNESDAY 12 APRIL Snow again Snow Again Snow again The T.T. did not come till 2 a.m. once more! I tried to be as stern as I could when she did come – but what is the good of that? [...] I manage very badly. I ought to treat her like a child in this. But in critical penetration her brain is superior to mine & more original. How then can I treat her so? [...] I am the worst person in the world to exercise authority over other souls! 'Tis terribly difficult to my whole nature – even the Black I can only command now & then in an awe-inspiring voice. I did awe the T.T. with such a tone last night but she, like a child, will forget. Well! after all I have her – a child – as my 'oaristes' 'οαριστης' 'to dally with' – the little Elemental! [...] I have had to write half a dozen letters today. How brief are therefore the precious hours that I get for my book & yet our future finances which are in rather a shaky state depend on my finishing this Weymouth Book by the Summer.

SUNDAY 23 APRIL After tea I did Re-write a 3 page letter of great Care to Mr Fadiman. She thought I ought to explain to him fully how different this Book is turning out from *Wolf* & from *Glastonbury* – an airy gay light whimsical water-colour book humorous & transparent & rounded with a luminous mystery, not ponderous – no thundering Purpose – no unified Philosophy! – the characters natural & easy. [...] As I listened to the T.T.'s words about my Weymouth book I was a little bit touchy! How funny that I should be so. For she really likes this book – in which she has the wise little Elemental taken really such a very large part. It is due to her that I changed it. For I began it in the back-wash of *Glastonbury* & with that foolish Conceit (boasted aloud) that I always thought more of the houses and the names of streets & the names of characters than of the plot. I had to learn by experience that this is not the way to write a book [...].

WEDNESDAY 26 APRIL Woke at 6 but hearing it rain I just held the T.T. with joy & pleasure & went through all my Beads & Paternosters for Two Hours, finishing 'em up completely! [...] Took Black via Mail to Prometheus. Saw Snow on the High Ridges. On my return I called the T.T. & then went to Bathroom & got thro' all my laborious Ablutions. Returning to the Parlour I met the T.T. just come down. She was in good spirit, smiling and playing with the Black but my one thought was to sink down on my couch. Then my Tyrant Soul said to my body tugging at its Leash – You think 'tis the moment for the couch – Not at all! 'Tis the moment for Laying the Table. So I went & got the cloth & pulled out the table & just at that second the little T.T. in high spirits said something to me & was met by a cold non-human or [a line here with ink-blots interspersed with the word 'Tears!' four times] rather animal look or vegetable look as when Lulu says I want Coffee (more Coffee). She said you look PERFUNCTORY & this broke me quite. I lost all scrap of Self Control & Howling on my knees did cry Give me a Thwack! Give me a Thwack! What a disgraceful scene for the God of Phudd & the Souls of the dead Indians to behold! O I was so ashamed of myself & when I did read of Circe the only word I could see was the word that means 'evil-minded' applied to her brother Æetes which I applied to me wone self! O Ailinon! O Ailinon! What a disgrace I be! The T.T. was so sweet & forgiving & took all the blame! But when I think – O the Bugger! The Bugger that I be!

SUNDAY 30 APRIL Yesterday I revised the part about Sylvanus & have daringly & boldly – to satisfy the T.T. – made him like myself with my trick of bowing to the elements etc., etc., etc. The T.T. is pleased. She thinks I have at last made him interesting! [...] Took Black to Tintern Abbey. Warm Wind. This Day is so like her own home & she is so happy that I actually heard her humming. No Hurting.

The effects of the Great Depression continue to be felt. Many visitors this summer: Masters; James Abell, a friend from New York days; the American writer Ruth Suckow – much admired by Phyllis; Mabel Pearson; Marian and Peter; Dreiser and many casual day visitors.

FRIDAY 5 MAY Mr Masters brings news from town that most Publishers are on the verge of Bankruptcy. [...] I talked to him happily about the authors till Supper. [...] Then we had a pleasant evening – he & I agreeing in our poor opinion of Robert Frost & how we liked Vachel Lindsay & of his tragic death of which he gave a most grim account. We then counted up the recent Suicides of well-known noble Poets.

SUNDAY 7 MAY There is grass everywhere now. Green grass on that mountain-like slope above the Black Dragon or Serpent Swamp. [...] All the little trees all the bushes are now in Green leaf. That Steitz Lane leading to the Gibbet Tree & the Skunk-Swamp is deep in rich emerald-green grass. And far off I can see fruit trees in blossom of a thicker whiteness than the airy-fairy Shadblow trees – whether they are cherries or wild plums I know not. The Apple trees are all covered with a misty-green & everywhere there is over all the spinneys and copses and bush-clumps a haze of green. This is my favourite season of the year – & I think the T.T.'s too. [...] But she did not like it when I sat in the door-yard, near her beautiful Rock Garden, with its tulips & a noble clump of Pansies (dark purple) & a lot of violets & Polyanthuses yellow as well as bronze-coloured – and the first forget-me-nots coming out too, no! she did not like it when I sat there in silence saying my prayers. 'You are not really a Hermit – why then ——?' Aye! I must be less of a Pharisee! They who make long prayers in Public! She spoke at breakfast of the deep irony of my books on 'Sensations & Solitude' when she on whom our harmony depends is so hit by Domestic things. The penalty. But she said I was not to blame. It was fate – it was the penalty & price of our harmonious life!

SATURDAY 13 MAY Yesterday I took Ruth Suckow & Mr Ferner Nuhn her young Mate to High Wood & the fallen Eagle Tree. [...] They both despise these clever ones who go to Paris. They are for America and for Iowa! She gave in the way she spoke & ate her meal & all, (said the subtle T.T.!) the exact impression of her Perfect Art to which all have to bow! Finished & complete is her art – inevitable – writes itself – she said how it wrote itself so natural while she was cooking for a house-full of Influenza patients. This was *Country People* a book I have never read. [...] Mr Ferner Nuhn is a regular Sainte Beuve of penetrating criticism. We liked him very much also for she was not at all like George Eliot with George Henry Lewes – not at all! She gave him free carte blanche to assert himself & he gave it to her also – a very harmonious pair of truly adjusted mates.

TUESDAY 16 MAY Last night Doctor Frink told us of the Suicide of our exquisite friend & delicatest of all Dentists at Great Barrington – Doctor Baldwin. He killed himself in his office with some kind of Knife. [...] I shall pour out a Libation of honey & wine & water & barley to the Powerless Heads of the Dead.

FRIDAY 19 MAY The T.T. stayed down till 4 o'clock reading the Novel [...] about 'Joe' & the old America. Deeply she meditated on the American Pathology. That terrific Driving Force for Unworthy Ends! She pondered on her own life – so this book read till Four of the Morn was not wasted! 'What is wrong with me?' she asked herself – 'And with all my Americans. A lack of philosophical enjoyment of the Routine of Normal Life or any life-routine in itself.' She needs an exceptional crisis to scheme & drive for – then a great wave of Cosmic power flows thro' her – which won't come for a Fixed Life which ever presents itself as Dull. But she said to herself 'I am only 38. I can change. And I will I will I will change! – change according to my own nature even if it can't enjoy like English, analyze like French, sob planetary sobs of the life-hysteria like Russians, feel philosophical Cosmic feelings like Germans! But change I will, even if I can't be like Marian, that mass of iron – that "Me in my Garden"!'

MONDAY 22 MAY James stayed late in bed today. [...] Found the T.T. Terribly Upset by the feeling of two Hulking Males – for she felt that I was hypnotised by Old James into becoming Male beyond my wont. The T.T. did feel as if her Petrushka was not any more her Inanimate Doll but Another Hulking Male. 'I hate Men, I hate Men, I hate men!' [...] It was unlucky that I went up last night after the visit of the Shaver family with the excuse of Exhaustion. [...] I had had – in our walk – no time to pray for Vivisected Dogs & 'All Prisoners & Captives' & Negroes in the hands of Southerners etc etc & Trapped animals etc etc etc & I saw no reason why the X-rays or cosmic rays of Taliessin-Merlin rays which I hurl out of my Tibetan Cave to the rescue of these Beings should be forgotten because of James being here.

SUNDAY 4 JUNE I saw the heads & shoulders & backs of the two White Horses. Sleeping standing. Above them was a sea-weed-green elm & above that a pure white cloud voyaging thro' blue ether. The shadow of the Blind Horse fell along the side of the Other Horse. Marbly white they were under that sea weed green tree & under that sailing white cloud & under the deep blue heaven! Mythological they were [...]. What a thing to have these Horses in our fields! I cried out 'Zanthus! Podargus!'

MONDAY 5 JUNE She had laid the table on the Porch. But the sun was too hot & too blazing there. This upset her & she could not help allowing words of extreme criticism of her Dolls House & even of Petrushka sitting there like Pangloss to pass the Barrier of her Teeth! In other words she fell to cursing the Construction of the Porch which is too small. She took her chair & fled. But presently lo! she returned sweet & repentant & not only so but having found a place! I took my *Iliad* & Lexicon & Translation & she did carry my wicker chair [...] to this new better cooler, more shadowy place. There I sat and read about Meleager & Halcyon-Marpessa of the lovely ankles [...]. And she dug kneeling on grass & made the earth look so beautifully deep Sienna brown & I looked at the Columbines (she says they are Mr Shaver's & that my constant reference to the wrong ones – is like when I said to Alyse – 'your next book will be a masterpiece!' How dunder-headed I am! Ailinon! Ailinon! Shall I never learn the secret of that gentle Courtesy & Tact so praised by Dante?) but she liked to work there while I read to her.

Schuster writes that they want to make Glastonbury *into a movie. Phyllis's mother, 'The Mistress', comes for a two-month stay.*

SATURDAY 17 JUNE [H]er feelings are all worked up in indignation at the idea of the Movies, these unspeakable Hollywood Vulgarians – lower than the lowest of the Mob – daring to touch *Glastonbury* or the Holy Grail. Other books of mine are on a different level – I think she is right. In the case of *Glastonbury* – such has been her eloquence at this juncture & the intensity of her feeling – I think I shall on Monday write to Schuster & REFUSE! [...] The T.T. is now actually making her mother's bed – and she says it seems as if the Dead were coming back – or some figure in a wild story faraway & remote like Mad Bet. She is very nervous, excited, bewildered, happy, yet over-wrought at her mother's coming. She is going to meet her at Chatham at Five o'clock.

MONDAY 19 JUNE Mailed my letter to Schuster refusing *Glastonbury* to the Muses. God! Think of writing Muses! I mean to the Movies but saying that I would let them have *Wolf* or *Weymouth* or any other book. Worked at Book about Weymouth. I am rather proud of my skill in gathering up the Various Puppets of this Planetary Book between Sea & Land – This book on the Beach.

TUESDAY 20 JUNE It is amazing how the Black has accepted The Mistress as the Missy's mother. [...] I don't know what it is! But it is a 'Complex Vision' of instinct & reason combined – in the old Black. [...] Am working on my chapter & also thinking about it which is very very unusual for me. I write extemporary as a rule but now I think about it in my walks & I would think still more if I were not compelled by my Conscience to pray so much! I am worse really than my poor Sylvanus!

TUESDAY 22 JUNE We sat together in our night-clothes her head on my shoulder – she was sad the T.T. – because she could not like my chapter XIII but had to criticize it very very severely. Too crowded, too rambling, too much repetition of old themes she considered. Too much havering. She wearied of Magnus & his sensations. [...] I did the things in a hurry very briefly. I took letters to the Mail. Then I took the Black & also my Pail & net – for (as in the case of my Mother) there is a tendency when you are tired to assume more burdens. It is a curious psychic tendency! You lack the strength to tell your Conscience to go to hell!

SATURDAY 1 JULY Stayed up till One writing my Last Chapter – while the Mistress and the T.T. went to bed. But the T.T. didn't go to sleep. From Twelve to One she lay awake reading [the] Diaries. Then she called me – Jack! Jack faint & wispy thro' the ceiling – Jack! just like that! I went up & she came out of room – her dear face her exquisite little face so perturbed so troubled – & it looked so delicious as I saw it.

THURSDAY 6 JULY Revisions are a struggle for a nature like mine, born to walk on & walk on & walk on & walk Past! [...] Worked very hard at my revising of the 'Brush Home' part & the Sylvanus part of my Last Chapter. I have cut out the actual destruction of the Vivisection Laboratory but introduced my Propaganda indirectly in Talk. I have made Benny's appearance a bit more probable! The T.T. is such a Critic for things being convincing. She does not like – nay! she won't abide – just childish fairy-tale writing & she is now working herself at this book revising the typed script very carefully.

The English edition of A Glastonbury Romance *comes out on 30 June.* A Philosophy of Solitude *is published by Jonathan Cape in England on 9 October. The 26 July entry is the first mention in the diary of his* Autobiography. *Albert marries Dora and they live with the Kricks. Dr Frink, worried about Phyllis's health, persuades her to go to a specialist.*

SATURDAY 8 JULY I have knelt & prayed in deep thankfulness to the great goddess Cybele to whose care I confined my Glastonbury Book – & in good hour I did! Aye! The Great-Earth-Grand-Mother sitting beyond Foulden Bridge with the

Towers on her Head. I prayed & prayed to her to let the Glastonbury Book come out! I began to fear it never would come out. I do so want it to be read in Glastonbury and to be sold in the Ruins to Visitors & Pilgrims there! What an incredible Honour & Grace of Heaven to have your Book actually drawn up into this Fragment of the Absolute. It is like I had written an actual Litany that ever & ever would be part of the Litany of Christendom. [...] I like the idea of Lane bringing out my book – the publishers of the Yellow Book & Beardsley. But what pleases me most is that it should be sold & bought in Glastonbury its wone self.

MONDAY 17 JULY When shall I have a dog who is a companion in my walks? Never! I fear. [...] Took the Black nearly to Merlin's grave. But the second leash was off he bolted away. He vanished into air like Mephistopheles! This desertion seriously upset me. I could not fix my mind on my prayers or on my invocations to Merlin.

WEDNESDAY 26 JULY Albert's Wedding. [...] I wrote letters & began my Preface for Cape's English *Solitude*. At Four I took Black for a short walk to Prometheus. Here I saw the two wives of the old Frog; I asked them about our new idea supported by the Mistress of Wintering in Hudson so as to save the T.T. from House work & also to save money. For we received from Mr Shimkin the Statement of what is coming to us from *Solitude* in Nov. And it is only $1300. And on this we have to live. I felt nervous – & thought of having to write Articles & even spoke foolishly of being driven to lecture again, yes I spoke querulously & petulantly thus! But the T.T. wisely bade me hold my peace! All this I revealed to the wives of the old Frog at the Stone. They replied not a word. But the old Frog from under the stone advised me to go to Hudson. But I suspect he wanted to get rid of my daily visits & converse with his Hareem. Then we all went at Six o'clock to Dinner at Arthur's. [...] I told him of my scheme for an Autobiography without a single woman in it [...].

FRIDAY 28 JULY After breakfast the T.T. in her new & now perfectly clean white dress – the one she upset the ink over – cleaned with milk – and the Mistress in a pink dress, were called for by the good, kind Dr Frink – who appears in my book as a Conchologist under the name of the old Welsh God Mabon –

1933 Dr Mabon. [...] And by Dr Frink are now being taken to Pittsfield to have a formal visit to the admirable Dr Paddock. O what will Dr Paddock say about the health of the T.T. [...] I shall now soon I imagine go to Gladys Studio to go on sitting for my Portrait in Arthur's German Student's cloak! [...] Doctor Paddock says she is all right except weighs only 90 lbs and ought to take more Food.

SATURDAY 29 JULY A hot Day. A very Hot Day. Up at 7.30 The T.T. wide-awake & full of tired detestation, quiet & tired disapproval of everything in her life. I stayed and argued with her, explained at length how it was possible to look forward to a cup of coffee & a piece of bread. Then hurriedly I did all the things omitting a few elaborations of a Sylvanus-like character. [...] Gladys took me off after we had listened – the Mistress & me – to an eloquent analysis of old Arthur's nature & writings from the T.T. So penetrating was it that I made up my mind to appropriate her wisdom & assimilate it & then when it is my own hurl it at Arthur's poor head. This I did half an hour after having heard it! And to good effect for once started by the T.T. I tend to become very eloquent on my own account & to think of many original psychic discoveries.

FRIDAY 4 AUGUST After breakfast the T.T. talked with extraordinary Eloquence about that experience of life – that thick, rich feeling of life made of up of a vast number of tragic experiences or of experiences observed in others or just intuitively grasped even if you live in one place all your days. This deep life-feeling she says is the chief thing! Shakespeare & Dostoievsky have it & Dickens a little too but not Balzac. Tolstoy has it a little. She says I spoil it in my books by Propaganda.

SATURDAY 5 AUGUST Both Albert & Dora came with the great Extra Saturday lot of Milk. I said to Dora – 'Are you still Happy?' She said 'Of course, sir! Have I not decided to be Happy?' I bowed before this Kindred Spirit! [...] The T.T. is looking thro' the envelope of a letter of Mr Schuster full of excitement, reading the word 'Raging' thro' the envelope. Is it about *Weymouth*? I insist on its being kept un-opened until tonight! Thus I understand children!

MONDAY 7 AUGUST I read all the *Theogony* & all the Hesiodic

Fragments & am now far in the *Demeter* which is some of the loveliest poetry I have ever read. I have never before even opened a page of the *Homeric Hymns* either in a translation or in the original. This *Demeter* is incredibly beautiful. But my Loeb translation does not please me. I don't like his ways. I don't like his bringing the word 'Sacrament' into the scene when she asks for meal & water & mint or 'penny-royal.' When Jesus said 'Take & eat.' 'This is my Body.' – no bloody clever Evangelist took on himself to inform us it was a Sacrament. [...] Then the T.T. came and stayed a while with me in the garden enjoying the warm-cool strong East Wind. I watched her mobile face like an Aspen Leaf.

TUESDAY 8 AUGUST After supper we commented on a letter from Mr Schuster which did not contain any clear hope of the Publishing of *Weymouth Sands* in the Autumn. The T.T. spoke very seriously of our financial fate.

What money they have is in the Philmont bank, now closed. Phyllis and her mother go to New York on 9 August for three days. A telegram from Alyse on 12 August informs them that Llewelyn is very ill with a tubercular haemorrhage.

SUNDAY 13 AUGUST The T.T. is perceptibly Better in Health & very much happier & more blooming after her holiday. That is what she wants, the change & excitement of a holiday without work. O deary I! Would it could have been longer. 'Too expensive' she says. Fuck! Damn! What a bread-winner I am, that can't give my girl proper holidays! [...] Took Black to Eagle Stump & Tintern Abbey & Merlin's Grave. I invoked Merlin on Lulu's behalf also Ceridwen the Earth Goddess of the Welsh.

TUESDAY 15 AUGUST I have decided to begin on this lovely day – the Day of the Assumption – my *Autobiography*. In that Assumption of the Mother of God – all Women, 'who lead us Upward & On' as it says at the end of Faust, call to us from some Heavenly Dimension & thus it will not be necessary for me to mention one single one of them in my *Autobiography*. My mother would not like to be mentioned. Such is her nature. And why mention any other? For the T.T. also shrinks in the same way from mention in this matter! I shall also go on with my work against Vivisection making it an attack on all the ways & hasty dogmas of Modern Science. I shall begin my *Autobiography* out of whatever is most adamantine & iron-like & slate-like in my Nature.

SATURDAY 19 AUGUST   I had to use all my philosophy to bear up against this blow about *Weymouth Sands*; Fadiman not liking it, and wanting to send it to England first. [...] The T.T. thinks that I had better go to New York when Marian returns & deal with them face to face. And I think this is exactly what I shall do. And before going I will get the T.T. to prime me in all I need as artillery for this Interview. It is very dark. Both this actual Day & also, also my decision and its issue!

MONDAY 21 AUGUST   I worked at my *Autobiography* [...]. The first chapter will include all my first seven years of mortal life. I have begun to talk of my Sadism – I hope restrainedly and without exaggeration! I must give a true idea of my Father & of how old Littleton & I were linked from the start.

They discuss possible places in America and England to which they might move. 'The Mistress' leaves on 26 August. Phyllis begins to go to Hattie Steitz for her mid-day meal. Obviously John has in mind at this early date 'my Romance about Merlin' – the novel that in 1951 is published as Porius.

FRIDAY 25 AUGUST   I thought a lot about this Weymouth idea – and asked the Mistress to [...] go with us – then the talk turned on the T.T.'s health – & this was too much for her – the little T.T. became upset & rushed out of the house. [...] The agitation, the agitation was soon over & we sat quiet after breakfast & spoke of the Mistress' passionate love of her home. [...] She spoke of our living out there with her but that if we did we would have to sleep separately – could I stand for that? The Lord knows! We can stand a good deal if Fate makes it imperative! [...] But the general drift of all these talks has made one thing quite clear to me. We must leave Phudd Bottom for this winter! But whether it will be to Chatham or Weymouth remains a great Doubt! It is Economy we have to think of and also the T.T. being only 90 pounds in weight.

SUNDAY 27 AUGUST   She is starting a new régime of having her dinner in the middle of the day. We talked of going to Wales

& I was 'elated' as Dr Frink would say. O deary I! How it all came over me that old longing to go to Wales and write something with all those Welsh gods & traditions & magic behind me! That longing which I can recall feeling on Brighton Beach & such a longing it was too and I read then everything I could get hold of Welsh Grammars, Dictionary, Poetry, History, but then came Burpham & the Birth of my son & I had to take up a different rôle from that of being an Avatar of Taliessin! But now the T.T. wants it more than all! So we want the Same Thing; & no one has ever wanted the same thing as I before! Well she had dinner at Two Thirty. But I found her wandering about the garden thinking of her mother. She said she felt Lonely. And when she asked me how I felt about leaving here & all I said was that the cows looked nice under the apple trees she said she felt still more lonely because I seemed so like an Inanimate & showed no Wishes clearly marked that she could match & weigh & balance against her own.

MONDAY 28 AUGUST Tried to explain my feelings about Wales & so on to the T.T. because I do not want to leave her lonely in her thoughts. Then Mr Johnson brought the Mail. A letter from Alyse saying that Lulu is really better.

TUESDAY 29 AUGUST I wrote such a long letter to Lulu & Alyse, together, all about our idea of leaving America forever & going to settle in Wales and for me to lay my bones in Wales! But ere that – I have an idea that with that background I shall write the greatest Romance of Modern Times, with the Welsh Legends & Myths to back me up. But the T.T. has many reactions now – O so many! in favour of this House – in favour of the ease, the comfort, the calm, the convenience, the familiarity of our life here. 'Here I have got in my own land such a perfect house and I have got such nice neighbours & a gas-burner & I must needs go & "stir matters up"!' Thus did the T.T. speak. But I answer to it all – 'I must and will write that masterpiece about Wales in Wales.'

THURSDAY 31 AUGUST When I came home we read a very important letter namely Schuster's own private Notes on Weymouth Sands. He does not like Sylvanus Cobbold. He wants to cut out all the scene where Gipsy May cuts off his mustache! And he does not like Mr Gaul or Rodney Loder. But he likes

Perdita and the Jobber. On the whole he likes it. He likes Gipsy May. But he also talks of publishing it in England first which is teasing. I do so wish, so wish that he had just accepted it & published it this Fall. But there it is!

TUESDAY 5 SEPTEMBER [T]he T.T. & I talked about Wales and how hard it would be to tear ourselves away from Phudd which the T.T. now says has at last in our 4th year become dear & home-like to her. 'The man' however is resolute for some move. The T.T. doesn't like the idea of my having to tell Marian & Oxford [wife and son] & face all my family & deal with Lulu & find a home in Wales all for her alone but I tell her that I have long long long thought of going to Wales. This is a Recurrence of an ancient strain of music, a sort of far off Pilgrims' chorus in my long life; so I only use – I explain to her – her longing for a change as my urge to make an effort I feel I am deeply destined to make!

SUNDAY 10 SEPTEMBER The only wild flowers now are Golden Rod. That little kind rather short that comes out last along with Silver Rod all over the fields – and Toad Flax – & the small faint-violet-coloured & white little Aster – with tiny daisy flowers & a lot of very filmy tenuous & thin-stalked foliage near the ground. In the garden Roses out again everywhere and Dahlias, pink, & amber ones too and best of all the pinkish raspberry-tinted Japanese Anemones – twelve blooms out now – beautiful against the brown earth. The Phloxes are faded & dead – the Hollyhocks gone. And those great beds of Spearmint in the field have lost all their blossoms and are faded tho' I still smell their faded leaves & the garden Sedum loved by Peacock butterflies are out as are also the wild ones in the field – one or two – I have never seen these out before. And there is one Periwinkle out.

John goes to New York 12-16 September to see Simon & Schuster. His request for better terms and an advance on his royalties is accepted. In return he agrees to revising Weymouth Sands *and to writing another 'philosophical brochure'* – The Art of Happiness.

FRIDAY 15 SEPTEMBER Poor Mr Shimkin was in rather an embarrassing position because my plain grave talk brought many moments of diplomatic concessions which he did not know were serious or not. But I felt friendly to both Simon & Schuster. […] I wore Marian's skirt under my overcoat like a Scotch Kilt.

MONDAY 18 SEPTEMBER I opened my Weymouth Book to make some cuts according to Schuster's recommendations! I must cut out little bits all the way along. […] I shall get on I think by cutting many paragraphs and certain pages too – such as I have never cared for myself! Have made one cut about the Jobber's mirror which has to be put back again, the T.T. insists!

TUESDAY 19 SEPTEMBER Up at 7.50. Did the Things. Took Black to Prometheus Stone. Came back via the Chicken Field because our Bridge is still down. And there was the T.T. coming to meet me across our orchard – with an open book – *Axel's Castle* – about Villiers de l'Isle-Adam in her hand. She spoke of the fatal effect of these French Books (Huysman etc. etc.) when she was young in bringing on her 'Unhappiness' – in fact a mental state that was really Deranged […].

SATURDAY 23 SEPTEMBER Had a happy breakfast and the T.T. said that she was wholly converted to Roosevelt because he was going to buy all the farm surplus & give it to the Unemployed – cotton, wheat, corn, all! What a wonderful thing. […] No Government has ever given the surplus of production to those who need it most. This shows the good of a Dictator – like Goering of Prussia suppressing Vivisection in Germany! No one speaks of this owing to the conspiracy of the bloody Scientists to hush up their doings!

SUNDAY 1 OCTOBER I fear it will be too cold in the bad weather for the T.T. to walk to the Steitz. And these Steitz meals are doing her so much good. She is really happier now than she has ever been since we came here. It is such a comfort to her not to have to get so much food into the house and not to have to cook! It simply makes all the difference to her.

MONDAY 2 OCTOBER Held the T.T. when I first woke up for I felt exhausted in mind & body but holding her made me feel a great deal better – in fact quite Strong. I hold her & hold the earth too when I walk even as Antaeus renewed his Strength! Death alone will be the Hercules who will hold me at last from off the earth in his arms & in that way strangle me.

SUNDAY 8 OCTOBER The Man's Birthday. Down at 6.50. Went to the Barn & lo! & behold! It was all Transformed. Instead of the mouldy Hay which I had been somewhat inaccurately saluting as 'Damp Straw' there was a floor of Wheat Straw and everything was fresh & clean in my Oratory. The Manger looked so nice with the old hay in it & the Picture that noble Oil Painting by a Great Artist had been washed clean & looked as good as new. And there was a rope hanging down & there were my broken pitchers as before. You can believe how I fell on knees & tapped forehead on straw & uttered a prayer for the T.T. – Her Mother, Llewelyn, Alyse, & G. & Mr B. – 'as long as'! And then went Oon & fairly 'off' & prayed for every fucking member of my family including my Son & his Mother! Albert had burnt the Paper so it was unbelievably neat & tidy. Take it all in all I cannot remember when I had such a nice birthday as this is! [...] There is a frog in the Fount – & the Cypress still stands. I said '*Numen in est*'! as Walter Pater puts it. Went on over Stein or Carl fence right down over the field between the stones I call the Skaian Gates to the hedge from which I saw & made my bow to the Dead Tree. I have never been so far as this before breakfast! O how lovely the rose tinctured leafy branches are of our Maple a delicate colour! I can see a glimpse of one branch out of my parlour window as I lie on couch – golden – a real Golden Bough against the blue sky! But from the sloping field it looked especially lovely. Had a heavenly breakfast. It was just ready when I came. There by my side the T.T. had piled up my presents. She read Floyd Dell's life of himself & we are both enchanted with this excellent Book – one of the best autobiographies we have in our tongue! But I must, must, must beat it and make mine better! The T.T. says she does not want me to bring in any moralizing into my book, but to keep it a story a story a story & let readers do their own bloody interpretations of it. Then we opened my presents. A Guide of North Wales and a lovely Itinerary thro' South Wales by that excellent Ernest Rhys. Also *Don Quixote* from Mr Schuster in the Modern Library. Then I opened the Sears Roebuck presents. A seafaring tarpaulin whole suit and a heavenly warm jersey of thick wool – very expensive! [...] Dr Mabel tells us of an available House in Cannes! We think of Aberystwyth.

THURSDAY 10 OCTOBER We have thought more of Aberystwyth and of that National Library of old Welsh books and of the Scholars there from whom I could get help for my Romance about Merlin & Taliessin than we have thought about that available House with a French Servant at Cannes! [...] Here we are confronted by living beyond our income and by a Winter that is too severe for the T.T. But she feels that we might be challenging Fate too far if we left this place of Refuge. She sat out on the porch yesterday & had a reaction against going away. [...] I feel my old trouble. At breakfast the T.T. said Cannes would be ridiculous for Petrushka – & I indeed agreed! but I feel a sort of shame not to carry her to some warm place.

WEDNESDAY 11 OCTOBER I took the Black nearly to Lesbian Wood & returned under the stars thinking all the while as I looked at the Milky Way & Vega in Lyra & Cassiopeia of that brute Deacon at Wildman's house [Sherborne] & how he used to ill-use that poor stammering little Puckle who later died. They ought never to have sent him to school! Such were my thoughts and I trembled with impotent anger as I thought of it all. But calm & deep & dark was the earth & the great Black dome of Phudd & the dark sweep of the hill over the crest of which I walked in pitch blackness save for the faint light of those stars.

THURSDAY 26 OCTOBER Albert has had a fight with the Bull at Radowitz Barn to whom he took 'Blackie' or Rose Marie. I hope the Bull in his dalliance & sweet usage (as Lulu would say) won't kill Blackie. But Albert in a most blood-thirsty way described his battle with the Bull & how he hit it savagely with a club but how it came on & how it is 'hung up' now by the Horns. Personally I am just a little – such is my feeble heart – a little concerned about this hanging up by the Horns – but I expect Mrs Radowitz will untie it presently when this young Toreador is out of sight. At least I hope so. But it clearly cannot mount 'Blackie' with its horns tied to a beam. So I think it will be let loose but I hope it is not suffering at this moment with its neck distorted – what events what events do go on in this country!

SATURDAY 28 OCTOBER O how this cold North wind did thrill me how it did make me so intensely happy & exultant. But for all that the T.T. looked so haggard & woe begone at breakfast – & I murmured in my weak fond foolishness about after all not staying here but she would not hear of such silly talk but she said that this place made everyone look like withered flowers – not rugged & gnarled but ivory-white, & pinched & parched & wilted & ugly to behold! She said Dora alone, save the Old Man of Phudd, looked really fit!

SUNDAY 29 OCTOBER The T.T. thinks and indeed I think myself that the time has come to curtail these rigmarole Invocations of mine which have grown to be a burden far too heavy and allowing me not a moment's chance to contemplate [...]. I am ceasing to be a disciple of Wordsworth and becoming a Monk of the Thebaid! This must stop; for I am making my head tick like an over-taxed clock!

TUESDAY 14 NOVEMBER She was reading the letters of D.H. Lawrence. This is what I longed for her to do for I had been so impressed & so was she. [...] She said he was positive, a new culture, not like Russell an old disillusioned Stoic supporting himself on the sad old battered wisdom of the world – but something fresh and startling and healing. [...] That miraculous 'Xmas Rose' or better call it Hellebore has come fully out again. She has put it on the old little Sideboard in the Study. There it holds itself Erect – as she says – like an Absolute. Beyond the Chaos of our life.

THURSDAY 16 NOVEMBER [S]he spoke of her passionate desire to have been a Dancer. [...] Deep in her heart is the desire to be not a Superior Person but a real trained Virtuoso in Dancing. [...] We were so thrilled by news from England about *Weymouth Sands* tho' I have to revise & expurgate that mad wicked talk of the old Captain Poxwell. Ronald Boswell is Lane's Reader & he says that in some ways *Weymouth Sands* is even superior to *Glastonbury* though not quite so exciting. [...] Now arrives this set of end-papers of [*The Meaning of*] *Culture* for me to autograph! Three or four hours work but our living depends on it to a serious extent so it must be done.

Despite the shortage of money and uncertainty about their future, in October Phyllis redecorates the parlour with a new carpet, paper and paint.

SATURDAY 18 NOVEMBER The chickadees were asking – calling, begging, scolding – for this Snow deprives them of any food. But no sooner had I taken up the bread & toast for them – than there was Sintram hunting them – so in the slipperiness I had to catch Sintram such a hunt. He ran up hill into bushes, up trees & twice escaped from my hands and once after I carried him to the foot of the hill he escaped & up the hill sliding slipping balancing holding on by branches I had to pursue him. Finally with garbage tin and stick in one hand & Sintram in another I staggered down. [...] Then I had an imperative Command from the god of Phudd to christen anew that white Stone of his that I jestingly used to call the Rosetta Stone – so I went to it through the still hushed silent snow – not a breath stirring. And I kissed that beautiful white stone & I did name it forever by the name of the MARBLE Stone. [...] I reached home after kissing the branch of the Saviour-Tree the Grandmother of the Gods I have named that old noble Willow – Rhea, the daughter of Gaia & Ouranos & saluting that mossy stone I call the Threshold Stone this side of our little bridge – I hurried home – & lo! & behold! There was Mr Shaver's car. He brought wire to protect the Hawthorn Hedge from Rabbits. Then there appeared none other than Daddy Scutt to measure for our new wallpaper. They stayed till nearly 11.30 so that the poor little T.T. had only a second to get my breakfast & the Black's which she did with incredible speed and without a taste or a sip of coffee or tea to rush off to go to the Steitz for her lunch!

SUNDAY 19 NOVEMBER I talked to the spirit of the Swamp as I always do about my Book on Merlin & Taliessin. Would I ever ever write it? All dead silence! Does silence 'give Consent'? I saluted the Lesbians & Laodamia & Protesilaus Trees. The Lesbians are Limes, the others Oaks. On the way down the side of the steep grassy hill I put my left foot deep in a Woodchuck hole & fell such a cropper. But so far – I touch wood – I am an extraordinary good Tumbler & Faller!

TUESDAY 21 NOVEMBER Did all very slowly & with every possible Rigmarole! Old Krick came by when my head was in water & I saw him put the Old Carpet of Parlour into back of his Truck. Then as he went off he blew his horn. This sound had a great effect on the little T.T. May such a horn blow often! for though she Scolded right fierce the man with dripping head, he had a heavenly sight of this exquisite little figure with bare feet & in nothing but white night-shirt & with little-girl braided hair going up stairs after Scolding was done! May I often be so scolded [...]. But behold now she do coom down all lovely & penitent! Thus did the Old Man of Phudd have it Both Ways.

SATURDAY 25 NOVEMBER [S]he told me how important she felt wallpapers could be & I – the fool! – mumbled only about liking old dark oak-panels, & she said this was Malice in me. No – it is only stupidity & clumsiness! She looks very very white & tired. Last night she suddenly had a reaction against all these changes she is devising – paper, paint, carpet, all! Her moods flicker like the moon on a running river!

FRIDAY 1 DECEMBER I could not help the image of those Skeleton Horses of Harvey's rising before me. When I came back last night the bitter terms of all mortal life was one pitch-fork threatening. [...] They were hauling wood. I touched their skeleton ribs & did not hesitate to speak of it to Harvey & he muttered about their having some complaint & not understanding it & giving 'em oil with their grain – God! I understand it too well – Damned little grain – Nothing but Damp Hay & little of that have those wretched animals had. But Harvey himself looks withered & gaunt & said he & John had applied for work under the N.R.A. & that Ray Becker had gone off with his horse from Stein's field – weary after half an hour of ploughing – & he had taken Mr Becker's place then. With one of these Skeletons like a Horse Death might ride on? No wonder the field is still unfinished!

MONDAY 11 DECEMBER As I cleared the Ashes out of Parlour Stove I dropped a hot coal – 'a live coal from off the altar' – on to our new carpet! I timed telling her of this till she was smoking her first cigarette after breakfast. But I never saw a terrible & loathsome mess from the cats' stomachs on the dining room carpet near Oleander. [...] I must stop this hurting somehow – or it will eat through & give me Peritonitis [...].

TUESDAY 12 DECEMBER Worked in Attic at chapter VI & VII of *Autobiography*. [...] Here I stayed till 3.45 & at four I set out. [...] When I got home I was seized with a Devilish Spasm of my hurting in duodenum. It made me feverish-sick & I writhed & twisted & actually on the couch kicked down the picture of Lord Nelson from the wall over my head!

On 15 December he goes to bed for a week to try to relieve the ulcer pain. Phyllis tries to contend with winter chores as well as Christmas presents. John distinguishes between 'my way' or 'in my own Tibetan manner' of making love and 'Lulu's way' or 'à la Lulu'. The latter means 'normal' sexual intercourse; the former sometimes masturbation and sometimes coitus reservatus.

MONDAY 18 DECEMBER The T.T. didn't come till nearly Three o'clock. […] The Stove in the Parlour went out on her & about one she had to go to the Barn for wood & weeping & praying & kneeling & collapsing the evening the night the early hours of morn passed over her poor little head. Why will she do such mad things? Xmas! Xmas! Damn! This morn she went with Black the Round & met My Lord the North Wind – Boreas! And this blustering Amorist did make rough love to she all the way; all the way long of Willow Path – so that she sank down Hysterical, as so often before! This is the familiar issue of the man's cure in bed! I know it, ah! too well I do. […] I fear me tonight it will be the same – & this is the Xmas we were going to give no presents! Instead of presents we seem to be giving the good calm of the T.T. – done up in neat little parcels & tied up with nerve-ends at two in the morning!

WEDNESDAY 20 DECEMBER The T.T. came at 3.30 Aye! but I was reckless! I was so thrilled to see her that my pleasure passed the limit practised by the Late Dalai Lama, whose death we read, & attained the level always spoken of by Lulu – when he writes 'I was Happy'. Oh, how tired the T.T. was in the morning. It did so deeply touch my heart. I shall never forget it. She kept speaking – & then her dear little head would sink and she would be fast asleep. I felt indeed that I had a child in bed with me […].

THURSDAY 21 DECEMBER It isn't that I hate the snow for I have at last acquired a sort of half-taste for it, though it is not quite natural to me – to me to like snow. […] No! – what I miss is the brown dead trees & dead grass and dead earth. I am a Necrophiliast! & I am enamoured of my great planetary dead Mother – poor Demeter by the Wayside sorrowing for Proserpina! I get a greater thrill from the dead Winter earth without snow, than from anything in Nature save the coming back of Proserpine.

FRIDAY 29 DECEMBER The Coldest Night ever known round here. Mr Czzirr had to come to unfreeze our Pump & he said he had never known such weather in 8 eight years. Mr Krick looked very grave when I saw him & said that this would mean Death to Many.

1933 SUNDAY 31 DECEMBER Catastrophe! Catastrophe! Catastrophe! What a morning for the last day of this year! What Agitating Occurrences! I went up at 11.30 […]. The T.T. went on quietly sewing I think till One! Then she went to kitchen to wash up and there found that the Gas Oven had been burning for Seven hours. Then suddenly the Pump stopped and she had had the electric Heater down there. […] No water – and the Boiler without its flow of water began to make menacing sounds. Would it Burst? I woke up with un-ease & because the room was so terribly hot, as I did not want to open window ere the T.T. came, I came down & there she was very very agitated – trying to bring down the kitchen-stove which in this South Wind was burning like Hell. She said she could not leave it. She took off her dress & shoes & settled herself on the Horse-hair sofa to sleep there, so as to be on guard. I went up but came down to ask whether I might open window or door into Anti-Attic. 'What? can you not watch with me One Hour?' I opened the door to Anti-Attic – but the T.T. fearful lest that would be worse for plants than the usual window came up and closed it. I slept then and she slept then. I was awaked about 4.30 or 4.45 by a frightening smell of burning – like as if the whole House were on fire. I came down. She was very agitated but yet brave calm collected competent like a Captain of a ship in a Storm. She had been woked up by strange noises in cellar & this burning smell in cellar. She went down. The Pump had started without water. It must have burnt out the Motor Engine. She turned off the Company's Main Switch! How did she know how to do such a thing. What spirit, What competence these brave American girls have at a pinch! I put on my clothes. She put on her dress. We looked at each other. The cats went on the Rampage. The Old Black came out. It was a crisis in the life of the Terminals! She discoursed on our being both of us so unsuited to live in the depth of the country. I agreed. I lay on the couch […]. She sat on the [words obliterated by spilt ink]. I said 'Do have a Rug.' She said 'Don't Fuss' [words obliterated]. I was worried for fear that necessity for my enema should suddenly seize me. […] How slow the dawn came. We had candles! First she had only the Searchlight. Then she got Breakfast. Coffee & Tea cheered us […]. She went to the Kricks. Albert came. A Miracle. He started the Pump. ENEMA Had to have two enemas.

1934

This is one of the busiest and possibly one of the unhappiest years of their life together. Despite the long discussions of the previous year, both Phyllis and John, for different reasons, are ambivalent about leaving Phudd Bottom. John has always loved Columbia County and Phyllis now feels 'at home' there. Their poor financial circumstances play a large role in the decision, but of much greater significance is John's determination to write his 'Great Welsh Novel' in Wales.

Although he has lived with Phyllis since 1923, his wife and son and some of his relatives still do not know of this liaison. When the decision is made to leave America, he 'confesses' to his son and makes a new will in the son's favour.

They sail to England from New York on 1 June, taking with them the Black, the doll Olwen and the Autobiography manuscript. On arrival the dog goes into quarantine, their belongings into storage and they go to Dorset to be near Llewelyn who is at Chydyok, still very ill. They move into Rat's Barn – a totally isolated cottage without any conveniences – one mile equidistant from Chydyok and Chaldon. From here John goes every day, either by the cliff path or dead horse valley, to read to Lulu.

They travel to London to see the solicitors about John's Glastonbury libel suit, brought against him by the owner of Wookey Hole. The settlement eventually costs them Phyllis's savings and most of the legacy from his Aunt Etta.

On John's sixty-second birthday (Phyllis is now thirty-nine) they move to a small flat in 38 High East Street, Dorchester. With their dog back, and their books and furniture around them, both begin to feel more comfortable. John begins to write The Art of Happiness – or, as he calls it, 'Be Happy, Damn You' – for Simon & Schuster, and, at the end of the year, makes a third start on his new novel, Maiden Castle.

1934

WEDNESDAY 3 JANUARY I saw an elm-tree stretching its seven branches out across the grey distance where the ridge rose. And this tree against the misty ridge gave me such an extraordinary feeling as if endless ancestors of mine had seen such a landscape in Shropshire – in Wales – maybe in Broceliande! I could hear a distant train, far off.

FRIDAY 5 JANUARY I fell down near the Ash-Heap and burnt my hand slightly in the hot ashes I was carrying. God! I have a way of falling down. I am always falling down! It is ridiculous.

SUNDAY 7 JANUARY Did All – in fact I did All too completely for when 'twas all done I felt rather exhausted. Took the Old up Stein Hill past Magic Fount to the High Fence – the Mountains hidden in rain. [...] We had a splendid Lesson. About Menelaus not to die but to go to the Elysian fields, 'where falls not any rain or any snow nor ever wind blows loudly' – and about that vulgar little bugger Zachaeus climbing up into the Tree & Jesus being so particularly lovely to him tho' he did only give half to the poor!

TUESDAY 16 JANUARY At the back of our house a Hundred Long Icicles hang as if on Dian's Temple & through the midst of them protrude so nobly & symbolically the Horns of the Three Cow-Skulls – those skulls that Mr Masters calls 'Bos-Crainium' That magic word I intone every morning! The T.T. had given me half a loaf for the birds. The Chickadees came & the red-headed Woodpecker. I did all. I said all my prayers touched every tree in our Hawthorn hedge & embraced the Hickory that I have named Berengaria! O I cannot tell you how azure blue the sky was above Phudd. Never have I seen such Blue in my life! [...] I must think of this eternal Blueness when I am fighting hard against the Devils! [...] As I stood down by Alders River beyond Spinney on which the Sun shone so strong as it rushed so black and glittery between its snow-banks there came over me another Inspiration or rather a powerful Impulse a Magnetic Imperative towards my Book about Merlin and Taliessin & Ceridwen & Welsh Mythology. Was it that Blue colour in the sky conveying to me the diffused essence of some Welsh Virgin Mother older older than the Mother of Jesus? I very foolishly allowed water from my leather boots to make a pool on my couch & with equal folly and laziness I sat down to breakfast in my green shirt one sleeve of which lacks a button & thro' which my vest did show. This lack of consideration did agitate the T.T. O I must try and be more careful about my clothes! She says I cannot – that I am a hopeless Inanimate but we will see!

WEDNESDAY 17 JANUARY The T.T. tells me about an automatic talk with her Father who told her she ought to write while Jack is still at her side to criticize. He said 'I will help you and give you Strength!' I feel very nervous about the little T.T. going to the Steitz in this icy weather – this is the sort of cold North wind that is the very worst thing for her. It makes her hysterical.

THURSDAY 18 JANUARY The T.T. at breakfast read to me the beginning of *Clayhanger.* She thinks Arnold Bennett is a really great Novelist – far above Galsworthy. She read about the little Darius being saved from the Workhouse by Mr Shushions. She cried & I cried. It was a triumph for 'A.B.'! [...] Miss Clough & Paul came. There is danger of the Mills actually closing for good.

SATURDAY 20 JANUARY I had a lovely awakening in the dead of the night – suddenly realizing the loveliness of my little slender bed-fellow & I did enjoy her in her sleep with such protracted & Saurian Lust like an Ichthyosaurus who had stolen a little girl. [...] After breakfast the T.T. spoke of Henry James more penetratingly more eloquently more passionately more humorously than I have ever heard him spoken of. I thought – what an intellect for subtle matters this girl has! No wonder she often feels Abused by having to look after a House! [...] The T.T. went to the Freehans as well as the Kricks. She tells me now about Mr Richardson's son she saw in that hardware shop whose father died of joy at shooting a deer. He is as frail as an elf – like Shelley – and has hair like the fluff of a milk-weed! [...] Old Krick – thik artist – was shocked at shooting a hurt horse in the street making blood for nervous ones – like Hattie – to see. But Mrs Krick spoke up & did say – a woman & no 'artist' – 'quite right to shoot at once & stop the poor beast's suffering – never mind where!'

The Philmont bank re-opens. Robinson Jeffers (1887-1962) was an American poet whose verse explored man's alienation from nature.

FRIDAY 26 JANUARY I ought to do something about what we

have got in the Bank! […] And the T.T. is very very very set on my going to the DENTIST in Philmont. These two things together the Bank & the Dentist do rather 'taunt' me poor mind. […] Talked to the old old Mr Tracey – 90 years old – the Cashier. […] Mr Tracey wanted to know whether we were going to go on using his bank. I said 'I do not know. She deals with these affairs!' Then later at the window talking with the ex-soldier, wounded, who is the amateur banker, the Missy began to say she would withdraw our money which was $200 – odd – over two hundred – but so agitated seemed the poor ex-soldier that in the middle of the transaction she changed her mind & got a cheque-book & said nothing – even forgot to take out a penny!

SATURDAY 27 JANUARY [S]he spoke of going to Hudson once every little while together on Saturdays. Well! We must try this. For she gets no comfort when I talk of drastic changes in our life. 'When you are hungry' she said 'you want to eat at once; not in the future!' So I must stop talking about the future: & really be alive-O for such little jaunts as she thus indicates. […] At breakfast we did – in spite of my vow not to talk of the future, discuss what it would be like at that University of Wales at Aberystwyth. […] Then we had a nice Lesson – Penelope's grief for her son's danger. How she lay down on the threshold. I note that even Homeric women lie down on the ground when they are unhappy […].

SUNDAY 28 JANUARY It is muddy & wet & thawing & I had those boots on I couldn't put off & on so I said to myself – this is unlucky. But I never remembered to get up the mud-marks from the dining room floor as is always my custom to do ere the T.T. appears. My head was very full of Blackie or Rose Marie & of the way we have to face life & death here in the country. […] Aye! – how silly of me to forget those marks on the carpet! I swore 'on my dying oath' it would not happen again nor shall it!

THURSDAY 1 FEBRUARY Our Mail was very agitating today – for there was a letter from Mr Shimkin – S. & S.'s Lawyer – to say about our Statement for what we shall receive in May, of Royalties – and he says only $600 which is much less than half what he told us in a letter, in the Fall, there would be and there was no word about *Glastonbury* at all! Not one penny from *Glastonbury* in England. […] What on earth are we to do?

SATURDAY 3 FEBRUARY The T.T. was upset and with reason too alas! when I confessed about scorching her best woollen gloves delving in the hot coals! Aye! I am a fool! [...] I have torn all my trowsers. The T.T. says that Petrushka, without meaning no harm, is terribly destructive of his clothes his boots his jerseys & of all forms of Matter that he approaches! No Man, the T.T. says, could be more difficult in this respect for the companion he has. Aye me! O deary I! But this morn & last night I did hold this tiny little Elemental with inextinguishable delight. I am not destructive to beautiful limbs when they are lying by my side! [...] Read Jeffers *Give Your Heart to the Hawks*. What a bloodthirsty bugger he is – a homicidal Maniac.

1934

MONDAY 5 FEBRUARY I was worried by the Black eating the little bit of fat I put out for the Birds – this brought me pelting down from caressing the old apple tree that I have named *Polutlas Arbor*! 'much-enduring tree' & before I had time to lay my Merlinish hand on the two Beech-trees up there & on the English Hawthorn Hedge or to pray for the soul of Canon Crow & his daughters by the dead stalks of the Phloxes. [...] Not having bread for the birds & not being able to stop the Old gobbling up their little bit of fat made me feel a helpless fool. [...] I like best to feel like my Father who 'would not be bullied!' or even like his father the learned & shrewd Rector of Stalbridge! But in my worries this morn I did feel like 'Johnny of Norfolk' who could only build a tall brick wall round his kitchen garden at Yaxham in Norfolk. I have not even built a brick wall round my garden here! I can only call upon different coloured angels to stop sadness in the world & the sort of cruelties that Jeffers loves so much to imagine!

TUESDAY 6 FEBRUARY She came at about 3 a.m. having finished the Waistcoat. I had prepared for this so I made love to her [...]. And I woke up too at dawn & made love to her. And she called out, 'Mother, Mother, come!' like a little girl on her bridal night! But she did not [know] why she called out 'Mother!' like that, though she remembered doing it. But Oh she is so sweet! Oh she is so sweet! She herself, as that bad mad seducer Afanasy in the *Idiot* said to Nastasya Filippovna, – you yourself are my excuse!

John's youngest brother, Will, whom he has not seen for many years, and his wife, Elizabeth, farm in Africa. They stay at Phudd 10-19 February. John's wife and son now live in Oxford.

WEDNESDAY 7 FEBRUARY Albert & Dora came just like children playing with a toy sledge. He put a coop on the sledge & perched her on the top with the milk can on her lap and then pulled & pulled laughing so proudly & so triumphantly! […] A telegram from Will to Marian says 'will dock at seven on Tuesday Night.' So they actually landed this very last night when it was so cold in this house! It was colder than I ever recall it to have been. Albert says it was Sixteen Below. But I had to put on a coat & wrap up in a rug and it was almost too cold for me to enjoy writing my chapter. I only longed to go up to the nice warm attic & go to Bed. […] The T.T. had begun her coffee when I returned & had to hurry off. I hope she will get an appetite somehow! There will be only half an hour between her breakfast and her lunch! She had time to read in paper of Terrific Riots in Paris.

THURSDAY 8 FEBRUARY Had a very agitating letter about changing my Will from Oxford. […] I am to change my will in favour of Littleton Alfred instead of his Mother. Wrote my chapter in bed as usual till 5.30 & then took the Old to Grotto. Aye! but it is Cold! It is colder than ever tonight. […] After tea I opened an 'ad' of a regular wicked Sadistic book. It would, I know, disgust me if I saw it & yet & yet. I was surprised & astonished how the description of it set my stomach shivering like an aspen-leaf & my pulses beating wildly! I was exactly like Mr Evans! It is wonderful the way I am able to talk to the T.T. about my Sadism and my shivering emotion over this Book. Went on reading *Dombey and Son* – got to Mrs Pipchin & Major Bagstock.

FRIDAY 9 FEBRUARY The T.T. came up at 2.15 a.m. & I held her tight trying as I held this little elemental to 'sublimate' that shivering that scoria shiver rising up from depths below depths of my inmost being caused by the 'ad' of that terrible book. Most of it would have been far too violent & bloody for my taste – for I am not a human panther – but little side-touches in it simply overpowered me swept me away like a Sirocco wind bringing back all those books – much more 'in my style' – Angels & Ministers of Grace, can't you understand? – than this bloody book thus sent in the form of an 'ad'. How can these things be –

The Powys Family, Montacute Vicarage, 1897
Back: Llewelyn, Marian, Albert Reginald, John Cowper, Littleton, Gertrude.
Middle: Philippa, The Reverend Charles Francis [Father], Mary Cowper Powys [Mother], Margaret [John Cowper's wife], Theodore.
Front: William, Nip the dog, Lucy.

John Cowper lived with his companion Phyllis Playter in Patchin Place, New York City, from 1923 to 1930. Here with his brother Albert [Bertie] and sister Marian on the right.

John Cowper Powys: 'Petrushka' 1929

Phyllis Playter: 'The Dancer' 1929

Phyllis [called in the Diary the T.T.] and John in the doorway of Phudd Bottom, their farmhouse in up-state New York where they lived from 1930 to 1934.

J.C.P. with their beloved spaniel, 'The Black', and 'Daddy Scutt' the Handyman, 1933.

In June 1934, with 'The Black' and J.C.P.'s manuscript of his *Autobiography* in hand, John and 'the T.T.' left America. After living in Dorset for a year, they settled permanently in Wales.

They stayed briefly at Rat's Barn to be near his brothers and sisters at Chaldon Herring, Dorset. Here with brother Theodore, another writer, in the village which was the setting for many of Theodore's stories.

'Chydyok' the isolated cottage between Chaldon and the sea. Philippa and Gertrude lived on one side, Llewelyn and his wife Alyse Gregory lived on the other.

[*below, left*] Sisters Philippa [a poet] and Gertrude [a painter] on the Dorset coast near Chaldon. [*below, right*] Llewelyn, the third writing brother, at 'Chydyok' in 1934, recovering from a recurrence of his tuberculosis.

[*above, right*] J.C.P. with his son, Littleton Alfred. [*above, left*] John and Phyllis lived in Corwen, Wales from 1935 to 1954. Here with his schoolmaster brother Littleton in 1937.

John was made a Bard at the Corwen Eisteddfod in 1936: the procession with the Welsh Dragon banner and the Great Oaks of Pen y Pigyn, newly cut down.

5 November 1939: Betty arrived with those wonderful pictures of Petrushka like Paracelsus calling up a ghostly T.T. his Undine. […] Oh oh oh I am so pleased to have this picture of the funny 'Terminals' – Petrushka & the Dancer!

I suppose this almost homicidal frenzy of Sadism is what sells well to a certain section of Americans – Ailinon! It is queer that what is not really what I like should start me off like this. Why is that? It must be that the idea of 'voyeurs' getting such wicked pleasures in itself stirs up my evil being even though the violence itself is totally out of my sphere! Certainly it shows that my sadistic tendency is actually – after all these years of austere & rigid control – and of steering clear of such things entirely for some 15 years anyway for 12 years – still exactly the same. I suppose nothing but my Death will end it. [...] What would Theodore make of this book? He would not endure it – no! no! And yet there is that element diffused in his work. I cannot understand these matters. Nor can I understand how Jeffers can go on with his homicidal blood-lust as in this *Give the Hawks* book of his – where his Hero takes to butchering Oxen ere he kills himself? [...] How can it be that the sensual nerve can work these madnesses? O Great Spirit of Dostoievsky you & you alone worked this through & got out on the other side purged and like a Christ-Satan! [...] This morning I had to do such hard things. The parlour stove was red-hot and too high! When I opened it blazing coals fell out & set on fire my newspapers spread out & burnt a little spot in her carpet – not much. [...] Then I had such difficulty in keeping kitchen stove just alight but low as possible. For there is no water. I say we have no Water! The kitchen pipes were frozen. Albert started Pump – no water still! He called Mr Czzirr the ex-sailor of seven years in a two-masted schooner on the Mediterranean. [...] By our thermometer it was 17 or 18 Below Zero this morn. This is worse than that other Day! Albert's thermometer is Thirty Below.

MONDAY 12 FEBRUARY Found the Parlour Fire very low & instead of leaving it with the draughts on I poked it down & shook it down as usual & lo! it went out! Just think of that! With Marian, Will, Elizabeth & Peter on the scene. Fire gone out! I did pray to the gods that the T.T. would nothing know of it but she did know – in a luckless burst of Candour I told she me wone self when I called her & she was terrible upset – terrible upset and there it is! [...] We had a very happy breakfast. Then they all went off sledging in the flat lot. [...] I keep noticing resemblances between myself and Will. I also seem to see him as resembling Theodore especially in his humour – I've heard him say things exactly in Theodore's tone.

1934 WEDNESDAY 14 FEBRUARY [W]e discussed seriously and most earnestly the Idea of going to live with W. & E. in Africa. The T.T. thought of it first! The T.T. would really like it. Yes she would really & truly like it; really & truly like it. I have always known she liked the idea of a landscape with wild animals in it. And she would have no housework at all and no zero weather and we would have no people with literary ideas!

THURSDAY 15 FEBRUARY I have explained to Will that I would sooner not decide to come to Africa. Though in the end it is possible that it will be the best thing to do but yesterday the T.T. had a reaction against it largely for my sake. [...] Today there came a letter from Mr Devoe about buying this house for $3000.

SATURDAY 17 FEBRUARY At breakfast Old Will held us simply entranced while he told of his first adventures in Africa & of being put out at Sunset in a plain and of an animal like a leopard coming out of the bushes and of the madman Seymour who said he would buy all cows in world & larn 'em to whistle & of how the natives used to click at him & he would chase them on his pony into the thorn bushes and they always escaped. He told me how the natives were afraid of the snow-topped mountain because the ghosts Marsi kept there – the ghosts of cattle – & how he told them he would go up & raid those ghost-cattle and how on a dangerous path they always put stones on the branches for luck as we used to do on the Yeovil road but they never took them away and by & by they fell down in heaps under the trees.

In February John hears that a libel suit has been brought against him by the owner of Wookey Hole, Glastonbury. With the sale of the house to Alan Devoe, the decision to leave America is made. From now until they sail on 1 June, the days are filled with various business arrangements, farewells to friends and neighbours, and packing. John finishes the Autobiography *before they leave.*

MONDAY 26 FEBRUARY I changed my morning tactics. Doing my shaving first. But this was agitating, for the Old was restless wanting to do Number One & it does so upset the T.T. when he does it on the dining-room carpet or even in the kitchen. [...] The T.T. gave way to a long pent-up outburst about my not enjoying with her lighter & more gay things and modern books – instead of always the New Testament and Homer & Horace and Dickens & Sir Walter! [...] I felt totally bewildered. But it is because of the 22 years I am older than she is.

TUESDAY 27 FEBRUARY [I]t is clear that the T.T. is very very nervous just now & very easily upset. I expect 'tis the house effort, the effort to be mistress of a house that keeps this little Elemental always in a state of tension. You wait! You wait till we are safe off & then I will see to it that never again will she have this kind of responsibility and all this effort & tension which so upsets her nerves. I must get this absolutely lodged in my mind. I must not forget as I tend to do.

WEDNESDAY 28 FEBRUARY Last night we opened Mr Shimkin's letter which agitated us terribly for he said he had already signed up with Jonathan Cape for the publication of my *Autobiography* in England. [...] I seemed to see myself landed to be exploited for ever & ever – and on the verge of poverty or driven to lecture or to write Magazine articles – my Books (as I write them) entirely in the power of S. & S. The T.T. pointed out that she had told me not to sign the *Weymouth Sands* Contract with that Two Books Option business but she said I was so proud of getting 15 percent instead of 10 percent that I would not listen or heed her. [...] I had great difficulty in gathering my philosophy and my spirit together to resist & to think that [...] I still was not, after all, in the hands of the Police – in spite of the Law case for Libel of Philip Crow of Wookey Hole! As I went to bed at Twelve after reading 'He's drownded: ain't he?' with such delight – my little T.T., my 'Heart's Delight' did say 'Well we can always forget our troubles by reading Dickens.'

THURSDAY 1 MARCH Found a Dead Starling on the snow under the French Lilac with its claws crooked & one frozen wing outstretched. I admired its brown spots & its iridescence & when the T.T. came down she did see, & wonder at long, its thin horny tongue between the opening of its rook-like yellow Beak. Then she got it done up to send to be Stuffed. The T.T. has a passionate love of stuffed Birds & animals. Her ideal would be to possess a Stuffed Zebra's Head.

1934 SATURDAY 3 MARCH Last night read Alexandra David-Neel on Tibetan Magic & the creation of living Entities by the power of the Mind. [...] Again at breakfast the little T.T. did read from this favourite Book of hers. She adores to think of Tibet.

SUNDAY 4 MARCH It is extraordinary to see the rush of water in the river & to hear the rush of floods and waters everywhere. I say 'All the Air is filled with pleasant noise of Waters!' but the T.T. says [...] that when she hears this universal noise of water she feels as if the earth were Sick! I have never known the T.T. so Upset as she is these days! It is this New Carpet of hers. This Carpet is the opposite of the Magic Carpet in the fairy-stories. It is a Carpet of Distraction. The T.T. says it has kept her warm this winter & that since her childhood she has never had such a nice Carpet. And she says that the effect of this Carpet with the gold Pears on the green ethereal sunset wall-paper & the salmon-coloured Cushion on the velvet couch gives her for the 1st time in life the Watteau essences she has so pathetically & desperately struggled for. The sort of delicate artificial – 'effete' – is the word she uses – Watteau remote beauty – beyond Nature altogether.

MONDAY 5 MARCH Took the Old via the Mail. [...] I took off my rubbers on the porch & sat on the bench watching the four cows by the river enjoying the brown grass now exposed in the thaw. Presently after shutting up the Old in Bath Room she came to see where I was & when she beheld me so quietly seated on the porch she burst into a flood of passionate tears. Poor little T.T. she was piteously upset again and cried & cried. She leaned against the open china-cupboard with big tears streaming down her face & pitiful words issuing from the barrier of her teeth – a barrier that these days is like a dam that is drawn up! I much prefer her to be very angry & to scold than to cry like this. Is it not strange – that I the suppressed Sadist – feel so very sorry for this sad little Abject when her whole slight being melts as if it would melt away in these flowing tears. The snow melts these waters are released and the tears of this Elemental are released. I shall never forget these wild disturbed days.

TUESDAY 6 MARCH She was very excited preparing for the Methodist Ladies' Party. The Man & the Old were fixed in Attic. Her 'Prodigious Cake' as in that old tale *Holiday House* that we used to love about the cruel Mrs Crabtree & Harry & Laura – that book that my little whore Lily of London liked so well when she was allowed to stay at Burpham with a view to her Virtue – her Cake came. […] The Ladies came. Miss McNeill first an hour before time, then Hattie & Mrs Freehan – the Man's favourite – and Mrs Paul Curtis – & then all the others. And up above there the Old barked like hell as they came. But Hattie opened the Meeting by the Lord's Prayer & without kneeling they all shut their eyes & said it. Then I heard them burst into peals of school-girlish laughter & giggling fits, these dear, hard-worked women.

SATURDAY 10 MARCH Just finished breakfast when T.T. noticed that one or other of the Cats had done Number Two on the Spare Room Bed – on the precious Blue & White Quilt. This decided us both to call for Dr Smith and put them to Death. […] I am aware of my Side today. This is due to my walking too far yesterday when I heard the Devil laughing like a Hyaena in that wood near the King Tree. […] It was a wonder with her Sickness hovering over her that the T.T. took this affair of the Cats as calmly as she has – having to decide on this Double Death; but the T.T. I note can rise to a drastic moment with more firmness & calm than when she suffers from much lesser trials! This is her nature – made for drastic moments like her Father.

SUNDAY 11 MARCH Snow again. The T.T. is SICK. […] I have seldom felt 'so fond' of her as Alyse said: 'I can understand why you are so fond of her' & in those first Wicked days of my insane desire for her lovely slender limbs it seemed a humorous expression to me. But now tho' if anything the purest rapture of my Wicked Desire is more rather than less, more rather than less, because she is such a very Docile girl I confess I have got rather 'fond of her'. […] The T.T. blamed her outbursts & her angers & her upsets for this whole thing. But the real truth is that neither she nor I have the necessary kind firmness for animals. This Murder which we have been driven to plot – using the Veterinary as our hired Assassin is due to our weakness, to our luckless incapacity with animals – certainly with Cats – we seem to deal with the 'Very Old' better but not too well! It was pitiful to me to see her wake up so miserable. She brought up some Blood out of her stomach – nothing else when she first woke up

& I liked not to see this Blood. But I've always thought her violent retching would break some little blood vessel. It was weird this Morn instead of being greeted by Sintram as I always am [...] to find those two silent forms one half lying on the other – Sintram the upper one as he was when they tussled on the floor – & wrapped up in thin coverings over their heads. There they lay, our two white companions of this hard winter!

THURSDAY 15 MARCH Felt Soreness in my Side like an un-healed Cut or interior Wound – not smarting but faintly raw! Did all & took the Old to Prometheus Stone. Met Albert driving a Big Wagon with two horses; he was wearing Dora's green cap. O he looked so surpassingly beautiful! [...] At breakfast the T.T. talked so very eloquently about Sadism and Masochism being equally evil and being entwisted with the System of Things from the very Start. This led to a discussion of Theodore's original sense of evil. [...] I think of the rose colour in the East of last night's walk to the foot of Becker Hill & I think of that walk by the Full Moon to the Downing Place when from the silver Moon herself rose-coloured rays shot forth! How we do let pass un-recorded so many never-returning never-returning Miracles. [...] The T.T. went to the Wambach's today with Hattie. She felt gloomy at the lack of Pleasure in these People.

WEDNESDAY 21 MARCH Came back by the Prometheus Stone for yesterday as well as the day before I kissed my Stone Daughter Perdita telling her I loved her well & I touched that round little stone her toy which the T.T. gave to her. The T.T. after we had finished breakfast which was only 10.15 for I was so early today spoke of her letters to her Mother & to Aunt Harriet which she felt were too bold & drastic stirring up these two poor old ladies to lay their bones in the Old World – while she herself meditates returning to lay hers in her Native Land!

WEDNESDAY 28 MARCH A cold North Wind with sprinkling of Snow. She came down as I was starting & it distressed her to see me standing on the Sacred Carpet in my Over-shoes. But it is a hard job to cope with these matters! [...] I read ere I went her typescript of my Praise of a Stoic life tempered by Tea, for *Wine*! [...] Then she did help me with my ENEMA & after that I must write my Confession to my dear Son. I have written it – Four pages long!

FRIDAY 30 MARCH Mr Johnson brought [...] my Will witnessed leaving all to my Son. This renders void my American Will & makes a Codicil not possible. I shall have to think about this. The T.T.! I'd better just write my last Wishes down about her for my Son in case I died. The T.T. is now going to Hudson to get an envelope to send these two documents off to Blundell & Baker Serjeants Inn. This letter from the Wookey Hole Lawyers in Wells is a great worry – saying the sum offered by the publishers is inadequate and that they are issuing 'a Writ' forthwith, with Mr Powg as Defendant. I find it so difficult these days not to spend my time imagining my Speech against Philip Crow in the style of Sir Thomas over the Seven Bishops! But I have also to imagine my speech to S. & S. about my English Rights & my speech to my Son about the T.T.! What a lot of Speeches to compose as I go about with the Very Old!

SUNDAY 15 APRIL All yesterday & today the T.T. has been working in the garden. [...] I noticed the feverishly quick & intensely concentrated way she worked. [...] I always derive a peculiar sensual pleasure from watching a lovely girl on her knees on the earth a kind of voluptuous mystical feeling especially now in this spring weather when she is feeling for the plants with her fingers & acting like a young Persephone. [...] The T.T. has been making a long list of all the things for me to do in New York. I shall not write to her. I carry her with me always.

John is in New York 16 – 22 April. They sail from New York on 1 June, arriving in England on 10 June.

THURSDAY 19 APRIL Marian talked very strongly about my doing justice to the T.T. both psychologically over calling her 'Mrs Powys' in our lodgings & so on & also that I must make a new Will telling my son clearly what I am going to do & leaving her certain definite things. She said 'I am devoted to Phyllis and have the greatest respect for her. You all to her owe yes – you owe all & not to Margaret, who has not —' Such were her very intensely uttered words & they made me feel as if I had been weak and cowardly over defending the T.T. at all points! It is a cowardice to say 'I think of her as myself.' She is not myself; she is a girl; and not a fighting girl either but a 'half-born'. [...] Thinking over the interview with Schuster I am inclined to think that they will flatly & firmly refuse to let me off those

Options – Options! Options! Options! This means one more non-fiction book for Schuster & Cape after *Autobiography*. And one more or is it two more novels for Lane after *Weymouth Sands*. But then I am free.

SATURDAY 12 MAY This morning when she first woke up, the sense of all that she had to get through made her collapse. [...] She said that like Madame Bovary she could cram poison even Arsenic out of a jar down her throat & she made the gesture of this! I too had to call up all the Philosophy I had to cope with things – '*rebus in arduis*' – I thought of the Libel: I thought of the Will [...]. I thought of the Septic Tank leaking at this moment of all moments & I thought of Poor Garland's neurotic anguish & that I ought to send her $50 towards her escape to Fred in the City. It was about 4.15 when Dreiser & Helen came.

MONDAY 21 MAY Very Warm at last; but a greenish sky since dawn. I am simply amazed at the powers of the T.T. The T.T. stayed up All Night. I stayed up til One finishing my chapter. When I got up at 6.30 there she was still packing the great wooden box, like a Coffin, on the Porch. [...] After breakfast Albert came with his truck that Old Ford Truck 9 years old that old faithful servant. He drove it clean against our steps so as to get all the luggage in including the Owl & the Duck and Falada – but not Olwen. Albert packed all into the Truck with extraordinary skill. [...] We saw the truck descend the hill by the Burchfield House where so many of our visitors have vanished out of sight. Old Dreiser like a Goblin & Mabel. [...] Mrs Paul Curtis paid a call. Mr Shaver came to ask about the lamp. Mrs Powell came. [...] Boissevain and Edna came straight from Lulu & Rat's Barn. Arthur came & I gave them all whiskey.

SATURDAY 26 MAY The T.T. set off to one thing after another that in these rushed days my memory forgets as soon as they occur. [...] Carl and Hattie & Albert and Dora were all together here in this room. It was like a Play. Exit – Entrance – entrance, exit! Then Mr & Mrs Watson came and then Miss Wambach came, with the Laundry? no! I mean the dressmaker's work – in fact a beautiful chinese silk evening dress. And then I took the Old to the Grotto and then we all dressed up & Arthur came for us. The T.T. has been to Hudson & did so like the Pier

[…] & the Steamer for Albany coming in with a lovely balcony Cafe! & the Captain & sailors & the flag & the bells. She did so wish that she had gone down the Hudson. But O deary I! the expense. Mr Betz' charge was $50 – & it was $16 to get the crated things to New York on the steamer.

SUNDAY 27 MAY Daddy Scutt appeared suddenly & talked to us while we had breakfast. We liked him so well. The T.T. kissed the old chap. […] Visited the old Stone of Phudd & tapped head on behalf of Lulu & on behalf of the T.T. & on behalf of the Devoes. Saw the White Horses & the 4 Cows. Took off my hat to the Willow-Tree & to the tree with One Breast which I have been secretly in the habit of kissing. I must today visit my stone daughter 'Perdita' & my stone son 'Tony.' […] Hattie came with Carl very gloomy & sad. I kissed her hand & bundled her into their car but I would not let her say good bye to the T.T. who was at the end of her tether. Indeed she has been at the end of her tether for a long time.

FRIDAY 1 JUNE Had lunch with the T.T. outside the Brevoort on little tables like Paris. Then we went to the Grand Central & drove with our luggage to the Docks. Then we drove from the Docks to the Brevoort where we left the T.T. & I went on to the Speyer home where I wrote a cheque for fifteen dollars & got the 'Very Old'. Then drove all in the same Taxi to the Brevoort where the T.T. got in; but not before we had great agitation over the laundry, which was late in coming. […] On the Dock by the Gangway I found that I had not got a ticket for the Black. […] I kept getting all my papers mixed up & I carried the 'Very Old' while the T.T. carried the MS of my *Autobiography* and also my heavy overcoat, the old one. Thus we crossed the gangway. There on the deck we found Arnold & Hattie & Marian & Peter. Arnold arranged all. It was like old days to me.

WEDNESDAY 6 JUNE Last night the T.T. watched them throwing dice for the racing of toy-horses in the Lounge. I read *One of our Conquerors* and was struck by how the jeering mental fanciful word-mongering style of Meredith had a certain resemblance to Joyce. But the writing was not obscure to me. When I had read it 40 years ago it was obscure and unintelligible. How clever I must have grown in my old age! But I don't like Meredith's Soul. I don't like his nature. I don't like his kind of mind.

FRIDAY 8 JUNE The sea was like the 'Glassy Sea' of the Apocalypse before which they 'cast down their golden crowns'. Oily it was & yet purer more jewel-like than oil of Lebanon. It was silver-white milk-white vapour-white moonstone-white & there were long gently heaving waves without foam where the ship passed. [...] And suddenly there were revealed to my Proteus gaze a herd of SEALS voyaging voyaging voyaging 'round the world for ever and aye!' It was extraordinary to see them put out their long necks black against the milky sea – like a row of dark-moving stalks of queer-shaped fungi going along!

They move into Rat's Barn, and Phyllis meets for the first time 'the Powys Clan' en masse. *Philippa and Gertrude live in one half of 'Chydyok'; Llewelyn and Alyse in the other half. Theodore and Violet live in the near-by village of Chaldon with their adopted baby daughter, Theodora (nicknamed Sue or Susie). The 'law-suit' involves Llewelyn, Sylvia Townsend Warner and Valentine (Molly) Acland, who have reported to the authorities a woman who runs a home for retarded girls in Chaldon. She in turn has sued them for libel. John goes to London on 14 June to see his solicitors, Blundell & Baker, about* his *libel suit. He also sees his son, who agrees to John's including Phyllis in his will. During this period there is much visiting back and forth. John and Phyllis spend a day in Weymouth, and they visit Littleton (L.C.P.) and his wife Mabel in Sherborne.*

TUESDAY 12 JUNE Philippa met us at Wool. [...] What a noble girl – what a ravaged countenance like a storm-tossed Mariner! We drove to Theodore's and stopped for a moment. Theodore made very humorous faces at me & we thought little Sue a most beautiful child. Drove on up to Rat's Barn or Down Barn but had to leave our trunks in the village. The T.T. was thrilled by this scenery. [...] But she doesn't like the lack of independence over getting provisions or the way you have to mind your 'ps and qs' or the fact that Rat's Barn has windows only North & East. Found Gertrude with the fire lit & had a cup of tea with her in Rat's Barn by the fire and on the old table from Father's Study at Montacute. Found the Montacute dining-room chairs here. I left the T.T. alone & went a little way with Gertrude & was just going back when I saw Alyse in the distance and so I had to wait a long time tho' I knew the T.T. was alone at Rat's Barn. Then I walked back here with Alyse. Then we went to Chydyok and found Lulu in a barn like a cloister. He looked like an Apostle or a Pilgrim or a worn out Palmer from the Holy Land with Cockle-hat and Sandle-shoon. We had tea with Gertrude. The T.T. and I sat by the fire of Down Barn till after eleven by candles. She cooked a fish. We heard a blackbird late in the evening and also a wild Will o' the Wisp's cry!

WEDNESDAY 13 JUNE When I looked out of window I saw 19 sheep in the barton some of them lying on the straw and chewing the cud. Out of our window – our bedroom window – we can see the path going up to a gate – one of those horse-track gates that have to be opened & shut. Opposite our […] sitting-room window there can be seen a patch of tall grasses & nettles & a few elder bushes now out in blossom and to the right of this hill a ploughed field slopes up to the sky. West of the house – on which no window opens – another ploughed field all strewn with flints, like the upland where Tess worked for the unkind farmer, rises to another sky-line. O it is such an unspeakable relief to me that the T.T. is so pleased with this wild & barren landscape. […] I managed with some care & effort to start a splendid fire but I was startled to see the T.T. in her butterfly-thin dressing gown getting water from the outside tap over the stone trough. […] Alyse hesitated not to get me into a fine row & scolding from Lulu over my way of talking to a shepherd with a crook & a hurt hand in shearing and my way of talking to 'Ruby Joyce' who I dared to say resembled Violet! This was a brick Lulu said. I will be careful! In fact I have just talked with a labourer in the approved manner.

FRIDAY 15 JUNE The T.T. was looking for me & came to meet me in the midst of the flock of sheep. We kissed in sight of the Shepherd. We had a very happy tea & told each other all our adventures. 'Molly' & Miss Warner the writer 'Sylvia' brought their Lawyer from London. I think Lulu will win his case over the mad girls and will turn that woman out. But it looks rather as if I shall lose this Libel suit […] & have to go Bankrupt.

THURSDAY 21 JUNE [In Weymouth] we went to the Esplanade. […] Then we went to the bathing machines and the Donkey Stands. The T.T. was very stirred and moved almost in fact quite to tears by the look of a Goat-Carriage and those

Donkeys with their names round their patient foreheads. It seemed like Grimm. It was a Fairy-Story to her and she felt that the aura of Weymouth was the happiest she has ever ever known. She wants very much to spend our winter here – with all the harmless bun-shops & the taverns & the silver-smiths & the market – it seemed with all these children with spades like an Ideal Children's Paradise to her – where she would be so happy to live always.

TUESDAY 26 JUNE As we were finishing breakfast Alyse came – such sturdy stockings & shoes and such characteristic chains & medallions, and a stick in her thin hands! [...] I went back with her to Chydyok and read to Lulu out of my Book – the *Autobiography*. He was in good spirits today. I hurried back at 12.30 when the T.T. helped me with my ENEMA yes with my ENEMA. It is Raining. The T.T. has been washing up, tidying house, and packing our two separate bags; for we are to be 'Miss & Mr' with separate rooms at Sherborne!

FRIDAY 29 JUNE L.C.P. & I talked in his car by the Almshouses; he spoke of how his feelings had been hurt by not telling him of Phyllis; but as he confessed he would have told my son I think I was in a way justified. [...] L.C.P.'s car had to go backwards down Gertrude's Lane & Lulu burst into a queer fit of wrath.

SATURDAY 30 JUNE I thought of the wild-quivering outburst of Llewelyn against his two brothers but he has been so cosseted by reason of his grievous illness & his nerves that anything is liable to make him 'Go up in the Air'. [...] By God! after his outbreak I do begin to see what Gertrude means by all her caution. [...] 'These are the words of an Honest Man!' he shouted with trembling voice to the two aged Humbugs sitting at his side.

SUNDAY 1 JULY I decided to use this disturbing morning to Empty the Privy. And this I did being afraid as I went of the Big Adder that Willie saw there. I also walked to the Obelisk rails & looked at Chesil Beach and I thought of how yesterday Lulu had teased me into a temper by jeering at me about my penchant for the Catholic Saints and I thought how weak & like a 'little girl' I really was – as the T.T. said I actually looked – like an alert but docile little girl with old Littleton. But I felt & behaved like an angry little girl when Lulu teased me [...]. So indignant was I that I walked nearly to White Nore! How I struggled to overcome my rage at Lulu's teasing. He said such things that I shook with fury in thinking of them! [...] I recovered from my shock of quarrelling with Lulu by thinking of myself as a little girl.

John and Phyllis go to London to see the solicitors. He writes an article for Bye of Scribner's Magazine*: 'Farewell to America'.*

WEDNESDAY 4 JULY [W]e went to the office of Blundell & Baker in Serjeant's Inn. This was an agitating experiment for tho' I liked Mr Blundell the T.T. had a violent Independence Day reaction against English Law. [...] It has become a passionate Revolt in the T.T. against all English ways & all English men. Her feeling over it has been more extreme than any feeling I have ever seen in her. The Libel and the Will & the £200 all were the cause of volcanic agitation from the very pit of her stomach.

THURSDAY 5 JULY It seems as if a fatality were possessing everything I do & say so as to drive my little T.T. to the breaking-point. It is a state of things that has driven my own soul to its final & ultimate resources! I am her lover & her adherent & I would give up almost all to make her happy but I fail & fail & fail. It is extraordinary. I shall never forget these days to the end of my life. All I can do is to hold on to her tight & pray that I can do wiser in the future or feel more clairvoyant in the future or change my nature in the future. [...] We went to Bertie's Office & I had to go alone to Blundell's to dictate a long Document about my Father's money. [...] Bertie enabled her to get a cheque of her Thousand Dollars for Blundell & Baker. We had Tea and Supper with Dorothy Richardson and Alan Odle.

MONDAY 9 JULY I took a taxi with the luggage to Waterloo. Then a taxi to Mr Blundell with whom before a Commissioner I swore to having been separated from my wife for 20 years and having given her all I have – my Father's money – my library – my house – which is of course most literally true, tho' never a legal document passed betwixt us. [...] The train was hot. She was very sad at Wareham. There was no water when we got home. Mr Webb took us to Iron Road & here the T.T. carried up hill a big basket she bought at Covent Garden. There was no water. No water.

TUESDAY 10 JULY I went over in the morning to see Lulu & I carried him the basket of fruit and I hoped very much to be able to have an Enema for I took my Hand-Enema over there & though Lulu wanted to decide the sort of ENEMA I was to use I used eventually the one I wanted to use and got on very nicely.

MONDAY 16 JULY The T.T. said that England seemed to her like a fragment of planetary Matter floating in space – not like the broad & deep earth at all! And the sea so hypnotized by the smooth deadly cliffs. She said it was a strange land.

WEDNESDAY 18 JULY After breakfast she started off [to Weymouth] very happy carrying her bag – the zip one in her hand but refusing – which I pray she wont have Cause to regret – to carry any kind of cloak. Then I wrote hard at my *Farewell.*

No! Oh patient unknown reader! I must be so confused by her absence as to have mixed up today with yesterday. I am supposed to be describing yesterday as today, I mean Wednesday, curse it all! & here I have precipitated myself into Thursday. I hope to visit Theodore soon & may be the Chance of Meeting 'Mr Weston' down there has turned Time into Eternity.

Lit both fires really today – the true 'today' of this Wednesday – and walked to the cliff as far as Telegraph post 100. It is a hot day a rather thundery-hot day. I wrote several letters one to Dorothy Richardson saying how we enjoyed our time with her & Mr Alan & I received one from her telling me not to let people disturb or 'rally' the T.T. [...] I found Lulu in a straw barn and enjoyed reading to him there very particularly. I asked him if he was afraid of death & he actually supposed me to think that he might, as such a Rebel, be afraid of Hell & Penal Fire. I never thought of this aspect & it shows how human beings get things wrong.

FRIDAY 27 JULY Heard from 'B & B,' my lawyers, who were – as the T.T. always so naughtily says – 'Blundelling & Bakering' along, very sagaciously to settle all – that they had settled all & that the Captain had accepted the money in Court. [...] I looked out towards Iron Road & lo! & behold! Mr Bryer Ash J.P. & his Jane Austen Lady & his two daughters, Margaret & K. The T.T. likes this family very much & is more interested in these girls than in the more literary figures of Miss Sylvia Warner & Miss Val Acland! Though to me Miss Warner remains the most retiring & the most modest writer I have ever met & I felt at ease with her & also with her 'dear companion': the boy-girl Valentine. Mr Bryer Ash J.P. felt strongly that I were wise to stop the publication in England of *Weymouth Sands*, altogether. But I doubt if Lane will like this!

SATURDAY 28 JULY Up at 7 precisely by the Cob watch which is fast. [...] There was a second letter from these wise Serjeant's Inn Lawyers [...]. This second letter announced that the Case was withdrawn & that I had to cut out the passages from the book describing the Caves as Phallic & describing the Seduction of Persephone in the Cave. [...] But I am relieved that this is all that has to be done. I have now written to Messrs B & B [...]. We have had a terrific time over this letter. Mine was Censored by the T.T. & hers was Censored by me! But Two Brains are better than one! O dear! Ailinon! Ailinon! but this B & B letter ended with Distressing Disaster for the T.T. got tied up with her version of it & finally in desperation started on her way of Automatic Spirit Writing which I always so greatly dread for her for I fear its an Elemental of a dangerous sort & not the spirit of her father at all who takes possession of her pen so tightly clutched. [...] She became hysterical & went up to her bed. I followed & read to her *The Wings [of a Dove]* till she went to sleep.

TUESDAY 7 AUGUST [Lulu] said why do we quarrel so over ideas now when in old days we never did? I said because our dear companions have blown up our conceit & egoism like two balloons till he fancied he was Voltaire & I fancied I was Rousseau! [...] Then Alyse came & I said for all her 'feminism' she was the most 'womanly' of women & gave herself body soul & spirit up to him. She took this very well. She has reached a point beyond all argument & anger.

FRIDAY 10 AUGUST At breakfast the T.T. did have her favourite of all dishes namely Creamed Chicken – but what must I do – brute that I am – but make a face when she wanted to open a letter from Lane to know if he was coming – & this look of mine spoilt her happiness entirely & she became very upset & her upset state grew worse as she recalled a very psychological conversation we had the last thing last night about her temperament being like grass that must rise up & assert itself against English ways & also against the 'Powys Cult' or rather not against this latter but in defiance of everything but its own Necessity to be Itself.

TUESDAY 14 AUGUST She had a longing for the tender care of her Mother which with all his desire the very 'climate' she felt of Petrushka's nature could not supply. She felt as if for the very sake of her life with 'the Man' it might be necessary for her to spend some months in her native land.

Phyllis goes to London for x-rays and to see Lane. On 22 August they go to Dorchester to look for a flat.

THURSDAY 16 AUGUST At this very moment – 10.30 a.m. – the little T.T. must be interviewing Allen Lane at Vigo Street near 'the Albany.' How will she get on? & very soon will come her interview with the Doctor in Wimpole St. – what will he say? Aye! my little T.T. Aye! my little Ballad Girl, what things do be occurring! And when will she get back to Petrushka tomorrow? And what will her mood be? I depend on her moods even as sheep on grass or turmits; or cattle on grass or hay. Her moods are the man's 'climate'! [...] I keep thinking of Dorchester as the Solution. I do feel so sure that if she was comfortable & near shops & out of the wind & away from everyone she would be all right. Met Mr Toomer with a telegram from the T.T. and then, old lady running, Mrs Toomer aged 76 with one from Lane.

FRIDAY 17 AUGUST I keep recalling the neat tidy black figure of Mrs Toomer aged 76 laughing so hysterically & rushing down the hill to follow Mr Toomer her son. She told me he had been never the same after an accident when a motor left him for dead. He was a funny one but O deary I! his Mother was queerer. [...] They were the most Dickensian Pair to be in Dead Horse Valley that I have ever seen – & they went off different ways, Mr Toomer the son by the road on bicycle & the mother by the Ash-Tree & Withy Bed! I shall never never forget it! It was so much more like a Story than like reality! I fancy all English life is more like a Story than reality!

SUNDAY 19 AUGUST All day she has had Nothing but bread & butter which is not the right thing for her & it does not give her any vital strength. I am 'up against it' over what to do for my little T.T. […] I simply don't know what is wrong or what to do. Perhaps it was a mistake coming to England but she never liked our house over there. She doesn't like Lodgings. My only hope is a flat in some town. I must do something drastic & make some move. […] Read about Christiana & Mercy, out of Bunyan to Lulu. His fever was high – but blood-spitting has quite stopped – but he was irritable & cross. He wanted to tell me about chalk carried by donkeys from a quarry & could not explain & it made him angry & sad. […] I go from the T.T. in misery in her mind to Lulu in misery with his body.

WEDNESDAY 22 AUGUST Well, this has been a day of Occurrences. Got fire lit with prickles & box & wood. We are running short! Had no time for Enema and the little T.T. was so terribly tired that I had to wake her five times. She had been thinking so late, so late, of her life – last night – just sitting down there & thinking – I think she was near the point of wishing that she had never risked coming to England at all! […] Well we got off & when we reached the Village the Car had broken down & we had to wait a full hour conversing with Mrs Legge & the T.T. walking up & down like a Sentinel outside till at last we did get off. […] On arriving at Dorchester we went at once to Damer's Road. […] Here we found Miss Sherry's house. […] But alas! her windows looked out on new houses and also on Allotments & on the Barracks. […] We had not come to England to look out on new villas & cabbage stalks so on we trudged – across those very 'allotments'! Then we walked straight down High Street till we came – after visiting the Public Lavatories near where Mr Hallett do bide – to the Phoenix. Here we drank Grove's Beer – I had two glasses – & then by a divine good chance we asked the Landlord if he knew of a flat. There's a party he said just gone out opposite here above Mr Davis the Grocer. So we went there – and lo! we had found what we both were craving so for. A tiny very old Attic bedroom a nice kitchen & a perfect front room with two fine wide windows looking over ancient roofs at ancient tree-tops. It was also near All Saints Church & All Saints old churchyard in which I sat for a while waiting for the little T.T. There was an excellent toilet & water-tap down one flight.

TUESDAY 23 AUGUST [A]fter I came back from a glimpse of the sea, all silvery round St. Alban's Head, I found her getting breakfast in a very desperate state of mind. I will not record the cries of wild trouble that at such times do pass the barrier of the little T.T.'s teeth! But 'the Ways of the Powys Family' do not seem to separate themselves as I could wish, & as I sometimes think I deserve, from the ways of Petrushka! But as soon as I showed signs of unmistakable emotion under her upset state she felt better & explained that I must understand how very very hard, for her, her present situation is, that is to say considering her life-illusion & all our circumstances. The mere fact of a foreign land to her and the difficulty of 'living with another person' and the way she is torn between her authentic love for Lulu & the furious maelstrom-like tyranny of his pitiful Sick nerves, is the cause, the cause of all, so she explained and she did feel better after explain[ing]. I woke up however quite fixed on our High Street Flat & Attic & resolved to carry it through. […] This I felt resolved upon & in being so resolved I really felt sure I was acting for the best – as well as Petrushka could see 'the best' in spite of his being one of this convoluted breed! – and not only so, but acting also as a Unit with her, which is what she always prays for. It was when I spoke of breaking it softly to Lulu that she was upset – for this particular tone – as well as the tone – 'I will be Drastic' has an agitating effect on her. The first with regard to my family and the second in regard to her private life-illusion of herself […]. But Lulu in his Sickness has in truth become most terribly tyrannical. He was always so in a sense but you could rebel when he was well but now it is hard to be independent at all. But I must & I will be. […] [I]t looks a little as if 'S & S' might be thinking of making me responsible, if they are made so, for the whole of the eleven hundred pounds paid to The Captain; unless the 'Tort-Feasor' clause in Contract is null & void. Tort-Feasor! What a word!

WEDNESDAY 29 AUGUST X This mark recalls a sad and bitter grievance expressed passionately by the T.T. as to the [word inked out] of being with me, as one of the Powyses whose manias [word inked out] their companions. And O I did so think I was different from this! O I did so think so!! But it is the fate of my being 20 years older & being what the gods have made me. What can I do now? This conversation this morning has made me more distressed than I have been since – I do not know how long! [...] Ailinon! Ailinon! Ailinon! This is the worst moment I have had since we came to England for this is really the T.T. not liking to live with me as I am & she says too that I cannot change! And if I cannot change & this with me is tragic for her what is to be done? – O O O what is to be done?

FRIDAY 31 AUGUST I walked to Lulu's Chalice & on to the fallow-field above West Chaldon where I can see Moyne Clump to the West and & the Tower of Winfrith Church to the East. Noted how much coloured (so deep the blues & purples; so clear the wet spaces) the English landscape is – & Egdon as seen over the green Downs is, ever, so purple, with spaces of bright green intermixed. [...] I gave myself an ENEMA and then while she began washing up she did all suddenly come over to my couch & say the words 'Forgive! Forgive!' & you can believe what Petrushka felt and how from Pit of Stomach he did feel what she were to he!

WEDNESDAY 5 SEPTEMBER Got the water for her pretty hot at 7.50 a.m. an hour after I came down. [...] I made some marks on the linoleum or whatever our floor is made of – & after the T.T. came down she beheld these marks – invisible to me! [...] She was so upset that I did not know what to do save to hold my tongue & look like a fool. But this made her feel far worse than if I had got angry. O I wish I could break down & cry without any – and yet I don't know. [...] She found it hard to fry her mushrooms on the fire for it was – tho' I knew the danger – too hot again but O its so hard to boil water quick with a little fire. But I be – & that's the plain truth & its all nonsense to hide it – so clumsy with feet & hands – so like an animal – or rather a great hulking Moujik – for animals are not clumsy – that I am a maddening partner for a delicate Watteau-like girl. [...] Did she manage to get into Dorchester? She could not have caught Mr Webb's Bus – she could not! [...] I ought never to have come to Down Barn. I ought to have known!

THURSDAY 6 SEPTEMBER After breakfast the T.T. described to me her feelings driving in to Dorchester after running and all the Village running to stop Mr Webb. Finally he did stop and she

1934 got in & then as she drove had the feeling of the absolute queerness of vegetation – & machinery & the whole cosmos – being so irrational & its Purpose Inscrutable. I discoursed to her on Hegel & his idea of Being & Not Being & Becoming.

SUNDAY 9 SEPTEMBER After breakfast the T.T. (who had been reading my Diary) remarked that there was less of the Shrew in her than might be supposed from my observations. [...] We set out half-an-hour late to Mrs U. & Miss Warner and Valentine and once more in my desire to please I made an ass of myself. [...] A very delicate & nice situation full of a thousand criss-cross currents & agitating feelings has emerged from 'the girls' as Miss W. & Val are called having got Mr Cobb to let them hire the Hut. There appear all manner of queer under-currents about this, complicated by the thousand & one passions & egoisms & touchinesses, and jealousies in East Chaldon.

MONDAY 10 SEPTEMBER The T.T. did not come to bed last night till 2.30 a.m. This was so agitating to me that I felt as if I lay awake near all the night afterwards [...] but what she spent her time upon from 10.30 when I went up till 2.30 – four hours – I have not any notion! [...] She looked very white the next day – today – & when I said 'you are dissipated' she said the fairy-story princess 'wore their shoes out in the dance.' But I heard no dance of elementals only the familiar wind of the downs and some rat saying to itself 'I must take shelter ere the weather breaks up.'

They move to 38 High East St, Dorchester. Schuster commissions a short book on the 'Art of Happiness' for which they will give John an advance. He agrees and puts aside 'my Dorchester Romance', begun in August.

MONDAY 8 OCTOBER Katie gave me as a birthday present *Theodolph the Icelander* the old original edition tied up with blue ribbon by my Mother. Gertrude gave me the Montacute Milk Jug from Stalbridge & Lulu gave me one of Uncle Littleton's Elephant Tusks from our Father's Study. Mr Webb took us to Dorchester and charged a Pound. [...] I came up to bedroom and lay on my bed while the T.T. went out to buy many important things – among them a chamber-pot & also to telegraph to Selfridges upbraiding them about the non-appearance of carpet and brooms. […] Started at Six p.m. for such a rapid walk & went to the very end of Poundbury. Here was a herd of cows & a twittering bat like a Homeric ghost. The men were still doing the sink so I could not put head in water but the T.T. helped me to wash my hands.

TUESDAY 9 OCTOBER Saw the sun rise over Stinsford Brook from the window. Saw Jackdaws. Heard Rooks. Saw the sunrise on the Spire of All Saints. When I first looked out there was no one in street save a little black & white Dog. Then I saw a man near the White Hart & a lonely woman advancing up High West. Then I saw a sad little flock of sheep, I think being driven to slaughter. Ailinon! On slaughter still the peace of Durnovaria depends – as of old. […] Read the *Odyssey* lying on bed & wrote letters! The T.T. discoursed on the Powys Family & then wondered if she ought to do this. I said yes! always – & so do I feel it is best. For there is a lot in what she says. […] She has her first proper fling. She has bought a lovely little chair & table & <u>will</u> buy a writing desk of ebony & a set of wonderful MSS drawers. She has bought too for 10/- an excellent <u>Couch</u>. She has bought too a poker & a Hob. Heard all this eve the Fordington Bells.

THURSDAY 11 OCTOBER Oh how it thrills me to my deep cold heart to hear her say 'In coming here from Down Barn I have come from Hell to Heaven!' How the T.T. did suffer from the difficulties & hardships there! In comparison – to her nature – this *Vita Nuova* in Durnovaria is <u>Paradisic</u>. She never once with me anyway walked up to Down Barn from the Bus without tears or without a deadly cruel silence and walking ahead of me dumb with misery! And this went on <u>for</u> <u>four</u> <u>months</u>. But it is over now – over now.

MONDAY 15 OCTOBER Tried to begin my Book for Schuster on the *Art of Happiness* under a title at present undecided. I think I must finish first though the first chapter of my Romance and then let it go till Xmas. I ought to be able to work fast on this happiness book and try & make it a real Handbook of Psychological craft for people teased & fretted by the sort of obstacles of a mental kind that I understand best.

SATURDAY 27 OCTOBER Up early – got fires. […] I must

remember each time I light a fire – moderate your mania for a bonfire, Mister. But how amazingly quick the T.T. recovers when she is upset – & to say the truth she has been hardly upset at all since we've been in Dorchester.

SUNDAY 28 OCTOBER Walked up the empty High Street & bought a paper, the *Observer*, read a teasing attack by Basil de Selincourt upon Poe a jeering unfair facetious clever attack. Damn the chap! Last night the T.T. went to the Circus. That of Hill Brothers of Bristol. She came home transported with joy.

FRIDAY 2 NOVEMBER Up at 7.15. Unfortunately I woke the T.T. by rattling the kindling & unfortunately I had not lit her fire first so that it was necessary for me to light it while she looked on & for to see my clumsy attempt at fire-lighting drives her distrastic distratic distracted & desperate and very very upset. [...] Then the T.T. and I had a yet more serious Misunderstanding in which we reached the final point of my saying How like a woman! And the T.T. saying How like a man! She wanted to decide it by tossing up & actually produced 2/6 for this but of course I refused. And later by 'obstinate water seeking level' I decided on a crafty compromise & after she went out & came back in a very good mood she was willing to let it be as I had 'decided'. Thus it was. The feminine winning entirely the emotional battle & going off with flying colours &, as soon as she was off, the cunning male digging a regular 'Poundbury trench' on his lost field of battle! It is the greatest nonsense to make out that women are craftier than men. That they are considered so is the greatest proof of man's craft!

He takes the train to visit Lulu and the others twice a week. Phyllis gets her main meal at the Wessex tea-rooms. The 'Old' gets out of quarantine in December.

WEDNESDAY 7 NOVEMBER I walked to the River across the fields full of cattle and the Stallion and the Great Goat like the Sign of Capricorn. He was just where I cross the ditch but he moved off to follow in a most annoying manner a poor cow with swollen, & I fear sick, udders. I met a tramp too gentlemanly to help but soon another like an animal with merry eyes to whom I gave a shilling and a thrill of lively satisfaction was shared between us. Then I bolted off to the train. Found Theodore in splendid spirits but Violet with a terrible cold. Theodore told of the Fireworks he had bought and had let off to amuse & scare Sue. He was braver in this than I could have been. One of them hit the window but didn't break it against which Sue was pressing her face.

THURSDAY 8 NOVEMBER Washed quick & called the T.T. who awoke with her accustomed misery as she felt life before her again & the cold of England before her again. For myself I was struggling to gather my resistant powers together to cope first with my enema & then with lunch at the Goodens which meant no work. I find that not to work – to have to pass a day without work – is a great effort to me. […] It is like being forced to sit down for a long time out of doors instead of being able to walk and I find the greatest difficulty in really enjoying Nature unless I am walking and really walking pretty fast. […] To take life in I prefer to be passing through it like a pilgrim whose real goal is beyond life. […] I like either to be working, or walking, or going to bed. I think to read a novel on a train-journey is one of my greatest joys for then the very landscape itself moves; & I read, & then catch a glimpse as I pass by.

TUESDAY 13 NOVEMBER She will never forget this Winter for she feels under a weight of water. She says it may be that she is recovering from a Nervous Tension – like recovering from a Breakdown – but I hope this down & out drugged numbed exhausted feeling isn't itself a sort of breakdown. She'd be all right if she had nothing to do for she is happy observing life. If she had nothing to do she would be very happy; if she could only lie back on her sense of interest in life & never have to be responsible for any thing all would be beautifully well with her. I did read my Chapter to her and she did like it. […] O thank the Lord! & the Great Kwang our Idol – who now is in a Drawer without a Head.

SATURDAY 17 NOVEMBER This book shall go to the limit in my peculiar points of view. The title has been carefully selected by Mr Schuster. The contents will be hastily concocted by the author: for it has to come out this spring which will be a bit of a rush! But I think I tend to write better sometimes in a rush & also I think too on a theme set by someone else – such is the indirect, or it may be the medium-like nature of my particular talent. I have to get started like a telegraph wire in the wind &

then when the wind gathers to a rush the tune emerges!

WEDNESDAY 21 NOVEMBER Alyse came & lay down on our bed in absolute prostration. The mark of her poor dear little head is still on my pillow above the T.T.'s pillow! She is on the verge of a complete collapse. God knows what is going to happen. Lulu does not realize in the least how bad she is. The best that could happen would be for her to collapse completely & go to a Sanatorium before she dies of it. Too long has it gone on!

TUESDAY 4 DECEMBER Young Mr Eliot a nice young man – the County Librarian – [...] told me of his difficulties with the rooted Conservatism of his Committee & how they censored the books chosen – banning *Wolf Solent* as well as Socialistic works. He said Mrs Hardy had resigned in disgust at their ways.

WEDNESDAY 12 DECEMBER I took the Old to the Frome. There were all the ditches brimming-full with water just as that Elfin 'Drowner' had said that they would be from the pulling up of the great Dam by the Hangman's Cottage & letting the water flow along the Ditch [...]. So full was one Ditch & so covered with scum that when I jumped over it – for in my love of watching ditches fill with water I have become a Jumper – the Old took the Scum for Land & sank out of sight, till I pulled him by the leash round his neck. Then we saw those Two Swans again. There is a poem of Yeats about Swans that I can recall with a lot of pleasure. I actually watched one of the ditches fill up with water that was empty before; I watched the water flow along this empty ditch and make a series of overflowings & miniature waterfalls at the points where the Drowner had left for what to me is so far an unknown reason small turf-dams, dividing each ditch into segments. Over these turf dams the water brimmed, cool and swift & deep & clear, over the grass & the earth.

SATURDAY 15 DECEMBER Up at I don't know when; for the T.T. had woken up to face what I foresaw would be a blow to her namely the State of the House after the man's frantic efforts to 'carry on' in her absence. Three times I tried to make her a decent cup of tea & at first it tasted of Perfumery. Finally I managed to get her one that confined itself to tasting of Incense. [...] For the first time in England I let the Very Old off the leash

– in that path between those two ditches, keeping him in front of me. […] When we got back I gave the T.T. the paper to read in bed – postponing the evil moment of her seeing the Confusion of the Kitchen – & myself lit the parlour fire. Then I had to go up to wash. But lo! the T.T. was up & out in the kitchen & all was sadness and scolding for she was sore upset. Next time I must manage better. […] All the day I worked at my easiest of all chapters, the way to be happy with a woman.

TUESDAY 25 DECEMBER As I lay on my couch yesterday before tea watching the T.T. hang up her Wreaths & Major Stanley's Holly she said she wondered why I looked on without helping in this task & why I had helped so little over all her Xmas activities! This question nonplussed me totally. It is odd how little we know! But I suppose I behave as my Father used to do at Montacute – watching all our activities with benevolent but detached interest.

MONDAY 31 DECEMBER O the little T.T.! I do hope I can make you happy in my country ere long. You do like the attic bedroom anyway & the fire-place for she said it was the best refuge she has ever had. I think of that word. Well I took her tea & went down to get more coal & lit both fires & took the Old to Hennings where I saw a chaffinch & a wren & a thrush & a blackbird and those two Swans but not Leda. A TERRIBLE Time over the ENEMA. Oh! I do feel so very sorry for the T.T. this little frail Being having to go through such an awful time with her Man-Doll. Why O why isn't [he] stuffed with Straw?

1935

The move to Dorchester seems to be a mainly happy one for Phyllis. Lacking the theatres and concerts of a big city, it none the less offers some of the 'distractions' she craves. John resumes the habit of two long walks a day that seem essential to his health and creativity. Poundbury and Maiden Castle are favourite destinations but the customary 'round' with the Old is in the countryside immediately to the north of their flat: Hangman's Cottage, the river Frome, the Saviour Tree, 'Henning's', Coker's Farm. He continues to visit regularly his brothers and sisters in Chaldon and Chydyok.

The main events during their time in Dorchester are the court case involving Llewelyn, Sylvia Townsend Warner and Valentine Acland; and the excavations of Maiden Castle being carried out by the Dorset Archaeological Society under the direction of Sir Mortimer Wheeler.

Despite their apparent contentment in Dorchester, John has Wales always in the back of his mind. During a holiday there, they are shown a row of modern cottages being built on a hill side on the outskirts of Corwen, North Wales, and they arrange to move to one of these in July. The last half of the year is spent in settling there – yet another house – and adjusting to a new pattern of culture.

He finishes The Art of Happiness *for Simon & Schuster in January, writes an anti-vivisection article and another article for* Scribner's *– 'England Revisited'. Most of the year is spent working on his novel* Maiden Castle. *The finds from the excavations excite his imagination, as does the great Jubilee bonfire, and he incorporates these into the story. As is his custom, he researches his novel extensively, borrowing books from friends, the library, the county museum. The three main characters are Dud No-Man (modelled on himself), an historical novelist; Wizzie Ravelston (modelled on Phyllis), a circus girl Dud buys at the opening of the novel; and Uryen Quirm, a mysterious Welshman who tries to get in touch with the old gods of Maiden Castle.*

TUESDAY 1 JANUARY Up at 8. Lit fires took tea to the T.T. Found her in splendid Good Spirits telling of how she put head out of window and saw [...] young people in evening dress & heard them bid each other Happy New Year in such crystal-clear voices – for once the T.T. did love the 'Cheerio' tone [...]. And she came & opened the Attic window so that I could hear the Fordington Bells that except for Maiden Castle thrill me most of all things in this town. And so I heard them, ringing wild & free out of the darkness. [...] At 4.30 the Black & I got his licence at the Post Office & set out to within half a mile of Maiden Castle. We both walked on air – we were both so thrilled. Why does Maiden Castle thrill me so?

WEDNESDAY 2 JANUARY [A] Builder in a Mackintosh with One Eye out of Commission & a Big Airedale Puppy held me Standing for Twenty Minutes. [...] Sturdily did he denounce the Government & Bolshevists too. Sturdily did he indicate the True Economic Policy of Public Works instead of a pampering dole. Sturdily did he tap his chest and speak of ex-soldiers 'full of Beans' that we had ruined by the Dole. O deary I! I remained polite. 'Absolutely – yes, I agree Absolutely' I kept repeating standing first on one leg & then on the other. A group of little boys with guns held me up later. 'Oxford or Cambridge?' they cried. 'Cambridge!' – 'Pass!' We had from Mr Bye a cheque for $250 – no! $225. But I delayed to put it in my Wallet. I sank into my writing! for I am at the end of my Chapter the Last of my Book. And when I came up to the top again – Alas! This precious Cheque was lost. It was Burnt with Rubbish & Envelopes & Papers! I will not describe for it was too sad & too distressing to think of or recall the effect of this Disaster on the T.T. It knocked her over totally & it was a terrible time. Finally she collapsed on her bed upstairs and covered herself with the Purple Rug & turned her little distorted countenance to the Wall in helpless despair. All the troubles of her life, going back to Hillsdale, rose up round her & she gave up completely. I sat in the new guest's arm-chair by the window of our sitting-room with the door wide-open lest she should go down unseen for I feared what she might go & do in her wrought-up state. But when she was quieter – at 4.20 p.m. I set out to recover myself with the Old and walked – careless of the effect on my Side – all the way to Maiden Castle. It was nearly dark there and I lost a glove like my Spectacles at Glastonbury. [...] But I got strength from my Bronze-Age ancient home!

1935 THURSDAY 3 JANUARY Heard the T.T. say what a good thing if we could get breakfast earlier and begin the day earlier and all. So I told myself to wake up at Six [...]. But I only [began] lighting her fire & was barely finished inserting kindling under the coal – when behold! the T.T. did wake up with a start – was it because I poured the whole contents of a pail of coal into the box on the landing? Was it because owing to red coals in the grate I had to scrape instead of as is my custom using my two hands with those gloves on that I did buy for sixpence at that shop where they were so very reluctant to lend me Sixpence to give to a tramp? Well anyway she woke up saying that the noise I made resembled that of a locomotive. And not only woke up but leapt out of bed & hurried into the kitchen to get herself tea. So you can believe I had to hurry up! for this business of her being up at 6.30 made the day Earlier with a Vengeance! [...] We had a pretty fairly happy breakfast but our talk ran upon economic matters & why the coal has vanished and why with things being so much cheaper our money does not go further and so on. Then we found we had lost the First Page of my Fourth or Fifth chapter and this was only discovered when the T.T. took out every one of the fifteen drawers of our Black Cabinet – which is certainly more like that old black-and-gold-cabinet or chest-of-drawers that Grandmamma at Penn House gave me than anything I've ever had since. But the result of this disturbance was that just as the T.T. was starting off to the Bank & the Wessex I begged her to tell me where the two important letters of this morning were. [...] They had vanished. The T.T. knew no more of them than I knew. They were gone forever. But the T.T. wanted to look for them in the Top-Drawer that Limbo of Lost Letters but I implored her to desist & after a while she did desist from this mad search.

FRIDAY 4 JANUARY This evening I read to Page 26 of my Last Chapter of my Happiness Sermon to the T.T. When I got to the part about Cigarettes she suddenly began to cry & then became very heart-broken & said that my cherished Philosophy was a Reaction [...] from living with her & against her ideas & ways of feeling as – she said – happened with all men and women. I denied this & explained the deep truth that it was my Protection against Reality & Responsibility. But what I felt, when for a second I thought of what it would be like if I gave up my Philosophy, was simply Fear of my Ancient Terrors, Manias

& Imaginative Morbidities. But I must think over what she said. She said we ought to try as at first lovers always do to be more like each other – not more different.

Llewelyn's court drama begins. John reserves him a room at the Antelope Hotel. The verdict goes against them.

FRIDAY 18 JANUARY I took the Old before breakfast to the Saviour Tree & called up it under the name of Rhea Grandmother of the gods to guard Ll. & the T.T. from Worries by absorbing them into itself. I knelt on my cap on the Henning Path where no one was & prayed to the Rising Sun to help Lulu thro' this Ordeal & to give him Victory. At ten we went to the Antelope. Colonel Doddington took the T.T. to Grand Jury Seat. I followed later with Gertrude. I did like the Judge, Justice Finlay very much. He is a just man & a merciful. He has acquitted a man for seducing under the Age of Consent – under 16 – and he has given the woman who killed her husband by throwing a brick only 1 year. I like his countenance very much & Mr Slade, Miss Warner & Miss Valentine's Counsel, is a very formidable man with a projecting chin and Mephistophelean eyebrows & a terrific bald forehead under his wig. [...] I had to go out to pump-ship & got lost among the cells in the cellarage & had to make water on the floor and could not find my way out! Gertrude said I looked pale when I emerged back in our Grand Jury Seat in the trial. The T.T. is wearing her Purple Hat of the kind she is going to wear to the end of her days. [...] I read to Lulu out of the *Mabinogion* about Pryderi & Manawydan out of the subtlest & loveliest of all Mythology after Homer. Then I took the Black to that Wood beyond the stone trough where the Owls were. On my return I had hoped to light the fires but I heard Lulu wanted me and so I went to the Antelope & read to him while Alyse went out. So when the T.T. came home at 5 o'clock there I was only just having changed my new clothes preparatory to lighting the fires. And finding the flat so cold she was terrible upset. But I made a disgraceful fuss when she was beside herself. I must try to act different at these moments.

SATURDAY 19 JANUARY I just greeted Lulu who has had a bad night & went with the T.T. into the Court. I took good care to ask where the Lavatory in the cellar was & I found it this time.

It was very very exciting and agitating seeing Lulu carried in in a chair by the Boots of the Antelope and others. Mr Pollock interpreted for him standing at his side and bending down beside him the doctor stood behind and Alyse stood near [...]. I came out to see Lulu go off driven by Mr Etheredge straight back to Chydyok & I embraced him – Lulu I mean – with emotion unusual in me – indeed it seemed from the way Alyse pulled me back that my emotion was liable to hurt him more than giving evidence.

SUNDAY 20 JANUARY The Papers ring & ting & buzz & hum with Llewelyn's coming to the trial 'as a dying man'. The *News of the World* has headlines about it & a Poster which I have got to show Lulu. [...] I took the Old to Hennings & the Swamp and the Saviour Tree. [...] I deliberately left unopened a telegram from Gertrude till I came back. When I told Miss Warner this she was astonished & reproachful but I like all to be in order – I like telegrams at proper times & I don't like my walk interrupted by telegrams. At breakfast we read all the papers. [...] This will mean that the Value of Lulu's Writings will go up!

TUESDAY 22 JANUARY I went into French's & bought 4 papers to read of the Verdict. *The Times* gave it in full even to the separate amounts of the Damages. We had a happy breakfast but I told her how when I heard the Foreman of the Jury come back & the Judge read out – 'They all had Malice' I thought, 'It's a trick of theirs to Lulu's advantage in some way I don't understand.' She said quite passionately & even angrily 'You are all like that, you Powyses, you twist everything round. It's your Egoism.'

THURSDAY 7 FEBRUARY The T.T. talks of the fact that here she – the Devotee of Fairy Tales – recognizes their real weight & almost terrible truth as the Only Hope! [...] I note how all these fairy things – Rooks, fowls, Ducks, cattle, the crescent Moon – which I saw for the 1st time this quarter today – & the Evening Star & trout in the river & the Prison walls & the Bugle in the Barracks and the trees & the ivy & the gulls & the White Owls – each so solid and stoical & preoccupied with its own life in its own place – are so near together in our little Island that [they] form a natural Drama or Poem with those limitations & 'Unities' of space & time which poetic drama – including Fairy Tales –

requires according to Boileau & other repulsive Pedants. But it looks as if this necessary smallness of the stage worked another effect more important – namely the quickening of a Shakespearean Imagination which knocks holes into a larger Time & a wider Space than Monsieur Boileau would allow for.

MONDAY 11 FEBRUARY I did all with slow leisureliness. Only I had to go down & get coal – two buckets of it – & empty the ashes. It felt odd stepping over those flagstones in the narrow yard in the grey early light. The T.T. was sad when she first woke up over-pressed by Life! She said 'Oh that we were both Dead!' But I said – 'don't 'ee make me die yet! I want to live to go to Wales & to write a shelf of great Romances – one a Masterpiece about Welsh Mythology.' I think though what really made her say this – was my telling her that the Blind in the Living Room – the 'Shade' – refused to 'go up' & I had left it for her to cope with. She said 'do you remember how at Hillsdale you always announced Calamities when you called me?' I said 'Yes I did – but not to trouble you but to prepare you so that it should not be a shock.' She then finally said 'you are not grown afraid of me, are you?'

SATURDAY 23 FEBRUARY Went to the Doctor's. Waited with the Old in his dining-room for half an hour. Got more and more miserable looking at a Garden Wall out of the window topped by red brick tiles. Felt very irritable felt more and more nervous till I hated all the little back pleasant places & gardens I could see out there – old queer shut-in tinkered little gardens adjoining each other & leading into vistas and greenery. But I felt caught by the quaint, the shut-in & the little – I struggled with this. I felt like an Old Bronze Age Man of the Elements submitting to the rules & regulations & little rock gardens & pleasances of the Belgic Durotriges and the Saxon Dorsaetae and to the Meticulous Laws of the Romans. [...] So in my megalomania waiting for the Doctor in his dining-room & looking out of the window I thought & worked myself up into a Katie-like Rage yes! a Rage just like Philippa! Then I could bear it no more. I then did just like Katie – I went off in a fine huff – leaving the door open – and full of nervous agitation I set out past the Hangman's Cottage. Here I saw the first Primroses I have seen this year.

MONDAY 4 MARCH Yesterday I watched for the first time the

Song of a Blackbird actually proceeding from its yellow bill! But as with some magical power the Blackbird flung out these deep cool mellow bubbles of black water of liquid sound, beyond joy & sorrow! Like Nietzsche's poem in Zarathustra – in praise of life. They hung about that yellow bill in the air & seemed independent of it as if the soul of the Blackbird outside its body were melting into this mystic sound that hovered like an aura round the bird. The sound was gayer than I had expected – and yet more than gay – a cool dark bubble of liquid sound floating away – getting larger and larger as it dispersed – and in some mysterious way suggesting the colours of green & yellow and black!

WEDNESDAY 6 MARCH Heard again for the fifth time, or thereabouts, the Wood Pigeon. Aye! what an effect on me this 'Take two Cows – Taffy – Take two!' really has! I cannot put the deep thrill I get from this mystic sound second to anything except the Church Bells [...]. But this sound seems so rooted – no! not rooted but bubbling up from under all roots – even the roots of the world that may have abscesses like my poor teeth! It comes from all sorts of race-memories – no sound more in England! All old parks – and old ponds under calm skies all old clumps of trees outside houses, outside villages – all ancient hedges & terrace-walks. [...] Those who only love wild cries such as of Seagulls, like it not! Philippa hates it. It is a calm sense sound! It is the sound of the unctuous Sabbath of the eternal senses! It has been permitted – it alone – in the whole of our Planetary experience to forget the cruelty of life. What would its sound be like to a person being tortured to death? The worst last straw?

THURSDAY 7 MARCH The T.T. had a very tiring day yesterday – what with one thing & another – & today will be worse for her. She ought to be allowed to live her own secret sense-life & hum & mum & drum & whisper & murmur & whistle alone in joy like a swaying grass-head in a quiet field.

THURSDAY 14 MARCH The Old was seized by Alma Venus last night & kept moaning. He wanted to enjoy a bitch-spaniel & there weren't none! He was terrible excited over every dog he met for he is as Homo-sexualist as any person! He is a bi-linguist as we used to say. Well! I took him to the end of the Straw Road before breakfast. 'Tis a windless overcast dark day, the sky looked low & it mingled with the smoke of burning weeds. The T.T. felt grieved at my not reading the morning papers for it seems – she said – unnatural for the woman to tell the man the news & seemed sad to have a partner so lacking in interest in the Great Panorama of Human Events.

SUNDAY 17 MARCH I had a very very happy time with Theodore. [...] I sat on my cap in the hedge while he sang Hush-a-bye to Sue & finally got her to sleep. It was a pretty & satisfactory sight to watch him [...] rocking the pram like a cradle & murmuring some half-song to her. The extreme ruggedness nay! stoniness of his visage & the sardonic looks under his heavy eyebrows & his old faded long black coat did impress me. We had a very friendly & very down-to-the-bottom conversation over the sleeping form of Sue [...]. I wonder what impression little 'Dudy' will recall of these long morning walks.

FRIDAY 22 MARCH On my return I found a telegram from old L.C.P. to say he'd come with [a Sherborne friend, W.E. Lutyens] at 11.15 & bring their lunch. [...] Lutyens did not like my kissing him. You are so 'gushing' Jack he said. [...] I have that peculiarity like an Old Maid. Went at night to hear Dr Wheeler lecture on Maiden Castle. He (Lutyens) jeered at Americans to the T.T. somewhat unkindly – not 'meaning' it – but asked her whether she liked 'Dream-Lands' meaning those awful those terrifying & awful Amusement Parks! Think of that! What is the real pathology of this perpetual jeering at Americans in my fellow-countrymen. Is it a kind of elder-brother friendly teasing? But it is not very friendly. They don't do it to Frenchmen or Germans. After [...] lunch we went in the car to Maiden Castle & walked clear round it. On the top is a temple to Minerva & some Gaulish God who has three horns and three heads!

SATURDAY 23 MARCH O deary I! The very worst thing the very worst almost that happens to me occurred namely the Window got Stuck & the T.T. leaping frantic from her bed 'with hammer & tongs' went, in her thin white night-shirt kneeling on the red chest to beat at it, struggle with it fight at it! This sight was so disagreeable to me that my philosophy broke down & I fled – and inappropriately enough recited my accustomed Stoic

Litany '*Integer vitae scelerisque purus,*' '*non civium ardor prava iubentium, non vultus instantis tyranni*' etc etc etc etc etc ending up with '*impavidum ferient ruinae*' while I lit the sticks I had prepared. But ashamed I returned – to find that she had given it up and was drinking her tea.

WEDNESDAY 27 MARCH I bought a copy for 4/6 of Hardy's *Mayor of Casterbridge* where (rather as in my tale) the man sells his wife. The T.T. says the 'aura' of Durnovaria encourages the sale of ladies!

FRIDAY 29 MARCH Last night the T.T. astonished me by falling into a very queer mood. She spoke of her Loneliness & how she missed that friendly reciprocity – never mind what is said! – of meeting people like our Hillsdale neighbours – especially Mr & Mrs Krick. In England she said every one cultivated their lonely egoism and were the same together as separate. She certainly felt in a desperate mood – but afterwards when I came downstairs to her late she called it all 'absurd' – but it was not absurd.

SATURDAY 30 MARCH Up at 6.10. Was absent-minded when I lit the fires for on both occasions I set fire to the paper before I'd put the wood on it! I think my head was full of my book which has reached a difficult point. [...] Today she has that feeling of absolute exhaustion & weariness – partly her cold – a slight touch of 'flu – but partly due to Wessex climate which seems terribly Relaxing to her taking her spirit & interest in life away. What shall we do? What a problem. Perhaps a Welsh Mountain? – but I am not ever going to land her in a remote country place again! For except for the relaxing air & this 'whoresome Lethargy' she is happy here. [...] Yes I worked real hard at my book – for I had an inspiration after I reached that impasse and pondered on it so hard.

FRIDAY 5 APRIL Coming round by the bridge at the end of our street where the same elderly gents are always leaning with backs to the bridge I saw two young tramps. Very young & very old tramps are sadder to me than those about my own age. They seem less competent & less inured to the Profession. One of these, in grey flannel trowsers torn & thin that hung so low that their seat was nearly down to the back of the young man's knees, looked foreign & superior but <u>very</u> cynical. He had <u>a</u> <u>book</u> in his coat pocket. When I gave him sixpence, he bolted without a word across the road into a Fruiterers. Was he thirsty? Or was he a fanatic who lived on apples?

SATURDAY 6 APRIL O deary I what an Occurrence when I took the T.T. her tea. I balanced her tray for a minute <u>on</u> <u>her</u> <u>bed</u>. I whispered '<u>Don't</u> <u>move</u> <u>now</u>!' But she waking suddenly moved her feet & lo! the tray fell crashing onto the Floor! Alyse's thrice precious tea-pot fell, full of boiling hot tea but it did not break – but a saucer broke & the little dish she loves so well with Fox Gloves on it broke [...]. But you should have seen her leap out of bed – & I fumble in vain bewilderment to find her slippers. It was a woeful and yet a comical spectacle.

TUESDAY 9 APRIL As I came back to High East Street I saw a super-natural tramp – like a sea man. Like Captain Lingard like the <u>Phoenician</u> <u>Sailor</u> of the Tarot Cards. He was so grand a figure this tramp that I dared not offer him money. In a black coat with bare neck he swung along so majestic in the middle of the road. [...] I watched him follow the London Road & my awe & my respect went after him like a page after a monarch passing by on the way to an unknown destiny.

SUNDAY 14 APRIL I ate bread & butter while the T.T. ate her early Osborne biscuits and drank her tea. She says it is nice when we have these little refreshments together – she calls it an agreeable encounter of Two Skeletons and not so much in the style of the '<u>Anti-Man</u>'. Went as [...] far as 'Coker Farm' & I got that indescribable feeling that has come to me all my life of some secret ecstasy in certain things that is handed down thro' the generations from father to son & father to son and has to do with some marginal sensations <u>not</u> of any particularly beautiful thing or pretty thing – but simply of the blank stucco wall of a house, like Coker House, with a great holly bush and mud a <u>lot</u> of mud & a few very ancient & decrepit apple-trees – but it's silly to list these things for the things <u>aren't</u> the point – the sensation is the point & it comes to us by inheritance down long long long long long ages – <u>down</u> <u>all</u> <u>the</u> <u>ages</u> – yes – down <u>all</u> the ages it comes, floating there – if we want to grasp it – just outside the margin of our ordinary works & days – no! not 'outside' – for it floats through it all & over & round it all – it is what the Theologians call 'immanent' – it is non-moral – non-spiritual – non-mystical – no it is not mystical at all – nor is it poetical – it is the plenilunar circle of the whole moon of life seen faintly from horn-to-horn of the young crescent moon! That's what it is – entirely materialistic & earthy & yet psychic – […] & it has to do absolutely & completely with the Past. It has nothing to do with the Future! The Future – any thought of the Future kills it. It is when your hold on the present is rather loose that it comes. […] Took the Old into Bear Wood & saw Bluebells out! Into Badger Wood nothing but Moschatel & White Violets. Saw Six Swallows by the 10 Weirs. I have already seen the first Pink Campion out in the Henning Shrubbery under the Beeches.

THURSDAY 18 APRIL Saw a great row of horned sheeps' faces pressed in curiosity against the rails opposite Henning's Garden – looking so like complacent rather stupid old ladies. I noted their eyes very very carefully – sheeps' eyes – at first sight they looked reddish under white eyelashes & then I saw the white part of the eye was pale yellowish & the pupil long & narrow and black, but tending to get round, as I say of my Wizzie's eyes, when very interested! The ears pink inside but concealed a little by the curling horns. Discussed at breakfast the tendency of Frances & Lulu (in their different ways) to rage against me & my refusal to rage back […].

FRIDAY 19 APRIL The T.T. heard a great Rush of Cars coming into the Country to 'see Primroses'. This did so amuse the T.T. It went on all the morning – a great stream of cars coming up the same way from the London Road. […] [I] read aloud to her the whole of Massingham's *Fee-Fi-Fo-Fum* – trying to prove that all the Neolithic & Bronze Age Civilization & Stonehenge & all & Maiden Castle & the Cerne Giant & all – come from Egypt. This the T.T. strongly & vigorously protests against. Why couldn't they invent their own gods & cults from their own peculiar climate so different from the Nile & the Desert! […] I must say I am swayed & deeply influenced by what the T.T. says on this matter. I must try & bring her ideas into my book.

TUESDAY 23 APRIL Today she went to her lunch at the Wessex & met Miss Good there & visited with her an Exhibition of Etchings which she wanted to support by paying for one just as she wanted to pay for a new piece of music to be played by the Band. She has an extraordinary tendency to bestow patronage as if she were Lady Phyllis Playter of Sotterley. But I refused 'to support Art' unless she was thrilled by what she bought & only two of these pictures really thrilled her – one of the Poundbury Farm & one of Coker Frome but these cost 2£ & 12/- each. I am miserly in such things I would sooner she bought china. […] I began an article on England Re-visited for *Scribner's*. I have finished my Anti-Vivisection article for *Whitehall* No. 47. Then I took the Old past Hennings. There were some boys & a little girl throwing stones for a dog to catch in the dam-pool by the Hangman's Cottage. […] This morning such a pathetic one was playing with a dog & insisted on jumping over the ditch herself with a touching desire to show off before the man & aye! what a quaint figure of a wench she was. The T.T. said suddenly to me 'Would it not be nice for you to fall in love with a young girl – a very young one?' But I answered & with precise truth – 'you are my young girl.'

THURSDAY 25 APRIL 'Twas a very anxious & very agitating night to 'Petrushka' for I heard my little Magician's Daughter groan & whimper & moan to herself again & again & Oh! how burning hot she was! But her fever must have dissolved in Perspiration. I kept muttering I recall in great agitation – 'Sweat it out! Sweat it out!' And when I got up myself to pump-ship I recall I felt myself all burning & perspiring from the electric contact with her burning spine! God! It was a night. I kept imagining the most awful things. […] I cannot imagine life without her. That is the truth. I do depend on she for my whole existence – weak little Reed tho' she be for a Cerne Giant or an Iron Man to lean on. […] I seem to have lost Ten Shillings when I bought her Tonic at Boots.

SUNDAY 28 APRIL The T.T. has been in a Perfect Mood all Day long. What is the explanation of this? Not I think only that her cold is less in her head. I believe it is due to two things. First that No One can come to call and that she can stay indoors the whole day without having to face anyone – and secondly that she has been occupied all day with her favourite of all tasks – changing the furniture & the pictures. […] She says that Alyse and herself are broken & draggled & keep fighting with their 'spurs' like wounded birds in a cock-pit! Whereas these Powyses with their tough egoism have nerves so strong as to be able to keep their purpose and their life-illusion unimpaired. She asks why is this so?

The bonfire at Poundbury, celebrating King George V's Silver Jubilee, plays a significant role in Maiden Castle. *John's Romance,* Owen Glendower, *was not begun until 1937.*

SATURDAY 4 MAY This Income Tax now that I've been forced [...] to delay so long after the official time is a deep bruise & Terror to me; it is just what I dread – I keep imagining myself in Prison & how should I get my ENEMAS in Prison? No one knows what I do go through in my fanciful mind over matters of this sort. [...] The T.T. was so touched with England's way of Celebrating – this word 'to Celebrate' being her favourite of all words – that she actually shed big tears as she read the Programme I got today from Mr French. England touches her heart & when in its irrational way it celebrates she says that every Englishman lives by Caprice & by Will & by Imagination against Reality. The last Englishman to be killed, she says, would die irrational & whimsical & defying reality to the bitter end! Raining today but let it rain before Jubilee really begins. The T.T. is in happy spirits today. Her flag flies free out of our window. [...] She went to Genges & bought a Summer Hat with Poppies & Daisies & Cornflowers such as she has not had for ages, not since she was 14. Think of that!

SUNDAY 5 MAY I worked steadily and hard if you can call it hard when its only too easy a vicious self-indulgence to me really, my writing, compared with hanging up my trowsers, or stamping my letters, or counting words in an article, or dealing with Income Tax [...].

TUESDAY 7 MAY [W]e did enjoy the Fireworks and the Enormous Bonfire. It became a Personality – this Great Fire – it became as it whirled & swept & curved up a regular Elemental Hephaestus. And the fireworks were striking but the best thing was to see the crowds silhouetted against the sky. They actually were like the old Durotriges for you could not see their modern clothes as the Bonfire lit them up & they might have been the old Neolithics under the Crescent Moon.

THURSDAY 9 MAY I feel such a tremendous longing for hours

and hours & hours & hours of calm quite uninterrupted peace in which to write my book. It is hard to be philosophical when you know you can write, when your brain is seething with desires to write, with ideas, with thoughts, with the will to write & you are held up by one thing after another of tiny little interruptions.

WEDNESDAY 15 MAY Got up at 6.45 & lit her fire & took the ashes & cleaned my teeth & got her tea. I sat by the fire eating my bread-and-butter. She does so love these moments & does so hate it when I sit munching my bread & butter & staring at the fire without a word – so I made the effort to talk, tho' I am always more inclined to just watch her form under the bed-clothes & watch the flames of the fire in happy meditation! But making the effort to talk I unluckily made use of my malicious Reservoir of unkind commentary on the belligerency of women. This suddenly to my astonishment completely upset the T.T. & she burst into an eloquent diatribe against the English character whose self-control she said always hid up a deep cavern of Malice that forever kept seeping out in furtive ways. [...] I think I do sometimes get waves of curious brutality of thought. I must remember & be more subtle & wise. All was well when I returned – but during my walk I felt impelled to give Ten Shillings to a mother of Seven children whose larder was empty. The T.T. was pleased when I told her this and was not in the least vexed! [...] She wants me to write a Romance about Owain Glydwr. Yes, she spoke eloquently of my Romance to be writ about Owen Glendower.

James and Tim Hanley find them a holiday cottage in Cynwyd near Corwen, Wales. While there they arrange to rent from Admiral Cotton one of his newly built houses, with electricity and an inside bathroom. They live here at 7 Cae Coed, Corwen for the next nineteen years.

SATURDAY 18 MAY As we went past Maiden Newton and past Pen Mill & Marston Magna & as we came into sight of Cadbury Camp or Camelot the T.T. was in better spirits & better heart than she has been for a whole year. She adores travelling. She loves trains: anything to escape everything!

TUESDAY 21 MAY Took the Old to the Village found all shut except Mrs Evans the Grocer; & to her (in my excitement & with my head full of vague ideas that all Welshmen talked only

Welsh) I made at her door the most eloquent signs as of one writing. This performance was an astonishment to this good lady who assumed that a Madman, led by a Black Dog, was arrived in Cynwyd. However, as she replied in perfect good English [...] that she kept no ink & that no shops in the place would be open till later, I went away. [...] I am sorry to say the T.T. woke up very very sad & upset even speaking of suicide which I have never before heard her do. It was the strangeness of all, the difficulty of all & I think the cold too; for it is very very cold this morning. [...] Took the Old a walk up the mountain or rather over the mountain's base. It was indescribable. It was indescribable! [...] If only I could convey to the little T.T. what I feel so that she might feel it too; for I am so and she is so – is it not sad?

THURSDAY 23 MAY Awoke at 7. But for twenty minutes I held her & made love to her with more rapture more deep enjoyment than I have felt in this kind since mornings in Hillsdale. Is it the Mountain Air? Is it the amorousness of Wales – is it the 'aura' of Owen Glendower's domain? Is it some mysterious life-sap emanating from these hills & valleys? And as I held her I was aware of a fragrance from her inmost essence the smell of some unknown magic plant! A little like hay – perhaps like Meadow-Sweet. It was not perspiration. Heaven knows what it was. The very fragrance of the little T.T.'s Soul. [...] There are so many little springs & I saw & kissed Primroses growing by tiny rivulets. The first Primroses I have really enjoyed since those ones the T.T. planted in her Hillsdale garden. [...] I looked down on Cynwyd & I knelt on the ground – no! I lie – I knelt carefully and even mincingly like Boissevain says proves my essential falsity & treachery & coldness of heart – on my cap and there did thank the Spirit of my Mother for the happiness of this place. [...] When I came back breakfast was ready the kettle on the hob & also her particular hot tea-cakes. All looked as I liked things to be. But during breakfast she spoke of this strange change in her – how she no longer cares for Nature or the Picturesque but has changed & by reason of trying against the grain to be practical has now atrophied something in her nature & now craves for life in a big metropolis like London or Paris [...]. I said that I would far rather live in a Metropolis and she be really deeply happy, than live in the country & she be sad. But just as I hate to sacrifice her so she hates to sacrifice me

& there we are! It's an impasse. But Dorchester was a compromise – yes but that was not deeply satisfying to either of us, not really!

FRIDAY 24 MAY I burst out too last night after Hanley left. He is so sociable & genial & good-natured. [...] He is so kind to us but has not the least notion of my mania for loneliness & it is hard for me, being such a Coward – just like the T.T. – to tell people the reality of inhuman solitude which I hide up under my indulgent & even obsequious manner! But it is absurd to put it on her, & be secretly truculent with her, when in such difficulties. These are things a person has to cope with himself. I don't want in this to resemble my Father who put all on my Mother & got angry with her when anything went wrong. I don't want to turn her, so independent & lonely & imaginative & pessimistic as she is, into a watchful & protective Mrs Gladstone. I must defend myself against life without dragging her in to help, or hiding behind her skirts.

TUESDAY 28 MAY [H]ad no time to do a single stroke on my Chapter – the morning glided by; the little T.T. struggling & collapsing & weeping & I writing my letter to Dorothy Richardson & feeling sad for her & wondering what to do – thinking that I must must must (above all) concentrate on her comfort & her having what she can cope with! Well! after Lunch Mr Edmonds, who had already been in, & talked to us – Mr Edmonds our quiet-voiced guide & guardian-angel here – came in & said he would take us to see houses where we could abide. [...] Then we went to a tiny little fairy cottage but aye! it was so damp & old but so quaint – the garden as high as the chimney! Then we got a lift & visited the Admiral's New Houses & then we boldly visited the Admiral his wone self – & told him we wanted No. 7. Will we get it? The T.T. is simply thrilled, & so am I, by Number Seven.

They return to Dorchester until 5 July when they move permanently to Wales.

WEDNESDAY 12 JUNE I hurried to Tizzard's where I found that Mr Tizzard remembered my Father – & in consequence gave me a present enough of his best coffee for the T.T.'s breakfast! The truth is that it is my Father's Memory & his

Personality after 50 years that has given me my Status in Dorchester in spite of our names 'Miss Playter & Mr Powys' so shameless writ above our door-bell in the Street! But the Durotriges of Durnovaria are great ones for respecting the Past & for a Feudal submission to any local gentry that have the gall to carry it off & assert themselves even by the queerest eccentricities! [...] We went together to the Bank to put in Aunt Etta's cheque which follows those of Aunt Dora's & Aunt Kate. What a debt we do owe to these sisters of my Mother & how good they are. My Father's money went to my wife & son but my Mother's money is thus come so long afterwards to us. I put the £350 to the account of the T.T. lest I should suddenly be Knocked on the Head! [...] Then I went to the Library & got out a History of Wales & also Rhys' book on the Welsh People.

THURSDAY 20 JUNE Her conversation this Morning 20th of June eve of the [longest] day was a very important one in my life as a Writer. Never has she spoken so eloquently or so strongly on what she feels about my Work. She says that in *Wolf & Glastonbury* I touch Reality but not in *Weymouth Sands* or *Skald* & never before *Wolf*. She says that I ought to take a simple theme of universal human interest like that of *Hamlet* or *Lear* & then be as fanciful & as imaginative as I like – but based on the old universal feelings of the human race – feelings that all can follow. She says this present book about Dorchester goes back to *Rodmoor* & is a curving back in a cycle to where I began & not an advance! She says there must be Reality & an interpretation of Reality for a book to be really great. [...] She says my fear of Libel is totally out of proportion & ought not to be allowed to spoil my work as it is spoiling this Dorchester book.

FRIDAY 5 JULY I have been reading aloud [...] a thrilling Russian book – we always enjoy Russian books of every sort & kind! – called *Semi-Precious Stones* where the fellow keeps a show-off Diary to be read if he is arrested. I 'sometimes think' or to speak more correctly – I have this second thought that this Diary of mine is just such an 'Apologia' when I am arrested by Death but it is also one of those things you are proud of doing just because it is difficult to do & it has always given me thrilling pride and pleasure when the T.T. reads it. She used, in her way, once to say that it was her favourite work!

TUESDAY 9 JULY I read *The Castle* of Kafka late last night to the T.T. [...] It is a most curious book everything made numb & muted as if by heavy falling Snow. [...] We have had such a nice letter from that critic of the *Argosy* called Adrian [Bury]. And photos done in Mr Cottman's studio by young Mr Frisby. Very very good! We had breakfast in Kitchen by the fire – O I like it there so! And the T.T. talked most eloquently about the thrill she got from her bath last night – and how in this proletarian house it was possible & permissible to get a childish delight from the material luxury of a hot bath – a luxury possible to our working class neighbours by modern methods of building houses – without feeling that your pleasure in a hot bath was a spiritual 'come-down' [...].

WEDNESDAY 10 JULY [W]e set out in the Rain to visit the Hanleys. We have decided that when people say that Wales has such a large rain-fall they forget to make any mention of the particular kind of rain that this rain fall consists of – namely misty rain, mountain-mist rain, soft vaporous rain, rain that is really entering into a cloud, which has not burst into ordinary rain yet, but just holds its rain in a diffusion of soft warm cloudiness. [...] Rain in Dorset drenches you to the skin very soon whereas after walking to the Hanleys in pouring rain, only it is not 'pouring' – that is the point – but diffused – we sat there talking without thinking of wet & I even put on my wet coat to keep me warm after tea ere they lit the fire. We had a nice time & like them well. But 'the Terminals' in order to satisfy their temperamental desire to be economically inferior, practically inferior, less successful, less competent than others took the opportunity of enlarging both to their own satisfaction & the interest of their sympathetic hosts upon their past financial crises & their future alarms. This brought all sorts of friendly advice & practical suggestions which these evasive demons – ourselves – at once began dodging in their customary retreats & evaporations!

THURSDAY 11 JULY We had a happy breakfast with a Registered Letter from the crippled poet Mr Branford discoursing on the Magnetic-Energy of the Cosmos. I answered this letter & then had a hot BATH very nice & used the big sponge – the most important of all one's possessions. [...] This sponge is the first I have ever had that does not smell of the sea – what am I to gather from that? Are sponges ever grown in fresh-water rivers – or does 'Boots' the Chain Chemist, extract the sea-smell from all sponges – or does a sponge bought from a woman not smell of the sea because of the oceanic character of all women that swallow up the mere material waveringness of the sea, substituting a psychic sub-marine element for the physical one?

SATURDAY 20 JULY Took the Old to the Post via the Gorsedd Stones & back the same way. [...] As I passed those Gorsedd Stones I hesitated whether to 'invoke' them; but decided against it. My Gods belong to 'Yr Gaer' that prehistoric Camp! Towards this I look when any bitterness or demon assails me! [...] I have come to use this old fortress as a stepping stone to the Next Dimension beyond this present Astronomical Universe. [...] Then I worked on my Chapter V. I must thicken out this book & make it have more weight – [...] even as in her aesthetic discourse the other day she hinted so austerely. I must end this 'frivolity' of my method. For as she says what I read the *Odyssey* for is its simple primordial interest applying to all time & all human beings everywhere. Took the Old to the Wood Bridge & on to the Dead Ash Tree. I have now at last selected my Saviour tree – the tree of Rhea [...].

MONDAY 22 JULY The T.T. was very upset by my Chapter V because she felt that I had fallen into a Cynical vein over the relations between Man & Woman [...] taking a low & harsh view – not tragic – but dealing with silly little bickerings. 'Is this' she said 'the result of our 15 years life together?' The mistake she made was not taking into enough account the maniacal convolutions of my reserves! As I left out my mother from my *Autobiography* so in dealing with Noman & his girl I dodged & avoided any introduction of the precious & indescribable pleasures of every sort that I myself have got from living with the T.T. Instead of this I just exploited, yes exploited! for my story many of the most superficial weaknesses of the feminine – of the 'eternal feminine' – in the T.T. as opposed to the philosophical & Sensual Selfishness of a man like myself & yet really not like myself! [...] In the morning after breakfast I made love to the T.T. à la Lulu in the Passage! And this pleased me; for this immorality christened, as it were, our dwelling!

TUESDAY 23 JULY The T.T. read to me – I adore it when she reads aloud my chapter – & I was amazed how well she did it –

the close or end of Chapter V – leaving them on the way to Maiden Castle at last! But then a very upsetting, foundation-shaking event occurred – namely the T.T.'s renewed Distress over the Wizzie part of my book & my hero's masculine reactions to little Wizzie's nervous outbreaks. [...] She got hold of the agitating notion that all my Socratic Self-Control & all my '*Aequam memento rebus arduis servare mentem*' protective-cement or self-evoked 'Stillicide' as I call it – wherein in self-righteous self-control the male soul tries to keep itself guarded from the up & down surging of the Feminine Ocean-tide like a Barnacle under the foam, gathering sea-grit & sea-sand and rubble to protect its interior softness & vulnerability like a Caddis-worm in its coat of stick-mail – [...] was a mean base & profoundly revengeful Hit-Back at the Feminine. She felt that in Wizzie's moods & in the relations between her & Dud-Dud I had betrayed this struggle & this detached self-righteousness that refuses to quarrel but conceals a deep grudge & brings it out in Books which is, she feels much worse than any personal & immediate anger or even a blow!

SUNDAY 1 SEPTEMBER After breakfast she told me the story of her Indian book by Mr Myers & read a little of it. It sounded very exciting. Then she did speak with great eloquence on the subject of my future writings – how – as in this Indian book, *The Flower & the Root*, I ought to bring in Reality in the more stirring & historic form of large national movements, both political & religious – & no longer be content with vaporous summer-lightning but by getting historic reality have some real thunder & some dominant subject – like in Shakespeare. All this I found very inspiring & I pray to be able to do exactly as she said. [...] I returned to revising Chapter VI which is my final chapter with poor old Dud-Dud as the chief mouth-piece. After this with a daring plunge I am going to strain it all – à la Henry James – thro' the personality of poor little Wizzie.

SATURDAY 7 SEPTEMBER I found a Blue Bead – a blue bead from the stones of the Dee. This I gave to my Elemental. [...] The T.T. hopes I didn't snatch it from the Nymphs but it is from my point of view a Gift from the Sacred Dee Itself. I am sure I don't know about the Nymphs – I used to give objects to my thought-born cerebral-born Eros-born daughter 'Glank', in that Missouri river, but there is no 'Glank' in the Dee!

1935 *Phyllis goes to London 7-12 September. John decides to learn Welsh. In October the house next to them becomes vacant and Phyllis rents it for her mother.*

THURSDAY 12 SEPTEMBER Up at 7.20 (late) – but lay for a while with that queer relaxed sensation in my leg-joints that I first felt with satisfaction in the Aunts' house in the 'Close' in Norwich, when, with my 'Mrs Powys' & my son, I was staying there & with unpardonable rebellion at heart was relucting at domestic life & writing the 'Death of God' & wandering with unsatisfied erotic desire about the Norwich Castle Grounds. [...] O how I tapped head to think of the T. T. coming back. O bring her safe back Great Little Kwang! [...] One thing alone is a little worry to me; & that is that I would O so much like the T.T. to help me with my Enema before we have our heavenly tea & before I go my little walk with Old – so that I shall have that nervousness free away & off my Mind & so I can enjoy her with a free & liberated spirit. But on the other hand I can't bear her to think 'He only thinks of his, or of the Old's Physical Necessities!' – as when she came back from Carnarvon I must needs have a bath & the other time when we came from Carnarvon I clamoured for my Enema at once! Oh but if she being back & if listening to her weren't such a Paradisal Pleasure to me I would not be so impatient to get such nervous, Physical Necessities out of the way! No one but one who depends on Enemas, like 'Petrushka' do know what funny cravings & so on, the mind do have! [...] Mr Thomas the Station Man came with Huge Parcels from London sent by the T.T. He talked about Llywarch Hên. Think of an English labourer talking about Beowulf!!!

FRIDAY 13 SEPTEMBER The T.T. got back safe. [...] She saw [the ballet] *Petrushka* who was she said exactly like myself! Not for nothing then has she selected that name for me. She went to tea with Dorothy Richardson & Mr. Odle who were very nice to her & she went with Gamel & Gerald to tea with Arthur Waley, the Sinologist, or authority on China. Aye how she told me of the Argot so sophisticated & airy of this Bloomsbury Group. [...] She bought a wonderful lot of Welsh Books including a Dictionary & two Grammars & a New Testament in both tongues.

FRIDAY 4 OCTOBER Got the *Times* & the *Daily Herald* at the Station. Saw on the outside page that the Invasion of Abyssinia had begun. Where is the great god Poseidon & the greater god Zeus both of whom were always going off to accept the homage of the 'Blameless Ethiopians'. News of the bombing of Adowa from the air & the killing of 1,700 [...]. When I told this in the kitchen to the T.T. her first feeling was furious anger against the Italians. She wept bitterly & raised her fists in a curse against the Italians. But a minute afterwards she regretted this & declared that if reading these things made her feel such anger she wouldn't read them any more. I consequently & selfishly & indeed scandalously hid the newspapers till we had had our tea & coffee. [...] I have written to Prague about the translation of my book – to Prague! fancy that!

WEDNESDAY 9 OCTOBER Tonight I hope to read Chapter VII to her. Will she hate it as much as the rest? [...] Have read Chapter VII – but it's no good. She really does condemn this whole book as unreal.

SUNDAY 13TH OCTOBER O what sad pessimistic thoughts she did have a few days ago at night as she stayed up thinking by the Cold Cinders. [...] I do not argue with her when she falls into this mood but all I did say was that she is physically handicapped by her childish frailty & little-girl fixation. Some EROTIC Nerve or Gland is very very sub-normal in her. But she says the effort of a house has killed her 'Inner Life'. [...] The T.T. said she wished we were both literary people with a charming 'affair', but not doomed to this work-house life of a 'House'.

FRIDAY 18 OCTOBER I had nothing but Letters to write. This is my second day of letter-writing. [...] If Lamb said his Works were in Ledgers of the Cotton Market – my Works are in the waste-paper baskets & old bureaus of my epistolary correspondents! I must be – unwilling – the greatest in quantity – of all letter-writers!

TUESDAY 22 OCTOBER Up at 5.40 [...] I saw the dying Moon, very very thin & the Evening Star – & the whole mysterious colour-process of the dawn from muddy rose to translucent watery gold & then it clouded for the day. There is no wind. But as I was looking at the Dawn in its muddy-rose phase with the glittering crescent in a blue-black sky I heard that familiar sound of a horse eating! And I saw its head just exactly the other side of hedge & opposite our door. How that sound could be made a primitive & elemental Symbol in an Orion-like Poem – of the earth waiting in hushed expectation and the earth-horse munching! […] We had a happy breakfast. But directly after that the Blow fell – ah! the blow fell – for we received the Income-Tax assessment which comes to 109 Pounds. This is a terrible blow & it brings many troubled thoughts. What shall we do & where shall we go? Shall we live in Spain? Shall we go back to America & live in New Mexico? […] I shall need (& am needing) all the best Philosophy I have to cope with this blow; & the T.T. feels pretty desperate & sits by the fire uttering profoundly rebellious & profoundly bitter & sad remarks.

THURSDAY 24 OCTOBER I started all the breakfast save her coffee & fried egg. But I tried hard when she came down to learn how to do these things too – so that at a pinch I could get her breakfast! I can see my grand difficulty would be to get the fried egg out of its pan and on to a plate!

FRIDAY 25 OCTOBER I met that corpse-like old man who couldn't sleep owing to his wife's death […]. He is without exception the least washed & the dirtiest old man I've ever seen – this is due doubtless to his wife's death – but tho' I am not very fastidious in that way & not one for many baths myself – I must say it was an effort to forget the look of this old man. […] Finished my article for *Daily Mail* on 'What I expect from Life' but it's probably quite unsuitable – well! I shan't change it or add anything but they can cut it as much as they like to. […] At tea the T.T. eloquently scolded me & very gravely for not restraining my manias about Tea. The T.T. said I didn't enjoy tea mutually but only privately with my own manias like a solitary wolf. Well, I must see what can be done.

SUNDAY 27 OCTOBER We had a very jumpy time before breakfast but a very very happy breakfast & a lovely talk afterwards about the Welsh character and about the astonishing way more 'a-moral,' helpless, weak, feeble, semi-imbecile persons can survive & defy the Darwinian 'Survival of the Fittest' here in Wales than is possible in England. Those old Dole-men on the bridge at Dorchester were formidable-proud diplomatists compared with the waifs who have pensions here; waifs, wraiths, and lathes of thin transparency these people are and you have to accept the situation & note a defeat of moral and intellectual Evolution and the permanence of the ill-constituted & unfit! The T.T. was so sweet to me at breakfast over my talking in civilized ways & not just thinking of my bread & butter & tea [...]. She was dressed beautifully tonight. She wore red stockings & her velvet.

SUNDAY 10 NOVEMBER Took Old to Yellow House on Cynwyd Road. Was thrilled by two things – first the extraordinary sweet smell of the rain-soaked hedges, ditches & dead leaves – like the very scent of Demeter's delicious bare flesh. Secondly the gaps spaces holes slits islands of open golden, silvery white, brown-red breaks in the heavy clouds to the West where the sunlight was so magically dying.

FRIDAY 15 NOVEMBER Watched a Welsh farmer arrange his sheep with a big dog & noted how Welsh farmers like to be dressed in a picturesque manner as indeed so do the very tramps here. All these Welsh go to & fro with a huge inner life-illusion of a dramatic appearance. [...] Worked pretty well at last on chapter VIII. I detect a faint tendency to excessive characterisation that goes beyond caricature into grotesque farce [...].

SUNDAY 17 NOVEMBER O what can I do for her. Everything with her seems to depend on outward conditions & her 'outward conditions' seem all wrong. She ought to be living the life of an Abnormal woman, not a normal woman – with some sort of Intellectual Work & everything practical done for her by normal women. She has the imagination of a poet-critic, of an artist, of a generalizer in Nuances – & what can be done to make her fate – as a normal house-keeping woman – endurable? [...] A SERVANT that is the only solution. As I have known for so long O for so long! [...] I was so saddened & shocked & disturbed. I overcame these feelings for it is silly to let her temperament murder my temperament and her 'unhappy' glands kill my 'happy' glands and her pessimism sap the fount of my moralizing & philosophy. So though I was too disturbed by her sad voice to remember to take a stick – think of that! I took my new gloves & did get pleasure from the rocks & stones & trees. I have to get something from these things – I have to! in order to feed my spirit.

TUESDAY 26 NOVEMBER At breakfast the T.T. asked me why it was that after Louis, Lulu & myself had been so stirred and rattled by Frances, that we could go on & relegate her so coolly to a place on the remote horizon. I said it was because the deepest instinct in all men is their secret Life Illusion of Themselves [...]. Frances attacked this inner self this deep inner self or life-illusion habitually; & thus all three of us have had to grow a sort of protective fibre round the wound she made. The strange thing is that while we have all changed, Frances has remained the same.

WEDNESDAY 4 DECEMBER I read all Chapter VIII to her. But with the same Result! She does not like this Book. It is wearisome & Pointless to her & all on the same note. To me it is not so at all! All my characters to me are very very very Real & each full of some particular response to & strife with the Cosmos, & the Cosmic Situation. To me this book is like the Second Part of *Faust* – one of my favourite Books – because of its struggle towards 'the Mothers' along so many different paths! [...] Mrs Peake came with Patty a fair-haired strong young girl with a resolute underlip.

THURSDAY 5 DECEMBER I got thro' my Morning Prayers which if you, Unknown, (whether Man or Woman) want to hear about I may as well by degrees let you know but it will have to take time & be continued. I begin by standing in front of the paper-stall on the west side of Weymouth Platform & buying for my Father the *Guardian* [...]. Then I go to Chesil Beach then to Portland then out to sea then to the St Alban's Head & the White Nore & so back by Lodmoor – to be continued.

FRIDAY 6 DECEMBER I pass those old Weymouth Houses beyond Penn House that I tell of in *Jobber Skald* – & then reach the Eastern Platform of the Station. Here I say 'Burdon Bus rumble back to the Burdon' & I say, 'Gloucester Bus rumble back to the Gloucester'. [...] Then I say 'My grandfather & grandmother & Aunt Dora, Etta, Kate, Annie, Gertrude, Uncle Cowper, "Rise to Immortality & Intense Happiness!"'

SATURDAY 7 DECEMBER To continue the history of my Daily Invocations – after Julia, the Aunts' servant, I move to Stalbridge & pray for the soul of old L.C.P. my other grandfather to rise to Immortality & Intense Happiness. Then for my Grandmamma at Penn House & for Uncle Littleton, dead in India. Then for my Father who I imagine always walking from Redcliff Bay & a rock-pool with little shells to Hardy's Monument & from there to Penn House & washing his hands in the bedroom looking at St John's Spire. [...] Took the Old to Post bought the Wrexham Paper for the T. T. & then went to the pebbles of the Dee where I tapped head & the Old drank. He now always stops at the Tree for me to pray. He knows exactly what is up!

MONDAY 9 DECEMBER The Doctor came yesterday and said the blackness on the top of her thumb was GANGRENE & that it was very lucky it had not gone up her arm. [...] To continue my daily Prayers or Invocations. I bring my Father into the Penn House drawing room & give him Tea there and I imagine his various thoughts & objects of contemplation as he eats & drinks but these would take too long to relate. I then give him the *Guardian* to read. [...] I make him drink tea looking at Portland.

THURSDAY 12 DECEMBER I [...] invoke the Four Elements & drink my orange juice and as libation a few drops to the earth & to the Chthonian Deities Below the Earth & then feed the birds. [...] We went on to the Gorsedd lane & thro' the cross farmer's field up the Rough Field to the Morgan Farm. Here I found Mr Morgan – a laconic individual who knows me – feeding his fowls. He said 'Plenty of it' to my enquiry about Butter Milk. 'She,' he observed, 'is in Cow Shed'. So I entered Cow Shed – & what a pretty sight met my eyes! There was my friend Mrs Morgan a young Intellectual like a Student with Spectacles & such a delicate intellectual face, on a four legged tiny milking stool milking their Black Cow. By its side in another cow-stall was a big black calf who licked at my milk-can. I waited enthralled by the spectacle – for it was a low-roofed warm dark place mellow & sweet smelling with great rafters above – aye! what a warm sweet snug place! When the pail was full – the girl gave it all to the Calf who put its head right into it & became a white-headed calf. [...] And then she went into the house with my Can and filled it with Butter-Milk.

SUNDAY 15 DECEMBER O how I long for a clear <u>4 hours a day</u> only 4 but I ought to have five to write my Book in! Of course by giving up the *Odyssey* & the Welsh *Testament* I could get 4; 4 for the most voluble & voluminous of writers. [...] Not a good walk for I was afraid I would keep her waiting & she was waiting even so, reading De Goncourts' *Journals* by the fire! Just as we were sitting down to breakfast I must needs try & put on a big lump of coal with the tongs O such a huge black Coal & lo! & behold this piece of coal was dropt by me out of the tongs – for she spoke of the storm today and her mother's crossing at that juncture & I have like President Wilson a one-track mind – I find it hard to cope with the League of Nations & with Communism at the same moment – out of the tongs, I say, into her saucepan of Coffee!!!! [...] I keep pondering on why it was that I failed to keep up the T.T.'s spirit! that dear spirit I depend on, of the little Elemental? Partly because of my Side being too much in evidence perhaps? But no! With a good topic I can toss that aside. [...] But perhaps it was purely that my vest showed under my sleeve. This was a thing that can be rectified but the ups & downs of exciting talk are harder to control. But what a poor Magician I am! It puts me to shame that I can't thrill a little Half-Born. Ailinon! Ailinon!

In Welsh myth, Bloddwyn (Blodewedd) is a girl the magician made out of flowers.

MONDAY 30 DECEMBER I talked to the T.T. while she had her tea & cigarette & I looked out of the window with delight. [...] I derived enchanting & ravishing pleasure from touching her – for during this cold weather until now she has been so bundled up like a little Xmas Parcel that I have not realized that she was the desirable little feminine Elemental that I made out of gorze-bloom & heather & anemones when I was Gwydion-ap-Don the Great Magician after I had practised on Bloddwyn.

1936

1936 is a year of acclimatization for John and Phyllis. Living in a small Welsh town involves a major adjustment. New York had been busy, crowded, anonymous. In rural Hillsdale, with its scattered population, they had made friends only gradually with a small number of people. When they move to Corwen they are plunged into village life and quickly forced into closer associations with neighbours than they had been accustomed to. The Diary suddenly teems with new characters: Ebenezer and his 'ooman' Hannah; Llew Williams the shopkeeper; Jones the signalman; Thomas the nationalist; the unfortunate Mrs Morgan and baby Fenna; Ellis Evans the chemist; Admiral and Mrs Cotton, owners of the Cae Coed cottages; Annie Davies from the almshouses; John 'Goch' the town crier.

For many years Wales has been for John an almost mythical land – the country of his remote ancestors, of his hero Owen Glendower, of the familiars of the Mabinogion. *Now he explores the 'real' landscape with 'real' people. Always a poet-bard in his own imagination, in May he is made an official Bard at the Corwen Eisteddfod – an event which fills him with joy and faint bewilderment. The style and content of the 1936 Diary suggest that, rather than 'centring' him, the move to Wales initially puts him off balance. However, by the end of the year he is beginning to move more easily between the interpenetrating real and mythical worlds of Wales.*

For Phyllis, Wales represents a safe remove from the Powys 'clannishness' although she wonders if, in the process, she has isolated him – metaphorically placed him on Glendower's hill fort of Dinas Brân. (His brother Bertie, who dies in March of this year, was convinced of this.) But Phyllis, too, has adjustments to make. She begins another new garden and sets about furnishing two houses. Her mother and aunt move next door. Phyllis's perception of her mother as an emotional support and a person who can deal, as she cannot, with everyday practicalities, is soon shattered. Although mother and aunt cook her the one good meal a day necessary for her health, Phyllis finds that they are otherwise totally dependent on her, emotionally and physically. She is as before but now with <u>three</u> *elderly people to cater for: John is sixty-five, her mother 'the Mistress' seventy, 'Aunt Harriet' seventy-four. They hire young Pattie Peake to help with the housework.*

John finishes Maiden Castle *in March. Simon & Schuster agree to publish it in America if many cuts are made. In England, after six publishers reject it, Cassell accepts it. In the meantime, he begins writing his anti-vivisection novel* Morwyn, *and simultaneously works on a book of essays on famous writers.*

WEDNESDAY 1 JANUARY Must get the DOG Licence!! I was very thankful that she didn't feel sick this morning for the champagne which she was so excited about & did so enjoy. [...] But it made the T.T. so numb & *hors de combat* afterwards that her mind wandered from my reading about Brân the Blessed & the Mistress had to rouse her & tell her it was Twelve o'clock. [...] I was so touched by the way a bare thin little arm of the T.T. was stretched out to touch my hand when she got into bed – just like a little girl dazed & overpowered by her first party. [...] Her excitement & then her prostration was so much more than twenty two years younger than I am. [...] She does so love Extras & it is such a struggle to her to be an ordinary grown-up person.

FRIDAY 10 JANUARY Aye! but what a terrific storm there was last night. [...] I brought this storm into my [*Maiden Castle*] chapter IX & made it occur during a crisis at Glymes! [...] Saw the Sun rise at the very exact top of the Bridge-Gorge so that it looked as if the waterfall came out of the Sun. It was an Elemental Sight! That burning furnace in the sky & water roaring down from its blaze over Rocks!

MONDAY 13 JANUARY In place of Lovers lying side by side we were like two chilly Hot Water Bottles! The poor little T.T. felt so cold that she edged against me till in the Morn we were hugged together on the edge – my edge – of the bed – & in the night I hugged her not from amorousness but from the misery in my Side. [...] All the land is White today with a Heavy Hoar Frost. [...] Dragged the Old to Town. Got my own cigarettes from Llew Williams & found him a standing bundle of congestion of the lungs. Phlegm bubbling up like soap bubbles in a Tube. [...] Took the Old to the Sycamore Tree by the Dee I call Rhea, the Saviour Tree – Grandmother of the Gods! I saw the Swan asleep – its long neck under its great Wings.

TUESDAY 14 JANUARY She Came to Bed with me! [...] 'Twas unlucky after this felicitous start to the night that [...] the T.T. found the Blanket – and 'twas our thick woolly Corwen Fair one – next her face! This is a Mania of hers to have the sheet neatly folded at the top of what she calls the Covers & I call the bed-clothes – & this caused the Devil's own disturbance in the bed of the 'Terminals'! She was awfully upset & detected by a certain queer 'hesitation' in my voice that I was too [...]. But very soon she was sweet & sorry & asleep like an infant. Girls can stand emotional upsets much more easily than men & they are much less serious to them. This is why Nature gives men more self-control – just because it's much more devastating to them & exhausting & upsetting to lose their self-control. I begged her in the morning [...] to explain exactly what this 'hesitation' in my voice is – that betrays the Storm Within! For it is strongly against my desire to thus betray myself! She says that we should accept ourselves & others just as we are. I take another view – the view that we ought to aim ourselves at becoming 'Superior' to such human lapses while we assume that others, all the others, have no free will in the matter at all. But of course, such self-control often leads to little sideways outbursts of indirect malice later in cold blood which she says is the vice of the English.

MONDAY 20 JANUARY Bad epochs of hurting in my side in the night. [...] A letter from A.R.P. says he is badly hit by his ulcers but is driven for business-sake to go on with his travels. He speaks sadly of old Littleton's queer fever going on so long – god! all four brothers are in a parlous way. Only old Theodore in good fettle.

King George V dies 21 January; Edward VIII becomes king. Their talk about making their own Selection *from the Diaries never came to fruition but the 'Dog Story' becomes his anti-vivisection novel,* Morwyn.

TUESDAY 28 JANUARY The *Telegraph* our newspaper has Black Lines & little in it but the King's Funeral. The T.T. feels [...] that only the English can organize such matters, not, not by mere feeling, like driven sheep, as the Americans – this is her word! – but by the combined weight of reserved characters & Personalities deliberately setting out to Organize Emotion – a thing impossible to all races save the English!

MONDAY 3 FEBRUARY Last night the T.T. talked of my Diaries, these very productions. And we decided that by far the Best Course would be to bring out a Selection from them our wone selves! while we still live. [...] Saw the Moon reflected in the Dee [...]. And how wondrous looked the Black Waters of the Divine River, as they reflected the blue sky with all the snow round them – these black waters assuming the Mystic blue of a magic Sword-blade.

TUESDAY 4 FEBRUARY The T.T. told me she'd been reading the Anti-Vivisection Paper & I told her that ere long I should write a Dog Story at the same time as my 'Pleasures of Reading'. She said bring the Devils in who enjoy it. The real devils of the Underworld. Make it imaginative like Dante's Inferno.

THURSDAY 6 FEBRUARY The T.T. had a BATH last night & came to bed like Aphrodite 'fresh-bathed in Paphian Wells' & was 'enjoyed' by her Satyr with enchanting delight! Not only so but she [was] especially sweet all the night & so docile in allowing me to swing her round so as to get her small figure exactly in the position I like. [...] The T.T. wants me to make my 'Art of Reading' or 'Read to Live' succinct & terse & clear & systematic – with some psychological arranged condensed System that shall please its academic readers!

MONDAY 17 FEBRUARY A Battle Royal going on between Sun & Mist. The sun & the mist [...] wrestling with each other, losing, winning, losing, winning over the Berwyns. [...] So fused with the Spring is the T.T. these days, of the thawing of the frozen ground, & this sun & mist battle, that I feel as if to embrace her with the faintest caress is to gather into my being the very essence of the Spring. [...] How a girl does feel the weather & express it!

SATURDAY 29 FEBRUARY At breakfast which was a particularly happy one the T.T. spoke of a revelation as to the secret of pain in the world & the meaning of pain & how to think of pain. It had to do with something parallel to the Normality of Sadism & Masochism – but she forgot the crucial point in her revelation.

WEDNESDAY 4 MARCH O how hard I find all beginnings! Ends are easy things. Ends write themselves! But Beginnings are the Devil! And I now am confronted with no less than Three 'Beginnings'! My Anti-Vivisection Story, my Article on Wales & my book on Reading to be called 'Read to Live'. [...] I am read[ing] that Russian Theologian Berdyaev with great interest. I agree with most of what he says.

1936 *John hurriedly travels to Hindhead, Surrey in response to a letter from Faith, A.R.P.'s wife, saying that he is very ill. Bertie dies from complications arising from a perforated ulcer. All the Powys brothers, with the exception of Theodore, developed duodenal ulcers.*

TUESDAY 10 MARCH Off to Hindhead via London. Faith's letter decided me. I feel it is 'the thing' to 'do'! It's a bit of an effort for an aged egoistical Recluse but there it is! Bertie got into his old head the erroneous idea that I wanted to isolate myself from all the family! So this will show the old Bugger if he is conscious! I do pray he is; but Faith's letter was certainly disturbing. […] Well I […] reached Paddington via Birmingham & Wolverhampton & Wellington (Salop) & Leamington & Banbury. […] Drove thro' the Parks to Waterloo. […] To my surprise I found that Hindhead in Surrey had no station. So I took a Return Ticket (a too confident thing to do in a world so tricky & shaky & in times like this) & got out about Seven in the dark at Haslemere. […] I asked for taxi & he drove me out to Stoneycrest Hindhead. […] I asked for Mrs A.R.P. & said I would keep my taxi for a bit. Then the boss of the Home came (a lady with a marked resemblance to George 1st & George II) & said I must stay the night as 'they' were going to leave the place at 4.30 a.m. tomorrow morning! I could not see what this meant. Then Faith came and said 'Bertie went last night' & I saw then that he was Dead. […] I kissed his forehead & prayed my usual prayer 'Rise to Immortality & Intense Happiness'! as against the Church's less optimistic & probably more justified, 'Give unto him Eternal Peace.' But I was absolutely shocked by the change in Bertie; he was not the same person. This husk I saw seemed to have no connection with the Bertie I knew. […] Lay long at night thinking of that form lying there on the same landing.

WEDNESDAY 11 MARCH Up at 4 a.m. down at 4.30 breakfast at 4.45 & then we left for the most strange unreal drive I have ever had in my whole life. Bertie's coffin […] went in front. So that all the way I could see it and the sign on the back of the car 'G.N. 5388' and a light burnt. Very very slow was the dawn to begin! But by six it was beginning. But the roadside trees looked so curious – many were Birches, many oaks – & very slowly the dawn came. […] We drove on & on & on with Bertie's Coffin always going ahead till we came down from a hill upon

Winchester. We saw the whole of Winchester grouped round that massive Cathedral. [...] Took Bertie to [Winterborne Thomson] church & left him there.

MONDAY 23 MARCH Woke up to see Rain-Drops on the Pane. How I love rain-drops on a window. Did the rain fall tonight on Bertie's grave? Looked out past the chestnut coloured hair of the T.T. upon rooks slowly walking in the field. How awkwardly Rooks walk on their two thin legs! And then suddenly the T.T. began to talk of the Mystery of her Nostalgia & her curious HATRED of England when we first got to Dorset. [...] She had expected that some old atavistic feeling of her English ancestors would make her love it but instead of this her atavistic feeling made her hate it as if her ancestors had shaken the dust of it off their shoes when they went to America. The twisted old trees seemed to her not able to expand & all the people seemed malicious & the very sea-waves seemed like the soft tongues of savage tigers! It was all so different the second she came to Wales. [...] But all is well now tho' she has sometimes the feeling that she has put me on the top of Dinas Brân. But I do reassure her – though she doesn't know – & never will – whether I am speaking the truth in my reassuring words.

SUNDAY 5 APRIL Met a Poacher with a lurcher very gaunt & slim [...]. The man was not pleased at my cheerful Good Morning. He had hoped all the World was safe asleep in bed & he might get a rabbit for Sunday Dinner. What a wicked shame it is that all the shooting & fishing should be in the hands of people who do not need what they kill for Food! [...] I keep thinking of the very sad & tragic letter I got from Frances – when she wrote about Bertie's death. I did reply as tenderly as I could. The most interesting object in the Rough Field is the Stump or Post or Trunk upright of an ancient very dead large Mountain Ash with new leaves out of its death.

WEDNESDAY 8 APRIL The T.T. burst out suddenly into one of those PROTESTS which the arrogant & Devouring Clannishness & Anti-Social Savagery of Solidarity & to Hell with all who are not Powyses so underlying my Family & inherited directly from my Father now & then rouses in our 'Dear Companions'! But the T.T. was in fine feather & good heart today. She came running downstairs with her hair flying loose to see what the 'Mail' had to say! You can, O my Good Unknown, realize the extremely laconic growl with which 'the Man' replied to this spontaneous interest of a young American in 'the Mail', from 'Some Place Else', on the verge of his setting out over the exact diurnal stepping stones, & grassy hillocks, & running rivulets, of his USUAL WALK!

SUNDAY 12 APRIL And it is now Snowing. The T.T. woke up thinking how I used in old days after lighting Fires to wake her with a story of Some Disaster or other in the House. And that now Pattie wakes us with tales not of Disaster but of Wonder. […] The T.T. decided it was far too cold for the Mistress to go to church at Rûg […] but the T.T. felt she had to go herself. […] I had a moral Struggle as to whether I would go too so as not for the T.T. to be alone & decided with an effort – for I don't like Rûg Services – that I would do it. So I kept on my boots & was all prepared. But the T.T. wouldn't have it! She recalled that Easter Service at St Luke's, Hudson St, in New York that caused me to fall flat on the Pavement in my fury at an unworthy Sermon. Her final argument that stopped me was that I ought to wear good trowsers & not my Great Boots. […] I feel a little ashamed to have thus deserted her & especially so since last night she came, to give me a Special Pleasure for Easter Eve, to bed with me – & did undress by my fire in this room – a situation of which – being so infatuated of her as I be – I took the most intense & paradisic advantage making love to her after my fashion (not Lulu's). […] The *Observer* says there are 2 million cars & 7 million cyclists on the roads this Easter. The Mistress is astounded – 'in this little Island!'

THURSDAY 16 APRIL I may […] have to go to see Pollinger our Literary Agent but at present Lane's Lawyer is reading *Maiden Castle* […]. I don't think it is Libel they are scared of this time but what is technically known as 'Obscene Libel' – Libel against Decency & Law & Order! And the trying thing is that our Schuster's new editor Mr Quincy Howe – with Bostonian Economy – is all for not printing my book till they can photograph it from the English Edition. This would be a terrible delay – of the gravest seriousness to our livelihood. So we have just now good reason to Worry about Money & I know the T.T. does worry about this dread matter. Perhaps it would be safer for us if I did too – a bit more than I naturally seem to do! […] And the T.T. is terribly upset too about the chicken wire put up by the Admiral opposite our house. And in addition to this when [...] I spoke of it being – & wrong I was to do so – being the Day for my enema that was the last straw & the T.T. became badly & violently upset – hysterical in fact – & frightened me as much as a Stone like me or a Post of Old Wood can be disturbed & frightened. But I always get wild notions into my brain & imagine her rushing down to the Dee to drown herself. [...] Oh that I could only give these things to myself! What a helpless idiot I am.

SUNDAY 19 APRIL The T.T. [...] spoke of authors & publishers, on the subject of Hanley's letter from Macmillan wanting him, <u>ordering</u> him, to cut out the Murder, which <u>he</u> thought (in the simplicity of an author) to be the subject of his book [*The Maelstrom*] & also of his next book which is about the Trial. But Macmillan says that if he gets <u>Mr</u> <u>Hicks</u> (of their staff) to help him write Novels, they will be able to 'put him over' [...]! The T.T. & I did however decide that if <u>Publishers</u> are arrogant & meddling; <u>authors</u> <u>want</u> <u>all</u>! – want to write <u>as</u> <u>they</u> <u>like</u> & yet want to sell very very widely. Want Glory & <u>wide</u> <u>fame</u>; & <u>yet</u> want to be true to their Muse.

WEDNESDAY 29 APRIL Pondered long & long on Frances & her proud unhappiness. Will my letter comfort her again? It is without scruple in its Praise. But that is what we all want & what we generally Need most of all! Not advice, <u>not</u> advice! But first Money & then Praise. <u>And</u> <u>why</u> <u>not</u>? How old <u>A.R.P.</u> used to try us by his Honesty! & how rarely Theodore praises except when he is scared! Life is so hard for all. I think you cannot praise too highly <u>any</u> <u>one</u>!

Katie arrives for a twelve-day visit. On 16 May John is installed as a Bard at the Corwen Eisteddfod.

SATURDAY 9 MAY Katie read her story to the T.T. until 10.30 & at 10.45 I went to bed & they went for a walk with the Old. Then they read Katie's story again till Twelve. Then Katie went to bed [...]. Then the T.T. found the Mistress – who had been in bed all day & had <u>no</u> <u>Butter</u> for her tea & <u>couldn't</u> <u>come</u> <u>for</u> <u>it</u> & she felt <u>Neglected</u> because of Katie taking up the time of the T.T. and she thought of her Death. [...] She said their time alone was at an end because of Aunt Harriet. Thus when the T.T. went over at Twelve after all the Beer with Katie she had to force herself to drink Malted Milk with the Mistress and she stayed there talking till Two. Then she had to wash up & she was not in bed until Three. [...] I got the TICKLES that terrible affliction I tend to get like the TWITCHES. It comes, both of these inflictions, from bad blood circulation & low blood pressure but it feels, the 'tickles', as if I were the victim of Lice!

SUNDAY 10 MAY The T.T. thinks of taking Katie to Llangollen [...]. They will climb Dinas Brân. This will thrill Katie. [...] [The T.T.] doubted if Katie & the Mistress were very harmonious. Of course Katie's passionate hero-worship for the T.T. must gratify the Mistress but I daresay the T.T. is right that there is some sort of horoscopic or national or psychic clash of temperament, hard to quell, between these two devotees of hers!

WEDNESDAY 13 MAY Her first words (I always regard her first words as an Oracle) were about my not going to have my hair cut before the *Gorsedd* Day for I have such a Bardic Look! Then she spoke of the excited & secretive way our Mr Thomas (the Nationalist) looked over the hedge & said 'The Inner Circle for Mr Powys because of his Interest in it!' Then she teased me, in the manner that does so please me, about 'Petrushka' being brought in to make his bow! [...] By great ill-luck the *Gorsedd* Eisteddfod Proclamation on the 16th Coincides with our dear Mistress's Birthday – a day which is more important to her than any other day. She has a queer childlike intense cult of this day such as no one else, as far as I know, has ever had for their birthday – not even Lulu for Aug. 13th!! [...] I went under Mr Thomas's instructions to call on Gwenllian Williams. Her I found at No. 6 – in that row opposite the station. She told me I was to be admitted into the Inner Circle & not only so but – as Dante says – 'much more honour was paid you even that I was made the Sixth' [of Paradise] of those to be Numbered among the Members of the Powys *Gorsedd*.

SATURDAY 16 MAY The dear Mistress is bravely trying, in these new surroundings, & on this very crowded day & with our dear Katie here too & the Man (being as we are) to keep up her old Birthday Cult. [...] She came over to breakfast. The T.T. [...] managed to get all done & the Presents by the side of the

Mistress. As I sat by the fire waiting to toast the bread I began philosophizing in a vague manner & began – 'The Early Christians — ' when the T.T. did say, 'If you have the heart & spirit to think of the Early Christians at such a moment, I have not!' But the T.T. recovered after her coffee & indeed she got through getting that meal & keeping up her Mother's Ritual with us two weird Cuckoos in the Nest, wondrous well. [...] Now we shall have to think soon of when we must start for the *Gorsedd*. I think I shall put on my Sunday Tweed Suit to go with my Ten-pound Burberry over-coat which I always feel is a bit too gentlemanly for me to feel quite natural in – but at the same time I feel grand & important in it, & ready to face the world – which is a good thing – but it is not exactly a life-illusion over-coat to me. But I was touched at the T.T. choosing it when she so seldom spends ten pounds on her own attire! [...] The *Gorsedd-Cadair* Powys was an extraordinarily thrilling event in our life. Katie heard the band play her favourite Men of Harlech as it came up the Hill. And the Cornet turning to East & West & North & South was most satisfying & the Horn of Plenty brought Ceridwen's Cauldron to my mind. But the chief thing was the Arch-Druid who is one of the best living Bards. Ioan is my name! Ioan Powys.

MONDAY 18 MAY Went up to the Morgan House [...]. Katie & I were both awed & deeply impressed by the way Mrs Morgan very solemnly shook me by the hand & congratulated me. And did mention my new *Gorsedd* name 'Ioan' – 'Yo-arn'! It was as if some Secret Glory had been obtained for us, like one who has blundered into a magic circle of fairies, & has by chance rescued the Queen's child by uttering, without knowing, some occult word! It was very weird, exciting, & a little awe-inspiring.

The Adsain *is the local Welsh paper. 'Aunt Harriet' arrives on 25 May to live with her sister, 'The Mistress', at 8 Cae Coed. John teasingly calls them 'the Ladies of Llangollen'. Richard Heron Ward wrote a biography,* The Powys Brothers, *in 1935. Sir Watkin Wynn of Rûg and Wynnstay owns huge tracts of land in Wales.*

TUESDAY 19 MAY I set out with the Old to the Post & up Pen y Pigyn – & round Rough Field. I was Shocked; for like Mr Phelips [of Montacute], Rûg has sold the noble trees of Pen y Pigyn Wood to a Timber-merchant & they are cutting them down – all the big trees.

THURSDAY 21 MAY Met that astonishing old Mole-Catcher his pockets full of dead moles which he showed me. He said – to my extreme surprise – that Moles did have eyes – [...] & certainly with one dead one he showed me carefully scraping its fur aside what to me looked rather like an eye. But the Mole-man himself had very bad eyesight & I had no spectacles. So there were 3 personalities, 2 alive and one dead, arguing about eyes with some dubiety. [...] I have composed a Sonnet called Yng Nghoed Pen y Pigyn on the subject of their murdering the great oak-trees there. I could hear them crashing down. [...] Pattie will take my 'pome' to the offices of the *Adsain.*

FRIDAY 22 MAY On awakening the T.T. – my little Oracle – fell into deep Thought – no word did she utter. [...] Then at last I pressed her, 'What are you thinking about?' & her reply was brief & conclusive. 'Money!' she said, 'I'm thinking about Money!' [...] And now there has arrived a Splendid Letter [...] from Mr Quincy Howe – Schuster's new Editor – saying that they will go ahead with *Maiden Castle* if I make a lot of small cuts. These he has worked out with infinite care & meticulous labour so as to improve, & not meddle with the general trend of the book. Just a few of old Dud-Dud's Ruminations. I do not mind this at all.

THURSDAY 28 MAY A lovely letter from Old Littleton. They will not be able to visit us this summer he says. He says Heron Ward is in Winchester Gaol in Prison. I must write to Mrs Heron Ward condoling with him. Whether it was just homosexuality or sadism I don't know. Oh dear! it is so risky to betray your perversities with young persons for they are so inclined to lead a person on & then betray them or blackmail them. Heron Ward is a genius & a funny one. I hope he has not to be in prison long. [...] Worked at this damned Revising of that man's cuts of my book – 'cutting the cuts' – but leaving many of them – O deary I! But some of them I confess do deserve to be cut – but others O ailinon! ailinon! I hate killing them off; but there is still the English Version – if only old Pollinger gets some daring Publisher in London to take the book! They cut for length in America but for libel and morals over here.

WEDNESDAY 3 JUNE When the T.T. woke up she was only silent from the teasing worry of her eyes [...]. But after a while she was seized with an Inspiration [. . .] & after an unlucky interval – when I foolishly tried to relieve her of her tray – which she said I did as if I were docking the Queen Mary yes the Queen Mary – she began after some coaxing on my part to talk of it. I stood at the foot of the bed & I shall ever recall the look of the Beech-branches & emerald leaves against the grey rainy valley & the look of her face with eyes rather swollen & blurred & her expression rather like the portrait of her by Mr Adrian [Bury] over her head. And she said – The New Intellectuals – the new young Einsteins – will give the Mind a holiday, or a time in gaol, or let it go & play as it likes. And then they will use what hitherto has hardly been explored at all – our sources of Knowledge independent of the mind – not necessarily the ordinary senses, but the impressions derived about the senses from our continuous stream of sub-conscious life [. . .]. As always, when she told me to go, she said it was 'Silly'. But I know better! The thought came into her head from thinking how she & I knew each other so well that mental knowledge had come to an end. We began with mental knowledge – & then came a point when she used to cry unhappily – 'We don't know each other any more!' but now she realizes that that was because of the beginning of this deep knowledge – outside ordinary mental processes – which takes the place of the other. In the same way at first we generalized about Wales but the more we live here the less we know according to mental logic – but really according to an illogical knowledge – we are slowly knowing more.

TUESDAY 9 JUNE The T. T. woke up today full of spirit & with small head full of a trip of Gardeners to the Gardens of France. I would greatly like to be able to send her off on this trip! We must ask about its Cost. I could for once give myself a hand-enema. She does so need a holiday. Tried a new walk. [. . .] I met too many people I know! And had too many encounters. I could not say my prayers in peace. I shall not go that way again. [. . .] Some perfectly lovely wood-cuts of Gertrude's – sent us via Lucy with the *Nouvelle Revue Française* that contains some lovely love-affairs of young girls. French writers seem all Nympholepts, just as I am! The French language lends itself to the winnowed sensuality of sterile eroticism of my own kind. [. . .] All is white with Hawthorn & the blossom of Mountain Ash. I am getting on with my cutting of Mr Howe's cuts. I think he will be satisfied. And yet I have retained my favourite passages.

1936

FRIDAY 12 JUNE This day the T.T. found her House – the Ancient House of the Powys princes. [...] She & the two Ladies of Llangollen are going to be driven by 'the boy' (Mr Jones' son) to World's End – to a sale starting at one something – at World's End, Manor House. Well – they went off about 2.15 p.m. starting late. [...] Yes the T.T. has found the House of Princes of Powys going back beyond Rhodri the Great to Eliseg. She seriously thinks of our living there! [...] It belongs to Sir Watkin Wynn & the T.T. does really & truly want to live there. What will the upshot be?

TUESDAY 16 JUNE A letter from Wynnstay Office to say the Manor-House at World's End could not be let independent of the land. So that is a relief! as it takes away any feeling of tantalization – & makes it easier to settle down where we be!

WEDNESDAY 1 JULY I set out still leaving her asleep & dragged the Old on the leash for the Old does not like hills. [...] Then read letters. Faber refuses *Maiden Castle* but Pollinger is still in good heart. Then I did find the little T.T. in such a sweet mood wanting Petrushka's life to be happy. [...] And I did recall how it was when I first found her – & how grave she looked – & knew not what young girls did when they had a lover. But Nature did whisper in her ear – 'Lift up your chin, little girl!'

Phyllis does not get to the Gardens of France, but they go to Chaldon for their summer holiday, 6 July-8 August, staying at Rat's [Down] Barn. There is the usual visiting with brothers, sisters and friends. John meets his son on 29 July for a day in Winchester and brings back Bewick's Birds *as a present for Phyllis.*

WEDNESDAY 8 JULY How the stillness of the night came in & the sheep so hushed & the Moon just risen opposite & the Great Bear above & Jupiter over the sea. Her long braid hung down to her waist & she hugged her shawl round her & looked long & long into the darkness & the starlight & the moonlight. [...] I took the Old nearly to 'White Nose' & worshipped Chesil Beach & admired St Alban's Head and Portland & saw St John's Spire at Weymouth. But I was giddy & dizzy and very scared of those deadly cliffs. [...] This is the first time I have seen the sea for a year. I cannot recall going for a whole year ever before without seeing the sea! And I have not heard a lark for a whole year. The

Old came back unleashed & we had a happy breakfast. The T.T. had mushrooms. The only sad thing was I had made the fire too hot. [...] I was so shocked by [Lulu's] skeleton thinness like a picture of starving people in the war! He talks of going to Switzerland.

SUNDAY 12 JULY A dark greyness and damp wailing wind from Sea. [...] And the T.T. was overpowered by the rain – & the darkness of this Down Barn & its not having any view. And going in & out with water & coal all the while. [...] She has no time for reading or for quilting even if she had a book or a quilt. She hovers round our sole volume – *Bleak House* – like a moth round a candle. [...] Alyse visited the T.T. & then returned to Chydyok. Talked on French Literature to Alyse – she was pleased to have a 'literary' conversation.

THURSDAY 23 JULY Sad Sad Sad The T.T. is! Totally overcome by Down-Barn Life. I must never let this happen again. I must remember [...]. When we first came she was happy as before for a couple of days but the isolation – the difficulties, the distance, the wind & the rain. [...] How I link these miseries with this place & our first coming! She was like one beside herself. It is her old 'unhappiness' coming back at these times. [...] Last night what troubled was seeing too many people & not being free to go off to Weymouth by her wone self! I tell her to go & let happen what may happen, & let be said or thought what may be said or thought! But having once won such favour in her flexible personality she hates to display the non-human & lonely side of her character & its wild & haughty & sensitive solitariness. The wind & rain howling outside & a dark cloud of wet mist rolling in from the sea, sadly the T.T. read Mrs Gaskell to herself. After a few hours passed in this cloudy storm of wet-rain-mist – the T.T. found herself equal to hear *Bleak House* & I read it all the morning & afternoon to her great soothing but it has been a very trying day.

FRIDAY 31 JULY I brought the T.T. Bewick's *Birds* as a present. The T.T. was thrilled at the idea of having a Bewick of which I've told her so much & explained ever since we met how deep a role from early childhood this book with its unequalled Vignettes has played in my Culture. It has all England's true country life & 'country matters' in its brutal, grim, ghastly, terrible, exquisite, sad, cheerful, lovely, fairy-like, solemn, traditional, humorous & with such a sense of the mystery of half-seen, half-felt, passed-by things of no importance as you go about the country. Stumps, logs, grasses, plant off-shoots, twigs, tussocks, pools, rock-pools, old walls, old posts, old desolated gates, old gibbets, cruelties to dogs and the same by dogs to others – graves, graves, Graves! I must now turn from Bewick to a still more important aspect of my 'Culture' namely the Worship of Eros. Never never never have I got such thrilling 'wicked' pleasure from any feminine form as I got from making love – or as A.R.P. used to say – 'making lust' to my little T.T.

WEDNESDAY 5 AUGUST Went to Lulu's & had to defend Old from their mother-cat. Read to him his article for St Bartholomew & for Bank Holiday the latter taken by *Daily Herald* the former rejected because his editor was on holiday. Read Cranmer-Byng's wonderful Preface to a great Chinese Materiant & Sens-ist – incorporated by the Taoists & mentioned by our Kwang – praise be his for evermore! Theodore Lulu & I are all Devotees of the Chinese Philosophers. They suit our family exactly.

SATURDAY 8 AUGUST I must tell you that both Collins and Chatto & Windus have rejected *Maiden Castle*. 5 publishers in all have rejected it now. What the devil is wrong with it?

TUESDAY 11 AUGUST A comfortable letter from Pollinger attributing the rejection of *Maiden Castle* to its 'length' & to the worn & dirty type-script which in vain he keeps patching up & re-covering. [...] Began my real Work again after this long vacation! I wrote on at my 2nd chapter – page 170 of my Anti-Vivisection Book.

WEDNESDAY 12 AUGUST I went as far as the Dead Ash of the Alwen. There were two great wagons full of hay in the field by the Dee that ends with the stile by the Saviour Sycamore which I worship as Rhea – 'Daughter of Ouranos & Gaia, Sister & Bride of Chronos!' I say 'Rhea! Rhea! take into your Divine Substance the worries of the Abject & Aunt Harriet & the Dear Mistress & of Lulu & Alyse & of Marian & Peter!!' Then I, as usual, did greet Blodewedd & tell her at Llangar Old Church that I am a more formidable Magician than Gwydion ap Dôn & that I could turn her back from an Owl into whatever form she pleased! Blodewedd! Blodewedd! I call over the river.

THURSDAY 13 AUGUST Last night I fancy that the T.T. must have had a bath for when I kissed her between her shoulder-blades [...] I was aware of this exquisite clean smell of soap! I confess I do like my little companion lying between me & the window to smell of Soap! Unable to resist this after-Bath freshness combined with my favourite silk night-gown I hesitated not to make love to the slender little Being in my own satyrish fashion with indescribable satisfaction to myself & (I do think) nothing of revulsion in the small object of my dalliance who lay like a little statue with her arms crossed. [...] We had a happy reading of the *Telegraph* though with bad news of this damned General Franco having got a lot of German & Italian war-planes at his headquarters in Seville. Oh we do so pray the Government will defeat these confounded rebels. But 'tis trained soldiers against the un-trained populace.

His nephew, Francis Powys (Theodore's son), and his wife Sally (for whom John has a variety of nicknames) visit 15-23 August.

FRIDAY 21 AUGUST Woke at 7.30 a.m. & lay awake not able to sleep & in a queer State of Mind. Not able to sleep again owing to a queer & curious brain-spot of unknown disturbance & yet aware of a little grit-like speck of deep extreme tiredness somehow in the very heart of the brain-spot of unknown worry! [...] At last I heard Pattie arrive – this was 8.15 – & I at once got up & was down at 8.30. I fed the birds & forced myself to walk up & down the Cinder-path by the T.T.'s beautiful flower-bed! I say forced myself because I dread so much being seen by our neighbours & it is impossible to avoid this when I go as far as the end of the cinder-path. But by fixing my eyes on the Flowers [...] I can fight against my dread of being peeped or peered at.

SATURDAY 22 AUGUST A Fine Day for the Powys Eisteddfod! [...] I called the T.T. & also Francis & 'Me' & then took the Old up the Lane to the Rough Field Gate. The Mist white & dense filled the valley between Rûg & the flag-staff of Pen y Pigyn! It looked a Marvellous Sight. Slowly in a god-like manner it moved from West to East as if it were a living part of the *Gorsedd* Ritual. We all had tea & bread & butter in the T.T.'s

1936 room downstairs. And then I set out with Niece 'Minnie-Me' to the Square; both of us in our Sunday clothes. Here we met the Clergyman [...] & he took us into the tiring room of the Central Hotel. [...] I talked to the harpist, a lovely little lady from Snowdon who had with her husband a farm on the mountain-side & keeps the harp warm in the straw of a Cattle Shed. Then my Niece & I helped to dress the Druid. I was more impressed than ever before by this Druid whose bardic name is 'Rhosier' but his real name Roger Hughes. His Dignity & aplomb & sacrosanct reserved manner is like that of a Grand Lama of Tibet. He is Perfect. I am a connoisseur in such matters & this man is incomparable at his office. Then we marched my niece and I behind the Welsh Dragon & behind the Horn of Plenty which we both furtively touched for Luck. It is the heathen Grail in a different form from the Cauldron.

WEDNESDAY 2 SEPTEMBER Stocks are a wonder – they look the heavy voluptuous Scent with which they are so sumptuously charged. No other flower except purple violets or roses looks so Sweet. Then as I set out I saw our Handsome Neighbour Mrs Gregory who is so averse to demonstration. I took off my hat, like a courtier, but she sweetly, kindly & gravely contemplated this man who was bowing in the Lane! Then there suddenly appeared, following me up the lane, the great Midland Lorry. I at once in my muddled way thought it must be my friend Mr Thomas of the G.W.R. So I shook hands vigorously with a young man crying out 'How are you my friend?' Then another unknown young man emerged and to him also – seeing him next as Mr Thomas – I extended my hand and cried 'How are you my dear friend?' They were bringing coal for the Mistress & in the end when I had calmed down I gave the elder one One Shilling & shogged off. [...] Went thro' the Morgan yard and down thro' Little Rough Field to the Small Reservoir. Here I encountered [...] that very handsome & very formidable man who looks I am sure much younger than he is & who has such green eyes. To him – just because he is a Strong Character & I am a weak character I must needs as is my inveterate way confide the most pressing worry of the moment of a decent respectable kind! and so I broached the problem of how to get a Welsh *Mabinogion* that Foyles say does not exist save the *Red Book of Hergest* at Four Guineas. He gave me the address of a Calvinist Methodist Minister at Bethesda. [...] I came home via the

Council Houses & that gate – our new discovery – but the sound of noisy children in those back gardens frightened me as much as the Old. Then I saw Mr Formaston far off & most indiscretely & impulsively SHOUTED to him how the 3 ladies enjoyed their ride – thus revealing an open secret. Then I met Miss Durrant & her rich bloom swallowed up my nervousness and tenseness as if I had poured it out upon a bed of roses.

THURSDAY 3 SEPTEMBER Woke late – at 8.15 – heard voices escorting Pattie to our door as if of her whole Family! [...] Had such a happy breakfast with the T.T. Oh! & I must tell you a great secret. I found in her room a piece of MS just composed by her – her old-conceived story of 'Miss Pastime' – will she go on with it? [...] Last night she looked so especially lovely & animated as she came here to me about 10 or 9.30 all primed & so radiantly amused to get a rise as they say out of the crusty old gentleman by showing him *TIME* that incorrigible & scandalous American Summary of What must not be Said! What a profound instinct each separate Entity – especially among two Lovers – has to risk & dare & stir up & see What Will Happen. And so she came with *Time* with all its Raw Exposures, like a beautiful butterfly carrying a scrap of a newspaper out of the Vaudeville of the World – and pushing it between the paws of The Great Bear & upon it he turns his little deep-sunk greenish eye anxious not to twitch his nostrils & yet anxious to suggest the Gullibility of this Newspaper brought by beautiful Swallow-Tail.

SATURDAY 5 SEPTEMBER I took the Old on Leash clear up the Mountain. It was incredibly lovely! Blue sky – wind blowing – diffused rainbows – the white clouds visible thro' a vapour of Irised light all flowing & fluctuating. [...] No sign of the mountains in the Arenig or Snowdon direction because of this iridescent Mist of fresh cloud-spray illumined by Sun. The whole sky was a rainbow wind-blown waterfall, interspersed with blue. Up there the Reservoir was dark blue – lapis-lazuli – & round it all tall wind-tost yellow Ragwort & masses of Rose-Bay! The grey rocks dotted with pale purple Ling which is now the flourishing heather & interspersed by a few plants of bell-heather & its brown dead bells. Those green ferns, so narrow, glittering with diamonds of dew & I heard two Grouse crying crossly 'Get away! Get away! Get away!' The hills towards Ruthin stood out beautiful. Rûg woods were black under a cloud in a sea of sunlit hills.

FRIDAY 11 SEPTEMBER We caught the train to Wrexham. Visited the Hughes printing place & bought another Welsh version of those Four Mabinogion stories [...]. Then we went to the VIVISECTION shop with its horrible 'ads' of shocking Cruelty and found the young man who came from Headquarters in London & Mr Parry & Miss Wordsworth and Mrs Owen. That was all & we all sat on a sort of low platform & felt sad & queer & as the T.T. says in some weird way under the aura of the cruelty, as if we were not the reform of the thing but the thing itself.

SATURDAY 12 SEPTEMBER Took Old to Reservoir but my mind was all upset by this atrocity of Vivisection [...] – feeling that I ought to go out on a speaking Crusade against it. I was also worried by this arrival of Helen Valentine to next door parallel with Gertrude's long expected visit here. And the T.T. has to cater for both houses tho' they do the cooking very largely for both. But Corwen shops are so bad that the T.T. will be kept on the jump all this fortnight [...]. Also after breakfast a letter from Ribbons & Winder, the Income Tax people saying that I owed the Government of Ynys Prydain [Britain] no less than £55 & that my income for last year was £900!!!!!! Think of that! It is incredible. Well there'll be a pretty little drop this year!

SUNDAY 13 SEPTEMBER The tiny little T.T. is Overpowered by the Difficulties of her life. Alone it would be hard for her Nature – even in a Convent it would be Hard for a *Grande Nerveuse* like her – but *à Deux* with a Man makes it harder – & now not only with a Man but with her Mother (always a puzzle to a younger feminine Creature!) & not only with her Mother but her Aunt & not only with these 3 persons but the 'Very Old' added & now my Sister, and Miss Valentine. [...] Then 'the Man' fooled about with his new shirt in that detached casual way calculated to madden a woman's realistic nature! [...] And the Mistress & Aunt Harriet came to breakfast – but I 'jollied them along' too grossly carelessly roughly & with too heavy a hand! – teasing them like a rough school-boy to make them giggle – that tho' they seemed to like it it was awful to the T.T. so much so that she retired to the Kitchen. [...] On coming to my room later the T.T. begged me to be different at these occasions & so I will. Then she spoke so eloquently of her difficulty to be herself in the moral cheerfulness of Ynys Prydain. She can be grim under tragedy but not cheerfully enduring of pin-pricks. Americans are quick-silver & they want, they want, they want, a mirage beyond the day's hours & work & sensations!

Gertrude arrives for a visit on 15 September but on the 23rd Llewelyn has another serious haemorrhage; she cuts her visit short and returns to Dorset. John goes to London 26-28 September to see his agent, Pollinger, and his new publishers, Cassell. 'La Belle Sauvage' (Pocahontas) was the Cassell device. He stays with Francis and Sally ('Minime'). 'The Perfect Child' is Theodore's adopted daughter.

WEDNESDAY 16 SEPTEMBER Had a very happy breakfast. Scurried through the paper. Could not read one word of the Welsh in the *Adsain*. Not one single word. How hard is Modern Welsh to me after the *New Testament* & the *Mabinogion*! Why is that? […] Gertrude seems very happy here for which I do thank Heaven! The T.T. is perfectly lovely to her. Worked at my Vivisection Tale which the T.T. thinks should be called *Morwyn* so as to mislead buyers of it. We'll see. Perhaps *Hell* is a little Crude.

THURSDAY 17 SEPTEMBER Now I must tell you that at two o'clock p.m. we all 3 or rather all 4 – including 'Old' – set out […] to WORLDS END & the Eglwyseg Manor of the old Chiefs of Powys – of '*Talaith* Powys'. […] The Eglwyseg Rocks are amazing! And the Stone Woman is like Ceridwen herself. It is a retreat for the old gods. The Gorge above it is full of Caves & one terrifying Hole, probably bottomless, whose peculiarity is – *hynodrwydd* – that it goes down to Hell. Near it is a Cave – a Dragon's Cave […] The green green grass was enchanted like emerald & the dark black pines where the sun dropped little pools of gold was like the Black Forest. Through the Forest we climbed till we got clear out on the Moor beyond where the air was Divine. Never shall we forget it! Worlds End. Worlds End!

FRIDAY 18 SEPTEMBER A thrilling Letter from Paris from Emma Goldman transported with joy (aged 70) that she has been invited to Spain to join the Anarchists who for the first time in History are 'Making History'. She – this old champion of Anarchy – talks of BAKUNIN as their great Sage. But a melancholy account of the way the Anarchists are ruling Malaga from Refugees. But of course Refugees are not always good reporters. But the fury & cruelty on both sides in Spain is not very pleasing to read of. [...] At 3 o'clock Gertrude & I & the Very Old set out for Pen y Pigyn & climbed happily to the top. We got a Bird's Eye View of the Horse-Show & the Fair. [...] Gertrude & I then went down to the church-yard & visited the Old Cross with its Celtic-Mercian look & I told her it would bring her luck if she touched it as such pillars are connected with the worship of Cybele in Crete! She touched with her fingers the cross of Glyn Dwr's angry dagger.

TUESDAY 22 SEPTEMBER YESTERDAY CAME GOOD NEWS GOOD NEWS CAME YESTERDAY in the form of a telegram from Mr Pollinger a brief but very very very very comforting & relief-causing & Happiness-bringing piece of News namely [...] 'Have sold *Maiden Castle* to Cassell.'

WEDNESDAY 23 SEPTEMBER Took Old as far as a few paces to the Left-Hand Rock. All the vale below was covered, yes, all the whole expanse of the vale below was covered with snow-white Mist, but I was soon above all this sea of fog up there with the sun warm on the Mountain & I saw the opposite Mountains rising above this White Sea. Gertrude's picture of 'Under the Bridge' is a Masterpiece. The wall, the green fern & one brook. She picked some Bog Asphodel Seed & showed us how it looked under the Microscope.

MONDAY 28 SEPTEMBER Got up at 7 and called my little host & hostess [...]. They eat a great bowl of Oatmeal just like a Nursery Meal! They opened the *Sunday Chronicle* & read about Theodore not writing any more because of Susie the Perfect Child & a picture of Susie. Then we all set out to town. Francis got out at Regent Street or Oxford Circus or Piccadilly. We waved to him from the bus. They both know London very very well. 'Minime' (as I call her) points out enthusiastically beautiful costumes in the windows but she is also just as alive to architectural superiorities & she sits in the bus exactly like Susan, the Perfect Child, with round eyes observing Mr Todd's pigs from her Pram. We got out, Minime & I, at Trafalgar Square & we walked down to the Embankment past Old Bertie's office. Gone, he is gone completely! gone gone gone gone gone. We walked thro' the Embankment Gardens past Cleopatra's Needle [...] till we reached Mr Pollinger's offices in Norfolk Street near the Courts of Chancery. I thought of Miss Flite & of the man who died of Spontaneous Combustion. [...] Then we went to Ludgate Hill & to La Belle Sauvage. I was enchanted with the *belle sauvage* & with Cassell's Office & with the history of the original Cassell & his Advocacy of TEA and with Pocahontas herself that real American! And I liked Mr Flower & also Mr Desmond Flower very much.

FRIDAY 9 OCTOBER The last white hen at the Morgan place has gone! No smoke from chimney. Are Mrs & Fenna gone forever??? No flower but yellow gorze left up Mountain even the last foxgloves are gone gone! All the bracken is deadly dead deadly deadly dead and the whin-berry leaves are livingly & brightly – dead too. [...] Just as I returned the Mistress peeped in ere we sat down to breakfast – Hanleys telephoning! It was Tim – bright, clear, compact, hard, full of life, holding up a brimming cup of experiences and adventures to share. But the T.T. prompted by Mistress & me cried off on strength of her hovering sickness & put them off till Monday – thus leaving her free for her greatest & secretest of all pleasures – a SALE in Corwen. [...] She felt remorse – she felt remorse – but there it is! A Sale is an event hardest of all to be robbed of! [...] As we looked round both of us for matches as we always do when anything nice is toward we thought how we would do just this in our first day in Heaven! [...] Found the T.T. returning in Triumph having bought a Great Cupboard.

TUESDAY 20 OCTOBER Last night she wrote a long letter to Marian & this I knew because when she writes letters, she riddles herself with cigarette smoke. [...] The T.T. advocated the idea that the First Cause was the Great Mother. I fancy this is the Tao notion of the cosmos. And I fancy in Hesiod the Earth is the mother of Ouranos. But it is we decided the old Antinomy – noted, once for all, by that old rattlesnake of a philosopher, Hegel – that Nothing & Something are the same thing and both must be there at the Start.

Ebenezer Jones 'of the one arm' takes over the tenancy of the Morgan farm. John's son now has a curacy at Wiston, West Sussex.

THURSDAY 22 OCTOBER Took Old nearly as far as the Stone on the Left. Found old Ebenezer waiting for me still munching his breakfast. He said he had 15 lambs arriving & dogs too & it was a joy to walk round his flock! He said he had buried his wife (three, we understand from another quarter) but that tho' he was bad at housework (he has only one hand) he held the view like Panurge that a 'bad' one is worse than none! He is exactly like a character in Rabelais just as ribald, shameless & un-fastidious. [...] The T.T. was extra touchy when I returned today. [...] But when our young book-postman who always comes later than the letter-one brought the *Letters* [i.e. *Diary*] of Alice James all was well! [...] Not for years have we been so thrilled by the arrival of a book. When they were children 'Henry' seated in a desolate garden in a swing, remarked 'This might be called pleasure under difficulties!'

SUNDAY 1 NOVEMBER Set out at 9.25 went to the Grouse-Gate. [...] Saw the back of old Eben in shirt & braces just like a Vignette in Bewick of Man in Pigsty – & he called me to see his new purchase – Sow & a Litter of little Pigs. I praised this young Sow very highly [...] till she turned upon me the largest & most lustrous and most ruby-coloured eye I have ever seen! [...] It was Pwll Pen Annwn who first introduced Pigs into Ynys Prydain from HADES! [...] Yes, it was extraordinary to listen last night to the T.T. tell about her evening of Gloom & Hatred of Everything. It was terribly like when she was so unhappy. But in the end after her mother had threatened to lie down under a rug in the dark & Aunt Harriet had sworn she would have nor fur nor stove nor radio & nothing would induce her to play Solitaire any more than anything would persuade the Mistress to play Bridge they all recovered, playing Euchre which made them think of their mother & old days at Girard, Kansas.

WEDNESDAY 4 NOVEMBER Last night I was very upset when winding the kitchen clock – & I did not touch the hands – the Big Hand, the Minute one, fell out & I fear landed in the Fire for tho' I got my Spectacles & groped about for long on my knees – & I have now told Pattie – there is no sign of it. [...] My glass of Orange Juice as I lifted it up to drink divided in half & the lower half fell on the floor spilling all! [...] A nice letter from Wiston acknowledging my £108 but their last servant turned out to be a Lunatic. They have they say, 3½ acres of woodland at

Wiston & my son is very happy trimming and cutting down their trees with his Boy Scouts. Wrote Nothing but letters [...]. I met & passed a tramp but I had a shock yesterday when a very miserable man said 'You can give me Nothing!'

SATURDAY 14 NOVEMBER Today there was a Rainbow & moving patches of sun & the colours purple & brown & green! The stone wall of Caer Drewyn with the red bracken when the Sun struck it was like an iron crown with a circle of Blood! [...] Pattie is going to leave us! Whom shall we have in her place?

SUNDAY 15 NOVEMBER How the rain howled over the purple waste of hills & was like grey spears against those double Beast-Rocks, like petrified 'Hounds of Annwn' on the top. Found the T.T. getting breakfast & Pattie gone! We had a very happy breakfast in spite of the Raging Storm. In Dorset it is always Windy; but here it is either great storms or beautiful quiet days! We talked in High spirits & with great amusement about what we are to do at this DOMESTIC Crisis of our life? Merionwyn is ruled out as too frail. Myfanwy is ruled out as too beguiling. Dear sweet Agnes is ruled out as not strong enough for bad weather. There remains BETTY Evans. She is the one most like the Good Girl we are losing.

FRIDAY 20 NOVEMBER I met them at 10 last night and the T.T. related most subtly & eloquently one of the most surprising & enigmatic Adventures of her life. She & Aunt Harriet were [coming home from Wrexham] in a carriage full of Welshmen & one young man asked her flirtatious questions & she said at last 'I do not like your tone.' Then they all spent the whole rest of the time obliterating this 'Insult' from her mind & enjoying this subtle process. They sang those elaborate Harp tunes called *Penillions* & their voices sounded non-human & of the Bronze Age & she said they made her feel like a ten-cent Woolworth Tin Toy as she listened. But I say her Mind – the Aristotelian *nous* – was alert watching & recording like a mirror for sound-mystery tho' her psyche may have turned into a little tin thing!

John travels to Dorset on 23 November to spend a few days with Llewelyn and Alyse before they leave for Clavadel, Switzerland, where Llewelyn hopes his health will improve. The news of King Edward and Mrs Simpson breaks.

WEDNESDAY 25 NOVEMBER Fog! Up at 6.50. […] Lulu got up & was waiting in the garden in Darkness of twilight-dawn all foggy. He was in his night clothes & all wrapped up in his eiderdown quilt & blanket. We walked out of his garden by an iron gate the hunter's gate given him by the Weld Estate. […] We were so thrilled to be walking together & on our return we both rubbed our hands for sheer pleasure in the moment; in our Father's old manner. I gave him a flint to take with him that I picked up as a sign of my heart of stone! […] Then I went to tea with Gertrude & there was Gamel with thrilling tales of her escape from Spain & all their adventures. Katie took me down the hill – fog & frost – & I hesitated whether to carry home the GRAMOPHONE Alyse has given to the T.T. – & which makes the T.T. wake up each day happy & thrilled. But I was scared of carrying it. But all my journey of nearly Twelve Hours had a background of shame because I had not done so.

THURSDAY 26 NOVEMBER She & the Old met me last night at the Station at Corwen. […] She related to me in the most entertaining & subtle manner the Drama of the Installing & listening to Aunt Harriet's RADIO. The Mistress hates it & will not have anything to do with it. The T.T. is thrilled by the idea of the populace being so solaced so she feels philosophically moved by it & contends that Christ would have used it – & she is also thrilled by any Symphony of real music. Aunt Harriet, whose Radio it is, is only thrilled by Dance Music – & so it is a dramatic criss-cross.

TUESDAY 8 DECEMBER I invoked that ancient Celtic or Mercian 'Cross' on behalf of Lulu who leaves Lausanne tomorrow for Clavadel. But O folly folly! I didn't go to the shop to get the *Sketch* or the *Mirror* which give more sympathetic details about the king than these Dominion-Ruled heavier Dailies! This was a frightful blow to the T.T. & completely spoilt our breakfast usually one of our happiest meals. […] I must just adapt my life-illusion to the idea of being a stupid, absent-minded, selfish log at an important crisis. Well, I had to make the same sort of mental adjustment seeing myself in this same unpleasant light – over not bringing that gramophone! […] Took Old at Four to the Meeting of the Rivers. Aye! but how dark it was! – almost pitch-black ere I reached the Highway on returning. But the River was very swift & full […]. The Swan expecting floods was on a little side-pond. I must remember to take bread for it, for it always says Nep! Nep! Thank the Lord after all the agitation we had a very happy tea – & a young lady, with rosy cheeks but with a tendency to faint did bring the WELSH FLAG which the T.T. says is the best of all flags – far the most heraldic and Mediaeval.

WEDNESDAY 9 DECEMBER A Magical Morning! very low opalescent clouds full of fostering milk as it were from the very breasts of Demeter, risen from the earth under the wooing of the air-children & ready to fall with fecund nourishment on all living things. The sun making vignettes, suspended in mid-air, between earth and clouds; here an emerald-green field, here a supernaturally large tree or a group of brown trees, here a column of smoke rising straight up like an enchanted lily-stalk & expanding as it rises, here a single gate, here a church-spire, here train-smoke, wandering and lost, not knowing which is the misty sun-sprinkled earth & which the opalescent sky! & the whole earth & sky held up as they are thus mingled together as if by the hands of an invisible Atlas! I have never known such a WELSH DAY.

FRIDAY 11 DECEMBER Alack the Day! The King's Farewell. […] A letter from Cassell's to say they are going to print the full complete MS of my *Maiden Castle* & not just follow the cut American Version. But this will be a business – correcting the proofs – but I deem it a very high Compliment – for it will be a terrific expense and make the book very much longer. Well I set out at 4.5 or 4.10. […] I met my darling old Mrs Davies my favourite 'ooman round here just as the Town Crier be my favourite man! – & she waved her stick in the air over the King's Business & cried ''Tis love! 'Tis love! 'Tis love! like his grand-dad for Lillie Langtry!'

MONDAY 14 DECEMBER Floods! Floods! Floods! […] This is a sad morning to me – I woke at 3.30 a.m. & found no T.T.! I hesitated not knowing the time – but 'something,' as the psychic young ladies always put it, led me to go into my room – at first I saw nothing – but soon I saw a brown object collapsed on the floor by an empty grate & half on the chair where she had been kneeling when sheer natural exhaustion overcame her. It'll be some while ere I get over the shock of this sight. It is strange how impossible it is for her to come to bed. [...] Set out at Four – raining heavily still! Heard that horses as well as sheep had been drowned in this terrible flood – the worst for many years.

TUESDAY 15 DECEMBER We heard of the rescue of 166 sheep by a man up to his neck in water kept going by a bottle of whiskey! & the sheep crossing a ladder to the railway line! It was a strange feeling that Rising of the Waters. [...] Set out at 4 – & took Old to Grouse-Gate. It was dark up there – & I noted the stone in the middle of the path beyond the Forest Post. Saw moss. Were followed by the Sow quite a long way & I thought of how [...] Gwydion ap Dôn followed the Sow to where Lleu Llaw Gyffes in the form of the Eagle was shaking down his own putrid flesh from the tree!

SATURDAY 26 DECEMBER Last night I found the T.T. sad as she was washing up & I never found out the reason why. But that Brook-Street 'Mrs Wood' might have well been a reason with her husband lying sick on the floor upstairs & she sick herself and the whole place dark desolate dirty & one candle balanced on a tin & those little children! [...] Took Old as far as the Rhea Tree in this strange grey misty weather with not a breath stirring. Saw Blodewedd herself in the form of an Owl. [...] Met Annie Davies & talked to her. Like a Sibyl she gave us her blessing. She has a sprig of fruit now in her old black hat.

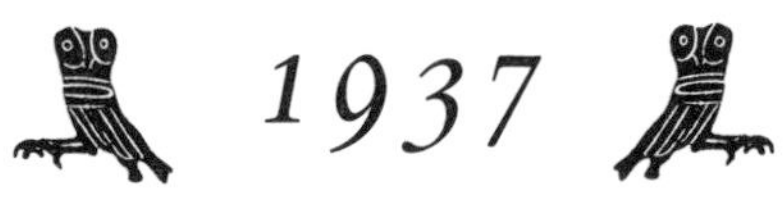

1937

By 1937 Wales, and the Corwen area in particular, has become their home. They are settled in the hamlet of Cae Coed and their new young maid, Betty Evans, relieves Phyllis of much of the heavy labour associated with maintaining the two houses. John seriously sets about learning Welsh. He is asked to compose a poem for the Corwen Eisteddfod and the gestation of this englyn, *with assistance from all manner of people, illustrates how much a part of the community they have become.*

Yet 1937 is another difficult year. Their income is shrinking and they realize that the cost of living in Wales is higher than 'in any place we have ever lived'. Maiden Castle *does not sell well. John finishes writing* Morwyn *in January and Simon & Schuster refuse it. Cassell publishes it in September but the book he considers 'the best thing' he has written gets unfavourable reviews. He begins serious reading for his next novel,* Owen Glendower, *but must set this aside to re-write his book of essays on writers. Eventually this is brought out in 1938 by Cassell as* The Pleasures of Literature *and by Simon & Schuster as* The Enjoyment of Literature.

Despite their worries, there are some very amusing occurrences in 1937 – such as the episode of the tadpoles – which John relates with increasing verve and freedom. In other ways, the diary is becoming more challenging as well as exciting to the reader, as Powys uses Welsh mythology to explore a growing complexity of themes and preoccupations. One example is the Mabinogion *tale of the owl maiden, to which John frequently refers. The magician Gwydion ap Dôn makes for his favourite, Lleu Llaw Gyffes, a wife out of the flowers of the oak, the broom and the meadowsweet, naming her Blodewedd (Flower-Face). She falls in love with Gronwy Bebyr, Lord of Bala, and the two conspire to kill Lleu. Javelined in the side, Lleu does not die but flies off in the form of an eagle. The grieving magician Gwydion finds him by following a sow to a tree from which putrefying flesh is falling. Gwydion punishes Blodewedd by turning her into an owl. In the mind of Powys, this story gives 'a local habitation and a name' to a further test of his own magicianship. Just as he once defied the power of the resident God of Phudd in Hillsdale, Powys, the 'outsider', challenges the established Welsh magician Gwydion. Eventually the struggle is transmuted into a memorable scene in the novel* Porius *when Merlin 're-creates' the blossom-bird-maiden 'in the strength of a magic that declared itself able to destroy all powers that ruled by force'.*

1937

WEDNESDAY 6 JANUARY Last night I finished my *Morwyn* Revision. And I told the T.T. that I held the view that this was the most valuable thing & the best thing I had ever written. If all my writings were to be destroyed this is the one – *Morwyn or the Vengeance of God* that I would most regret! This is the one I would select to be preserved of all if I had to choose!

TUESDAY 12 JANUARY After tea Agnes brought our Teacher of Welsh Miss Evans. The T.T. was frightened by such a Professional Teacher; but I was rather pleased that she was professional; for I know you have to have a real teacher to learn Welsh!

FRIDAY 15 JANUARY [Betty's tooth] began to hurt like the Devil. She lit all 4 no 5 fires in the Houses & then went home & her mother took her to the Dentist [in Corwen]. I said to her 'How brave you are Betty' & she gave me an answer that had in it all the feminine endurance of twenty-five thousand years! [...] I find up here in my room where I write & where [the T.T] sat up late last night a most curious & most fascinating Document! – several big sheets of paper inside the Oxford Dictionary! It is an original Idea of hers! She is making a Dictionary – going right thro' 'A' of what her actual real Proustian Feelings are about each word – what nervous & imaginative & sensitive & subtle Impressions and Images are actually called up by every single Word. I shan't tell you what word she wrote opposite the word 'Abject'!

SATURDAY 16 JANUARY I got to the Grouse-Gate & back in exactly one hour & ten minutes but only by cutting short my rigmaroles! [...] Had just time ere breakfast was ready to read one single verse from Deuteronomy with my Welsh Dictionary about what to do when you find a man lying dead, a murdered man, in a field, near foreign cities! Although I cannot expect such a situation to present itself to me personally – you never know! & I have ere now wondered what I would do.

MONDAY 18 JANUARY I encountered all those men who work on the river-bank with sacks over them to protect them from the cold sleet. The snow is melting melting snow & sleet & rain together – a wet wet day. A day for writing but not for tramps. The knife-grinder came after a cold starvation Sunday in the workhouse. He is off to Bala workhouse to try it. He had a hole in his boot! ailinon! […] Our Second Welsh Lesson. The little lady is a good teacher!

SATURDAY 23 JANUARY A beautiful heavenly soft fresh cool perfect mountain-wind scented with peat & moss & heather-roots. My favourite kind of Day (or nearly so). For 'tis a Wind of Memories. 'Tis a wind full of the over-feeling & under-feeling of the whole race and a Day when you can […] leave your limited body & even your limited individual soul & flow into earth-mould & heather-patches & the roots of emerald moss & of rusty-red moss […] & grey fairy-cup lichen that do bide under clear dark cool water & when you can flow into grey rocks and into these little new-grown sturdy spruces & scotch-firs & into the red-gold leafless larches & into the shapes of the mountain tops & into the heavy dark wild lowering clouds & as you flow into these things all the race-memories come rushing to be part of this psychic diffusion & this merging of the man John into other living things so that 'on such a morn as this' you seem able to stop raging & beating & gesticulating & howling for personal immortality […] & you actually take the first step in the direction of being so 'diffused', as to be content that life should go on while John as John is dead just as old Bertie is dead. […] Betty could not sleep last night again. She has NEURALGIA. […] And yet there was I up the mountain enjoying this Wind of Memories of the Race while Betty lit our Six Fires in our two Houses with Neuralgia.

WEDNESDAY 3 FEBRUARY I must make the best of the bare and naked branches for this particular kind of beauty will not bide long now. The field opposite our bedroom window has that curious yellowish green of long rained-on grass. […] It is very warm almost overpoweringly so to me in the absence of wind. The absence, I mean, of all wind. Wind & air – for my Favourite Element is ever the Divine Ether – are necessary to my power. I feel exhausted today for lack of wind. I took 'Old' as far as the Rocks on the Right. I got in all my complete Rigmarole of Commands to invisible but very particularly coloured 'angels'. I made my head hurt by the things I had to force myself to remember as I went through these interminable litanies.

He goes to London 4-6 February to attend a private viewing of his sister Gertrude's exhibition of paintings.

THURSDAY 4 FEBRUARY Had a pleasant send-off from Mr Davy Jones our intellectual Porter [...] Gertrude met my train. I was so thrilled to be with her, she had tea ready making tea herself at a gas-stove. She is in a huge great old Private House in Dorset Square looking out on the Square with Plane-trees. Thro' the grey rain it was such a Dorothy Richardson scene – the big windows & the trees & lights outside in the rainy twilight & Gertrude's room the old high Drawing-room with marble mantlepiece & frescoed walls & ceiling.

FRIDAY 5 FEBRUARY Well we took a taxi to the Cooling Galleries in New Bond St. [...] We went up the steps to Gertrude's exhibition & I was at once struck by the freshness & beauty of a completely new picture – her very latest! This was a picture of that road known best to me in the whole world between Lodmoor & the Sea. Gertrude has painted it as you would see it standing with your back to the old Coast-Guards & looking toward Weymouth. Patches of emerald-green grass & yellow moss in the foreground & then the line of the sea-wall with all those wooden breakwaters so familiar to me & the spire of St John's faintly & Weymouth in a mist & the hill behind the backwater in a purple mist – a town in mist & the pools of Lodmoor & then an indescribable real Tang & blow of the spray from the sea blown up over the sea-wall at high-tide with an unbelievable freshness against your face.

THURSDAY 18 FEBRUARY Today is our Welsh Lesson & this is sad for the T.T. as it shortens her afternoon so. She had a terrible wave of dejection & rebellion against her life after breakfast, feeling it to be an English & Welsh enduring life, a life of ought varied by small suitable sideways pleasures instead of the American life of a Margin of sheer adventurous & reckless Joy. [...] Oh I pray the T.T. will find some way to enjoy her life & break up the weight of Ought.

TUESDAY 23 FEBRUARY She is off to visit the Birmingham 'Coronation' Industrial Fair! Oh, I hope she enjoys it! – 'girls like Fairs' – as much as she enjoyed in New York the Russian Exhibition. [...] The T.T. came [home] safe – but – it was – but – but – but aye! the T.T. all machinery – all iron & steel! The Fair was all iron & steel.

FRIDAY 26 FEBRUARY Every day all this February I have had

to change my trowsers & rub the Old with a towel. What a month of Rain it has been. […] Old Eben came running out with a magic gift for me held in his Mouth! 'yn ei geg' & it turned out to be a noble PENNY 'ceiniog' of George III. […] I am thrilled to possess it & very grateful to Old Eben. He said 'I will give this to Lord Powys!' What an actor he is. […] I knelt down in intense joy before a new Primrose that has just come out at the back of our houses opposite the door of the Mistress' House. It is what we used to call in our childhood a French Primrose. It is a heavenly lavender. It is after lilies of the valley perhaps my favourite of all Garden-Flowers. That peculiar lavender-pink is ravishing to me! I am rather disappointed with Gruffydd's book on Math fab Mathonwy. […] Oh! none of them have the Imagination of old John Rhys! he was the one! he was the 'God Discoverer' of Welsh Mythology.

SUNDAY 28 FEBRUARY The WORST SNOW we have ever yet had in Wales & about the worst I can recall at all in Ynys Prydain. […] I took Old along the Bryntirion Road. […] Here I found our Mr Thomas the Nationalist & his wife. […] They had for 2 hours been digging out their sheep but they had got them all. […] Then I talked to Mrs Evans, Betty's mother at her toll-pike door & she had just sent 'Walter' to look for her Geese. Then I returned to find the T.T. terribly upset because of the Old being 'balled up' (as we say) with caked snow on his paws & me too being so drenched. Nothing is more awful to the T.T. than to have to cope with snow before she has had coffee. And my snow-storm voice talking of birds & sheep in too cheerful a tone was the last straw.

MONDAY 1 MARCH DEEP SNOW. […] Aunt Harriet is deeply convinced (erroneously we all three feel) that she has a Tumour in her head.

FRIDAY 5 MARCH I funked the hill this morn & took Old to Llangar. We went thro' these big snowflakes and thro' a heavy mist – like the enchanted mist that fell with thunder upon the 'Llys' of Pryderi & Rhiannon his mother. […] Had such a happy breakfast with the T.T. & such a perfectly charming letter from a lad called Casey in Glamorgan who is a passionate lover of Keats, & how wisely the T.T. discoursed on Youth & its Plans & how I ought to say to Gerard Casey 'DRIFT!! Enjoy your youth & DRIFT.'

SATURDAY 6 MARCH Aunt Harriet is so thrilled to get her Radio back at work – but the Mistress hates the Radio so that the T.T. who was enchanted by the wondrous concerts she heard & classical symphonies & modern music has decided not to listen to it because of the Mistress's implacable hatred of it. Was there ever so docile & gentle & considerate a daughter? For she was thickening out her musical culture very greatly by hearing all this first rate music. [...] I found the T.T. returned from the Doctor & he says Aunt Harriet may be free from all Alarm.

Pietro Aretino of Arezzo published I Ragionamenti (Discussions) *in 1534. The 'discussions' are vivid and scurrilous descriptions of sexual positions and perversions: 'all the ways and all the postures by which one may thread or get threaded.'*

MONDAY 8 MARCH Last night the T.T. came to bed with me again & aye! how I enjoyed her! – 'à la Lulu' as I discreetly say – & you my Unknown Reader can use your Imagination, & get as envious as you like, & think of Aretino's 357 ways of 'making love'!

SUNDAY 14 MARCH Took bread for NEB the Swan. But he wouldn't eat it! I'll never take him it again. I believe I have misunderstood his rapid pursuits of us along the Bank – he in the river I mean – & we on the bank – I believe he is driving us away, driving us off his Preserves!

TUESDAY 16 MARCH Another Snow-Storm from over the Berwyns! [...] Fed Birds; stood sentry to guard against the Rooks taking all! The Robin sat singing to me within reach of my hand – what a lovely dove-grey a luminous grey – the most beautiful of all greys it has; against its orange-red. The Thrush came. He must have known of the new Storm of Snow. The Blackbird came boldly & filled its sweet belly. Two pairs of chaffinches came – no tits. Took Old to top of hill by Reservoir beyond the Forester's Post saw the Left Rocks & the Right Rocks in the distance. The Snow was Frozen hard. And this put the Old and the man in a splendid temper. I can see him now with his tail erect in High Feather.

WEDNESDAY 17 MARCH The T.T. came to bed with me but suffered one of her sad far away pensive flights when her Lover has to be as gentle & tender as if she were the First White Butterfly. In the end by recalling old, old memories I succeeded in decoying – as if with little gossamer seeds – this wayward pensive sad one back. […] We received Lulu's *Twelve Months*, a Perfect Book – the prose as beautiful as poetry – the Sun 'turning on his golden heel!'

THURSDAY 18 MARCH Found Old Eben with one hand at work, & his stump assisting, stirring a jorum of corn-mash of some sort for the sheep & lambs in his barn. He discoursed most lyrically like a Psalm of David on the coming of Spring & how good the Lord was & of the grass on a thousand hills! He said that when he was a boy the women in the Farms blew long Horns like Trumpets to the four quarters of the earth – 'Utgorn' is the Mabinogi word – to call the men in to breakfast. But he said no Horn calls old Eben from his fields now & no horn calls 'Lord Powys' from the mountain – 'but they are called all the same!' & the old chap tapped his Belly & made a skip or two as is his wont when we separate. […] The Mistress appeared to bring the great news, eventful, & naturally to her & the T.T. a little sad, that she has sold 'Wildacre' for $900.

SUNDAY 21 MARCH Took Old up Mountain with Betty's washing-pail & got all the Frog-Spawn from the path. […] And this Frog-spawn in Betty's Pail I took to the Grouse-Gate Pool where I deposited it with the rest! I hope this pool does not dry up as it did last year, when Katie was here, & I had to carry away the Tadpoles.

Rhys connects Brân, whose name means raven or crow, with Urien, another hero-god who has the mark of the crow on his breast. The killing of a rook upsets Powys, who associates it (and himself) with the mythological crow, symbol of magical, creative and prophetic powers.

THURSDAY 25 MARCH I met Hubert & little Geoffrey who had a hurt or a young Rook which I begged them to let go in the wood which they did. But did they go back to it the moment I was gone? […] Its claw got stuck in my button-hole for a while. Did it want me to keep it?

SUNDAY 28 MARCH My mind ever since I heard of the death of that young Rook has been more remorseful than over anything I can recall. Even more – what a lack of Proportion – than over [word obliterated] when, owing to my kind of Love-Making, she lost her Wits. The little boys who were with Hubert came running up to me to say 'Hubert killed that Rook.' Then it came over me with full force what I had done. Its claws had clung to my coat as to a possible Rescuer – but I deliberately let Hubert unfasten this despairing clasp & take it away to kill it. How did he kill it? [...] I certainly have received a curious shock to my life-illusion which will remain till the end – & like Brân – Bendigeitvran – I shall have a Rook or a crow engraved on my Chest.

FRIDAY 9 APRIL Our money affairs look Bad. My books are not doing nearly as well as they used to do – *Maiden Castle* in America only made $600 (dollars) and in England they've only sold 1700 seventeen hundred copies. I am so scared that this poor sale will discourage them from accepting *Morwyn*. I am now – as she is – seriously struggling to economise. [...] She finds our expenses here higher than in any place we have ever lived!

MONDAY 19 APRIL I hurried up the lane rushing thro' my prayers or my superstitious Rig-ma-rôle at a devilish speed like a hedge-priest mumbling his mass before entering a pub. [...] I raced home fearing to keep the T.T. waiting but she was only just down & very nervous – moments most dreaded by the very Old! But she soon picked up after coffee & there was a letter from Faith asking for a title for Bertie's book of Essays on Building with a Preface & Memoir by Sir J. Squire. I shall suggest *From the Ground Up*.

TUESDAY 20 APRIL Rain overtook the Old & me as we returned & I had to Pray Short (with a selfish hardening of heart which I find is an absolutely necessary gesture for it seems to be my Peculiarity 'cynneddf' not to be able to be either Bad or Good without a Philosophical Decision that embraces the whole Cosmos!) [...] *The Book Tribune* has a Grand Picture of Virginia Woolf. The T.T. & I are deeply prejudiced against this famous *Littérateuse* – & it's obscure to me why we feel like we do? But, I fancy, it is on Behalf of our admired Dorothy Richardson who is a real Genius – simple, honest, direct – a great Sibyl – where the notorious Virginia is only clever & modern & what Lulu, when he wants to disparage, calls 'fashionable'.

1937 THURSDAY 22 APRIL There came from Wrexham a demand for Income Tax amounting to – O deary I! – amounting to not less than £104.40. Think of that! We ought (both of us together) to pay a visit to 'Ribbons & Winder' pointing out that it is very unfair that I should be taxed as a Single Man when I am supporting Two Families. How the wind howls round this little house! But how beautiful those Hyacinths planted so nonchalantly by old Wright are now coming into Bloom outside our front windows. [...] The T.T. went to town & had one of her dramatic high-comedy talks with our friend in the Bank.

SATURDAY 24 APRIL There was a letter from Pollinger that pleased me more than any event I can recall in all my Literary career. Quite as much, if not more, than the reviews of *Wolf Solent* that freed me from lecturing & bought us Phudd Bottom at Hillsdale – for it talked of Cassell's accepting *Morwyn*. Oh, I am so grateful for this! The T.T. & I went to VALLE CRUCIS where in the Chapter House I began my Romance about Owen Glyn Dwr.

FRIDAY 30 APRIL A very nice letter from Faith saying that Dent has accepted that title for Bertie's Book *From the Ground Up*. I am glad of this. [...] I took the Post and did register the £100 for Wiston. It is useless to wish that the Stipend of my son was a trifle higher! I don't exactly know what it is; but he tells me it is small.

SATURDAY 1 MAY Thick Fog everywhere. [...] But up on the Mountain there was warm & bright Sunshine & I looked down upon a great Wavy Sea of Snow-white Mist. Since we came here I have never seen this familiar phenomenon of Mountain country that I read of in books – about watching the peaks of the hills emerge from a great wavy sea of Mist! Today, up the lane, I was looking at the dead branches in the hedge under the grey wall & suddenly I saw half a dozen or more little white pear-shaped globes very white & round & shining in the dead bracken – [...] the first flowers of WOOD SORREL. Their 'oxalis' leaves (like shamrock) were concealed in the dead bracken; but these white Drops of loveliness showed clear.

During March and April John rescued frog-spawn and tadpoles – his Hillsdale ritual – transferring them from shallow ponds to the Grouse Pond.

SUNDAY 2 MAY Went to the Grouse Pond. Oh, but it's getting so low! If there isn't Rain soon I shall have to rescue Tadpoles [...]. The T.T. took the Ladies at 2.35 p.m. up the lane, past Eben's, past the Larches, actually as far as the Gulley Bridge. Here they finally made a nest for themselves in the warm dry heather dead & free from all moisture & the young freshly-flowering Whin-Berries [...]. They heard & saw a grouse, a curlew & a meadow-pipit. But aye! the T.T. says they touched her heart, for they looked so frail & so exhausted & so quaint & foreign & so old! The T.T. is so sweet to them – so like a boy would be; she does play the part of a son to the dear Mistress who is certainly a super-feminine old lady. As for me I took [...] the Old to the Post & posted a letter to Emma Goldman telling her to use my name to the limit for the Anarchist Conference at Barcelona – & to the Author's Insurance sending Five Pounds – damn! – as against Libel Action by the Vivisectors! over *Morwyn*.

WEDNESDAY 5 MAY I feel singularly exhausted – but why I cannot tell. I often feel this exhaustion but especially today – which is peculiar, as the wind is so strong & so cold! I praised old Davies over the wall for the wall he is building for us. He is a perfect Genius at Wall-Building without Mortar. As he describes the art of it his whole body sways in rhythm to his words & his arms sway (like he was swimming) & his face grows illuminated. It must be people like him who built these old bridges and who built Valle Crucis & Dinas Brân.

THURSDAY 6 MAY At breakfast we found the Contract for *Morwyn* from La Belle Sauvage [Cassell] & also a heavenly letter from Dorothy Richardson about it [...] & she did say, off her own bat, that 'twas the most real description of Hell she knew! The T.T. has been rushed off her head & feet today. Up & down stairs I have heard her run at top speed – opening back door – front door – knock & knock! Cooper's Order arriving – tramps, gypsies, G.W.R. men; old Mr Davies; Katie's Bottle of Rum [...] – & also the revision & doing up of both *Morwyn* & *Pleasures of Reading* for Schuster in New York. And after all the rest she went to town to the BANK. She was rewarded at the Star Grocery however by a present they gave her as a good customer of a metal tray with the rose & thistle & shamrock and the LEEK!!

FRIDAY 7 MAY I [...] saw quite a lot of FERN FRONDS

beautiful & magical they are above all things – & I am so devoted (in my Bookish Magic-taste!) to the mere word 'fronds' which is one of my favourite words in all our language. I always smell the damp earth-mould when I set eyes on a frond! They are sacred to Demeter & to Cybele! [...] Our own hawthorn hedges still have that indescribably fresh lovely light green which alas! darkens, oh so quick! – often before you have time to concentrate on it – & to say to yourself – 'There is the green of Spring – the green flesh of Persephone – the green blood of Persephone – the green hair of Persephone – the green soul of Persephone – the green goddess.'

SATURDAY 8 MAY I took the opportunity of going to the Grouse Pond & there I can tell you I received a sickening & startling shock for it had completely dried up. [...] In one single spot I saw blackness ominous blackness composed of the dead & dying Bodies of TADPOLES that directly owing to my stupidity were perished Miserably of hunger thirst & loss of breath! I have begged Betty to [...] fix a jam-pot with string for me to see if I can rescue any of these victims of my stupidity this afternoon. I certainly shall be a tiny bit punished for my Neglect & for letting 1000 Beings perish out of pure Neglect & Stupidity by having to go up there this afternoon which the Old hates so greatly & I am so scared of lest carrying my net & jam-pot I encounter Colonel Wynn or his gamekeepers. But when I think of the clumsy helpless selfish-padded way I go on – like a Venerable Archdeacon – not quite as bad – only less bad – than that fucking bugger, the Archbishop of Canterbury – may the silly old gentleman live long! But that is how I feel when I think of that young Crow whose claws clung pitiful to me Oh so pitiful – as if it were the crow carved on the chest of Bendigeitvran himself & that I handed over to his Murderer.

SUNDAY 9 MAY Tadpoles!! Aye! the Tadpoles of yesterday! Tadpoles. ENEMA. [...] I set out at 8 & got to the Grouse Pond – no longer a pond – a dry hollow! I took the jam-pot which has One live Tadpole. Betty showed it to me for I was too blind to see it among all the Dead, & I went down to that Pit of death & put a few more dead into my jar with a vague thought – no! not that so much as just because I was there & to give a cause for carrying the jam-pot. But I pray the one live one will live till I take it to the river-pond! I expect I ought to have separated it from the dead but I was too lazy to do so. […] Today the T.T. is […] looking at her flags for the coronation. […] She likes to be as our neighbours & not to be coldly superior & grandly indifferent. She likes to feel the pulse of the commonality beating in her veins & to join in national celebrations & I commend her. 'Tis good that she is as she is with a bugger like me as a counterpoise of cloddish Diogenes-in-his-Tub evasiveness. Well! I set out at Four & took the Old in good heart till I came to the first Pond – & lo! & behold! I had totally – aye God help me! – I had totally forgotten, after all that fuss – to bring the tadpoles dead or alive, with me!

MONDAY 10 MAY I feel a tiny bit hypochondriacal today about my Side owing to that tadpole business yesterday & my walk to the pond. That living tadpole was one that for a whole hour lay on our hard black cinder yard after being spilt out of jam-pot by the 'Old' jerking me! All the dead lay at the bottom of the pond when I put them in but this one swam up to the pond's edge & I could see its microscopic mouth – or so I thought – opening & shutting like a miniature whale. It really must have been devouring little mud animalculae but it seemed to be saying to me – 'a life for a life you wait! I'll repay you' – & all the way home I wondered how it could be possibly worked out that a tadpole could save the life of a man: of course a frog could, by waking him up or by turning a viper's attention away from him.

They join the Cae Coed coronation festivities and listen to the service on Aunt Harriet's radio. John finally decides to get all his teeth out. Eben buys a woman ('ooman') at the Fair.

WEDNESDAY 12 MAY The Coronation. Rain in London. God! what a day! […] We had breakfast at 9.30 but after it the T.T. felt impelled to comb & decorate with Ribbons the 'very Old' which occupied precious time – then my damned enema occupied more precious time so that we missed the descriptions of the Processions to the Abbey. When I got across we were in the Abbey waiting for the King & Queen. […] But what thrilled both the T.T. & myself most of all was the Bells of Big Ben – & then the trumpets! She & I were constantly on the edge of tears – & the dear Mistress was suddenly taken back to her childhood by the massive majestic dignity of the Prayer-Book words. But

Aunt Harriet – that staunch Republican disciple of Tom Paine remained sitting up straight in the parlour below mending her stocking!

FRIDAY 14 MAY Everything is now a lovely Spring green – but even yet there are [...] a perceptible number of big trees not yet out & still Brown especially in the Rûg Woods. What trees are those slow lingerers? ASH mostly for the oaks are already in their golden yellow leaf & the little Oak up the lane has even its flowers out [...] such as Math & Gwydion did use in the manufacture of Blodewedd who – when made – like a Magician's Eve – refused to obey orders & chose her Lover for herself. Good luck to her! but alas they made her into an Owl but I know her where she now do bide in the old yew-tree at Llangar & every day I encourage her with a message from Gronwy Bebyr Lord of Bala her Lover. [...] The Ladies went to town and had such an amusing time in the Bank with our friend there that the recollection of it throws them into a laughing-fit & the T.T. was overpowered with laughing when she related it to me at tea.

MONDAY 17 MAY The important event for my own secret & most private life was my Decision during this walk on Whit-Monday to Have Out those two great ominous Back Teeth [...]. I have at last now that the discomfort has reached my ear showing the spread of the poison from the abscesses decided to submit to fate. The mental struggle over this decision to overcome my cowardice – a cowardice that has last[ed] for two years at least! – has this morn [...] caused my bowels to feel so uncomfortable that I have to have an enema a day before the time! Such is the magic potency of FEAR!!

SUNDAY 23 MAY Had a very cheerful & talkative breakfast with the Ladies over here in the T.T.'s parlour where she has Lilies of the Valley and Lilac & where Olwen looks as if she enjoyed being a princess among flowers. [...] Up at Eben's the cherry blossoms have strewn the ground & gone just as, before them, the plum blossoms have strewn the ground & gone! Now the Chestnut blossom at Eben's is out. So far I have not been privileged to catch a glimpse of the mysterious shy ''ooman' aged 48 & called Hannah whom Eben bought or obtained 'with her Box' at the Fair when he bought his next lot of sheep.

TUESDAY 25 MAY The Mistress swallows Iodine! Great agitation when in place of Cascara Sagrada the poor dear Mistress did Drink Poison! The T.T. telephoned Nurse Jones – then Doctor Edwards our Corwen Welsh doctor – Out! Then Doctor Satchell the Irish Doctor the one who attends the Admiral. He came. But before he came the T.T. got in touch with our dear old friend Mr Ellis Evans the chemist who – though himself suffering from a terrible illness & only to be saved if at all by a Miracle – gave very wise advice thro' his daughter over the telephone. But Dr Satchell came with a Stomach Pump – but it was not necessary as it later appeared that the Mistress had only swallowed half a teaspoonful of Iodine [...]. However, Dr Satchell is a very Careful man & he is taking every sort of pre-caut-ion!

THURSDAY 27 MAY Took 'Old' to Blodewedd actually round the churchyard going by the Road. Had to hold up my best trowsers, as an old woman her skirt, one with each hand, while I also restrained the Old from making water on the graves. [...] I had the rest of my teeth out.

SATURDAY 29 MAY The little T.T. was Overcome with the pressure of her life & its events & persons TOO MANY. [...] She made me think of an Elemental who has been dragged back from freedom into the Burden of Human Beings. Like Ariel she was – imprisoned in the cleft of an oak & forced to do tiresome nay! well-nigh insupportable Tasks for a lot of Human Beings – forced in fact to change her nature! [...] I met Eben's ''ooman' up there feeding the ducks a swarthy sunburnt very diffident gipsy-looking person, very very nice. I like her. Nelly the 'Hwch' when we were talking stood on her hind legs & put her head & great flappy ears over the top of the half-door of the shed to be let out for her breakfast. Hannah 'the 'ooman' does think highly of Nelly the 'hwch' – who as Eben says is a kind pig.

SATURDAY 5 JUNE I passed a forester going up who hid behind a wall & on my return he pretended not to see me – what a queer lonely shy in-human anti-social life these foresters seem to live! Had a happy breakfast reading about Samuel Hoare's Prison reforms in the style of Elizabeth Fry – & I think of my great-Aunt Elizabeth Patteson who belonged to the Hoare family. But then there came from this young Improver of my

Works – Mr Quincy Howe, S. & S.'s editor – a GREAT BLOW to me! Which is very very very serious for he doesn't like my long essay of 200 pages on Saint Paul! This raises a very hard problem for if I leave it out – what a delay till I have written other essays to fill its place! Damn!

SUNDAY 6 JUNE Mr Ellis Evans our friend the chemist died yesterday afternoon. Myfanwy's father is dead & that Cynwyd baby. Betty says that Deaths always come in Threes! May Ellis Evans & old Hughes & this Baby all 'Rise to Immortality and Intense Happiness!' which is my private prayer [...]. But as the T.T. says 'No one knows what unknown Solution of all Griefs may be offered by DEATH.' [...] I met a Tramp with his young 'mate' or 'minion' or what-you-will & he had a bit of a look of [Dostoevsky's] 'the Idiot' but he told me he was a Genius which the Idiot wouldn't have announced.

TUESDAY 8 JUNE A sad day for me. The T.T. going away for the Day to Chester with Tim Hanley. [...] I DON'T LIKE IT when the T.T. be gone away! Talked to Eben in his Pig-Stye. [...] Then Hannah came all dressed up in new clothes & straw hat & I rallied her so tenderly on her appearance that old Eben waved his stump *sans* hand & cried 'she be a young 'ooman!' & Hannah looked so pleased & shy with two men teasing she in Pig-Stye! [...] Oh dear, I pray the T.T. will get back safe & sound from Chester – with Tim. I don't like it. I don't like it. I don't like it. I like to hear her voice & know she is in house or in garden. Then I can go on with my Book in peace and quiet & content!

SUNDAY 13 JUNE Last night CRWBAN the tortoise came to live with us! He stayed in the Bath last night. [...] I coaxed the Old up to the Reservoir. There I heard the Curlews & the Cuckoos. And I saw the grey rocks and the light-green Whin-Berry foliage against the unbounded rain-washed blue sky. I got that rare & heavenly sensation of being upon a Planet in Space. The Ladies came to breakfast. We put 'Crwban' into the garden on the cut grass but he walked away – took no notice of his saucer of milk – indeed he walked straight thro' it – & went off into the long grass in the direction of the Quarry! Have we seen the last of Crwban?

Littleton and Mabel arrive for a holiday, 15-28 June. Littleton's autobiography, The Joy of It, *is published in the autumn. He urges John to confront several financial and legal problems: his income tax; the generous allowance he sends to his son (now aged thirty-five) despite their own poverty; and his will, which does not provide for Phyllis.*

THURSDAY 17 JUNE We sat up till Twelve, last night, discussing the Important affairs of State – a blood & iron Discussion on My Will & preparation for my DEATH & what will happen then with regard to the T.T. & the Royalties on my books. We finally decided by Old Littleton's wise & most drastic ADVICE to write to Blundell & Baker asking for a copy of my Will to be sent to me. We also decided that the T.T. & I had Best Visit in person Ribbons & Winder in London & see if we can't get Income Tax reduced by claiming that the T.T. receives a SALARY as my Secretary as it used to be managed by our excellent friend of 'the Inner Sanctum' Mr Leon Shimkin, S. & S.'s private Lawyer. Old Littleton also thought strongly that the T.T. should have her own English Solicitor independent of Blundell & Baker who tend, we feel, to regard me as a Scallagag-writer & the T.T. as an adventuress!

FRIDAY 18 JUNE Last night old Littleton read to us his chapter called My Brothers a criticism upon Ll., T.F., & J.C.P., as writers & criticisms on Louis' Book & Heron Ward's & [a] few passages about our sisters – I wish there had been more of these! But he brought in quite a long letter from old BERTIE that was very good & gave a kind of voice to it all. If as Bernie says our parents were the trunk & roots of one single tree, this letter of old Bertie was like the voice of the general wind in the tree-tops of the whole Tree. Set out at 8 a.m. Met old Eben & he walked half-way up the Larches path with me. We agreed that it would be a good thing to get our Mr Jones the tomb-cutter to cut in those great deep Rocks up there just by the Gate leading to the Colonel's Grouse Preserve the words 'The Hills are the Lord's' in Welsh! Something for the Grouse Shooters to study as they set out! [...] Old Littleton wants me to write to the Librarian of the Bangor University Library to ask when we could visit it. So I expect I must do this. My Manuscript arrives with her corrections as a stern proof-reader from Dorothy M. Richardson. [...] Then came the Secretary of the Corwen Eisteddfod to ask me to be chairman of the Chairing of the bard & to compose & recite an 'ENGLYN' in Welsh.

1937

SATURDAY 19 JUNE Took 'Old' out at 8.10 walked up hill with my favourite Postman who has such a pleasant smile. I asked him about 'Englyns' this complicated form of poetry in a Quatrain that I find in the *Mabinogion*. And off went his pack from his back & down he squatted in hedge & wrote one from memory on a torn envelope [...].

SUNDAY 20 JUNE [Eben] walked down the hill with me & told me that 200 years ago the Greatest Welsh Bard – this was concerning my having to compose an 'Englyn' – was a young woman called Gwenwil Bychan or Fychan to whom came competing & rivalling & contending bards from over all the mountains & two of these put their heads together to fool her & composed a bawdy Rabelaisian poem (referring to her chief difference from a man) but instead of being reduced to shyness or confusion she replied in a poem even more shameless & a good deal more witty. The gist of which I found it hard however exactly to follow as Eben spoke it but [...] note that it is wit & art & intellectual deftness rather than inspiration that is the mark of Welsh poetry. [...] We discussed my Will & today old Littleton is working hard at the difficult question of how to revise it & what to do about it & to say to Blundell & Baker on the subject of a New Revised Will. For according to this present one the T.T. would not have what is now in her house! This of course is an unthinkable proposition! And I am glad old Littleton in the T.T.'s interests has made me rake it up & face the matter.

TUESDAY 22 JUNE A letter from Blundell & Baker saying they would make a New Will & that the 'Lib Declaration' was legally binding. These documents I post to my son. [...] Well! we went to Bangor & Littleton & I visited the Library & found Mr or Doctor Richards studying old mediaeval Latin Parchments like St Jerome in his cell. He lent me Lloyd's *History of Wales* a wondrous work & some Cymmrodorion essays on Bards. Then we went on & on to Carnarvon. Then from there we went all round Snowdon [...]. We past Beth Gelert & saw the hotel where Theodore & Littleton and I stayed as lads aged 19, 18 & 17 & the actual path of which we made use – with Littleton's help! – to get to the top of Snowdon!

WEDNESDAY 23 JUNE I have the sensation of being 'bit' as Swift would say with a vague sense of the evil-eye of Gwydion ap Dôn – in revenge for my championship of the Lord of Bala & his love for Blodewedd & his killing of Gwydion's pet 'Lleu LLaw Gyffes' whom the magicians married to Blodewedd. I am also a trifle overpowered by work at this juncture. […] I must do something about making use of the elaborate & most careful corrections in *Morwyn* made by Dorothy Richardson which are of precious & characteristic interest – like Charlotte Bronte correcting the works of Mr Peacock or of Harrison Ainsworth! And ought to be kept for posterity! But what to do I can't think for I like my slip-shod style. I deliberately use it. Then I have with Miss Evan's help to compose a Welsh speech & with John Morgan's help to compose an Englyn in Welsh. All these things – & Income Tax too & my Will in the offing are a bit heavy to my 'Hudoo'ed & wand-stricken state as the opponent of Gwydion!

Littleton drives them to places which figure in John's next novel, Owen Glendower.

FRIDAY 25 JUNE The day has been still, hushed, calm & full of hot sunshine from Dawn to Eve! We drove or rather old Littleton drove us on Highway 5A past the Viaduct & past my imaginary Tassel Inn & past the route taken by young Rhisiart ap Griffin from Chirk towards Valle Crucis – through Gobowen & thro' Oswestry to Meifod where we had lunch near or even in the churchyard where the school children were having their lessons. It was a beautiful church with Norman arches & Norman font – & one ancient sarcophagus-lid of the old Celtic Design of some ancient chieftain with a little naked man on it and strange star-fish & most heathenish & mystical ornamentation. […] Then we drove on, Littleton with the great Church-Key forgotten in his pocket, thro' honeysuckle hedges, thro' roses & wild roses, thro' hay-fields, oh, so many hay-fields & the incredibly beautiful hills & woods in the valleys of the Vyrnwy & of the Severn of the County of Montgomeryshire the old land of Powys. […] The Sexton had told us there were three Maen y Meifods one of which we believed was our ancestors' abode but we saw none of these but […] we finally arrived at the grand & supreme point of our Journey. This culmination of our pilgrimage was MATHRAFAL the palace of the Princes, built by none other than King ELISEG. I cannot describe to you the romance of this place. It was more than magic, more than mystery – like a thousand years of high reveries of an intense imagination, of lonely thoughts separated from everything – alone – an airy castle above tree-tops.

SATURDAY 26 JUNE This letter from Schuster's is the heaviest blow I have had in my literary work since I wrote *Wolf Solent*. It practically rejects both *Morwyn* – this very viciously & contemptuously – and my *Pleasures of Reading* unless I cut it, cut out St Paul & add three more Essays. I shall surely, I do surely, need all my Philosophy & whatever practical Wisdom I possess to deal with this blow. [...] I am so profoundly comforted, sustained, & strengthened by the T.T.'s wise advice & sagacious counsel 'cyngor' over this blow from the 'Inner Sanctum's' young men & their attacks, I have scarcely any need to call up from the vasty deep the spirits of philosophy for she is my Sprite & at her wand the Demons fly. Besides I feel so heavenly free from the black magic of Gwydion ap Dôn after my visit to Eliseg's proud, sad, high, remote, 'Llys' above the Vyrnwy – that I am much more able to take these blows of fortune with equanimity.

SUNDAY 27 JUNE I went up mountain beyond the Bridge & Gorge & down the path above the completely Dried-up Waterfall. Heard Curlew, Cuckoo & saw Wood-pigeons, & a Pipit, imitating a lark. On my way down – there was Eben & Hannah. Eben walked down hill with me & I took the chance of carrying out Hannah's instructions, yes the instructions of Hannah & begged him to keep her for it looks as if her only Alternative was the Work House. She has done Farm work all her life & cannot do domestic work & there's nothing for her to do for her Hero Eben, save gather wood & faggots. So she goes out long ways to do this & once Eben said she came back at Midnight with a huge bundle of firewood. The Gwerglas Farmer didn't stamp her Insurance Money Cards – for her right arm & hand crippled by a fall on flagstones. Eben is writing to the Authorities about this Insurance Money. If she had a few shillings each week it would make it pay to keep her but otherwise, he said, she'd have to go.

MONDAY 28 JUNE A lovely letter from Lulu he adores Switzerland the home of our Moilliet ancestors & sends one photo of himself with a little child a little Moilliet cousin of ours. [...] The T.T. & I have made clear our very great gratitude to old Littleton for settling that most difficult matter, & most complicated, of my Will. [...] Well – they departed! We carried the heavy things down on my heavy sycamore stick to the car in the road & off they went down the hill. [...] Old Littleton spoke of how they enjoyed themselves here. I think they really did. [...] I took Old to the Mimulus-Marsh & listened to the wind in the great Sycamores. The T.T. has that sense of something gone that comes after a long visit.

WEDNESDAY 30 JUNE Yesterday night at the Morgans was an experience unforgettable. The old Master-Bard – our Tailor of Corwen – took in hand at once the fixing up of the rough & crude poem I had composed – in outward look in the shape of an 'Englyn'. But he explained all the technical difficulties of this sort of composition, all the repetition of inside consonants, their alliteration & rhymes interior of the words. He showed me an analysis of the hard 'Englyn' art. And both of them helped me with my Speech which sounded most thrilling when old Morgan recited it! And then I left him to work out my poem in ordinary verse; keeping my crude ideas but putting them into a new form. A Welsh lyric but not an 'Englyn'. [...] The T.T. & the Mistress go to the Circus.

THURSDAY 1 JULY My Will has arrived. We brought Betty into the Parlour to hear my speech & she – for she understands Welsh – said she could follow it. Hurrah! [...] I have now come round again to Book XI of the *Odyssey* which thrills me most of all the poetry in the world. I am now reading the speech of Agamemonon – Agammemnon – Agamemnon – there! I've spelt it right at last – which is the most wondrous & beautiful of almost all poetry ever writ.

FRIDAY 2 JULY The same dark grey warm weather. The Farmers want – & don't want – rain & this question between hay in the fields – & roots in the earth – must be upsetting the unity of their prayers to the gods – who simply don't know what the human race wants at this curious juncture! [...] [John Morgan] has written a Welsh poem on the exact line of the rough one I gave him & also a real 'Englyn' for me to recite! [...] I must devote a lot of time today in practise of my speech & of these two poems. At breakfast the T.T. read some eloquent most eloquent articles in our Anti-Vivisection Magazine & indicated

1937 horrible & perfectly useless cruelties of keeping animals awake, torturing them awake to prove what we all know – the necessity of sleep! It is unbelievable as the T.T. says the madness of these vivisector's brains.

SATURDAY 3 JULY EISTEDDFOD. [...] Up at 7. Took Old as far as Bridge Gorge. [...] I admire all these tall fox-gloves against the grey walls & the grey river! And the hayfields everywhere being cut & turned as the hay is made fill the air with fragrance. And the Wild Roses here are heavenly to see – one single heart-shaped rose-carmine & white petal of which is according to Walter Pater more precious than the Absolute. [...] Well, we must be down at the Pavilion at 1.30. The T.T. has put on her Straw Hat. It looks very nice. Thanks be to Bendegeitfran I got thro' all right.

SUNDAY 4 JULY As I looked out of the bedroom window ere I dressed I saw an Extraordinary Sight. I saw Reflected in the glass of our open Window quite clearly – an active thin Sheep climbing with celerity up the Beech tree. I gazed in mute astonishment at this sight & then to my further Amazement I beheld the dear Mistress in black velvet & silk – like a Turkish Lady from a Hareem – & with her familiar Red Shawl ascending the same tree in pursuit of the Sheep! What it really turned out to be was the high flight of Stone-Steps going into the garden which were reflected in the glass of the window with the background of that tree. I hurriedly dressed & went out & there was the Mistress in her night-attire at the top of those stone-steps & a sheep was in the garden. She went in rather shyly [...] and I pursued the sheep thro' drenched grasses while the Old guarded the approach to the T.T.'s garden. The active sheep leapt to the top of the 6 foot wall, walked along it & jumped down the other side. [...] No sign of Eben or of Hannah. I feel shame and I think, yes, I feel deep shame as a Neighbour when I think [of] Hannah aged 50 going [to] the Workhouse [...].

MONDAY 5 JULY A letter from Wiston – my 1st family are struggling with much the same problems as we are! My son depends on a car to do his parish & 'tis a big rectory. O deary I!

TUESDAY 6 JULY This season of ROSES is wonderful. To see cut roses in vases is one of my chief pleasures – & yet Old

Hypocrite as I be – I would not pick them myself! […] Came down lane with Eben & have decided to sacrifice the bulk of my Tramp money namely 3/- as a weekly subscription that & towards & hereafter HANNAH will be able to stay with Eben tho' as he explains 'It cannot milk or use its crippled arm – & yet "It" has a healthy desire for food'! But thus my hope is that Hannah wont be packed off, with 'its' Box, to the Workhouse.

SATURDAY 10 JULY Last night the T.T. came to bed much earlier than usual & I snatched at the chance of keeping her awake for a short time! How does a Satyr, O my unknown reader, in your age, keep a girl awake? On this occasion I scrupled not to 'make love' to her 'à la' my rogue of a younger brother Master Llewelyn! I suppose one of the simpler ways recorded by 'the Ribald of Arezzo' in his famous work about keeping ladies from their sleep. This morning therefore I surveyed her head on her pillow with the well-pleased & proud look of satisfied Desire.

MONDAY 12 JULY Today the T.T. has begun reading Faulkner's *Absalom* & she is thrilled by it & I shall read it. She says it is a real Book at last like Conrad & Henry James. Last night the Old & I thro' the wall heard great laughter & bangings about in Aunt Harriet's room (thro' the wall). Aunt Harriet was in wild spirits changing her room I mean changing the contents of her room.

They take the usual Chaldon holiday from 16 July to 6 August, but stay in lodgings this time. The Five Marys are grave barrows on the high ridge between the village and the heath to the north.

MONDAY 19 JULY Gertrude treated us all – Gertrude directing all & paying (out of money she had earned by her etching covers for Lulu's books) for us all – to Mary Webb driving us all the way to MONTACUTE. […] We went to the Graves of my Father & Mother & of little Nelly & found them well tended & the grass cut but the Phelips graves deplorably neglected – grass growing long and rank. We went into the church & saw where my mother always sat by my Father's reading-lectern […]. Then went to the Vicarage & the T.T. & Gertrude & Bernie went over the house while I sat on the steps of the front door with the Old & 4 Ghosts sat there by my side – Father & Mother, & little Nelly & Old Bertie.

MONDAY 26 JULY The sad thing in all this 'holiday' is the fact of the T.T. not being able to get off by herself to Weymouth. I ought to have seen to it – that she could get off by herself but the difficulties are great. As I look at this Diary day by day there has been something intervening. It isn't only the family – it's outsiders as well – this Russian Spanish Left meeting tonight & Miss Gillman tomorrow & then Mr Hopkins & Miss Eleanor & old Littleton – one thing after another. But it gives the T.T. moods of desperation & rebellion & wretched tantalization & it fills me with impotent pity and shame.

MONDAY 2 AUGUST I worked at revising *Morwyn*'s Page Proofs & then set out to Theodore's with one of the *Morwyn*s for him to read. He said at once that the way it began arrested him, & that it was more writ 'from the Centre' than my, my other works. If he does read it, it will be the only work of a contemporary he has read for Ten years or so! [...] Theodore took the Old & Sue & me to the top of the highest 5 Marys where we all sat and enjoyed ourselves among the Harebells and the Thyme & the Scabiouses looking at the valley & Theodore recalling how in old days he would survey my approach from this point across Morton Heath & I telling him how well I recall once when I had had difficulty with my little pupil Margerie Edwardes of Burpham how I made up my mind looking at this same Egdon Heath from the hill that the only alternative to erotic obsession was writing romances. This was when I had not yet written any story.

THURSDAY 5 AUGUST I [...] met Theodore & Sue & I went with them into the churchyard – & Theodore showed me the place at the back of it – where the un-christened children do bide – where he wishes to be buried.

On their return to Corwen John begins writing other essays for Pleasures of Literature *to replace the long 'St Paul' essay rejected by Simon & Schuster. American friends visit 'the Ladies' and Phyllis.*

SUNDAY 15 AUGUST I must [...] plunge into my work – if work it be – to copy out passages from Matthew Arnold with poor brief comments, but I have come to regard my old 'dithyrambic criticism' as somewhat irrelevant – thrilling in conversation or lecturing – but rather irrelevant when written down.

MONDAY 16 AUGUST I tried in vain – how weak I am & how my Philosophy fails me at the fatal hour between Two & Three when people die & the tide of existence ebbs! – to avoid agitation in the pit of my stomach when at that low pitch of life I find no T.T. at my side! And yet natural enough to ladies (meeting or parting) seem such protracted swallow-like gatherings on the telegraph wires! I expect it's easier for them to live on their nerves than for an old cart-horse like Petrushka! They have a resilience – a something – either from their hearts or their nerves which is beyond me. These things are mysteries. [...] I felt very tired as I struggled on with my commentaries & glosses upon Matthew Arnold & more so still when in warm damp still air I took the Old – after rain – to Blodewedd. I met Ffoukes Jones whose countenance flickered into radiant life from being a driven leaf in the way Welsh faces do.

FRIDAY 20 AUGUST They all go to Chester. [...] Rain & Showers about. [...] Well! there'll be the Cathedral to shelter in – not much comfort though for Aunt Harriet – our gay one – in that! – but there may be a Movie to delight her if it is too wet to wander about. [...] It must have been about 3 o'clock when I heard terrific barking & a faint knock at the front door. [...] I went to the window – & saw Mrs Cotton her wone self. [...] I got her to sit in Aunt Etta's golden chair for about a minute & a half & was so proud of this capture that I let her do all the talking; & didn't even refer to my grand topic, my absence of Teeth! [...] They all returned at 6.15 having had a happy time at Chester & Aunt Harriet had Turtle soup. 'Turtle' she ordered, very stiff.

TUESDAY 24 AUGUST An important psychic Event has occurred. For today, pondering on money-troubles & contemplating our mortar-less Stone-walls – the T.T. had a REACTION against Wales! She seemed to feel the existence of a Demon under all the ideal spiritual mists – yes, of a Vampirizing Dragon that clutched & clutched & clutched & devoured & sucked the Good up leaving only grasping remorseless Evil! And from which the only cure was to Go Away! Now how can this be explained. She says that any good honest material Success in Wales is impossible – you have to Go Away to succeed. Witness my present ill luck over my writings since we came to Wales!

THURSDAY 9 SEPTEMBER The T.T. seems to have [had] a very frank heart-to-heart talk last night with both the ladies – even bringing up the idea that they should both return to America if they really feel sad over here. She was perplexed & troubled by the Mistress's down-hearted state, & by Aunt Harriet's passionate Home-sickness.

FRIDAY 24 SEPTEMBER Have finished revising all my typed essays & have mailed yesterday, or the T.T. did, the MS of my Goethe essay. So today I shall take out of my drawer the MS of *Owain Glyndwr*. Hurrah!

SATURDAY 25 SEPTEMBER *Morwyn* arrives – which is the Best Book I've ever written. I here & now witness, confess, acknowledge & declare So Help Me God! that the sole only complete & entire Originator of this idea is, was & will ever be none other than this little Elemental whose polished limbs are my Paradise [...]. And I am so pleased that *Morwyn* came out on the Autumnal Equinox.

SATURDAY 2 OCTOBER We have the Literary Supplement of *The Times*. There is an unfavourable review of *Morwyn* in it. I have not found one single good Review or friendly Review so far.

SATURDAY 16 OCTOBER Felt a tickling (the T.T. says it is an Imagination!) a tickling in my back where I couldn't scratch & in my head – where I could. But the T.T. says it's enough for the Bath to be Out of Order for me to want a bath with desperation. Found the T.T. only just up, but began sternly reading Jeremiah in my Welsh Bible! But aye! what a deep exciting burst of prae-palaeolithic Wisdom & Protest this astonishing little Elemental launched into after breakfast up here in my room. [...] The T.T. spoke of the way the Males of the human race with their logic & reason have neglected & put out of sight the Primal Feminine Principle which is the Origin of All Things. [...] Set out at 4.30 & came home in the dark or nearly dark! Saw the lights of Pen y Bont on the water for the 1st time. Saw a huge great Bird – was it the Owl Blodewedd or was it the Grey Heron. It made a cry a cry a cry a cry an awful cry like that of Lleu Llaw Gyffes when Gronwy Bebyr javelined him.

MONDAY 18 OCTOBER I saw the Gaer rise up just like an

island in the Sea above the White mist [...] then even as I watched, the mist rose – & I have often noticed these things – & covered the Gaer! It was a sight to see. Mrs Hardy is dead. She was out in her garden on Saturday but today she is dead at Max Gate. Found breakfast nearly ready in the kitchen. And our long prayed-for & hardly hoped-for letter from the Home Office signed by the Assistant Secretary of State allowing the T.T. to be my paid Secretary. [...] This Decision will just save us. It will mean a saving of no less than One hundred & Twenty pounds.

SATURDAY 23 OCTOBER Never in my life have I seen so many dead leaves a torrent of dead leaves as lie deep & deep in the Wood & on the path! They are piled up like beautiful corpses.

TUESDAY 26 OCTOBER Took Old at 3.30. It was an astonishing Day. [...] We had no sooner crossed the Duddon than that Ox with white horns that point down instead of up came rushing from 'way off' & leapt that little ditch like a deer & began jumping into the air tail on end till it reached us when it licked my coat while I caressed its neck and tapped its broad bull-like brow. [...] Then we saw 3 great Herons. And one of these Herons made a strange cry! Another was pursued by a Rook. It was a Dionysian Day. A mad day.

Both continue to give away more money than they can afford, to what John called in Wood and Stone *'the ill-constituted'.*

FRIDAY 29 OCTOBER Dense Fog. [...] The T.T. works in her Garden – before her tea-lunch next door, & after. [...] Her face when the Old & I greeted her as we set out at 4.15 had in the fog a wavering & fluctuating & mysterious smile; like that of some Nymph of the streams (as Homer says – 'the daughter of Zeus!') [...] I took Old to town & paid for the tramp's boy-shoes, price 6/6 & praised the girl there for the touching way she knelt down at the tramp's feet – he had no socks at all – to help him try on these boots. It had an Early Christian look this gesture!

THURSDAY 4 NOVEMBER A Terrifying MENTAL-Physical ATTACK took me suddenly last night at Midnight. I had slept an hour & woke up with the Mania that I couldn't breathe properly! And yet not exactly that. Rather that I suddenly became horribly aware of the PROCESS of breathing & a feeling as if I had consciously to breathe & that it was a thing that needed my full concentration. […] I tried to recover by looking out at the stars & feeling the cold wind blowing in thro' the open window. No good! […] So in Desperation I went next door at 12.30 for the T.T. She got me a high pillow & a scarf & sweater so that I could lie with head raised. […] The T.T. had lit a candle – but after sleeping a little with her there (& deep relief to me) I got up & put out the candle & all was well.

SUNDAY 7 NOVEMBER Grey November Day. Grey Clouds! Grey Mist! Grey Air! Grey Sky! […] This is her Birthday Month & this is her Cimmerian weather, about which she wrote her first story. Took Old as far as the Little Grey Waterfall on the way to the Grouse-Gate where only a segment of the Planet is visible all brown & burnt sienna colour with little green firs & bare thorns: held up an orb of dusky purple brown into an infinite grey space! Heard many Grouse. And oh it was so wonderful having my new GAITERS so that I had not to walk like a careful Cat! […] Worked at my IVth chapter of *Owen* & practically finished it so I shall read it to the T.T. tonight. One of my greatest thrills – nearly equal to making love to her (& it is making love to her) is reading to her a new chapter.

MONDAY 8 NOVEMBER A Day of Disaster. […] Met two old, old Tramps! To one I gave 6d & he said of the other 'poor old chap, he is so shy' so he called him (with difficulty) & I gave him a 6d too! […] And our breakfast was a sad one because of BAD NEWS Bad news bad news HANNAH came crying crying crying crying. I gave her 1/6 of my Tramp money & the T.T. gave her Five Shillings of her house money. She is going to a place in Carrog. But it is her heart that is mostly hurt. […] And now on the top of Hannah's disaster Betty brings the news that Nance Davies has sold her beautiful Dresser to buy warm things in Liverpool but 'they' have not paid her!

WEDNESDAY 10 NOVEMBER There was Good News for Mr Pollinger (that Good Agent) writes that Mr Flower (that Good Publisher) likes a lot & has accepted my St Paul. Hurrah! Hurrah! Hurrah! This is very satisfactory. Only I have to do a short essay on Dickens & another on Hardy. But he will give £100 advance. [...] No word from Howe of S. & S. Has he got my new essays or are they lost. The T.T. was very cold in the night. At breakfast she spoke so eloquently on the necessity of making an honest choice between modern humanitarian relief for the masses & all this old world leisure & beauty and decency & quietness! One thing or the other!

THURSDAY 11 NOVEMBER I wrote such a long explanatory letter to Old Littleton telling in detail about my exact financial state & how I have only about £100 income from my pen to count on from this Nov. to next Nov. [...] It was incredibly lovely this evening! All the sky cool cold clear gold – the outline of every hill darkly silhouetted against an infinite depth of pale gold. And the Half-Moon travelling in the river along by my side! How seldom I am thus accompanied by the Moon!

MONDAY 15 NOVEMBER Took Old to Rocks on Right. I was especially struck by the effect of this warm wet moist still November Day upon the power of Colour. The mosses, stalks, dead leaves, living leaves, the purplish leaves of a wild pea that grows there – all these seen to the rippling sound of the water from the earthen-ware pipe to the great earthen-ware Homeric Crock that suddenly appeared soon after we settled here – [...] all these did thrill me very much.

THURSDAY 18 NOVEMBER Had an Attack of my curious Breathing Insanity – but I got over it without waking the T.T. It was a help to me during the crisis of this singular Madness to imagine myself DEAD, when breathing whether thro' nose or thro' mouth would no long[er] be necessary whether conscious or unconscious. My Mania is the mania that I can only breathe by taking thought of each single breath! It is the mania of bodily self-consciousness & it proves how right I am in saying that the art of escaping from yourself in various sensations is the art of life!

WEDNESDAY 24 NOVEMBER Saw two Grouse on rocks outlined against the Sky that I pretended – all my life is pretence – to shoot with a Bow & Arrow.

TUESDAY 30 NOVEMBER Am thrilled by a request from Monsieur Wahl of the Sorbonne to translate excerpts from the works of 'Mr Powg' for the *Mercure de France* – & sending an article for the Sorbonne putting John Side Face your servant in the highest company. It has always been my highest ambition to lecture at the Sorbonne – but I suppose it is almost as grand to be lectured on there!

THURSDAY 2 DECEMBER The T.T. goes to town & returns miserable, because of the Day and because of the Poverty in the Air. Terribly Dark & Wet! And a cold North Wind! I prayed for the wind & by God I've got one!

MONDAY 6 DECEMBER The T.T. did a lot of typing very happily in her parlour with the Fire we had for the Ladies. Aye. The little T.T.! How she would like it if we could afford the coal for 3 fires in our little House. But No! we can not.

FRIDAY 17 DECEMBER I went thro' the churchyard & prayed for Lulu as I always do at the Cross & for Owain at his Dagger-Print. Home by the Road & how soon the town is left behind for we live in a little hamlet reached, really, by a country road. Saw a haggard dole-man with an empty sack & he said he was going to get a branch for his fire that he had noticed hanging over the edge of the little brook below the Gorsedd! I keep my sixpences for tramps but on my soul half the tramps I talk to are less haggard & necessitous. At tea the T.T. spoke so wonderfully of the difference between the Welsh & English about Death. And how the English love an actual place – Bradford Abbas let us say! with every gate; but the Welsh live a timeless life & seem without a local habitation or a date.

SUNDAY 19 DECEMBER Got thro' my Prayers, but not the extra Sunday Rigmarole about Chesil Beach etc., etc. I find it so hard – so tough & rooted is the plant of my Perverted Conscience – to chuck this crazy habit of prayers. And I must work & think of my work – instead of praying like a Carthusian Monk! I am well into Chapter VI of *Owen* & this is my chief Joy & Pleasure. And yet all last evening – I did lavish my Inspiration on a long letter to old Maurice Browne on his Autobiography. A discourse it was on the Metaphysics of the Circus!

SUNDAY 26 DECEMBER I decide to stop praying & invoking & sending Angels on Errands of Mercy. I have given up my

Angels. [...] Took Old to Rock on Right – no further! To Grey Waterfall & saw a magic apparition of sunshine with mists above & clouds below (& all insubstantial) except 4 hedges dividing 3 fields isolated from the rest of the world. It was only an apparition of 3 fields & 4 hedges but as it floated in a white sea of mist with clouds above & beneath – it was an Island of the Blest.

MONDAY 27 DECEMBER Well, I have kept my Vow. [...] I have, like Prospero, broken my magic wand & released all my Ariels.

1938

By 1938 the ritual walks are well established. The naming of features in the landscape, so characteristic of the Hillsdale period, is repeated in Wales: the Grouse-Gate, the Rocks on the Right, the Homeric Fount. The walks are accompanied, as always, by what he calls his 'rigmaroles', his long prayers, but at the end of 1937 he makes the important decision to end them and let his 'Angels of Mercy', the 'Ariels', who carry his prayers, go free. However, as 1938 progresses, the prayers and the multi-coloured angels creep back.

Phyllis continues to find the management of two houses difficult. Caring for Aunt Harriet during her illness – which extends over the 1937 Christmas season and into the New Year of 1938 – exhausts her. Later in this year, a visiting Playter relative who remembered a Phyllis always ready for new experiences, who in New York 'drew around her a choice circle of interesting minds', finds now 'a quiet subdued woman who lives in a far-away village at the end of No Where and whose only companions are an old mother, an old aunt, an old lover and an old, old dog!'

Their savings almost exhausted, John and Phyllis try unsuccessfully to live on five pounds a week. The only light in the dark of deepening poverty is the telegram from Schuster in the New Year. He finally reads the manuscript of Pleasures of Literature *himself and decides it will become a best-seller like Durant's* Story of Philosophy. *However, this means that, having already rewritten the book for Schuster's editor, Powys must begin again, adding eight more essays at Schuster's request. Meanwhile, Cassell, the co-publishers, object to the change of plans and refuse to pay any more advance. The involved story of publishers' conflicting demands reveals Powys not only as an immensely erudite and versatile writer but as a persistent and patient professional.*

The impending war takes up more and more space in the diary. Despite their isolation, they avidly read the papers and listen to the radio, attempting to understand the tumultuous events and their own responses to them.

SATURDAY 1 JANUARY A day when the earth turns like a child just born to the eternal ether – hardly breathing but down there at the very Bottom of Life a faint turning on its Back & waiting for the stir of new Life – a day not yet spring but aware of Spring coming! coming! A day of Persephone thinking of the Upper Air.

TUESDAY 4 JANUARY The T.T. was terrible Sick all yesterday alas! like old days – not quite as bad for I never heard her cry out 'What will I do?' but I saw her fingers extended nervously clutching at beating at the wall when at her worst.

FRIDAY 7 JANUARY Up to the Rocks on Right I went but felt the cold wind so much that when I returned the T.T. said I had a grim & severe look. I explained this by telling her I was pondering on my Chapter, which made her laugh, for my domestic reputation has not yet reached to quite such intellectual heights! [...] I met that old Stone-Deaf Ex-Postman with his plump black dog who said the said Dog had nearly killed a Pheasant. God! it must have [been] a stone-deaf pheasant. Then at tea [...] we talked of Realism & why all realism [...] – all fiction-realism any way, is tragic, shocking, terrifying & gloomy, disgusting, pessimistic & stark & grim? as if God himself were a savage realist. [...] At 7.15 I went over to the other house & found Aunt Harriet downstairs but very sad & holding her hand to her head & the Mistress looking as grim as a 'realistic novel' but I tried to cheer them up & risked reading my verse – & the Mistress did brighten a little bit!

SATURDAY 8 JANUARY It is getting to be too much – an Inferno of domestic 'love-tasks' in these two houses – & she is pining & pining to get out – into air – into her garden – into Paradise out of Inferno. And now by some devil's chance like the Last Straw comes the telephone – Oh that curst telephone! – to say the HANLEYS are coming! Of course they can't know, these kindly slap-dash friendly ones, on what a tight-rope of domestic misery the T.T. – that little dancer – has been balancing herself all this long Xmas & New Year 'Holiday' since Aunt Harriet first got ill. How can they know? No one who hasn't lived with the T.T. knows what a *Tour-de-Force* her domestic goodness & submissiveness is! [...] Last night in her revolt & her distraction & desperation she made a vow never again to Celebrate Xmas or indeed to celebrate anything. [...] The Hanleys missed the Bus & never came!

FRIDAY 14 JANUARY Last night when the T.T. came up to see me at 9.30 with a vague idea of my going on reading RABELAIS aloud to her which we have begun (at the very beginning) with great pleasure to both of us – she brought her accounts & these ailinon! ailinon! proved a shortage in her week's budget in dividing it as she now so meticulously does in her heroic struggle to live on 365 pounds a year – and on Five Pounds a week – among envelopes which is her own Invention as a Chancellor of Exchequer. [...] And last night after this bottom-rock talk of low finances & of our doubtful future when at the end of this year we have spent all the T.T.'s careful Building Loan Savings made under her Father's wise advice when I say at the end of this year we have exhausted all our Reserves as we have already exhausted 'Aunt Etta's Money' & when I shall have to reduce my wife's informal Alimony upon which my Son's comfort & certainly his very necessary motor-car depends – I had as so often happens on the night before my enema one of my Very Worst Dreams – I, the sworn hater & destroyer & opponent & persecutor & deadly enemy of Dreams so that I do not bear to see even the word 'Dreams' used in poetry! I hate the very word & everything to do with it. Well, I had, as I say, my Worst kind of Dream-Horror of terror & sick loathing & Disgust. It is the sort of Monstrous Insect Dream that Dostoievsky the supreme psychologist in his profound insight – far deeper than Freud – links up, absolutely correctly, with the erotic, sadistic nerve. [...] Betty came running up the lane after me with a telegram. This turned out to be a long Cable from Mr Schuster himself who – for the first time – had read my *Pleasures of Reading* & wants to change it into *Enjoyment of Literature*, adding Shakespeare, Cervantes, Melville etc., etc., etc., Went nearly to Grouse-Gate. This Cable of Schuster's has given us HOPE when we were in pretty good want of it!

SATURDAY 15 JANUARY The Dee is 'Out'! Floods. [...] Yesterday the T.T. at breakfast told of how she had been influenced by life in Great Britain – & how deeply it had affected her and even changed her. She wondered, however, if this Cable full of Hope from Max Lincoln Schuster this Napoleon of Publishing who snatches ideas out of the electricity of the air &

turns them into meteoric planets of blue fire growing bigger & bigger, […] she wondered, I say, if this cable, which is so welcome to the two Terminals, is a sign that she should not give up her Xmas Celebrations!

MONDAY 17 JANUARY Looking down our lane past that Oak Tree on the road the Dee looks as big as the Mississippi. […] I could see absolutely no sign of the Road into Corwen from the Gaer over the Victoria Bridge. It is completely under the water in some places even the hedges are invisible in others just faintly to be seen. […] I have at last heard from old Emma Goldman. I thought of her this morn – for she has been seven weeks out of hearing in Catalonia but now she is back again in London. I think I shall send 10/- cheque & my name (for what 'tis worth) for these Catalonian Anarchists are, as politicians & builders of the desirable state of things, more idealistic & more un-practical than any other group! & I confess that it seems that they alone (idealistic & unpractical as they are) represent a Society that is humane and free – the only set in the world that do!

Phyllis goes to London for a day to see Gamel who is now safely out of Spain where she lived with Gerald Brenan. They meet Gerard Casey, who is to become part of the family when, in 1945, he marries Lucy's daughter Mary.

WEDNESDAY 19 JANUARY Took Old past Rocks on Right, & even past Grey Waterfall – but not quite to Grouse-Gate. Pondered so deep on Chapter VII that I seemed to return flying thro' the air so little did I see or hear on my way down for I was with Rhisiart & the Lollard & the 'Fathers'! Had a very cheerful breakfast. […] I asked her advice about my Book & she says – to go ahead as I feel inspired & if need be to cut afterwards. […] At tea up here in my room the T.T. talked of Gamel how she is the only Person in the world she longs to see – the only one. And we discussed at length with the Railway Guide the agitating question whether the T.T. should go to London – if Gamel is there – for one night. I did not want to dissuade her from the Quixotic Enterprise. For after all if they were lovers what would 4 hours each way in the train for one sight of each other be? Nothing! And after what the T.T. said about Gamel their relation is really a rarer & more delicate one than that of lovers!

SATURDAY 22 JANUARY I pray the T.T. is all right & will get

back safe! I do hope there will be no fog & no accident on the railway. I was a bit shocked to see a Railway Accident on the L.M.S. not very far away – from Northampton to St Pancras – & a lot of injured & one killed! [...] Aye! but think! But think – it might have been the T.T.'s train! [...] I have been watching Mr Wright [...] digging in his own garden – & in about 20 Minutes he has with his spade dug the whole thing up! [...] There he is – a man leaning on his spade in his garden – at the end of the Winter! [...] The T. T. has come home safe!

SUNDAY 23 JANUARY After breakfast we read the Memorable Letter of Schuster as to what new essays to write. Shakespeare, Cervantes, Dante, Montaigne, the Bible, Melville & Poe, Proust, Joyce – & for the T.T.'s sake I'd like to add Gogol – if not Scott & Henry James. A heavy Task eh? eh? eh? but since I have to earn my living & S. & S. promise me $1,000 advance royalty straight away, 'tis better than trying to lecture again or to struggle to get – always the worst and most difficult thing for me – some journalistic work [...].

SATURDAY 29 JANUARY Aye but the Cold today from my viewpoint is the worst we've had this Winter! I had on, I have on, two cardigan Jackets and a Blue & Red Scarf. [...] Fed Birds; called T.T. & set off to Station to meet Gerard Casey. Dropped his bag at Mrs Peake's & took him to the Cross & the Dagger & round by Gorsedd. He had breakfast with us up here in my room. He is very nice & rather like Poor Dickie. We both like him very much. [...] He is the next oldest in a family of ten! A Catholic Irish family!

TUESDAY 1 FEBRUARY Set out at Four – in an ice-chill sleet storm whipping the Two Old Men as they crossed the Bridge. We went via Tyn y Cefn & by lane to Glan Alwen. Here we met the Town Crier 'John'. He talked like Culpeper giving Welsh names of plants that cured Piles & Boils. Perhaps I left him too abruptly when he showed me the scars of his cured Boils – but he refrained from showing me scars of his cured Piles.

THURSDAY 3 FEBRUARY The Doctor has come to lance that Boil or Swollen Gland in poor Aunt Harriet's Neck & I seem to imagine the poor lady crying every time I hear the wind! Betty has had to go home early because her Father and Mother have gone to Liverpool – for her father to see a Specialist. [...] What things are happening just now! Betty is thinking so much about her Father who may never be able to work again – & the Mistress & the T.T. are thinking so much about Aunt Harriet who has turned fiercely against the Doctor whom at first she wanted so. [...] Poor Aunt Harriet! I fear she'll put it down & attribute it to being over here. How things come suddenly in a person's mind! At that second – as I was thinking of Aunt Harriet – I suddenly felt myself in an avenue at Cambridge, the other side of King's College – where the cricket & playing fields are! Why was that?

FRIDAY 4 FEBRUARY Yesterday I saw the First LAMBS I've seen, in the Pen y Bont field – between railway & river. I saw one Mother-sheep going down to the Dee to drink & the tiny Snow-White Object like a perambulatory Snowdrop trying to copy its mother & drink of the full-brimmed Black Flood! [...] Hurrah! a letter – hurrah! – a letter – comes from Norton that Noble Publisher of *Culture* our only book that brings a constant Income – sending us 218 Dollars & of this I am fixed, inflexibly & unalterably resolute, to give the T.T. eighteen Dollars for her Garden! [...] A long letter from Quincy Howe which means I think that this *Pleasures* or *Enjoyment* Book will not be finished till June which will mean a late autumn publication. Well, well, well! I must just go steadily on [...].

SATURDAY 5 FEBRUARY Took Old to Doctor to get Aunt Harriet's Medicine. I had not known what a Rumpus there had been at No. 8 & how Aunt Harriet had sternly dismissed the Doctor saying that she would send for him when she wanted him! [...] Then came a long letter from Pollinger saying that Cassell's wouldn't give me any further advance on this book as it was Schuster who wanted it & not they & they were ready to print it as it stands. So I wrote and said all right to this only I implored them to keep my St Paul in its entirety as they've got it in their Galley-Proof [...]. I also heard from Mr Howe & have answered him very civilly & very genially even as Grangousier did reply to Picrochole when that testy personage had slapped him in the face & tweaked his beard.

MONDAY 7 FEBRUARY What teases me over this essay on Shakespeare are memories of the innumerable lectures I've given on him. It is a peculiarity of mine to hate saying again what I've said before – for my chief thrill in writing is a new & fresh discovery but luckily it isn't hard to make new discoveries in Shakespeare but to make this essay really fresh & new means that it may read rather crotchety cranky & quaint – & lacking the obvious reactions. But this can't be helped. [...] This mystic DAY has now turned out Incredibly Beautiful. Warm, still, Misty Spring Sunshine! The T.T. will soon be (I hope) for many uninterrupted hours in her Garden. [...] [Aunt Harriet] liked the Doctor better though today. Probably because he was grimmer & more like herself – after the jolts she has given him. The Mistress thought his feelings had been hurt by Aunt Harriet's despotic ways. But he told the Mistress herself that she ought to go out on this unusual day. And so directly after my enema at about two o'clock the T.T. – sacrificing her pleasure in garden like a pious daughter – took the Mistress for a walk. [...] I set out at 3.30 & drove back the excellent cows that give me milk who – by a mistake – in the absence of the 'ffermwr' were issuing out into the Highway near the Bridge. I saw Neb the Swan & his Mate on the River side by side among some reeds. I saw the Sun sink above the great solitary Poplar and make a path of deep rich ruddy gold on the Dee.

WEDNESDAY 9 FEBRUARY The T.T. [...] saw how bothered I was by Joyce's style. 'Tis my fastidiousness combined with my lack of cleverness & scholarship – & it really is my simple naive young-girlish idealism & romance that makes the particular tone of Joyce a very great effort to me! But my pride relucts at dodging dodging, dodging this admired Modern! [...] At breakfast today we talked of mutual erotic vices!

SUNDAY 13 FEBRUARY I saw for the first time this year – a great sign of Spring too – Frog Spawn! Yes there were two great Sponges of this singular Stuff in that little Grouse-Gate Pond, which today had a thin Coating, (you know those rippled, wrinkly, criss-cross lines, when the mystery of a watery surface becoming solid is just beginning!) a thin coating of Ice! I hope that pond won't dry up like last year before those tiny black pin-heads turn into Tadpoles but how you do feel as if you were present at the stir in the original protoplasm of the Cosmos when you see Frog-Spawn. That Tom-of-Bedlam in *King Lear* who was a fraud – just as I made myself at School – swore he ate frog-spawn – & any one might well do much worse!

WEDNESDAY 16 FEBRUARY Oh dear! O dear! O dear! here comes a novel for me to say some nice things of in advance of its publication & it is a little too psychoanalytical for my Taste – I am too easily shocked. It is a peculiarity! But we all are mad; & we all prefer our own madness. Mine is a little different from that [of] the author of this work who is all the same as the Americans say a 'warm personal friend' – tho' I have never yet seen him.

MONDAY 21 FEBRUARY Last night the T.T. kept bringing Broad-cast news of Cabinet Crisis ending at eleven with Mr Eden's Retirement & at breakfast we read in the *Telegraph* [...] the difference in Policy between him & Chamberlain.

TUESDAY 22 FEBRUARY Dark! Dark! Dark! [...] Took Old his favourite way all along the side of Pen y Pigyn above the town – heard the mediaeval clock strike 9.15 – 9.30 – 9.45 & a lot of dogs came out & barked up at us & an old lady of 'Brook St' held her hand to her eyes & gazed up at us but on we went on our dizzy way as Dante would put it one foot always higher than the other – & I thought & thought of Dante & of the Inferno as we went: with rocks above & broken slate stones below. [...] At breakfast the T.T. discoursed with great eloquence on the mistake of trying to prove extra-sensory psychic phenomena by scientific mathematical means! Then we read at length the speeches of Eden & Chamberlain. Principle versus Expediency & the T.T. & I feeling that the late war showed the futility of Principle took the side of Chamberlain.

FRIDAY 25 FEBRUARY As for me & 'Very Old' we went on struggling to end Dante well & nobly but finding it Oh so hard. Then at 4.45 (later than usual) we set out & posted a letter to S. & S.'s Mr Howe telling him that Cassell's (& the Author too) do not want to include Joyce but want the Book to be from Homer to Hardy.

TUESDAY 1 MARCH Heard Miss Durrant our neighbour break her coals for her fire at 7 o'clock. [...] Took Old along Path of Sheeps' Dung above the town – the river far away towards Glyndyfrdwy beyond Carrog looked like one of those great landscapes of the Old Masters with water in distance & haggard desolate trees, broken trees [...]. I do so love these landscapes that resemble Pictures! [...] I have now finished Dante. The T.T.

1938 hates the 'Inferno' so for its savage Sadism that it only distressed her to listen to my essay. But now we are together studying *Don Quixote* with Delight.

SUNDAY 6 MARCH I took Old, as 'twas Sunday, down by the River for a change. I met such an intellectual & epicureal Tramp & gave him two sixpences. [...] Then I saw a dead sheep in the reeds by the water's edge with such a peaceful expression. If a living one of these Welsh sheep is lively and alert a dead one seems to return to the eternal passivity of all sheep! Dead! Dead! Dead! dead dead was that beautiful sheep! its head out of the water resting peacefully in the river-reeds! [...] I have so humoured the Old that this tendency of his after his supper the second we are by ourselves to try to bugger me has become too extreme.

Llewelyn has written an 'imaginary autobiography', Love and Death. *After another severe haemorrhage in December 1937, he wants Phyllis and John to visit him in Switzerland. Will comes to England for a long stay, in part to consult doctors about a possible ulcer. While he is visiting Chaldon, Theodore suddenly has a stroke.*

TUESDAY 15 MARCH A very important & exciting letter from Lulu about his new Book – a poetical version of his grand love-affair with [Gamel] with a Preface by his indulgent & philosophical New England wife, our dear Alyse. And also news that he is putting aside a present he has had from the lady I call 'Esmeralda' of 40£ in order that the T.T. & I may (in September he says) visit them at Davos! [...] Well I am now reading hard at Montaigne with a view to showing how like Lulu he is!

SUNDAY 27 MARCH I am now struggling with Aeschylus, Sophocles & Euripides. What a Task! How easily I used to lecture on these when I was twenty-three! Well – I must now use the Lemprière that the T.T. gave me. [...] After tea up here in the man's study the T.T. & I discussed – such is the warlike mood that Hitler & Mussolini have thrown us into – the relative values of National war-like airs & we decided that the *Marseillaise* was far & away the best of them all. I sang it to the T.T.

MONDAY 4 APRIL Bad News is the order of the Day! [...] Theodore was suddenly unconscious & Violet an invalid herself

& who hasn't been to the village since Dec had to leave him unconscious & go to the Post to telephone for Doctor. […] Luckily Will appeared at that juncture & put off his visit to London. […] Now there arrives a long full letter from Violet which says that both Doctors agree it was a stroke and some kind of X-ray instrument showed the dissolved Blood Clot in Theodore's Brain. O deary I! […] Now comes a letter from Will himself speaking of taking us in his car leisurely down to East Chaldon via all sorts of places! He says his X-rays & Specialist say there is nothing wrong with him save the need for more regular meals. […] Gertrude is still in bed with a slight temperature every afternoon. Good Lord, what a shaky lot we all are!

TUESDAY 5 APRIL And with a wild dithyrambic eulogy upon Euripides I must close this Greek Tragedy Essay which is about the longest of all in the Book. I pray old Quince won't cut it & that Mr Flower will like it. It's a 'funny little essay' as James Hanley would say! […] At tea our conversation drifted to Theodore having had a 'Stroke' & from that to how nice Theodore was to Violet & she to him & from that to the topic of lovers; & why love-affairs 'on the side' so often come to grief that begin so generously unselfishly & nobly on the woman's part but end inevitably; by her scenes & her sorrows & perhaps an abortion; making the man into a Cad & a Brute & a Bounder tho' he is just the same as he was at the start!

SATURDAY 9 APRIL Went along the Dante Path imagining myself a great Giant; so that to roll down the Precipice would be like tumbling down a little bank! It was very cold, so I wore my sweaters (3 of them). Met only one tiny little boy. […] Another letter from Emma Goldman with instructions as to what to write for her paper 'Spain & the World'. It is hard for selfish old gentlemen to know what to say when bombs are the order of the day. […] I feel like Euripides in Macedonia, with an S.O.S. from Aspasía (aged 80)! […] I begin my essay on *Moby Dick*. I am simply thrilled by *Moby Dick*.

FRIDAY 15 APRIL [Good Friday] I took the Extremely Old past Eben's door (closed). […] The only living soul I met, but I saw a dole-man drifting in a weary under-fed mood along the foot of the hill, was our Epileptic lad Billy. And with a Shameful effort I stopped to talk to him about Neb the Swan & his mate.

Isn't it shameful our human shrinking from the smitten of God? The T.T. confessed this morning & with a great deal of emotion – scolding me incidentally for my English off-hand casualness of response to a subtle analytical point – her feelings of violent distaste for the deformed & distorted & inarticulate *Egg-Woman*! [...] Then she spoke of Aunt Harriet's taste in Books – & of the Mistress's – & of her own which was for absolute bomb-destroyed *Chaos* out of which very subtle *clues* of identity between pluralistical vignettes of gnomic significance in the midst of litter, of confusion, might be drawn, like the honourable gestures in Henry James [...]. As for me I tried to do justice to the *Death of Christ* but all I could think of was the Death of the two wretched Anonymous *Thieves* – one on His right and one on His left! who represent the unknown myriads of sufferers who were *not* God in disguise! [...] Yesterday I was aware that I once had trouble in my Side.

THURSDAY 21 APRIL Last night I read to the T.T. my essay on Melville & Poe & the part about Poe at the end of the essay stirred her feelings more than I have ever seen [...]. No, it is extraordinary how our emotional imaginations are identical – 'The *T.T.'s*' & '*The Man's*'. It is a *mystery* considering how, when she came in that big young-girl-of-24 hat with brim I caught her wrist as my white slave for purely wicked reasons – never did I know (when I wrote her name in the dust) how our emotional nervous imaginations were destined to display absolute identity. But so it was – when I read the end of my Poe to her 'twas like wandering with 'Psyche, my soul' 'down an alley Titanic, of Cypress'! The T.T. is the most imaginative human being I ***have ever met***. That is a conceited thing to say after saying she was 'like me' – but I always ***feel like*** all the deep and strange identities I encounter & for the time I *am* like them while I follow their thoughts. But she sees round me, as I don't have the power to see round her.

FRIDAY 22 APRIL I ought to have *read* it – begun properly to *read* it – this book she likes. Instead of which I turned the pages of this Big Print, looking for I don't know what – & missed it all. The whole thing took exactly *two minutes* – and then the T.T. took the Book away because I could only *hum & haw*, simply because I hadn't got it in any sense at all. [...] I hate not liking what the T.T. likes well! It is impossible to say why I only turned the pages in place of reading it properly. I simply can't tell you why I acted like this. [...] I am puzzled. The T.T. took it away so quick. She is very proud. I was certainly reduced to weakness & helpless passivity and to the state of an elderly jelly-fish that could only undulate on the wave of events & seemed to have no hard philosophic 'I am I' to fall back upon. 'The "Cushiony Worm" exposed' might have been the caption of this Portrait of Me – rather like the Portrait of T.S. Eliot by Wyndham Lewis rejected by the Royal Academy – which looks as if he were waiting helplessly for the Devil to Come For Him!

TUESDAY 26 APRIL Last night we read the first Seven Chapters of Lulu's Book [*Love and Death*]. The talk of his lovers is un-natural & too sentimental but no one in the world has ever piled up the beauties of Nature – & realistically too, to such a tune. It is a Phenomenon – & it doesn't bother me very much whether it is art or not. I think, as a matter of fact, it is not good art. It is too monotonous!

SATURDAY 30 APRIL The T.T. has Pleurisy. [...] We had Great Agitation in the Night for the T.T. suddenly found that pain in her lungs pass to the muscles of her HEART & hurt a lot & we were Alarmed. [...] We propped herself up on Five Pillows for only by sitting up & indeed at first only by leaning over could she get this sharp pain to cease. She was bad. She didn't like me to speak or to move – & I didn't know what to do but just to lie by her side as still as a stone in the dawn! – for it was dawn. Yes it was at 4.30 a.m. that this event took place & it seemed the middle of the night but so quick there came a white streak and a golden streak in the North-Eastern sky. And (after all) in half an hour it was five – but at the time the night rolled away behind 4.30 & in front of 4.30 and huge spaces of time were on both sides of the T.T. propped up on pillows & leaning forward over her knees & sometimes crying 'O My! O My!' [...] Returning home yesterday via Eben's we were first chased by Nelly the young sow then persecuted by Peggy the young bitch, then nearly run over by a huge Mysterious Lorry coming down from the Mountain.

TUESDAY 10 MAY I pondered a little on my Essay on Old Testament. This is very rare for me ever to think of what I am writing. I write by 'Inspiration' as Katie would say. Not that I

1938 don't think of philosophical matters for I do constantly: but I think of how to sharpen or harden or dissolve or assert or suppress or enlarge or narrow or change or project my own Self-Soul; in relation to the Cosmos and the Hyperthetical Power behind the Cosmos and I think how to arrange direct re-create my inner soul with regard to others – how to react to shame, frustration, shocks, humiliations, disappointments, mockeries & slaps, well-aimed, stinging slaps in the face. Thus do I think.

MONDAY 16 MAY Old Eben has made a barricade across his yard. Was that to prevent the 'Old' & 'the Man' going our usual way past his place? Or was it to prevent Nelly the Sow from wandering? It must be Eben who has barricaded the Rough Field where I prefer going! The Welsh are great lovers of these barricades. And you never know when you are going to come to some Barricade put up over night against you – & by a person who has talked so friendly the night before! [...] The Landlords are as bad as the small farmers. Rûg announces in the *Adsain* that you have to ask the leave of Mr Beadle [...] to do what Rûg calls 'take the breezes on the Mountain.'

WEDNESDAY 18 MAY I begin to read *Swann's Way* & am thrilled by Proust's way. [...] It has been raining since twelve I think. The T.T.'s Brain is moving with extraordinary rapidity today – owing to the Rain [...]. She is maniacally sensitive & responsive to the weather. When the rain was hovering but had not fallen she was cross & miserable – now it is actually raining her spirits are nimble & eager & flitting about like fire-flies. Nothing can annoy her today – & she has shaken off some ten or fifteen years – her face is full of radiance [...]. She would be pleased if I were to suggest the maddest enterprise. I feel like her grandfather who might say 'go out and play hop-scotch; only come in when I call!' In my Questionnaire sent me by Mr Clemens Mark Twain's son I have to say what quality in women I like the best – I shall most certainly say 'childishness'.

WEDNESDAY 25 MAY Had loathsome Dreams. It is my inside, with a touch of dyspepsia & also my dependence being un-realized on enemas & my memories of the times when I had not saved myself by enemas being still dominant in my dreams! Yes that is what it is – the heavenly Salvation & Redemption of the enema has not yet arrived into the land of dreams! The word dreams is to me the symbol of all evil & loathing – but all the same I have had dreams of heavenly beauty but the evil dreams in my coward's mind outweighs the good dreams, so that I am a Dream-Killer, an Oneiro-clast! – not an Icono-clast! Took Old up lane by Eben's where he has left a little space past his singular barricade in the yard – to the end of Dante Path. As I heard that divine Medieval Bell strike Nine I stood like Aaron between the horrors of Decomposition – my Dreams – and the intense absorption of my soul in all the fronds, & ferns, & new leaves & the Church Tower & the Gaer 'yr Gaer' & the Gorsedd & the circle of fairy branches put there by the children of the Orphanage. I have come by a thousand tricks & wiles & crafty ways to balance my mind – for I always take for granted these perpetual forms of madness – to balance my mind, I say, between going too far in facing Horror – which is a bad thing to do – & running away too quick & too universally from Horror, – which though less bad than the former, is, I fancy – unless I am deceived by my Puritan Conscience calling on me to be braver than my Nature & great Creative Nature allow or than is in my *Ker* or *Moira* – is also a bad thing to do. But the great trick is to fight all the time & with fighting to have Faith in my power of Forgetting [...] but there is behind & beyond this yet another trick – a sort of rearguard advance – which I used to use in old days – & this is Trust in Nature & lying back on the flow of the millions of little impressions offered by the stream of Life as it flows past my senses and trust that they will drown the Horror, as I float, as I float, without this cheerful obstinate Cheerio O! Anglo Saxon spirit! Of course these Dream Horrors as of conscious Decomposition of the most loathsome sort are quite different from those outrages to my life-illusion which occur so often that I can cope with them very easily. And this I do by a process of imagining myself a 'pet lunatic' & a skipping Boswellian 'Cushiony Worm' like my great grandfather Johnson of Dereham who was a Tanner. By having the Tanner's life-illusion I get on beautifully! I think it must be reading Proust that has loosened my tongue in this scandalously unreserved manner!

FRIDAY 27 MAY Oh how sweet she was after she had tasted her coffee & then all was well. She went upstairs for my spectacles once – for my cigarettes twice – so that I could loll at my ease & look at the slim sylphs with very little under their 'frocks' in her *Vogue* – a paper which I like now & again to glance over with a lecherous eye. I can recall how my Father once said to me very gravely 'John, Pictures are a temptation to me!' They are certainly a lascivious joy to John. And then she launched out into the profoundest remarks about Proust & the Madeleine that I have ever heard her use. Oh how deep into the mystery her words did sink! I listened to this 'golden stream' from her lips with a most practical & stealing ear for use in my Essay. I believe I shall steal from her words today the best paragraph in this whole collection of essays!

MONDAY 30 MAY Oh how nice the T.T. was today! Yesterday she became a Different Creature – as 'they' can beyond all the Metamorphoses of Ovid! She brought it about that I felt it to be an outrageous imposition that I should long for her to 'make tea' [...]. This Bizzzarrrre Image of the T.T – this Constantinopolitan T.T. had come back from Mrs Bailey's, a different person, from what she set out – and the two chief pillars, bases, props, foundations of my life – tea and enemas – trembled under the feet of this new T.T. My mind reverted to the old hand-enema & I got 'kindling' from the oven to light this fire up here [...] thinking in my heart 'at least I could boil the kettle up here.' But today the T.T. has dropped her Byzantine mask.

Phyllis and Aunt Harriet go to London for five days; they see Noel Coward's Operette. *She suggests John give himself an enema on the third day but he does not. He finishes the book of essays and begins again on* Owen Glendower.

SATURDAY 4 JUNE I shall never forget those 3 enemas in the Bath-room. Met the T.T.'s train last night. [...] But directly we got in I asked for the ENEMA & aye! if it hadn't been for the T.T.'s skill & competence & keeping her head & her heroic lack of any disgust, repulsion we would have had to have got the Doctor or the Nurse. How could I have been so foolish not to have done as she said? The whole bath-room was my privy. [...] Took Old this morning to the Duddon. Felt exhausted & shaky after last night. [...] She has just been talking [...] about London – considered as an actual ENTITY. She spoke with Proustian subtlety of this at breakfast & I listened intent. And the T.T., speaking of *Operette*, Became a Dancer: yes the T.T. saw Herself as a mysterious Erotesque Dancer!

SUNDAY 5 JUNE She was shy about [having] told me she was like a great Dancer. 'I hope you didn't think I was vain' she said. I do so enjoy it when she feels embarrassed. The great thing is to tease her in some subtle sideways manner & make her feel shy all suddenly – I can make her even put her fingers against her cheek! I do so like it when she does this. I like playing on a girl's self-consciousness, like you would play on a piano – tra-la-la-la-la! A girl is a harp – and you can flick the strings without striking them […].

TUESDAY 21 JUNE I am pondering a little now & again on my *Owen Glyndwr* which I have begun again. It […] will be interesting to see if my recent studies of all the Best Books of the World have any effect at all when I come to write myself! I am […] also working at my Welsh Story called the 'Cushiony Worm' in Welsh – 'Clustog Abwydyn' Cushion Worm.

FRIDAY 24 JUNE Set out with the 'Old' at 2.30. […] The T.T. [*sic*] did Number 2 as we walked along. I kept him on the leash & went along the Cynwyd Road. […] We got as far as the Beast House when lo! Mr Ervine's Car & his friendly chauffeur & he stopped & said 'I am alone. Come & see my books!' […] He showed me a Sir Thomas More & I took it for Erasmus but he tried as always for he is a born Diplomat to spare my feelings. The kind chauffeur took me home. It was an Event. […] Then we went to tea with Mr & Mrs Baker. […] After my talk with the Postman over the churchyard wall yesterday when he told me how in his childhood they used to go to the slaughter house to see the Butcher drink blood, I was in the Post Office & a very very beautiful young man annoyed me by his beauty for his beautiful eyes seemed to mock me. So I looked like the oldest of Ichthyosaures into his beautiful eyes & said 'My dog came by sea in a cage – in a Monkey's Cage!' Now wasn't that a queer thing to say looking into the eyes of a beautiful & mocking young man?

SATURDAY 25 JUNE I like to be out of sight before Betty comes for that gives me a feeling that I have got up like a soldier at the bugle, and not like a Rector waiting till the Maid has done his Study! I carefully correct my wandering thoughts as I go. This is an old astonishment & bother to me – the ridiculousness of the thoughts I have! […] The two subjects that frequently I tend to revert to – both very 'unmeet' are literary conceit & social conceit & their respective rufflings & shocks & absurd disconcertings [...]. Thus I condemn my thoughts wandering upon any book I have written especially the last. [...] And not only did I have to beat those thoughts out of my mind's austere cell but what do my thoughts fly to at every opportunity but Mr Ervine and his Big House – why don't they fly to Mr Baker & his little house?

MONDAY 27 JUNE I thought so much about Theodore during my walk. I think he is so faced with the thought of Another Stroke that this fills his mind to the exclusion of all else. He has always been very nervous about his Head, covering it from the sun with leaves on the top of his head under his hat. And he has always been subject to Interior Withdrawings from all outer contact – especially from his brothers & sisters – & I think he has now allowed this withdrawing inwards its full scope & indulgence. So that he can sit & knit letting the whole world – especially his relatives – go. I suppose he retains links with Violet and with Susie but that is all he can manage. [...] If he wants to see anyone I presume he'll insist on seeing them; but if he doesn't, as apparently is the case just now, well! this must be just accepted and he must be just left to his own secret Mind.

Will drives them via Oxford to Dorset for their holiday, 8–15 July. In Chaldon, Llewelyn is an absent presence, but John spends more time than usual with Theodore, who is still recovering from his stroke. Theodore's reference is to Jonathan Swift who in later years became reclusive, suffered from a brain disorder, and was finally declared insane. Llewelyn gives an account of Walter Franzen's death – 'Falling in Full Sunshine From a cliff' – and his burial in Chaldon churchyard, in Earth Memories.

MONDAY 4 JULY Went the 'Round', pondering (making myself ponder) on my Eighth Chapter of *Owen Glyndwr* about Dinas Brân. [...] At breakfast – & I had just time to read to the end of Joshua's murderous and outrageous victories over the aboriginals and his killing them – men women children & animals 'by the edge of the sword' & hanging the 5 Kings after the people 'had put their feet on their necks.' All this 'the Lord commanded'! Meanwhile we hear from Vienna how 'Big people treat Little People'. [...] Then I told the T.T. tales of Wyaston

House which I begged her to let me show in Oxford if we do actually stay the night there, and of Ralph & Alice & 'Bertie Moon' & Walter & Jeanie and the T.T. said all the characters in my life – and all the characters in the lives of my family were like people in Proust – & as if they had been invented by the same Author.

SUNDAY 10 JULY We feel at home in Dorset. [...] Woke up at 7 got up at 7.30. Thought of Lulu. Was glad he was safe in Clavadel. But I saw his gold-fish & the Inscription on his threshold about Mirth and Cheer & the joys of love in bed! Took Old as far as the new Coast Guard Station past the Obelisk. Looked with familiar old memories & deep satisfaction at Chesil Beach & Portland & St Alban's Head & the Sea. [...] This time I am completely puzzled & startled and feel un-natural not seeing Theodore as usual – only under these weird conditions. I cannot understand it. I am puzzled by it all. But I do what I am told to do.

MONDAY 11 JULY O how hard, O how hard I do try [...] to adapt my life-illusion to that of a lean bony worldly failure, and mental failure and love-denier or love-effacer, and a skeleton walking who is made cheerful by burning sticks under a kettle – and who would be beaten if ever he tried to compete. [...] I went to see Theodore. It is clear he is fighting for his life, whether it is his body that is instinctive in this fight or his mind I cannot tell. It may not be a mental thing at all – it may be a purely bodily instinct the body itself fighting for its life – and not nervous sensitive mental manias or what I fancied it might be.

TUESDAY 12 JULY What I had fancied was that Theodore was using his illness – as I can conceive in my anti-social heart a person very well doing as an excuse to avoid everyone – to do what Bertie quite erroneously accused me of doing & consequently never came to Corwen when he was at Oswestry but now I have changed my mind. I think now that Theodore is fighting for his life – and forcing himself not to feel things & not to have emotions & not to risk love or wrath! [...] He spoke of wools how when he did a scarf for me he would want so many ounces of wool – an ounce to a ball of wool. I said 'I have learnt that it is safest not to do things than to do things.' He said 'I am glad to hear you utter those words for it is Eternity in that direction and yet — ' This he said in a very low voice – 'it is natural to fear.' Then he said that sometimes he thought he had the same disease as Swift. He said his Mother taught him – only I noticed instead of saying your mother or my mother he said 'mother taught me' & then he said 'she always told me to keep both hands upon it and I never could do that and cannot do it yet.' [...] Will came & painted me – 'tis a wondrous picture & not unlike – & Gertrude painted the painter & the object too. [...] Then at 2 I set out with Katie & Old & walked to within sight of White Nose Coastguards where Lulu used to live. [...] I experienced that lively terror of the cliffs which I feel nor was this lessened when Katie showed me the very exact spot where Franzen Walter Franzen fell into the sea & was killed.

WEDNESDAY 13 JULY Set out at 8.30 a.m. Walked nearly to Dippy's Farm. [...] And the sea was cerulean hyacinthine azure halcyon lapis-lazuli Blue & white foam was there where the Cow & Calf rocks rose up in the blue & more beautiful still – of all things, save the mother-of-pearl with green of certain shells, the most magical in colour – purple under sky-blue – where under the sea was sea-weed! [...] I drink up the spirit of the blue Sea.

FRIDAY 15 JULY Last night I started reading in my style Eliot's Waste Land a poem I love tho' I heartily despise Eliot himself & disagree with every single one of his opinions. [...] Well I love the Waste Land & I love intoning it but the sound of my voice made Katie Hysterical with misery and anger because she hates everything that suggests church! She rushed away upstairs screaming 'Don't come near me!'

SATURDAY 16 JULY Will returns home to Dorset alone. [...] Oh Oh Oh! how I did Enjoy sleeping with the T.T. again. It was like the 1st time of all; but not quite, for it was ten, twenty, fifty, a hundred times more wonderful to me than the first time – for she did not struggle so much; & was less nervous than the 1st time. [...] There was Hay Making beginning in two fields down there. Very sweet to smell & nice to walk through – the death of grass – the battle field of dead grass-blades!

SATURDAY 30 JULY The T.T. today is doing the pictures, changing them – re-hanging them – & this always means that with her head on one side she has to survey each wall of each room from every possible angle. I do so like this picture of a sunset behind a castle with a flag at the foot of its flagstaff & obscure figures & a feeling of the sea! 'Twas from Gloucester Terrace it came into Katie's hands and she hated it & gave it to me! I simply love it. It is dark obscure and unbounded & it's the kind of picture that I seem to have seen thro' five or six reincarnations as by a warm fire – with everyone else gone out – I feverishly turn over the pages of the old *Spectator* for passages of that vicious & lascivious kind upon which my Imagination fed.

WEDNESDAY 3 AUGUST Had a very happy breakfast with the T.T. who discoursed so eloquently on the Japanese (for whom she has a deep secret weakness!) & on whether this Row on the Frontier with Russia will lead to a World War. The T.T. thinks 'tis more serious & dangerous than either Spain or Zcecho-Slovaks (to spell it is as impossible as to predict about it) but the T.T. has a Tarot Card & Old Moore's Almanack Instinct for future Events. I hope her fears will not be justified.

Marian and Peter (now aged seventeen) visit Corwen 4–13 August.

FRIDAY 5 AUGUST Had a most lively & exciting evening with Marian & Peter. [...] Peter talked freely & easily of anything that glided through his head. Had a very happy & lively breakfast. Marian's opinions are as usual very strong & very strongly expressed! [...] I have returned her half of the hundred dollars she gave me to buy new teeth. 'You are disgraceful' she said – like the person in the Waste Land. 'Get some teeth,' she said. But I didn't [...].

SUNDAY 7 AUGUST Called Peter & at 8.30 set out for the Round. Peter & I have the most exciting conversations about religion, morals, philosophy etc., etc. He said he was tired of telling me stories & wanted to ask me all sorts of questions about religion, philosophy, etc., & even about the circumstances of his birth & parentage & about his mysterious & evasive progenitor. I shall have to enquire of Marian exactly how freely & frankly it is best for me to speak [...]. Aye! but I cannot help wishing that his origin was yet more mysterious & unusual than it was! I will say no more.

WEDNESDAY 10 AUGUST Last night I read my Second

1938 Chapter of *Owen* to them [...]. But both Marian & Peter got tired of it & nearly went to sleep! Now what does this mean? [...] Peter protested that my giving sixpences to Tramps was only to satisfy my own ego but I explained that if it gave me pleasure & the Tramp pleasure it is unnecessary to analyze the kind of pleasure (whether moral or immoral) that both of us get.

THURSDAY 11 AUGUST Went the 'Round' with Peter & talked all the time about Ibsen & Aristophanes both of whom Peter had enjoyed in the Modern Library translations. He told me very vividly the play about Gabriel Borkman. We talked as we do every day to Mr Williams 'The Greek Professor' or Road Man who had epileptic fits and who has leant me, lent me Welsh literary magazines. [...] We are now going to Valle Crucis and also to World's End [...]. I protested a little but Marian said it was because I hate picnics!

SATURDAY 13 AUGUST Marian insisted on continuing our talk till it was 5 minutes to train-time. She does not, cannot, will not realize that in this country all goes smoothly if you take plenty of time. [...] She lingers so and rushes so at the last! Well, we got to Station & then like a lady – like a woman travelling – I could hear her protest at the ticket window very vigorously as to the expense of the trip. [...] Then the train came in and stood. Where was Marian? Peter was upset and so was I! but less than he. [...] But Marian did come & got into a 1st class. And I got our porter to put all her Twelve bags into the Guard's Van – but I pray she isn't too forgetful to have them all labelled at Ruabon. The T.T. feels as if all her world had been shaken by their departure & nothing left.

SUNDAY 14 AUGUST Well! well! Marian is at Chydyok – I might say 'at home' since Dorset (my Father's Home) with Weymouth as its Centre; & old friendly Dorchester; are more home to me than Montacute ever was or Shirley either!

MONDAY 15 AUGUST After tea yesterday I spoke to the T.T. about my *Glyndwr* Book & how both Marian & Peter seemed exhausted by the 2nd Chapter. She explained this – & also said that I must after this Dinas Brân chapter swing to Owen himself & make him into a HAMLET but a Hamlet who really (hardly knowing how) becomes a great Prince of Denmark. She also said

I mustn't waste precious time over my conscientiousness over details; especially over getting my character from place to place (exits & entrances) as if in a Drama.

The cost of the trip, the difficulty of obtaining passports and visas, and the threatening war finally decide them against going to Switzerland. Will, Elizabeth and family arrive in Corwen on 2 September, but two days later Will is hospitalized with an ulcer.

TUESDAY 16 AUGUST She dreads Oh so much! the expense of our visit to Lulu. She says we are so poor that we are best quietly plodding on & not having shoes or underclothes or overcoats but if we go to Lulu we shall have to buy some of these things & she says we simply can't afford it no! not even tho' Marian has subscribed & Lulu will subscribe.

TUESDAY 30 AUGUST The T.T. came up at ten to my room & said we would put off going to Liverpool to get our tickets till we knew what was going to happen in this Czechoslovakia Business; & these cursed Sudeten Germans; who are, it now clearly is shown, the obedient & humble tools of the 'Third Reich' & its Demoniacal Boss. [...] Betty went home to do the wash as usual & we – the T.T. & I – talked long of many matters – principally of the Chinese & the Japanese. The T.T. is secretly extremely pro-Japanese & profoundly suspicious of, terrified of, tho' not 'hostile' to, the Chinese; but she is outraged by the bad & evil behaviour of the Japanese Militarists. Then we read an exciting letter from Casey at Chesil Beach whose conscience tells him he has no right to be as happy as he is.

SUNDAY 4 SEPTEMBER The 'Old' doesn't like climbing Pen y Pigyn any more but I go ahead. When I look back he stands still, looking reproachful & asking for the leash – which always he likes to have – for it makes him feel very very safe & helps him to climb – but when I stop looking back, he comes on at top speed, and is always there catching me up. [...] Had a very happy breakfast. Will teased me about how in old days I made them all Superstitious & made them stand on sacred stones & by sacred wells & go thro' many invocations and conjurations. [...] Will goes to Ruthin Castle Hospital.

WEDNESDAY 7 SEPTEMBER Last night at Ten Elizabeth was

telephoned to that Will's gastric Ulcer had PERFORATED his stomach; that he was in great pain; had morphia. And that a Surgeon had been called from Liverpool. Elizabeth set out at once – would not let me go with her – & we waited. At Twelve Midnight she telephoned that the Surgeon had arrived & they were already giving Will the anaesthetic. […] Elizabeth got back at 7 p.m. saying that the Doctors swore to her that Will was out of Danger of Peritonitis which is the fatal thing it appears. […] Will's heart & pulse are amazing them all.

SATURDAY 17 SEPTEMBER Up at 6.45. Found Elizabeth up before me & having had already a cup of tea was busy ironing on the iron-board with the New Electric Iron which I believe we are Paying For by the 'In-stall-Ment plan'. […] I thought of the dangers of War all the time & of the partizan ideology which is the Curse of our age. I thought how human beings are roused so much easier to Hate & Destruction than to friendliness & construction. I feel it all in myself! When I think of the war as just solely a means of humbling crushing and humiliating Hitler & Mussolini I feel a secret longing that it should break out! That is the feeling of most liberals, radicals, socialists & communists! We feel much hatred & fear of Hitler & dread of having to say Heil Hitler! or be tortured to death with every shameful insult by these waspish & cruel young Illiterates who are the heart of Fascism that we secretly Long for War. What a confession! So that it is only with our reason that we – I say only with our Reason that we admire our splendid old Chamberlain who has enough sense & reason, & also I suspect a certain kind of vivid imagination, beyond ours to realize what a War would really be & to want to postpone or stop it at all costs.

TUESDAY 20 SEPTEMBER There ought to be a Referendum or Plebiscite among the young men who will actually have to fight. All these people advocating 'firmness' & 'stand by Czechoslovakia' our middle class leaders, & all the labour leaders too, are they not middle-aged or old men who would not have to fight? […] But it may be that this popular belligerency – that I myself confess to having to fight with in my secretest heart! – is the Method of Great Creative Nature, & the step she has resolved to take! Perhaps this is our only chance for a hundred years of putting an end to these Tyrants. […] It looks as if we may avert War by yielding! I think I'll put off my Enema till tomorrow. Another Dark Day. It looks as if we were forcing Prague to yield up the Sudeten to Hitler. […] The Dark feeling of yielding to Hitler almost but not quite over-powers the Relief at escaping War. But lots of simple poor people in these islands do not feel called upon to Die for the Czechs. But there is a feeling of Shame. There is no doubt about it we all in France & England feel Shame Shame Shame. But it is better to feel Shame than to let Science loose to Destroy the World! Science loves to be in unscrupulous hands! […] The indignation against Chamberlain is rising among all the liberals & especially in the U.S. where they are safe from bombs.

FRIDAY 23 SEPTEMBER Is Hitler responsible for the blind ferocity of the German Press which is the most Brutal Reading I have ever heard. If he is responsible for this there is no hope but in war; but are Gobbbells & Gorrring & these accurst young Nazis out of his control? […] Can these damned madmen represent the average German? If so all you can say is that this race understands nothing else but BRUTE FORCE. Our farmer & milk purveyor, Mr Jones said this morning that Chamberlain is a Birmingham Business Man; but we ought to follow Winston Churchill for it 'takes a Bully to stand up to a Bully.'

SATURDAY 24 SEPTEMBER 6 More Days of Grace! but the country is getting Restless. […] This morning she looked so lovely in her sleep aye! aye! what a thing, to have won such an one by my Oratory & by my Petrushka Dance! Once she said in her sleep these words: 'Do you Need anything?' All my life I shall remember those words. […] Mr Chamberlain talked till two o'clock last night with Hitler. No Good! He has now to come back & summon Parliament. The French are mobilizing; the Czechs are mobilized. What a terrifying word – Mobilization is! O deary I! O deary I! But the country is against Chamberlain in his peace moves. Actually the Socialist leaders are in favour of Conscription. Think of that!

TUESDAY 27 SEPTEMBER News dark dark dark. Parliament tomorrow will end all hope of Compromise. Hitler hates all Democracy & a Parliament is his *bête noire*; and all Parliaments hate Hitler. So from the moment our Parliament meets all hope of Peace is Over. Our only chance was before the speeches were let loose! Once let loose & we have Demagogue Mesmerizer

Hitler, confronted by what he hates most, a lot of Demagogues in Session! We all listened to the Broad-cast last night & most interesting was it to note our various reactions. I listened to my English compatriot Mr Harold Nicholson with profound dislike, suspicion, distaste & distrust. The man's sneering sarcastic manner – his lack of all strong feeling – his middle class faintly cockney accent – his ill-bred jokes, comparing the Czechs to a bird in a cage – this is the sort of person from whom I have suffered all my life. He is […] that sneering legal-journalistic attaché type who lacks all emotion & all imagination just exactly the person for the B.B.C. A sort of Anglo-Saxon Gobbbbbellls. After this sneering emotionless facetious tone – Hitler's hysterical theatrical prophetic speech, weeping, shrieking, weeping, boasting, was I confess more what I could sympathize with!

WEDNESDAY 28 SEPTEMBER I think Chamberlain is a really 'great man', whatever that is! How absolutely sincere & direct & realistic his speech was last night! […] & how honest of him to boldly say I am not ready to bring disaster on millions for the sake of Honour! […] He has said 'your Honour is less important than the killing of millions who don't know what it's all about!' But he is absolutely alone.

FRIDAY 30 SEPTEMBER The PEACE IS SIGNED! & a faint discomfort troubles our Conscience! A beautiful Day of Hope! Everyone in the world (all people who know what is going on at all) feel an indescribable RELIEF. Elizabeth took the Old clear to the Top of Pen y Pigyn. […] We both tried to make Elizabeth shy by praising her ways as a guest; & her ways are those of an early rising quietly-flying Bird.

SATURDAY 1 OCTOBER We spent a long time the T.T. & I over our breakfast reading the paper & all the praise of Chamberlain. The *Telegraph* however expresses our sentiments when it says that enough has not been made of the Sacrifice of the Czechs! […] When one contemplated the grinning Mugs of the Cabinet one could not help thinking of the Day of Mourning in Prague – at least that is how my mind led by the quick-changing mind of the T.T. felt towards it.

SUNDAY 2 OCTOBER Her walk last evening & now this one […] have brought back her Cough. […] Oh deary I! now that the agitation of the war is over the Terminals relapse into their own tribulations. The Truth is we can just get on – the T.T. can just manage to look after the Ladies & her two Old Gentlemen when we are alone. But visitors swamp the boat. I tried at breakfast to make her see that now after the Doctor's reassuring words that my trouble is merely a nerve into which my cold settled – not pleurisy, not shingles, not lung – it was her bad cough that has gone on for nearly 3 months and that any walking in this damp climate makes worse that is our real danger spot. She is so thin – so little & this great cough takes entire possession of her. [...] I acted like Lulu with Alyse! I ought to have made the Doctor sound her chest! He may have said 'You, young woman, are the one in danger now; not the Hulking Hypochondriac at your side. You ought to be in bed.'

WEDNESDAY 5 OCTOBER The T.T. set out about two o'clock and walked with the Old to Cynwyd. Here she went to a Sale [...] & she came back by the 4.20 train with some Cut Glass tinkling chandelier-beauties; diamonds & bells & music & sun-sparkles & ruby lights! [...] Had the T.T. a little baby daughter called Perdita she would like to lie for hours staring at these beauties swaying & gleaming & sparkling like a thousand crystals & diamonds!

THURSDAY 6 OCTOBER Mr Jones our Farmer brought the Paper with hints that it contained bad news. And so by God it did! News so bad that the result of it was to swing the feelings and the mind & the whole prophetic soul of the T.T. into a Wish that what we were preparing for last week, namely a World-War, had come! [...] What makes the T.T. now say that she wishes we had followed youth with its Ideals & not old 'business-age' with its experience is the news that Benes has resigned & that the New Czech Government is Pro-Nazi & Pro-Fascist & are already flying to Berlin like that Austrian Nazi did who betrayed Austria to Berlin. [...] What do I feel myself? Well the T.T.'s prophetic eloquence bewildered & be-numbed me – but I cannot feel that it foreshadows any change towards Fascism in the really democratic free countries. [...] I think Masaryk & Benes were great men & Democrats but I doubt if their subjects were quite the same.

SUNDAY 9 OCTOBER An episode of very curious interest

occurred last night. The Ladies were expected to come over here as it was the Man's birthday but I was content to wait, reading the *Brython*. I gradually became aware however of some long continuous performance on the Radio going on *sans cesse*. [...] At last at 11.15 there came the T.T. in a piteous state of pouring tears & sorrow & remorse! She had disobeyed the 'voice within' – the Quaker Monitor – or the Compass-needle pointing 'ar y Gogledd' [north] & instead of coming down to bring the ladies across for the Man's Birthday she was caught absorbed fascinated in mental & spiritual interest by a Play of Priestley's very realistic & very good on the Mystery of Time. It was very very hard to persuade her that Petrushka is not one to be particular or touchy about Birthday Events. [...] The T.T. spoke of how 'mixed up' she was, but how that point of the compass pointing to the North remained the only thing to be followed in all the miserable confusion of our life & of our blundering Fate. The wind has torn her willow-tree from its post.

MONDAY 10 OCTOBER Last night it was astonishing Moonlight. I did not see the Moon herself, at this full, for I am very slack & inert in this business of observing Nature! I am like my father – & have a tendency to draw the curtains & sit over the fire – whereas my mother, like the T.T., would be out looking at the moonlight or at least peeping out, between my father's curtains or shutters!

Will comes out of hospital. After a brief visit he returns to Africa on 17 October. Gerard Casey will go to Africa to work for Will and Elizabeth.

THURSDAY 13 OCTOBER At ten Gerard came & I tried to encourage him to ask Will questions about what he would have to do but Will seemed to imply that he could only find out after he was there. But since Gerard is a very silent & shy chap; & so is Will – this is not a very & never will be a very easy thing.

SUNDAY 16 OCTOBER Had a happy breakfast. After it we had a great Barber's Scene of cutting hair with a sheet. Will cut his own & E. did the back of his head. And then the T.T. cut mine under Will's direction. Then Gerard came & they three went up the Mountain & talked business. He is to go D.V. D.V.

SATURDAY 22 OCTOBER Suddenly last night I was clearly

confronted by Monsieur Financial PANIC! for no Cable of 'Homage & Congratulation' has arrived from old Schuster & yet according to what Pollinger said the *Enjoyment of Literature* appeared on the Seventeenth & for five days or six days it has been Out. So that alas! I begin to feel it cannot have been that spectacular success which old Schuster gambled on; à la [Durant's] *The Story of Philosophy*. It was this Panic that came upon me for we have been living for a year on the thousand dollars advance on this book & if it is not a rather marked success there won't be much more for us & no more of any kind till *Owen* is ready.

SATURDAY 29 OCTOBER I pondered on [...] that passage in Dorothy Richardson's *Clear Horizon* about Being – & its importance its Superior Importance – compared with Becoming. Spinoza as against that crafty Snake, Hegel – how I must try to enjoy as often as I can moments of sinking into Being – while I shave – while I watch the 'Old' lift his leg – while I hang up my coat – and at all manner of other moments – but I am very bad at sinking into Being! I am always afraid when I am not active that I shall think of a spider or of some other nervous maniacal Horror. How can people be so brave & so healthy as to dare to stop their activity?

MONDAY 7 NOVEMBER Golden leaves flying, grass emerald green & in all the little streams astonishing fresh green leaves & shoots & new little tiny weeds in a sort of Renaissance of the spring, in the very midst of the Golden Descent! Up at 7.30 – out at 8.30. Decided to let the Old go his favourite way today as the poor old bugger limped with clamped tail of misery – why I have simply no idea – all the way up the lane. [...] How happily the Old – completely recovered – what an old Malingerer he is! – headed for the Gorsedd & gambolled up his well loved Pen y Pigyn!

FRIDAY 11 NOVEMBER It is tragic reading – this German Revenge for the assassination of their Paris Envoy. And after all, this revenge of these ten thousand times accurst Nazis is so outrageous that it'll turn the world against them – for that these fashionably-dressed German Women holding up their babies to see the Pogrom – like lynchers in America – should clap their hands in glee while the world looks on in disgust – shows up the

Devil that has got hold of the Hitler Ku Klux Klan – & will be a hint to us all of what we are to expect if we don't arm! arm! arm! I wonder what the Pacifists will feel at such goings on!

TUESDAY 15 NOVEMBER Saw old Eben at his door. [...] I tried to make him understand the peril of constipation if he now starts as he desires on a completely milk diet – but there seems to [be] a lack of a Welsh word for 'enema'! [...] A nice letter from my Son suggesting our meeting in Dec – Dec 21 to 23 just before Xmas & he suggests a small Hotel in Chester! I must talk to the T.T. about this! It is very good of him to think of taking the expense & effort of that terrific long journey! [...] Now I am engaged upon the close of Chapter XI, very very difficult for I have to devise a sort of psychic bridge over which the readers & the author can pass together from the consciousness of young Rhisiart to that of the middle-aged Glendower!

Eben goes into a nursing home and Zach Williams moves into the Morgan farm. Enjoyment *sells badly in America and John considers various ways of earning some money. Llewelyn sends him £50 and Gerard Casey arranges a lecture for him in Bridgend in December. This lecture (sans teeth) not only brings a welcome fee, but also a meeting with the Welsh poet, Huw Menai, who becomes a close friend. The occasion is a very happy one in a discouraging time.*

THURSDAY 17 NOVEMBER The T.T. is now ensconced in The Spare Room under the window without a fire typing my Anti-Vivisection paper for that Manchester editor! The article that James [Hanley] got for me! It is a sort of evening edition (cheap & popular) of the *Manchester Guardian* & I thought they would refuse such an article. But they accepted it! [...] The T.T. typing my article has found silly arguments – old sentimental tags about spiritual progress being better than mental progress & scientific progress when the T.T. says they are equal in value – but whether she can cross it out I don't know. She often curses a thing & yet doesn't change it. I wish she would more often change things.

FRIDAY 18 NOVEMBER How strange EBEN'S House looks all empty. But there was Mr Zachariah Williams who has newly married a lady with many children – of Brook Street. And Betty says the little boy of 8 is one too many for Zachariah. But 'tis a great comfort to me that Zachariah (& none other) is to succeed Ebenezer as my nearest neighbour. I do not at present feel any fear of him or of his very large step-family & personal family, all mixed up. [...] Did I tell you of that occasion when by the Gorsedd Stones I heard a Rushing & a Mighty Wind – [...] different from a falling tree – some Mystery fell!

SATURDAY 19 NOVEMBER During my walk I pondered on our alarming Financial Situation for Schuster's letter of yesterday contained only talk of how 'noble' the book is; and that he had difficulty in getting it Reviewed at all! He is keen on it I know but even he cannot make Americans buy. And Pondering & Pondering – I decided to devote my mornings – or a portion that is left after my 'lessons' and my letters – to composing another of my tiresome little tracts for the Times, or lay-sermons – the last of which *The Art of Happiness* Lulu condemned as the lowest depth to which my talent had ever fallen!

SATURDAY 3 DECEMBER I go to South Wales for the first time in my life & meet there Huw Menai. A beautiful day. Took Old to Llangar Old Church. Found that a pink lichen of a lovely shell-like tint was beginning to cover up the flat tombstone of Peter Lloyd Bard & *Ofydd* which has such a great interest for me & has had ever since I came 3½ years ago. *Ofydd* with its green ribbon the 3rd order of Iolo's Druidical *Gorsedd* really was the scholarly critical philosophical & philological grade of the Bardic circle of Initiation below but different from Druidism White & pure Bardism Blue. [...] I got to Bridgend an hour too soon – but there was Gerard my darling Peredur, now to sail on his Quest [...] for the Magic Cauldron. And there was Mr Ben Roberts our *Ofydd*, of the green grade, with his literary head whirling round & round & his little Ford Car bumping up & down & his brain far more absorbed in books than either his Bard or his Druid! [...] Then I had the glory of meeting the greatest man save Dreiser & Hardy I have ever met, *sef* HUW MENAI! I Felt like Panurge meeting Pantagruel – & 'they loved each other at first sight.'

TUESDAY 6 DECEMBER Rain turns to loveliness. [...] At the station there was a crowd of Seven Friends including Huw [...]. John Lewis, Boss of the Congregational Union & Saddler, [...] said at the end of my endless harangue the night before – 'I have only one quarrel with the speaker that he said 'you' instead of 'us' – 'look at him!!' Wasn't that a touch of true Welsh Art! eh? or rather of […] beautiful artlessness such as Pwyll found in the Bride of Hades.

SUNDAY 11 DECEMBER As we passed, the Old & I, Zachariah's Abode lo! emerging from the door with a sauce-pan held in her hand was The Girl! Her head was adorned with a great cloud of flaming golden-red hair. […] I began Chapter XII & have plunged into the Consciousness of Owen his wone self. […] Then I took the Old to the Grave of Peter; Bard & *Ofydd*. The Lichen is — the lichen is —. Lichen covers the word *Ofydd* on a Bard's grave.

TUESDAY 13 DECEMBER The little T.T. says I act like a Demon – like a Devil – in encouraging all her weaknesses & helping to dissolve away the grains of 'character' in her Spine. Yes, I fear I do do this. It is true – & I shall always do it. For the one thing I completely lack in my character is Moral responsibility for the 'character' of those who are part of my deepest existence. I give them – I give her my soul & my intelligence & my imagination & my sympathy – but what I never give is a grain of the damned little 'character' I've got myself! Here I am a secretive Miser – very possibly because I have so few of these 'grains' & I've got to make them go such a fucking long way! […] Yesterday I saw a Thrush – it may have been one of the ones that I've heard singing by Pen y Bont – sitting in the ditch by the road with head erect, defying not only Death for it had been dead many days, but defying Putrefaction & Decomposition! I thought of the words of Job – 'Though my flesh worms shall destroy; yet in my flesh I shall see God!' […] Today my wife & son in Wiston, Sussex will receive the £50 I sent – the last money I can give them for some while. They are both going to Bath to recuperate.

WEDNESDAY 14 DECEMBER I was so tickled by old NEB the Swan's behaviour. […] He was so cross with the cows for making a noise near him that he flapped his wings at them but when he saw that not only cows had the temerity to exist and 'to be counted among the living' in the same world as Swans but that a doddering old man & a grey-beard dog displayed the same assurance he could no longer contain himself but uttered his own name 'Neb' like an angry incantation.

MONDAY 19 DECEMBER Our pipes Freeze just like Hillsdale! [...] Very quickly with burning torches of paper & the sharp poker Betty unfroze great bits of solid ice from outside pipe of the bathroom. Then I asked what to do about the Frozen Hot Water which was frozen up-stairs in the pipes. She referred to her Father. I said 'I'll go there after I've put my head in water.' But Betty said 'It would be best to go now.' So I went. [...] At last Mr Evans, Betty's Father, what a subtle face he has, did make the hot water un-freeze – O Laus Deo! So Betty & her father saved us.

SATURDAY 24 DECEMBER The Papers say that Dorset roads & Sussex & Surrey & Kent roads are all Impass – able! The weather here has sunk into its own self into its own soul – & just left 'Matter' to revert as near as possible to its pristine Nothing!

MONDAY 26 DECEMBER Yesterday's tea & Presents under the EXECUTIVE of the T.T. was a success & we were all 4 so pleased & happy that the T.T. must feel that all her exhausting labours were Rewarded. [...] How lovely the T.T.'s little Xmas Tree did look! Olwen came down.

WEDNESDAY 28 DECEMBER I have decided that my living & the T.T.'s depends on my getting ahead with the *Owen* Book! Lulu wants me to try short articles & gives me – so magnanimously – addresses of his pet editors – & wise instructions as to just what they want. I still have at the back of my mind a feeling – almost of a prick of conscience – that I ought to take measures – go to Bangor or to Aberystwyth or even Cardiff so as to prepare for the worst by having some sort of lecture work but against this is my dependence on the T.T.'s helping me with my enema & also the fact of our social situation, being Mr & Miss. So my conclusion is – & also my line of least resistance is – to get on fast with my *Owen*.

FRIDAY 30 DECEMBER Icy cold rain showers short brief swift rapid – snow gone – bursts of Nordic golden lights, like melted queens. Their rings of massy red gold. [...] Well! up the lane I went with Old on the leash for he generally likes that best, the quaint Old, but dragging the Man in his wake! [...] She has been inspired by the idea of privately printing & selling in Instalments, or Serial chapter by chapter on the Book Stalls at the Stations my *Glendower*. She also had the idea of living in one room. Our heads the moment we are silent together turn like compass-needles to the Cold North of our coming Penury & what we shall do???

1939

1939 is a extended threnody. It begins with the death of 'the Old' and ends with the death of Llewelyn. In between it recounts the death of nations as the war deepens, and the completion of John's novel with the death of his hero Owen.

Lulu's death, John writes, 'is the beginning of the end of all of us,' but it is the loss of 'the Old' and the way in which John uses all his philosophy and his magical powers, so long in the learning, to come to terms with the meaning of death and with his own pain that is the main theme of the 1939 Diary.

Each year the diaries have become more abundant, the content more explicit, the style more idiosyncratic. From 1929 until 1939, stories are skilfully carried forward and other story lines added; preoccupations about the inter-relationship of 'the three incomprehensibles' – sex, nature and religion – gradually worked through; the creative 'slippage' between the mythical world and the real world ever more complex and assured.

The 1939 Diary is both the apogee and a finale. He signals his intention to change the character of the diary in the entry of 1 January 1940, with which these selections end.

WEDNESDAY 4 JANUARY More Snow falling! falling! falling! […] Fed the little birds scraping a place with my boots. Then went up lane & fed the rooks. Then I visited the Garden & knocked off – aye! but how I recall doing this at Hillsdale – the heavy snow from the T.T.'s precious Douglas Firs, the lower branches of which were bent down. Then I shaved & Betty came. Then I took the Blue Elephant as I ever do into the T.T.'s room, as a sign I've called her & have gone my walk – tho' she doesn't always wake. Then off up the lane. O how Brave – Oh how Brave O how resolute & brave was the 'Old' – four walking Snow-balls with a black mat on them – was he.

THURSDAY 5 JANUARY Frost – Frost – Frost! This freezes up the Snow & is a wondrous comfort to the two old Gents. The man & his Dog. […] I had Dyspepsia which I haven't had so long – but […] Damp Snow when it's new-fallen is ever a menace to me & the Old. It drags us down & chills us to the bone. But today with this divine frost & sun on the mountains all is well again. I feared I had done for the Old for he had a cold the first cold the old bugger has ever had!

SATURDAY 7 JANUARY Letters from my wife & son happily in Bath where the waters seem so to cure them both. […] The T.T.'s cold beginning all over again! due to her doing housework in these cold rooms. […] We are at a low ebb, a low ebb; our money low our prospects low & the T.T. bowled out with this cold. […] Took Old to Llangar Rectory. The Dee is out in Flood.

FRIDAY 20 JANUARY The T.T. threw the paper away & beat the air over Franco's advance (O damn the sleek little Traitor!). The Puzzle is – What are Chamberlain's real Motives? Is he a Pacifist? Or is he a greater hater of Reds than of Fascists? Or is he simply & entirely for Big Business?

SATURDAY 21 JANUARY I made the Foolish Mistake of discussing what the T.T. describes as GABBLE namely possible lectures in University Towns as a 2nd string when our Funds end. […] But some 'S. & S.' Advance may save me. But I mustn't think aloud my wild schemes to the T.T. for it upsets her. […] A lovely letter from Albert and Dora. […] The nicest and best Four Persons in the world! – Mr & Mrs Krick Senior &

Mr & Mrs Krick Junior. Also a very exciting letter from Peter at school thinking that he'd try Harvard for a year. [...] I did get such a thrill of that feeling which is the most wonderful I have about Nature – the accumulated sensations of long past generations pouring thro' me as thro' a Medium when I heard that Thrush singing in those trees yesterday by the marsh.

MONDAY 23 JANUARY The Fascists & Nazis are becoming so purely a set of reckless gangsters that it looks as if War couldn't be prevented even by our great Pacifist of Big Business. All the present fuss about 'Terrorism' of the 'Irish Republican Army' strikes me as purely Comical; when you think of Barcelona & Spain or of anything really serious.

TUESDAY 24 JANUARY The fields are green; but over this greenness, just as over the blue of the sky, hovers this curious faint spring-like diffused atmosphere, too faint to be called mist. We were anxious last night about the Old – for he had (poor aged one!) a fit of vicious indigestion that seemed like a Heart-Attack or an attack of the lungs. The T.T. put it down to the chocolate. But this morn in our walk his spirits were full of life. He went up the lane in front of me without a leash. And in front of me like a real hunting dog he scampered among the rocks of Pen y Pigyn.

TUESDAY 31 JANUARY The Vet arrived at Six last night. I was impressed by the Nervousness of the T.T. as if it was herself & not the Old the Vet was to Examine! But he was a very nice man – very gentle [...]. He said the Old suffered from bronchial & heart trouble due to his Teeth. At 7.30 the T.T. called me over last night to hear Hitler at the Reichstag. He was less of a lost soul & more of a real leader. [...] The Old decided not to go up Mountain, or up Lane even, this day. So I took him over the big Bridge & to Duddon. Here I hesitated feeling myself a great craving to go further. [...] I think after listening to the T.T. that I must be a bit more careful how far I take him for after all I still fear it was that walk in the heavy snow when he got snowballs great heavy snow-balls on every foot, that began his trouble. Yes, I will be careful for the T.T.'s heart is so troubled about the Old – & I don't want my 'courage' on his behalf, which is of course, really, my selfish imperviousness, to do him any harm. This Morning arrived the National Service book which the T.T. is studying – hesitating between putting down her name to take a refugee – no! not a 'refugee' but an English Evacuated City-Child – or to take First Aid Lessons in Corwen. In my own mind I am inclined to doubt whether American Citizens are included – but this point we will waive. The worst blow to us would be if all American citizens were compelled to return to America – but so far nothing has been said of this. But over this 'evacuated child' the T.T. hesitates because all our health anyway the health of the Ladies & (in a sense) my own – is a bit shaky & uncertain & doubtful. Reading the *Welsh Review* the T.T. is puzzled by the Mania in the Short Stories for the physically Disgusting. Is this a Welsh characteristic? Or is it that being so strongly spiritual they turn to the Disgusting as an aesthetic novelty; & can play with it? as we of English blood cannot do without going mad like Swift. Last night the most important psychological event with us was a strong Reaction – (after listening to Hitler's speech) – in favour of Germany & against our own subtle Propaganda against Germany; is not that odd?

WEDNESDAY 1 FEBRUARY Yesterday while I talked to John Jones the delicate religious Baptist Road Man there passed by my favourite of all tramps a tall gaitered sombrero-hatted big stick big bundle with a noble ruddy face & aquiline nose & as content & carefree & joyous as any man, well! a good deal more than most! [...] He had been in the 'Great War' at 'Mons' & he launched out into denunciation of Franco's bombing of those Fugitives. This he said was unknown in the Great War. He wished that Foch had been allowed to march into Germany. He wished we would speed up Armaments even more than we are doing. His attitude was patriotic & conservative. How queer that I have met many religious Tramps but never once a Socialistic or a Communistic one!

FRIDAY 3 FEBRUARY The Hardest Frost we've had this winter. [...] Betty unthawed, with torches of paper, the outside of the bathroom pipes – but I set out at 8.50 a.m. & called at her Father's; & he has just come – the competent but invalid Mr Evans. [...] On the way back near Mrs Evans (Betty's Mother's) toll-pike cottage there is water on the road – this had frozen. And I came striding along, like my father, making faces of joy after my walk [...] and in a second, owing to my steel horse-shoes up went my heels & crash! I fell bang on my back on that

1939 hard adamantine road. I hesitated – well! not much! about telling the T.T. but when I did she cried for sympathy – the tear of Tityos. 'Tis strange what pity of an imaginative kind the little T.T. can feel! I pray this Wren's eye of Pity exists – along with the rest – in the complex mind of the First Cause! I think the T.T. does good by being like she is.

SATURDAY 4 FEBRUARY Went as far as that little Thorn Tree by the green bank of the river to the right which I shall henceforth name by the name of Little Prickly. [...] I shall often refer to it as the Terminus of my walks now the Old's illness has shortened them. It grows quite alone on those clear bare green banks – 'Little Prickly' is its name! – for I cannot easily get near to kiss it as is my custom with small trees to which I have given a feminine name! [...] The day before yesterday I saw a Heron standing in the river & yesterday I saw a large Cygnyt (I can't spell it) I mean a little Swan only this one was as big as Neb but he had grey wings or brownish-grey wings! Is he Neb's son?

SUNDAY 5 FEBRUARY The T.T. tells me that she had one of those Terrible Arguments with Aunt Harriet last night about the trouble over Mr Roosevelt whom Aunt Harriet calls a Booby. The T.T. fled & sank down in her kitchen into a Pool of Misery! [...] Slowly & very carefully – very leisurely I am advancing with Chapter XIV – trying to gather up every old thread I've dropped since the start of the book – trying too to indicate how out of chance & confusion a certain stream of destiny begins to move; gathering all the rubbish of sticks & leaves & rubble & dead fish, like a flood – aiming at the river's mouth & the sea! My back still feels shaky. [...] I took Old nearly as far as Little Prickly but not quite. He has now had his medicine – which must have opium in it. He loves it & is so sleepy after it.

MONDAY 6 FEBRUARY Mynydd y Gaer was lovely & magical in the swift-floating lights & shadows & all the bare trees of the park & fields below the park seemed to be surrounded by a thin atmosphere of their own sap stirring under the Sun in every branch & twig. Returning I picked up a Snowdrop on the bridge & put it into a tiny wine-glass on our wood-block table by kitchen fire with our breakfast cups & there when I turned away my head for one second – this little girl-snowdrop too shy to do it when I was looking at her suddenly was open to the warmth of our fire – displaying her green heart! [...] I see Neb & his son Warp!

The Cymmrodorian is a cultural and patriotic Society whose object is to co-ordinate and direct the endeavours of the Welsh people in the fields of education, social reform and the arts.

TUESDAY 7 FEBRUARY Yesterday it was very exciting for me to see Neb with his wings extended, well! curved like sails, in wrath, advancing against wind & tide towards the reedy spot where Warp feeds so content! Warp said 'Warp' very bass. Neb said 'Neb' very treble; but Warp just remained in the centre of the stream watching while Neb invaded his feeding ground. [...] Last night the young Miss Jones of 'Henlwen' came to ask me to fill an absent one's job on her Cymmrodorion Meeting next Friday – & 'twas decided [...] that I should lecture for an hour (not a minute longer the T.T. decides) on Owain Glyn Dwr. I believe I shall have to make Notes to use for this lecture – the first time I have used Notes since living at Southwick I lectured in Hove! [...] However, I want to do it – for it is the Proper & Dutiful & Pious thing to do in Owen's own patrimony!

WEDNESDAY 8 FEBRUARY A letter from old Littleton yesternight. He has been in bed for a week he says with duodenal ulcer! Damn! [...] The T.T. says it is our family's morbidly puritanical & ascetic & aesthetic (all un-healthy) attitude to cooked meals that causes our ulcers. [...] I had the distressing task of telling my family at Wiston Rectory that I could not pay a 'sou' of the 'allowance' which I pay from my income though of course they've had all my patrimony all this year. It looks like unless *Owen* is taken by the Films!!! [...] I noticed last night that 'Warp', Neb's son, remained on his isle of reeds – & Neb had vanished!

SATURDAY 11 FEBRUARY The Vet came. He says the Old has a growth in his Bowels – whether cancer or not he doesn't know. He says in a week he will come again – he's given us some more Medicine – and give him a dose of Morphia & take out some of his teeth which are the cause of his bad heart which is the cause of his bronchitis. I took the Old today in Rain no further than the end of the path by the River to where Neb & Warp now are happy side by side. Is 'Warp' perhaps not Neb's

1939 son but his daughter? Aye! but we did so enjoy – the T.T. & 'the Man' – but poor 'Old' had to be left behind – the lecture on Owen. I had written 20 pages of notes but only used one but I think I hope I stopped ere the people were worn out. [...] I received my first Welsh cheque for 1 Gini! I was pleased.

SUNDAY 19 FEBRUARY The T.T. did launch forth on one of the most eloquent discourses I have ever heard her utter directed against St Paul and against all these ideas of men that trouble the world. Her revolutionary idea was that our entire notion of the nature of suffering comes from our own mind and is a mental idea & is worse than the real reality. She finally said she wished that Jesus & his mother had founded Xtianity on feminine lines, instead of St Paul on his masculine lines. Yesterday we had an absolutely thrilling letter from Dorothy M. Richardson about First & Last Things. The most deep & exciting letter we have ever had from the greatest & best Woman Genius in the British Isles! And a nice letter too from Gwyn Jones of the *Welsh Review*.

TUESDAY 21 FEBRUARY Took Old to Gorsedd. [...] These walks to Gorsedd being so short & easy prevent my having that physical tingle in the blood & deep breaths of the lungs and that nice effort of climbing & the heavenly excitement of a possible sight of Snowdon. [...] Thus I be thrown back on my 'elementalism' – that is my struggle to get a formidable happiness from Nature & the Elements [...] while I talk to another pair of staring eyes in some passing neighbour! [...] But the Old likes doing No. 2 at the Gorsedd because of the variety of dog smells, so I have to stand about round those stones. On this spot, as I stand & wait & Contemplate the Cosmos, two devils have bothered me – one a great big Turd, if you know what I mean, that the devil persists in suggesting ought to be popped into my toothless mouth – the other that curious old neurosis about my old flat chest growing into vast women's breasts! Thus I contemplate the Cosmos.

FRIDAY 24 FEBRUARY Hard White Frost with Ice! White Frost with Ice! Ice! Ice! Ice! Last night – I, the Great Weather Prophet – said to the T.T. 'Well! there's Snow about but one thing is Certain there will be No Frost!' [...] Took Old to Gorsedd. Met an unknown old man who was talking to Zachariah Williams (Zach the lucky captor of Missy-Red-Head with her pretty engaging soft eyes & her dole-bringing children). But the Old thinking I intended to climb *Pyg y Pyg* advanced resolutely before me past those three fortunate & *sturdy old oaks* who escaped the slaughter, when *purely for the cash*, 'they' cut down the Druidic Groves that used to adorn the hill. But when he saw I was not following him up the hill he sat down – and oh the woeful figure the poor Old did make – chattering with his teeth – dropping saliva & rheum from his grey beard & half closing his life-weary, struggle-weary, heart-weary eyes. But he is, as we, poor creatures of the Experimenting & Lively, & Gay, & Careless *First Cause* – adapting himself to his Affliction & getting *used to it*.

THURSDAY 2 MARCH *The Floods are out again*! Our Pen y Bont Mr Jones says he has lost no sheep. […] But the sheep & the Lambs are *everywhere*. Never could there be any spot on earth of like dimension, with so many *sheep & lambs*! You see them from our window – they are in our lane – in our road – jumping over the old tumble-down walls & the lambs following the mothers wherever they go – whenever the *floods are out* like this we get surrounded by sheep. […] I note that in clear frosty sunny weather thrushes use their shrill treble high-pitched *violin* notes the notes of a *stringed* instrument; but on a warm wet day like this they have a *liquid sound*, out of full throat, sometimes very nearly reaching the notes of a *Blackbird*.

MONDAY 6 MARCH The last event of yesterday was upsetting to the T.T., namely the sight of *the Man's feet* which the T.T. swore were worse than *any tramp's* – dirt – fluff – & raw flesh all mixed up together. But water is bad for eczema so the T.T. as Dr Davis at Cerrig y Drudion advised got *olive-oil* to clean them with ere putting on that miraculous ointment of Mr Lewis the chemist & binding them up. But today – for they respond to treatment – these *Gorilla toes* – I can walk with ease & comfort. […] But it was a horrid job & a very upsetting one for the little T.T. It bowled her out. I ought to do it regularly in some way myself.

WEDNESDAY 8 MARCH At breakfast the poor Old was tired – too tired & too weary to come out from behind the Man's armchair. The T.T. discoursed on the *Random* trials of life – one thing *by chance* on the top of another – and often together like bricks falling down. [...] There was the Old's illness & Morphia & now there is our worthy neighbour Mr Hughes pulling down the plaster – as he tries to undo the original mistake in the building of this house due to the lead-roof sloping inwards instead of outwards – pulling down the plaster in the ceiling of the window of the T.T.'s parlour. She wishes she had covered up her Purple Chair! New Random Bricks of Chance falling on her head. Mr Hughes as well as an unknown man as well as Mr Garner all came in & out of the T.T.'s Parlour. [...] Betty came to tell her it was still leaking & the T.T. told her to tell these three men: but the men had got into a Tavern mood & just teased Betty. This the T.T. heard & was indignant & went in. But they were very rough & uncivil to the T.T. And where was – 'the Man'? Where was the Man when 3 men were uncivil to the T.T. & Betty?????

After an initial misunderstanding (she tears up his newly-built terrace in a rage), the T.T. & the new gardener – whom John nicknames 'the Ghost' – get along well.

SATURDAY 11 MARCH The T.T. works in her garden with her Ghost Gardener. [...] I must tell you that feeling so clean after my Bath & always being so particular I thought proper to take advantage of my little slender Captive & so I did – making wicked love to her both after my fashion and à la that Master of the 'Glory of Life' Lulu! [...] Met Will Goch & gave the poor half-starved devil Nothing. But I forgot Will Goch's under-nourishment on the dole by noting how well the Old did No. 2. [...] At breakfast the T.T. discoursed upon the Cult of Simplicity & the Elements in our Family & our feeling that cooked meals are disgusting compared with tea & bread & butter. She eloquently described Marian's conversion to American ideas thro' Peter & how different Gertrude was from all of us – being interested in French things & having an artist's bohemian eye, & yet being traditional like the Aunts. And how Katie's ways & fastidiousnesses & driving impulses are those of a man! tho' they shout the 'love' of a woman.

TUESDAY 14 MARCH The T.T. doesn't like so much space in my Diary devoted to 'No. 2'! I suppose it is the result of all the crises in my own life when not being able to do No. 2 has made such a dent on my mind! [...] We have decided to try the experiment of only taking him as far as the Home in the morn – not up that Gorsedd hill – for the T.T. thought he looked so dead beat, as he came thro' our back yard. […] A mysterious Mist fell when up Mountain yesterday. And the only letter was from Huw Menai – full of Mist & Mystery about Messengers of the Graal; & quite as Obscure!

THURSDAY 16 MARCH Hitler's troops occupy Prague and 'Brat-o-slavia'! Mr Chamberlain confesses Munich Pact not kept. Mr Eden calls it Anarchy! Hungarians occupy Carpathia. Poles & Romanians begin to feel very uneasy. 'Hitler', says our 'ffermwr' of the Dee-Floods, 'Hitler is out'. […] I only took [the Old] a little past the big Ash – for last night his heart – it's his heart, not his digestion – was so bad about ten and eleven that the T.T. thought he would die. She gave him her own pillow. After leaving the Old in kitchen I went up Lane alone as far as the Gorge-Waterfall & Bridge – near the Homeric Fount with its broken Bowl – the Cistern is Broken at the Fountain – where that little Larch has come out as it always does in early Leaf.

SATURDAY 25 MARCH I set off up lane – & overtook a little boy aged 8 not long aged 8 I fancy! – who with incredible effort had got on his sturdy back – he has the chest of a Hercules! – a sack of coal (Sack to Zach!) for this was the 2nd son of the Red-haired Girl. His name is Wilfred Edwardes. I couldn't have carried that sack 2 yards but I did bear some of its weight as I helped the child tho' it rested on his sturdy little back. […] Today is the arrival of the Ghost to help the T.T. in garden. He will bring an Iron Mallet borrowed from Betty's Father. Oh I pray while the T.T. holds those Hurdles steady this Iron Mallet wielded by the Ghost won't strike her to the earth. Last night I finished Chapter XV of *Owen*.

SUNDAY 26 MARCH I managed more gently more tenderly with the Old in his No. 2 walk. Instead of dragging him by the leash when he wanted to give up & sit down I carried him in the way the T.T. does which is much easier than my way. Thus I got him into the sight of the H.R. Jones Houses & as far as the Cauldron steps. Then I let him go & he trotted in front of me every now & then turning his head round to see how the Man was getting on just as he always does. This method was a grand discovery or invention – for he didn't dribble in that way I dread so & he didn't look at me as if I was a vivisector. […] Then went alone to the Rhea tree & also to a pond which had sunk terribly. Neb I saw alone again. His young daughter-bride has left him.

TUESDAY 28 MARCH The Old Dies. The T.T. wraps him in her quilt. The T.T. will get the Ghost to dig his grave. We went out in snow & choose his burial place. The Great farmer-Butcher brought his meat. We showed him the Old dead on Goat-skin & said No more meat. The Ghost came […] and the T.T. carried the Old to his grave & laid him in it. […] Last night the Old went under sofa in bedroom till after we had gone both of us to bed. But I caught a look in his eyes when he was lying in my room – so wretched that I DECIDED that I would tomorrow – that is now today – call up the Vet & tell him to come & kill him. I woke at 7.50 with this in mind & it was far worse than I thought it would ever be to have to decide to call the Vet up & say 'Come and kill my Dog.' […] In my agitation over the Decision to call up the Vet I forgot to visit garden and I even forgot to call the T.T. & to take Blue Elephant into her room as a sign I had called her. But I took Old out. He was in kitchen in the centre of the floor. He did No. 1 very freely the second he was out against the garbage can & I let him do it. Then he walked down the lane – but kept stopping with his head turned to the wall like King Hezekiah. Then I carried him. We met that curious little boy who looks so sturdy & never speaks. I rested twice. I passed a dying Worm drowning slowly as they do on the road. But I went on carrying the Old & didn't stop to throw it over hedge. Got to Cauldron & un-leashed him. O how slowly paw by paw of his four legs he walked home by my side. He stopped to cough once or twice. I told him of my Decision to call the Vet to kill him. I told him that Oscar said we all kill the thing we love. For the last few days he has been abstracted from us cut off from us absorbed in the mystery of dying – & alone like all of us when we die. But walking he was not like this. He returned to full awareness & his eyes said 'carry me home' but I said 'I want you to do No. 2.' But his eyes said 'It is not necessary but I'll try just to please you.' And he made the little run he does before doing No. 2 but gave it up & walked on. He chose to come up the drive instead of the lane. […] 'I'll get home & go behind arm-chair as I always do in Kitchen' he said to himself. But on our mat by the Kitchen door he fell over on his side. I lifted him in and set him down. He fell over on his side again. I patted him & he jerked up his tail & jerked his head forward. Twice he did this. Then he was still. I went up and woke the T.T. & said I think he is dying. She came down in dressing-gown. He was dead.

WEDNESDAY 29 MARCH So much of her existence side by side with 'the Man' has been poured into that Old black form that she feels that her life is cracked & rent in some way. As for 'the Man' he is more selfish & tough & hard & impervious. But at the same time he do think & think of the Old continually. There has very rarely been, among people of the human race, a love equal to that – a devotion equal to that – an obsession & infatuation equal to that – which the Old had for 'the Man'. I see his face all the time. Well – for I don't want to lie about the Old – at intervals so constant that the Old would be pretty fairly content if he could know. […] What I feel is how irrelevant how trifling are all ideas save the idea of living things that can cease & yet cannot cease. But the look I think of most & shall see before me till I die is the look he used to cast round as he went in front of me on our walks to make sure I was behind him. I wish I had started carrying him before I did. For that did soon end the foaming dribble stained with blood that I used to have to remove from his grey-turning chin with sticks & straws out of doors & with paper when he lay down exhausted on what Katie so beautifully called 'the dog-lain mat'.

THURSDAY 30 MARCH Yesterday the T.T. cried so much over the Old that I shall always to the end of my days see how her whole face was distorted with grief. Her profile when she begins to cry is like an Intaglio of Grief already printed on my mind from the earliest days in Patchin Place. […] Yes, 'tis of the Old in his illness I keep thinking. But my conscience – that treacherous mis-leader – tells me it was that fatal walk up the lane in the heavy snow when he had snow-balls on all four paws. […] Well I was destined to kill the Old with my peculiarities. […] With 'Peculiarities' we save and with peculiarities we destroy. […] If I hadn't killed the Old that snowy day sooner or later I'd have done it by taking him – deliberately – too far.

SATURDAY 1 APRIL All Fools – All Fools! We are all Fools! […] Visited the Old's Grave & thought of he – lying so still on goat-skin down there & wrapped up in the T.T.'s patchwork silk quilt of such bright colours. [...] I looked at the view past a certain fir-tree beyond the Dee Bank field whose branches floated and swayed – and still – though he is dead – float & sway in the grey blue air against the vast distance & the slopes of Moel Goch just as at Montacute one of the firs near the Phelips' Drive used to float on the air against the blue smoke of the village as I noted it from the Dressing-Room of my Father; where, thro' the wall, I heard Nelly, in the Spare-Room, say to her Mother, my Mother, 'Why don't you say Good-bye to me?' when she was dying.

SUNDAY 2 APRIL At breakfast the T.T. uttered on behalf of the Old the very words uttered to Gertrude by my Mother – her only comment upon her approaching death – about being 'afraid of the spirits'. [...] The T.T. came up to me very stirred – & sad about the Old – whom she cannot help think of as himself ill at ease in the spirit world & not able to come to 'the Man' for comfort as she can. I worked for an hour at chapter XVI. [...] After tea the T.T. stood looking at the sunset. How lovely she looked! The T.T. was extraordinarily eloquent about the impossibility of personal life vanishing in annihilation or having anything to do with the dead corpse.

MONDAY 3 APRIL Took Blue Elephant in to the T.T. & told her 'hush! hush!' Up mountain as far as Grouse-Gate – Aye! what grand cries & curves & far passionate flights of the Curlews! [...] Oh dear! it's so important to get *Owen – an Historical Novel* finished & in their hands by June. Can I do it? Well – we shall see! The T.T. begins to think it looks doubtful if I can – & she doesn't want me to spoil the book by rushing & crowding the final chapters after building up so long & so careful a base, a foundation, & getting all the people so slowly realised and solid & established, and making them, or trying so meticulously to make them, actual & conceivable! Yes it would be a pity to spoil it all at the end of the book – the best part, & the easiest part, & the most convincing part, by rushing it all too fast.

TUESDAY 4 APRIL Rain! Rain! Rain! Warm rain! April Rain. April Rain! Growing Rain. [...] As for 'the Man' – he was confronted with – a very very rare thing with him! – a difficult Problem in the Construction or Architecture as Hardy would say of Chapter XVI. The 'Man's' chapters as a rule grow like oak-leaves in a Druid grove of their wone selves & with mystic slowness but this time – & we'll see what comes of it in Chapter XVI for it'll probably never occur again – it'll be all a damned premeditation.

THURSDAY 6 APRIL Met poor old Will Goch whose infirmities are increasing on him – gave him sixpence – one of these precious Tramp-sixpences – for cigarettes. But when I Boasted in my Smug Bourgeois way of how I lived on Milk – not referring to Orange juice & raw eggs! – he pointed out that it wasn't easy to 'diet' in these elegant & refined ways on Ten shillings a Week.

SUNDAY 9 APRIL I fed the Rooks & visited the Very Old & thought of all it meant when his four legs gave way in one collapse – & then a second later his head gave those two jerks & he was dead. Oh I wish I'd had a last word with him – one last word – as I followed his laborious ascent of our sloping drive that morning – & followed him round the house. He fell so completely & then was unconscious forever unless our souls are immortal – dogs & men alike – for we stand or fall together – of that I am absolutely sure. If we do not survive the Old doesn't; & if the Old doesn't we don't! […] I could see the Old lying in that old Patchin Place patchwork silk quilt. I saw the wall – like that of Romulus, built without cement by the Tiber! And I saw the tiny stream itself running running with its rippling sound over a big flat stone – and I thought, 'here are the two opposite paradoxical things we have to do – let all memories, all relics of the dead be embalmed & lie in Egyptian Monuments thro' all time – such is one aspect of our act of faith – and the other is to, yes, to sink as far as we can all memory, reverence, love, lastingness, & relics of our dead, aye! and our own fond struggles towards survival into the Nothingness to which all things flow, flow, flow, like this little stream near the new wall built by the Ghost and near the Old's grave.' […] The sun-sparkles on the Dee were like Weymouth Bay.

SATURDAY 15 APRIL Last night […] I was seized with complete exhaustion. I struggled on with a page or two of Chapter XVI – the most difficult chapter by far of all my book! Then at 8 p.m. the T.T. came up & told me to go to bed. […] I was glad when the T.T. came for I had a hurting in my bowels, a new thing of unknown cause – but when the T.T. put her arms round my waist it slowly vanished. And I slept like a log. [...] I did do my Greek & Welsh lessons! These I shall do on the eve of the Judgment Day or the Wrath of Hitler. [...] The T.T. found two Blue Hyacinths – fragrant Towers of Bloom like young Sohrab in Matthew Arnold's poem – blown off by the wind.

MONDAY 17 APRIL At breakfast the T.T. gave me some very grave & serious Criticisms of my Book. 1st that by dandifying him so I had made Owen un-sympathetic to myself – a fatal flaw! Second that I have been too fussy about details & getting my characters in & out of cupboards & closets & chambers & dressing rooms. Third – that I have so many characters with weird names that it is confusing to the reader – who has to look back to see who this or that fucking person is! This is very serious. Well! tho' she says it's too late to improve & to rush forward with a clear simple dramatic tale – I don't think it is too late.

SUNDAY 23 APRIL O deary I! Elizabeth wrote privately to the T.T. that Will would probably have to have Gasterenterostomy but the family knows nothing of this & Will himself only refers to X-Rays that he'll have shortly. Perhaps the X-Rays will show he needn't have it – but I have no confidence in X-Rays. Aye! how well I recall old Dreiser taking me to that hospital in N. Y. when he saw my operation.

MONDAY 24 APRIL I suffered from that discomfort in my belly not having [a] real stomach but my bowels & I only drank one bottle of milk last night. I have now come to the conclusion that what I've been suffering from is gas wind a longing to fart – crack! crack! crack! in grand old Rabelaisian Gargantuan style – but an inability to do it because the 'wind' or gas hasn't got far enough down towards its vent. By damned ill luck just at the very second the T.T. came to bed I did break wind at last – in a terrific explosion & I cried out 'look at that Star!' wanting her to go to the window but she disregarded these words & afterwards when she was in bed said quite quietly 'Where is that Star?' & in a second had turned over & was asleep. But not so the Man who was too shocked at this untoward coincidence to sleep at once. [...] The Gwyddelwern Dairy is going to supply evening milk – so I am, at the T.T.'s advice, inclined to drop the Pen y Bont evening milk. Certainly I've never suffered from the 'wind' before. Babies are sensitive on these points & I'm like a baby.

FRIDAY 28 APRIL We all 4 go to dinner at the 'Hand' in Llangollen with an after-glow of the Gaiety of the 'Regency' & 'the Ladies' & see Shaw's *Pygmalion*. Very good save for his tiresome ideas. [...] Visited Old's grave & garden. Noted how the Hyacinths drooped on their great cool stems & how her special favourite, the Bleeding Heart (now in bud) drooped too – due to the White Frost & I noticed how there were long lines of frost curious to see on the green grass where the long shadows of the poles of the Wash-Line fell. [...] Had a most entertaining breakfast for the little T.T. was in her happiest & most humorous mood – aye! she nearly gave the Grave 'Petrushka' a laughing-fit by reason of her mischief – & how pretty she looked – like a gay happy mischievous little dancer sitting there before me on that hard chair while I reclined in my arm-chair. [...] But what threw her into so gay a humour was a book, a grave yellow-covered scientific-looking book, on Vegetarianism, by Anna Kingsford. [...] She opened at a lurid passage about the heroine moaning & shrieking & swooning. And what made her want to go on reading was the question what had this swoon to do with Vegetarianism. But the grave 'Petrushka' had to retire to his Study ere this link between swooning heroines and vegetarianism was made clear. Aye! the mischief of a girl's amusement over the contrast between this chaotic world of reality & the ideas in the brains of men!

TUESDAY 2 MAY Went all the way to Grouse-Gate – where I waited listening to the Curlews. I got the peculiar pleasure I do get from imagining myself a Gorilla, slowly walking along, feeling the grass & heather & moss under its feet & enjoying the cold north-east air. And I thought that though all living things produced by the earth perish & leave no individual soul behind, yet – so I am absolutely assured – the material cosmos, in which a Gorilla like me walks, is not all there is! I was so struck by the vital energy, careless of the cold, with which the new brown buds of the new fir-shoots rise, burst, break, explode upwards, turning into lovely green candles of conquering life! And how the Stalks, the main sky-aspiring thin trunks, of these fir-trees force themselves above the green larches into the cold blue sky and sailing white clouds!

SUNDAY 7 MAY Yesterday, in the first field across the Bridge where that Hole, designed for drowning children is, I saw several

Cuckoo-Flowers. [...] The sunshine on all, but no human being save 'the Man' without his Dog – to see it! [...] Up his favourite Pen y Pigyn. [...] I stared at the gulf & chasms & precipices & the glyn of the Dyfrdwy winding into the mist – into the 'niwl' – & the Mist was hazy with Sun. The Mist had the power – how I envy the Mist! – of mingling into one all the four Elements. Water, earth, air, fire – all were Mist. [...] Had an exciting breakfast with the Old – I mean with the T.T.!! I mix my two Pet Animals, the live one, & the dead one!

FRIDAY 12 MAY Visited Old in Grave. Visited Garden. Fed Rooks. Shaved. Greeted Betty; & set off. [...] Went to Alwen straight across the fields. Met Serjeant Davies who stopped his car to ask if I wanted another Spaniel. [...] The infinitely tender & gently-sad smile he gave me when I said I'd never have another dog I shall not soon forget. For the 'Serjeant' knows what it is like to lose a person. [...] I forced myself to look into the Drowning Hole – where those little corpses are floating.

SATURDAY 13 MAY Oh my ignorance, my dull ignorance, of bird's songs! How it annoys me – really annoys me. When I think how my wife at Burpham one day taught me the songs of 30 Birds all heard as I stood by her side in one spot by the Arun. Think of the Rivers of my life! The Dove, the Frome, – (repeated after 55 years!) – the Yeo – the Wissy – the Hudson – and now the Dee. The Sacred Dee! I thought of the World-Soul inspiring one individual life after another & enabling each to draw from its predecessors strange ecstasies from the repeated sensations, under sun & wind & flowing water & hard stones, of twenty-thousand years of individual lives – strung together – strung together like beads of receptivity on a string of spirit – and able, when they are in certain mood of attention, to catch the sensations stored up in this Immortal String!

MONDAY 15 MAY 'How completely the Dead vanish' the T.T. wept thinking of He, '& we go on living!' Yes they pass & we – we go on with our living. [...] Rain! Rain! Rain! Up late at 8.15 Put on 4 Scarves but no over-coat to feed rooks & visit Old's Grave; & go on trampling down grass for a path. Up lane, up mountain as far as in sight of both Rock on Left & Rocks on Right & in hearing of stream under those flat stones where I always stand to worship the Four Elements. [...] I saw – high in the clouds which were blowing darkly from the North East – two great Buzzards as big as Eagles – soaring, swooping, hovering! […] The T.T. found one of the Old's familiar Biscuits which so devotedly she would chop up for him while he sat by her side as she crouched on the floor. The Tears Rained down from her eyes & fell on my hands where I licked them up.

WEDNESDAY 17 MAY And now I wish, O moral Reader, to reveal to you what may be a unique fact in the amorous history of our race namely that when I said as I always do in my most seductive & dulcet tone good morning to Olwen as she sits up, so sweet & alluring, yes, alluring, […] in her little chair in Aunt Etta's golden chair – & as I lightly touched her 'glowing side' as my Lord Byron would put it, I enjoyed what Walter Pater grossly & crudely calls a physical stir; but which I, to spare your moral feelings O paragon of virtuous Readers, will content myself with calling a Phallic Lift or excited Up-lift. Now, do you suppose, O Reader, that even Papa Karamazov was quite as responsive to feminine charm as that? for little Olwen cannot be much more than a foot high!

THURSDAY 18 MAY Yesterday at Two P.M. we opened a French Journal of *Métaphysique et de morale* & read old Professeur Jean Wahl's exposition of my crazy Ichthyosaurus Sensuality book. God! I feel an 'Impostor' (as a leading writer pronounced me to be – & God! in a sense he was correct!) – when I read the Perfect Lucidity of Monsieur Le Professeur de la Sorbonne directed to my irresponsible outbursts. […] Up at 7.45. Fed Rooks. Visited Old's Grave. 'I've got No Dog! I've got No Dog! Where is my Dog – where is my Dog?'

MONDAY 22 MAY Went up the lane past Zach's where I greeted my 2 year old friend, Vera, & out popped red-haired Missy-Mummy to see who was seducing her simple child & out popped old Zach to see who was seducing Missy-Mummy. […] Stared at a Cuckoo-flower to note certain tiny purple lines on its four lavender petals & as I did so listened to the Cuckoo. Noted carefully the purple lines or purplish-lavender lines inside the petals of Wood-Sorrel. For now ere it perishes – the Wood Sorrel opens her petals like a cup held upside down or held up before being emptied of its libation to Demeter! […] The T.T. claps her hands because the Government had not the wit to ask the Mothers about Evacuation before `arranging it! The mothers refuse to leave their men or to let their children leave them. This pleases the T.T. who is very very opposed to the whole idea of evacuation.

SATURDAY 27 MAY [The T.T.] told me at breakfast that she woke up with very disparaging thoughts of her character & personality, & in a thundering voice – which made her cry 'hush! hush!' lest I be over-heard by Betty upstairs or a very aged respectable tramp nearly seventy in the yard – [I told her] that the ultimate triumph for any girl was to give complete, exquisite, & unbounded delight, infinite delight to a man at Bed & Board – as perfect between the sheets & the cause of immense pride & satisfaction by her talk & her listening. *Voilà – en bref –* it is enough! Her own 'creative work' & manias are legitimate side issues.

SATURDAY 3 JUNE Woke at 7.30 & stayed with eyes tight shut in blazing Sun – enjoying with purity – how odd! – the feel of the T.T.'s little form huddled as she instinctively always does in her sleep against my Iron Spine. [...] As I lay with eyes tight shut in that Blaze I enjoyed what I used to enjoy as a child that is to say the Colours of Dark the Colours of Black the Colours of the 'Abred' or Bottomless Abyss. [...] Purple & Blue are to me the colours of the Abyss of the original Nothingness out of which all came! [...] Thought of Old's black body after he died & lay all morn on kitchen-floor – for I liked to see him lying safe dead. The T.T. put the goat-skin under him; & then did wrap him up decent and comfortable – but I slipped my fingers under the quilt at intervals in the day and tugged at his hair, saying, like the Cardinals to the dead Pope – 'Very Old are you there!'

SUNDAY 4 JUNE I find I must have lied or remembered wrong about the Colours of the Ultimate Dark; for tho' I was absolutely correct about the Purple which was more luminous & resplendent than I even expected – there was no shade no tint no tinge of Blue! Did I invent that Blue? A lot of brown a lot of yellow & this Luminous Purple but no blue at all!

MONDAY 5 JUNE The 1st thing I was conscious of was the T.T.'s slender white soft little arm raised as she lay on her back to shield her eyes from the Blazing Sun. [...] I know she wants me to pull the blinds across the open window. Instead of that I just lie with eyes shut enjoying those Colours thro' my shut eyes! [...] Fed Rooks. Visited Old & chanted to him 'I've got a Dog! I've got a Dog!' as I used to do to control his amorousness. I don't think he liked that chant & yet I chant it now when he is so helpless! I chant it when he sleeps – just as I enjoy the blazing sun when my Other Pet Animal sleeps! I am a devil – but neither of them mind for they know that though I am a Turk she is under my ribs & he is leashed to my Memory.

TUESDAY 6 JUNE She read a bitter, savage, unkind attack on Lulu's *Love & Death* by Muggeridge. How these young men of a left tendency do loathe Lulu. Why is that? Why should Muggeridge of London loathe Lulu while Jones of Cardiff worships him – because South Wales takes seriously Sex – Nature – Religion – these 3 Incomprehensibles & worships them – whereas Mr Muggeridge knows all about them – they are not any longer Mysteries to Mr Muggeridge. But to Jones & to me & to Lulu, tho' we quarrel about them, they are everything.

WEDNESDAY 14 JUNE I have changed since I came here my attitude to happiness for I now believe in letting happiness come or go as it likes while I concentrate on the act of — enjoyment. This act of enjoyment is a diffusion of the act of love by which I mean what Casanova not St Paul would be thinking of! I mean I ravish the 4 elements and embrace them & mix myself in them & completely forget myself in them except as their 'ravisher' – no! hardly that even – except as a point in the space with the awareness of enjoying them in this sense of ravishing them or possessing them. Now since this process of enjoyment is an active process it is independent of independent of independent of all my chance moods and feelings. It is a feeling but it is an active 'feeling' which is independent of all the passive feelings that come & go outside our will. This is an Act of the will & nothing can stop it save great pain and death! How much better therefore is this deliberate and willed enjoyment of this Cosmos of the 4 elements than the 'happiness' in which I used to believe; oh! how much much better – because in my power. [...] Oh! how much better than that old ecstasy I used to so elaborately plan ways of attracting down.

MONDAY 3 JULY Up at 7.45. Fed Rooks. Visited Very Old

down under sod & thought of every detail of his death & of those final jerks of his old head – & then that terrible grim look – like a hooked Pike – an expression of savage defiance of Death. An expression I've never seen on the Old's face in life – a look of abysmal wrath with Death! The protest of Living Matter at Bay.

SUNDAY 9 JULY Everyone says 'we've had enough rain' & I think that is true as far as the Hay & Gardens are concerned – & true for the River too which is now full & swift & brown. But it is not true for what I enjoy most of all & go by most of all – 'sef', as we say in Welsh – the Mountain Brooks; all these are still very low as is what I call the Homeric Fount! […] Just as I wrote that, the memory of Northwold came on me with very overpowering force. It was because I've just had breakfast after going by the river-path & the drowning-hole to the Duddon which is very black & full of water! […] I decided this morn walking to the Duddon that the only thing to be really proud of would be to put our 'I' the 'I – I – I' the 'ego' aside & live in the 'I's or 'ego's of other living creatures! The T.T. contemplates a Book on the 'I'. The T.T. returns at 2 o'clock from her visit to Dee Bank in high excitement which excitement, which childish excitement and high spirits was soon brought a peg or two down, by her 3 elderly Teachers.

TUESDAY 11 JULY Fed Rooks. Trod Paths. Made love to Old in grave clinging to his form much as he used to cling to me – & he knows it not! […] At 4.45 I set out. Went beyond Rhea Tree; watched with delicious & lewd joy the Lesbian love of two heifers, both tall & comely, one mottled & the loved one black. Saw that the tadpoles in the 'Estuary-visited-by-the-Moon' were gone – Where?

WEDNESDAY 12 JULY This morn I got the greatest thrill possible to me from any Garden – to be vividly conveyed back down the years to Northwold by smelling a Phlox. Aye! aye! that smell of Prussic Acid – beautiful! like the smell of those old killing-bottles for butterflies – the reverse for them – but for Powys Ma., & Powys Mi.! How they bullied Powys Ma. for writing his name like Powys sha as if it were Powys Shag, with the 'g' of 'shag' left out! but at Northwold oh! oh! how happy Littleton and I were – & the smell of Phloxes over all! The happy-smell the smell of pure happiness!

John meets his son in Cardiff for the day and then joins Phyllis at Chaldon for a brief holiday. His old friends Bernie O'Neill and Louis Wilkinson visit.

MONDAY 17 JULY   Woke at 8. Called my son & kissed him, shaved in his room & we fell into such an exciting conversation that it was nearly half-past-nine ere we went down to breakfast. [...] I told him I was like water seeking its level & he was a good egoistic child getting what he wanted by sweet persuasion & firm will. [...] Then we talked till lunch in my room or his he lying on the bed I in armchair. We talked a great deal about lust of various sorts, about madness and about mental tricks & devices – and about harmless & perilous lust & about the confessional.

TUESDAY 18 JULY   Arrived at Chydyok. [...] Pouring Rain. [...] I heard the Reef bell of the Light-Ship on the Shambles so loved by Lulu. Looked out of the window at the Weeds in Lulu's garden – at the weeds in Lulu's garden – the weeds the weeds the weeds in Lulu's garden! The Weeds!

WEDNESDAY 19 JULY   Up at 8 didn't go to bed till 12 – either yesterday or today – but was recalling with violent outbursts loud & Rabelaisian those ancient wayside episodes & characters & above all Sayings – *logoi* of queer ones & of naughty ones & of reckless ones of the remote past – all dead. Thus do I live again the Past; our Past, which was Imaginative then & is Imaginative still – with BERNIE. [...] We meet as if we had never parted & yet we only see each other once a year! Gertrude doing it all as she does all for Katie – all for Theodore – and used to all for Lulu; and did all for my Father. [...] I had a lovely walk along the dangerous grassy cliff – down toward the White Nose. Gazed at Portland & at Chesil Beach and at the Nothe or rather Wyke Hill. Saw a Marble White Butterfly – a Marble-White – these butterflies remind me of old Littleton of my Father of Maiden Castle of Redcliff Bay! They carry my Memories on their wings. Those black dots are my memories. Black dots of Marble Whites! The Memories of a Maniac.

THURSDAY 20 JULY   Louis comes & goes! [...] I walk back with him to the White Nose; look at Lulu's house & Alyse's boat. All was lonely & bare. [...] Then I walked down to the village & visited my old friend Mrs Legg. Then I visited

Theodore & tho' Violet tried to hush him for fear of it exciting his wounded head, where a blood-clot goes pulse! pulse! throb! throb! tick! tick! all the time. Yes where a blood-clot a Blood-Clot a Blood-Clot dances a devilish dance in his great head – he talked very very freely to me of his feelings in this illness; he exposed himself and his feelings & his self-contempt and his unequalled Originality. Theodore's Originality into which even as I came down lane towards him I enter – with an awed sympathy & became Theodore who is far Oh! by far the most interesting and unusual Person in the British Isles – in Europe – perhaps in the World Today! [...] He has a depth, an originality, a subtlety, that makes a popular chap like Thomas Mann seem a Tedium of the Ordinary – & Bernard Shaw a pedantic Clown. I listened to his fears, his terrors, his fancies, his extraordinary remarks, with awe and reverence. I became a boy listening or rather a young lady listening & I felt devotion for him.

John and Phyllis leave Chydyok on 21 July, stopping off in London and Cambridge before returning to Wales on 24 July. While in London they see Stravinsky's ballet Petrushka *in which a magician brings to life three puppets – Petrushka, the Ballerina and the Moor. Petrushka loves the beautiful dancer but she shuns him, feeling only terror at his bizarre behaviour. The magician turns Petrushka back into a puppet with a head of wood and body stuffed with straw. In the last scene the ghost of Petrushka appears on the roof of the theatre.*

SATURDAY 22 JULY Yesterday afternoon we went after we arrived at the Hotel to the London Library. Here we paid Seven Guineas and ten shillings & gave Lulu's Swiss address & Ralph's grand name – & a great Personage in a velvet jacket called 'Sir Charles' did appear before us & caused to be brought to us to take away at once Lloyd's Life & Carr's Life – not of Lloyd & Carr, as this sounds, but of Dostoievsky. All this is in connection with S. & S.'s desire that if I can do it as they want it done I should write a proper life of Dostoievsky. I felt like an extravagant Gambler at Monte Carlo with 'Sir Charles' in his velvet jacket as the 'Croupier' at the Roulette Tables. [...] Then we had tea – I entirely forget where – & walked to Covent Garden. We went to Covent Garden Theatre. [...] What we went to see was PETROUCHKA & it was far more moving than I even had expected – in brief – Petrushka watched his DOUBLE.

SUNDAY 23 JULY Yesterday it was such a thrill to me the

greatest since I have returned from America to take the T.T. round Cambridge. We had Coffee & Tea, no! I had Malted Milk at Thurston's, opposite Emmanuel College a place which I nickname 'the Lesbian' because it was always full of lady students from Newnham & Girton. [...] The 1st College we entered was Downing. Then we went to Emmanuel & then to Christ's – but we didn't see the Mulberry Tree. Then we went to Corpus & looked at the Old Court and St Benet's Church. Then we went into Queens' after looking at Catharine's & the Master of Queens', a grey haired layman like 'Sir Charles', saw us peering through the bars into the hall & summoned a Scullion from the Kitchen or Buttery from ovens that had cooked for Erasmus to open up the hall. [...] Then we sat on a seat by the water-meadows watching Jersey Cows enjoying themselves & listening to the Wood-pigeons.

MONDAY 24 JULY Here at the London Library the T.T. left me at 10.30 & went off to do her shopping. Then, God bless my soul! what a frightening & teasing & vexatious time I had – trying to find out among those Iron Shelves books for myself on Russia & on Dostoievsky & all I could find were the books of old Dreiser & Dorothy Thompson & the works of Trotsky! The moment I left the protection of these well known names I staggered over the dizzy iron bars with Notices at every turn 'Put out the Light!' 'Put out the light' & then 'put out the light!' I seemed to come bolt upon innumerable works upon Needlework. What a Purgatory for a writer to wander about on iron lathes hunting for Histories of Russia; & forever returning to the same spot with all the works in the world on Needlework! At last the T.T. came. She took me to a little tea-shop where she had coffee & I had malted milk & she gave sixpence to the lady-like Proprietress. I grudged this largess. Then I poured out my woe about the books to the T.T. till she spoke to me quite severely & told me to pull myself together and even went so far as to tell me that we had better hurry off to the British Museum for a list of books on Dostoievsky if I couldn't do better & show more wisdom in this Club of 'Sir Charles's'! I begged her to return there with me before we assumed that I had thrown away Seven Guineas at Sir Charles's & so she did & at once all barriers fell before her. She boldly explained to a competent Mr Fallon what exactly it was we needed – & this made it possible for me to describe my wretched groping between those iron gratings &

Mr Fallon did chuckle & he said 'Tis too big a Library for that – you must have help! So he brought out about seven huge Catalogues & even a drawer of files & both the T.T. & I took notes of useful books on Dostoievsky & of one absolutely indispensable history of Russia in 4 volumes – an absolute Masterpiece. All this we owe to the T.T.'s talk, so direct, to Mr Fallon.

WEDNESDAY 26 JULY I talked to Betty about a little cousin of hers aged 14 whom Mrs Evans, Betty's mother brought back along with a Parrot who used to use Obscene & Foul Language taught by Sailors but is now reformed – out of Mrs Evans' own Salopian village – Mrs is a Salop – Mr a true Welshman. Little episodes from our time in Cambridge pass thro' my mind — how we sat in the cricket-field of Jesus watching tennis-players & seeing 'coloured' undergraduates, as we would say in America. And how the official on the look-out for Irish bombers told us of the activities (differentiated) of the Gardener & the Grounds-man. And I recall, as we walked by the Boat-Houses studying their armorial bearings & trying to see fish & seeing a boat with four oarsmen & no rudder – how there passed by, having evidently tantalised most exquisitely a pipe-smoking respectable common-grass-frequenting 'voyeur' who (like myself in former times) got ecstasies of transport from such sights – a girl of about 16 with a younger girl whose skirt – catching in a flash the vice of Petrushka – she wickedly did rumple as they walked past together evidently feverishly excited by the excitement of the timid, respectable citizen on the bench. This little Vignette of ravishing obsession, now so mild & easy to forget, but formerly unforgettable – I discoursed to the T.T. upon, as we made our way towards St Andrews St. And now it comes to me mixed with the smell of the red rose on my table!

THURSDAY 27 JULY Made love to Old in his fashion – which after all isn't so very different from my own! [...] How I used to drag him from my couch to the chest of drawers, clinging with all four paws to my left leg – & thus I had to move across the room 'clop-clop-clop'! like a cart-horse being loved by a little Bear!

MONDAY 14 AUGUST Found the Fields drenched with Dew & the Sun in little tiny diamonds of divine white light glittering on the flowing water each one of these glitters like a microcosm yes I say a microcosm of the Holy Spirit. Dazzle! Dazzle! on the dark waters of the Abyss! [...] Then I followed the flood-ponds & there was green pond-weed – duck-weed green as sea-weed in the glittering sun against the brown clear water. In that great Barn of the old battlefield was an open door & a grey rump of a heifer with its tail swinging in the way Hardy loves to describe, one of these anonymous generations, & the reflection of a huge red-trunked Sycamore in the flood-pond & that trimly-grown very ancient Elder-Bush by that old Barn, where the Tramps sleep, became an actual tree. [...] Worked contentedly at the tragedies of Others in my Chapter XIX.

MONDAY 21 AUGUST A day like yesterday (no sun, no wind, no sky, no rain, no dew) a Neutral Day! à la Thomas Hardy. All waits – all expects – a queer ominous day a day of Menace a day of the waiting for War to break out. A day of feverish activity in Danzig – but of hushed expectation all over the rest of the world. Up at 7.30.* [...] Found a little pool of water – surely it must have rained in the night, or could that be dew or melted fog? or was it the tears of Tityos, the Titan, over the Imminence of War.

WEDNESDAY 23 AUGUST Russian Pact with Germany – this is a Catastrophic Event to which all these sultry dark hot days have been moving. Well! the issue is now clear! DEMOCRATIC CAPITALISM against both Tyrannies! Will America show her hand at last? Any moment now we may have War. But still the T.T.'s Old Moore's Almanac says 'Peace'. Will the Stars save us? The two unknown Factors remain America & God! Both of them hesitating!

SATURDAY 26 AUGUST At breakfast we talked of the war from every possible point of view of the fact of the ordinary quiet Germans (so exactly like us) & so much easier to understand than French or Russians – all sitting just as the T.T. & I are over our kitchen stove & not wanting war at all – feeling it inevitably rolling up. What is the Mistake we are all making? Here we all are heading for a ghastly world-catastrophe – & even yet at the bottom of our hearts we common people are not [...] convinced Pacifists. Why aren't we? That's the question! If we all were & if these shameless rascals, like Hitler Stalin Mussolini Winston Churchill Lloyd George, could be kicked out by us how excellent it would be. But we are not philosophical Pacifists; still less Christian Pacifists; we have a lot of stupidity & simple patriotism & simplicity and heroism and Rhiteous I mean Rhighteous – fuck the word! I can't even spell it today – Righteous Anger & our Rulers' propaganda exploits this! Hitler has the power of working up war-hate, war-frenzy in himself, as well as in others. [. . .] The weak un-righteous aspect of our Democracy is Capitalism, tiresome stupid blind chaotic brutal Capitalism! This Capitalism – fuck it! O fuck it! you see pure & calm Reader how your garrulous old gentleman is rendered violent by the war. The Old Clown (safe in his arm-chair) sees it through! This Capitalism uses our Empire to its base personal ends. Oh how I hate our gentlemen with their Investments!

WEDNESDAY 30 AUGUST After the Thunderstorm the air is cooler & there is an East Wind. [. . .] [The T.T.] says that here in the old world people are used to preparing to give up their lives & to suffer privations & other sufferings and all for these old fields & walls & gardens & buildings that they do love – more than love. And they do all the while, even in peace-time think of — I were born at Longburton — Do'ee know Piddle-Trenthide? — Me wold dad came from Petter's Irrronmongers, Yeo-vil! — think of as in some way more important, beautiful, precious, valuable, & lasting than the generations who have lived there – or the individuals whose grand happiness is getting a holiday to walk thro' these vistas of Memory.

THURSDAY 31 AUGUST Went up Mountain to Rock on Left & thought of being dead & of others millions of others being alive. Tried to analyse & dissect my feelings about the war. I find desire to stop the physical pain that the war will cause to so many. I find a deep animal-like annoyance that Hitler & Mussolini (& above all Franco) shall not be forced to say the words 'We are beaten.' Oh how much more do I hate Mussolini than Hitler & how much more do I hate Franco than Mussolini! I find a love of the pure dramatic excitement – as Homer says – a tragic situation & a world-crash – that there may be a 'subject for song' for the men to come on the earth. But I also with all my reason & soul & body feel I must constantly hope that the war – however it may gratify various monstrous & outrageous instincts in me – should be avoided. The T.T. says that if it weren't for propaganda we should understand the German or at least the

Nazi feeling towards Hitler. She says we are all the victims of propaganda. I have an impulse to contradict this; but she may be right. A letter from MEA [Sally] describes the birth of John Francis Cowper Powys at 7.40 A.M. on Saturday August 26th. This is Nature's retort to the prospective slaughter of the human race – another Head appears & forces its way into the world to off-set the 'powerless heads of the dead'.

FRIDAY 1 SEPTEMBER War Begins. [...] Up at 7.40. Heard John the Town Crier – just as we have always imagined we might hear – but instead of 'the English are coming!!' he announced we must all get our GAS MASKS today in Corwen. [...] The Ladies – our ladies – the Mistress & Aunt Harriet are elevated & exalted & thrilled & excited – think of that! over 70 & Aunt Harriet 75. They are keen on going down for their gas masks. Their excitement & war-sympathy is rather a trial to the T.T. who is thus compelled [...] to do what she describes as lick her own wounds in solitude & harden herself when she goes to the Ladies. [...] She decided – to my wonder & respect – to go to Mrs Doctor Edwards the organizer of the Evacuated Children & offer her services when they arrive tomorrow.

MONDAY 4 SEPTEMBER Fed Rooks. Trod path 4 times. Talked to Old in Grave & thought of how amorous of 'the Man' he used to get after his supper when he used to sit up by my side as I lay on couch writing until I would have to rise & respond to his absorbing intense amorous love. I used to sing – then – but I think that he didn't like my singing then – as an amorous man wouldn't like a girl to hum & drum when he was making love to her – so that now by his grave I tend to dodge – so as not to remind him or myself! – this memory of how I would sing: 'I've got a Dog! I've got a Dog! a Dog I've got! I've got a Dog!' I think this was teasing. And what a cruel devil I must be in my inmost bones to tease an absorbed lover so, to whom his love was such an irritant & urge! But this I can say that I used to force myself to get up from lying down 3 times sometimes! May be 'twas the effort of making myself do this – copying the 'Little Flower', St Thérèse, who would leaveher sewing at all interruptions at once – that caused me to sing this cruel song! My conscience could force me to get up but not not to be teasing to the Old Bugger when I did get up!

SATURDAY 9 SEPTEMBER I was up at 7.30. I looked – as per

usual – out of my window at the new houses, one with a chimney over which we have lately seen such a queer-shaped Moon & over which I now see the sun thro' the fog rise above the Severn. Looked at the wall [...] & at that old Mare I know so well with a white star on her brow & a short tail always working – to brush flies away from her beautiful buttocks! I wish they wouldn't dock horses' tails so short! 'Tis painful to me to see that short tail working – working like a little Piston – not able to reach the spread of those noble curved buttocks that fill 'wicked me' with bestial admiration. But then I turned & looked at her on her pillow – her face upwards but drooping just like a flower on her abnormally thin neck a little sideways. Not a wrinkle on her face – her eyebrows arched so clear & definite. Her eyelashes – not so very long but as lovely as any long ones, closed against faintly flushed soft as velvet cheeks – her mouth just open – oh how engaging, winning, perfect! & her face a perfect Oval a drooping oval of a girl become in sleep a very young girl – a grown girl become a young girl again! Her filmy brown hair that descends – unlike that poor horse's tail clear below her buttocks – not visible at all – only that oval face exposed drooping, drooping, drooping sideways with the lips open. Had she been a girl after her first night, and after being un-maidened she couldn't have looked more bewitching & I thought: Mine! Mine! Mine! Mine Mine! Mine! Mine!

MONDAY 11 SEPTEMBER Last night I heard our big Clock [...] strike THREE when the T.T. had just come to bed [...] But still, seven hours of oblivion – for this little creature who so often says 'I wish I were dead!' – is something. Seven hours of a sort of living death! It is of the greatest interest to me to compare my intense wanting to go to bed – and even when I'm neither sleepy or tired my feeling that I ought and also for some reason – I want – to go to bed! Now profoundly-psychological Reader, does this mean that in spite of the T.T.'s constant expression of a wish to be dead that in reality she is less pessimistic than 'Petrushka' who hastens and hurries [...] to drink the heavenly Nepenthe of Dream-less sleep!

TUESDAY 12 SEPTEMBER Put my coat [...] over the Grouse-Gate & looked at the green path that goes on further & at the Padlock. [...] It is the Mania of all Welsh [...] for barricading with old bedsteads & old doors & old kettles & old wire & old barbed wire & old brambles & old perambulators and old logs and old curtain-rods and old locks & keys any bit of land they have! This curious Trait I noted 25 years ago when lecturing for Mr Lloyd George's War Aims Bureau, in Pembrokeshire & Gwent. I tried [...] to go for the sort of walk I would have done at Bedford or Huntingdon or Stoke-upon-Trent – not possible! – for the smallest Welsh freeholders padlock little enclosures of nothing but Nettles!

WEDNESDAY 13 SEPTEMBER Yesterday I forced myself as I went up Mount to look with enjoyment at my own Shadow! This is very very nearly the most difficult philosophical thing and neurotic thing I could do; so terrific is my Anti-Narcissism & so fast & frantic do I the arch-sensationalist flee, away from my self.

FRIDAY 22 SEPTEMBER Darker still & rain in the Night. [...] Over North Wales lies a Druidic 'Niwl' – 'Niwl' – 'Niwl' [mist] as if the whole thing (with a clap of thunder) might meet its 'difancoll' [perdition]; &, like its leader Owen, vanish out of sight! carrying us, like Pryderi & Rhianon off to Gaer Side! Up at 7.20 but I woke at Seven. In future I must keep my fucking Voyeur's eyes – I speak here very very literally; for a true Voyeur like me, a powerful Voyeur, does yes! does actually penetrate erotically the resistance of what is surveyed – i.e. – it literally ravishes; plunges its bumble-bee-like proboscis into the maidenhead of the Scene it hovers over. I must keep my Voyeur's eyes open after I first wake up so as to miss nothing of the look of things out of window – & also to avoid going to sleep again.

MONDAY 25 SEPTEMBER Sometimes when I put my face in water I do what I used to do as a child at Shirley. I press my knuckles to my closed eyeballs & look at the beautiful colours & very rarely – today it was so – I see, like this, a multitude of heavenly Blue Stars. [...] I go as far as in sight of the meeting of the Rivers. No Tramps at all. What has happened to the Tramps?

TUESDAY 26 SEPTEMBER I was up at 7.15 & then putting my hand in my left trowser pocket for it was a cold morn I was astonished at a crackling there & it did turn out to be, not my cod-piece breaking up owing to old age, but an unopened Telegram. I put this funny little yellow envelope how much less noble telegrams are than when I was young! and how unpleasant a yellow & how little they are! They used to be big and a noble leafy brown hue – on the window sill till I'd dressed. [...] It was from old Littleton wanting the address of Mrs Meech the typist of High West Street, Dorchester; that Best by far of all typists. So I hurriedly fed Rooks. Embraced the Old, trod path once – did not shave – put my head in water with the only rigmaroles of a sacred kind, that I have regularly allowed myself still [...] – & they are all about Weymouth and Portland and my brothers & sisters & my Father & Mother and about Chesil Beach, and shells & sea-weed etc. Then I did hurry off to the Post. [...] On the top of Pen y Pigyn I did see one of the GRANDEST SIGHTS of my whole life – namely a great Brown-Bay Horse with one white star on forehead & one white fetlock [...] standing solitary in the white mist – misty steam issuing from both nostrils! – its back against the similar back of the Berwyn Range. I gazed with wonder. The horse stood like a Centaur on a Rock with its head & ears erect!

SUNDAY 1 OCTOBER Hugged the Black Image of Perfect Love & in mind did carry him to the Cauldron Steps & in mind saw him do 'No. Two' And in mind, & with my fingers in over-coat pocket where his leash still is – answered his love with weaker love.

TUESDAY 3 OCTOBER Made love or as old Bert used always with blunt honesty to protest 'Made Lust' to my little Bessarabian. [...] Sat on 1st bench looking at Lilium Speciosum – a pretty carmine lily. On 2nd bench looking at the Dee the Sacred Dee & the deep reflections of the Alders in its black mirror-steel water. 3rd bench looking at Cemetery to right & White Cock & grey walls & bracken to left. Hugged in a sort of ecstacy my Very Old. Is it not strange that now he is dead I love him as (though feebly in comparison but still in the same way) as he loved me! Yes, honest Bertie Master Absolute & my dear brother there is such a thing, & from Old I've learnt it, of love & lust working together! [...] Then in lovely sunshine & every grass-blade soaking wet with the Melted White Frost, under burning hot sun I went to Grouse-Gate where I roused a grouse. Here I leant on gate & looked at the green path, at the railings of chicken-wire & at the little larches. Here I forced myself to contemplate Nature; that pretty little path, those larches, that chicken-wire fence & far away, Moel Morwydd in thin clouds. And coming home I forced myself to enjoy the sun in my bones & with my knees and hands & skull like a gorilla. And I forced myself to enjoy my own Shadow. This forcing myself to enjoy my own shadow and to lean motionless on gate meant of course that I was flouting & defying my Anti-Narcissistic Mania according to which I run away oh so quick & always from myself. Thus – as I knew would happen – tho' I foxed the black-out – yet there remained even in the black-out, those queer nervous and quite mad physical-psychic feelings of all my pulses beating & a sort of swelling of interior Breasts!

FRIDAY 6 OCTOBER Last night the T.T. was more Eloquent than I've ever known her. And the more she talked the more Beautiful & Lovely she looked – which is by no means always the case with feminines! It was like watching a flower on a very thin stalk sway in the wind & utter words. Oh how thin her neck looked! That is to me one of the chief beauties in feminines – a thin neck! The thinner the neck the more excited I get & my fingers itch more feverishly to put them round this thin neck! When I was young my favourite quotation from the Poets was: '& with his fingers long & lean he strangled her in fiendish spleen!' [...] Up to Rock on Left I went – & stood as I always do on those gray flag-stones over the brook that crosses the path just this side of Rock on the Left. There are ferns in the cavernous space under these flat stones & these ferns stretch out between the stones. On these stones I stand daily and think of the Old's elephant ears when he gaily ran to catch me up and I think of the brittle slenderness (so it feels) of the T.T. 's waist – & I think *en masse* & *tout ensemble* of all 4 elements & I make the rippling trickle of water under my feet the voice of earth air fire water and I think of all the universe reduced to a tower of water; rising bell-shaped, from Nadir to Zenith. And then I think [...] how the resources of Life are not limited, nor its boundaries ended, by the Material Universe. Betty's mother came & had a cup of coffee & talked of how, in the end, sometime, Dad had to be told things; but better wait till a suitable hour & day!

FRIDAY 13 OCTOBER Talked alone in his shop with my dear old friend of whom we asked where to find a house when we first entered Corwen from Cynwyd where we were staying in the Spider House whose Mr Spider I have to so constantly Will to Forget by my private Black-Out! For, as you wise & profound reader aided by some super-Freud or Krafft-Ebbing must already have discovered (See how my hand shakes even writing of Spiders!) I am a Spider-Phobiac. […] In truth I am an Insect Phobiast or what might be called an Insect-Horrorist. I associate this with my peculiar Brand of Sadism – a curiously Feminine kind – for Dostoievsky over & over again – tho' his Sadism was more mental & spiritual than mine – introduces the Insect-Horror & even describes Imaginary Insects – & speaks of lust as The Insect in us. […] Well! I started this repulsive inset on insects because I associated. Oh how the war in my members or the inner war of my life including among my enemies 'dreams', as they are called, those Insects of the Unreal! is associated with this thrice-accurst association!

SATURDAY 14 OCTOBER Dark! Dark! Dark! no mist no dew no rain no sun only low-hanging CLOUDS very, very, DARK. […] I hugged the 'Old' with a flash of memory almost always available – & then I sway over that patch in the grass like a lover sways when he 'makes lust' […]. I am confronted with an interesting psychological problem today. Why during the last couple of Days I have been feeling a Wave of thrilling Happiness??? […] Well I would say the real cause of these Thrills of happiness is that we are now come to the Octave as the Catholics say of the birthday of that lecherous serpent & cushiony-worm John Cowper Powys that is – for my Mother kept her first-born in bed with her too long after he was born, for it was her thrill so to do & I commend her. All should obey their thrills unless they are directly – I'm not talking of in-directly – cruel! But it was at this time & in just this Derbyshire-like dark wind that I first was in the open air.

THURSDAY 26 OCTOBER Betty's Father is Better; thank the Lord! But they were all roused at the Turn-Pike 'bwthyn' by an accident to the Mail for the Mail-Cart ran into the 'Bryntirion' drive gate knocking down a Stone Post & so wounding the upper lip (cutting it clean thro') of the Mail-Man that he could only knock at the toll-pike door; […] he couldn't whistle to them for he had two mouths & thro' the upper one the wind kept whistling! 'Jimmy' took him to the doctor to have his second mouth sewn up. Fed Rooks but had to put the crumbs in the hedge owing to the rain making the lane a brook. Hugged &

loved the Old & carried him to the Cauldron steps – in thought! only in thought! But all – I say all – is in thought.

MONDAY 30 OCTOBER The great event of today was Betty photographing us as Nostradamus or Bishop Valentine and his Bride of Lammermoor's Ghost, or lost soul found under the Oak.

SATURDAY 4 NOVEMBER Up at 7.45. Then there emerged the Episode of the Indigestible Cake like a chapter in *Holiday House* – the Prodigious Cake. For in the special Tin a pretty ornamental Tin where the bread for the Rooks is kept away from Mice I found a bag of stale chocolate biscuits & in a paper-wrapper Half of a Plum-Cake. These objects seemed to me too good to be given to the birds but the Cake felt so sticky & looked so thick and so impossible to digest – in fact it made my stomach ache to contemplate it – that I hesitated about giving it to the Rooks for the sake of their stomachs. I thought 'the lane will be strewn with dead rooks!' but the biscuits were very dry & stale. […] Well, I gave it all to the Rooks, tho' God! how I had to wash my hands after breaking up that sticky cake! But what do you think?? Both Cake and Biscuits had been bought yesterday for our Visitors by the T.T. & cost nearly two shillings. Fed Rooks – God! Jesus! Ave Maria! Mary! Joseph! fed the buggers only too well!

SUNDAY 5 NOVEMBER Up late at 8.5. Fed rooks – trod Paths. Loved Old in Grave & took him his short walk. How warm his body is when I take him out of his Basket! Walked with him down lane – picked him up – & remembered how he looked at me before I took to carrying him to those Cauldron steps; & this time I followed him up drive which he chose rather than lane, watched him hesitate whether to pump-ship against the variegated bush & decide he hadn't the strength – followed him round house to the door where he fell on his side. […] Betty arrived with those wonderful pictures of Petrushka like Paracelsus calling up a ghostly T.T. his Undine. What a triumph for the T.T. to have done this under the Oak in the road & for our Betty to have taken these Photos. […] Far far the best Picture of the Man with his Bessarabian Captive ever taken! Twas only that Dead-Girl Mask, that Ghost-Girl, that Undine-Spirit, the 'White Lady of Avenel' Mask, that persuaded

1939 my Abject, my Choice, my Immortal Sprite to consent to be photographed at all. Oh oh oh I am so pleased to have this picture of the funny 'Terminals' – Petrushka & the Dancer!

MONDAY 6 NOVEMBER A wild Storm in the Night. Rain! South-West Gale! The River Rises! The Streams foam & rush down! [...] Fed Rooks and they were glad of it for their black forms were tossed about, like great ragged torn leaves! Could not tread Paths for each path was a stream! And when I told the T.T. this she said I had better stop treading Paths save now & again when I happened to think of it. This means never with me until I am specially told for as I tried with great difficulty to explain to the T.T in the Material world of Action I have a self-preservative way of not thinking for my self at all! I save yes, I save my energy in this manner – by never thinking what I am doing but doing it always by habit custom & conservative routine. I can do anything like this for I am very very Industrious but the one thing my deepest self-preservative instinct refuses to let me do, yes, refuses to let me do, is to think! [...] The T.T.'s garden brook was foaming down. It looked white with foam as it rushed into the fount at the bottom of the T.T.'s garden, the fount full of dead lives of leaves.

SATURDAY 18 NOVEMBER A Neutral Day a Neutral Day yes, a Neutral Day but if you dig into this day & winnow it & plummet it & analyse it you get a wonderful amount of subtle originality – showing that all Neutrality is a Cloak & a Camouflage. Showing that the Normal the Ordinary the Negligible the Commonplace – the casual, the unimportant, the undistinguished is really a 'false-face' like that Mask Rhisiart sent us from Glasgow that the T.T. put on & that was so Half-Born & Abject that it was indistinguishably like my Cimmerian Sylphid. Up at 7.45. This was less easy – I mean to get up – than always because my slender little Bessarabian Captive had drifted like a lovely little bit of flotsom on the criss-cross tides of this star-lit night into a position exquisitely provocative alluring entrancing to me. [...] Met as I came back swinging on a tree just above the worst turn of the hill & liable to [be] killed at any moment by a car – those two little perfect darlings little fairies – both boys 'Tylwyth-Teg' [...].

MONDAY 20 NOVEMBER Last night the T.T. WEPT for the OLD. I told him all about it this morning. She thought of his resolute & unconquered unconquerable Personality not that he loved her particularly she thought or that he enjoyed being Alive particularly she thought but that he just loved with the force of a black Bullet. He had the pecularity 'cynneddf' of being able to love. [...] That is what made the T.T.'s visage, if you can use such a word for such a half-born natural 'false-face'! distort itself & tears, as big as golden-crested wrens eggs, to trickle down cheeks.

TUESDAY 21 NOVEMBER Never have I seen Moel Morwydd look so like its name Mulberry. It was a great black-purple orb of rich wine-dark fruit. And the Arenigs & Moel Fammau were outlined very clear – between grey sky and black earth. [...] I was up at 7.35 & visited Old & took him his walk in a rush – but he did not mind – he minds nothing now! – & his little black figure under sod lies still on its side just as it did when it fell so sudden on door-step. That is a stab in anyone's side! Why didn't I kiss him before he was dead instead of after? You see the truth was I was so inordinately relieved that he'd taken things into his own hands & died just as I had decided to get the Vet [...] to help me kill him. [...] But a telepathy from 'the Man' – made him resolve to strain his heart to the breaking-point; & die to spare me the annoyance of calling up the Vet.

Gamel, Llewelyn's former mistress, is visiting them when Lulu dies, 2 December.

WEDNESDAY 29 NOVEMBER Here is a letter from Alyse saying Lulu has not had even a drop of water thro' his mouth for 4 days – owing to haemorrhage from an ulcer in the stomach 'due to trying to get nourishment from cream & honey'. He is riddled with ill-health and sickness. Think of this being in his Stomach – & not lungs at all. I must soon go and meet Gamel & maybe send a telegram from all to Lulu.

FRIDAY 1 DECEMBER A Telegram from Old Littleton who has had a reply to one he sent to Davos saying Lulu's condition Critical. O O O ailinon! ailinon! Damn! Damn! Damn! Gamel has no thought of flying to him & of course I am too selfish a coward to contemplate such a thing. But it looks bad. However! He has got through so many, so many of these last moments without any one of them really being the last moment. [...] But I don't like to see this word critical critical critical! [...] Yes, the rooks were whirling in a huge flock round our chimneys and trees & lane & garden! Just like 'Owen's Ravens' in the *Mabinogion* [...].

SATURDAY 2 DECEMBER It was when Gamel & Phyllis & I were in the T.T.'s parlour at breakfast – that someone came with a telegram. I imagined what it was & said the words 'Lulu's dead' as I opened it & then tho' I hadn't my spectacles & they had writ the telegram small I read it to Phyllis & Gamel 'Lulu died this morning'. We all three felt Numb & cold & not believing it or realizing it or understanding what it meant. Nature made us Numb & dull & cold – we became three cold lumps of Stupid Being – three cold stones on the side of a deep sea-tide. Stupid Beings & Numb & Dumb we became – and cold & calm talked of what Alyse would do with the Body. Whose body we hardly took in. And the word we need on the whole event is not forthcoming – for it is Lulu's own word we need; the word of Lulu, who has died so many times that we cannot believe it now. [...] I think one of them – was it Gamel or the T.T. uttered the words There it is! with true bone-rock red Indian American stark stoicism – but I bent this way & that very slowly in the wind – an old stump with a shoot and a stone beneath it and a stone caught up in its substance. O Lulu I want you to read all I am saying here for you love these exact details of death. Lulu listen! I am writing all these things for you – about how Gamel's face looked almost old & very white & how her painted lips were a little open – & you couldn't see her teeth or her tongue. And how the T.T. was like an intense puzzled frown on the face of that Hamadryad (Lulu) what you always showed us in the Moon. The T.T. recalled Bertie's death & she thought of Lulu's Brothers she did, & she said how it was the Stomach that bowled them all out – us all out – in so great a variety of different ways. Will Alyse bring your body in its coffin to bury it on the cliff at Chaldon where you wanted – or will she have you burnt & bring little bones & ashes. None of us have any vision of you Lulu; but then we know you were ever against such gullibilities. This is the line with which my daily Homeric Lesson begins on this morn of Lulu's death *ὥρη μὲν πολέων μύθων, ὥρη δὲ καὶ ὕπνου* 'there is a time for many words and also a time for sleep!' said by Odysseus before telling them about the spirits of the heroes & after the spirits of the heroes' loves & wives &

daughters. Gamel took my telegram to Alyse – 'and what may quiet us' I sent her – from *Samson Agonistes*. [...] The truth is we do not accept Death. We say our *ave atque vale* & lo! He is walking by our side! [...] I carry a stone for his cairn from the Gorsedd brook up the Mountain.

SUNDAY 3 DECEMBER A showery day – thin rain but bursts of sun but the rain will win. [...] Up at 7.30. The whole East was rose-colour *Couleur de Rose*! The T.T. noted it with a funny gasp or sigh or cry & then was asleep again. I forgot to say how since Gamel has been here – – I think it was on Thursday night – I made love to the T.T. à la Lulu! How fitting how right – that that name of his should have come in my mind anyway to be identical with making love! [...] I was horrified by hearing Tessy the dog bark in that shed at Zach's deserted house. But lo! while I was passing, she leapt out of that hole in the shed which she must have been enlarging with her paws all night and was free.

MONDAY 4 DECEMBER Yesterday we all 3 went up the Mountain to the spot a little to the right where you 1st get a glimpse of the Grouse-Gate where there is a 'llannerch' or a clear space in sight of the other Carnedd Llewelyn of Eryri & here we have made a Carnedd Llewelyn ym Mhowys. We carried milk & honey mixed, exactly as Circe directs – the daughter of Lulu's Sun – & sweet wine and meal & we got water from that deep rut in the way & John played the part, 'the Man' played the part, of the Priest of Dis – & did kneel & say *πολλὰ δὲ γουνούμην* [Pray long prayers] & the two girls did answer *νεκύων ἀμενηνὰ κάρηνα* [for the powerless heads of the dead]. And the silver light on all the floods of the Dee & on all the pools in the path did light us down.

TUESDAY 5 DECEMBER Snow several inches deep over all! Snow on Lulu's Body. [...] To my amazement after for so long hearing of its difficulty & reasons against it completely puzzling to me the T.T. suddenly told me last night that our bed was in the Spare Room now. I forgot & went into our usual one – & how flat & desolate – just as if it had been Lulu's Bedroom – our bed looked. But I was so delighted once more to have my Girl between me & the Wall. [...] And to have this advantage over the slender shape – formed as they be – is a wondrous satisfaction to my tough & peculiar and conservative nature – the great advantage is that you can in my fashion (tho', may be, not in Lulu's) make love to them so continuously that there is none of that embarrassed shock that I am not keen on – you can 'make love' like that and they don't know or (which is the same) are compelled to pretend they don't know, to what usage they are being put! […] I got my stick & beat the laden branches of the T.T.'s Douglas Firs. […] What pleasure it is to knock snow from fir-branches and see the branches leap up so thrilled to be released from this heavy heavy heavy weight.

THURSDAY 7 DECEMBER Damn! I cannot keep my bloody fucking blasted spectacles on my nose my characteristic nose – so aquiline & hawk-like & yet so broad in bone like a Berber's nose! broad with the breadth that reveals my profound Commonsense. Our true essential character is most of all revealed in the shape of our skull and second to that in those dainty bones of the Nose that so soon fall away leaving that hole that hole that hole in the centre of our phys., that all skulls reveal! That's what skulls have: 4 holes – 2 eyes, one mouth & a nose-hole. The massive commonsense of my nose will not last as long as the intense fanatical shape of my skull! Then I forgot – thinking so hard was I about finishing my book for the T.T. last night hurried me up reminding me that me Money was very soon coming to an end & it is necessary & I know well for myself it is – to get this book off to the Publishers so as to come out in the Spring. I took 2 stones to Carnedd Llewelyn.

MONDAY 11 DECEMBER Went to Old's Grave & took him his usual short walk which he is now getting used to, knowing very well his incapacity. He wants to be carried all the way. But I make him walk back so as to do No. 2. And he falls dead on doorstep. […] Here are two letters from Alyse one Dec. 1 before Llewelyn's death & on Dec. 3rd – after his death. They have taken a Week coming but are not opened by Censor. The Censor must now realize that it is a matter of Death – if not of Life & Death – if not of 'Love & Death'. […] The T.T. has – well! we talked about such things after tea *à propos* of Alyse living on at Chydyok – has a notion of our moving to Weymouth to be near the family. I am very very sluggish to this idea for I am very happy & wonderful content where I now do bide! We also talked – *à propos* of Lulu's Death – which is the beginning of the end of all of us – about the T.T.'s future life when Petrushka be that Ghost on the Roof.

THURSDAY 14 DECEMBER Up Mountain to Carnedd Llewelyn. How wonderful Zach's House & Eben's & Mrs Morgan's (for all 3 live there) looks Empty – with 2 fowls, two heifers and a flock of sheep, in full possession! [...] When I came down I had to struggle with my fuss fuss fuss about my enema the T.T. having been literally forced by me & by the Mistress to stay in bed. [...] Then she got to feel cold & miserable & nervous in that chilly bedroom & so she had the Mistress's coffee by my fire & now is putting on her clothes; thus will she be able to 'give' me my 'enema', but I am awfully fussy about 'enema' & the mistake is that I can't manage it myself & so be independent. I tend to fuss so & work myself up about it. And thus it is an extra worry when the T.T. is shaky or ill. Damn! I am a weak blurter! I walk to little Prickly & Persephone in darkness.

FRIDAY 15 DECEMBER I woke early & the T.T. as I held my arm across her felt burning hot. [...] Girls asleep girls asleep girls asleep how like dead girls they are. I said at last when I got up: 'you are bad, you are burning!' She said not so! feel my forehead! So I did & behold it was cold as snow, but cold with the natural coolness of a girl's forehead not with the ice of a dead girl. So joy did pour thro' me – pure joy!

MONDAY 18 DECEMBER Up at 8 for I heard our World's End Clock say so in its high pitched Powys-Fadog Forceful & yet screaming voice! Fed Rooks but waited to give the Sparrows & blackbirds their chance. Had a long conversation with Old in Grave but he said he would rather sleep on & take his rest. However, I dragged him out because I am so fussy about his doing No. 1 & No. 2. Then I let him go thro' the process of dying & he was so glad to lie down in quiet & so I left him. 'I'll see you again' I said – but he made no answer.

TUESDAY 19 DECEMBER The T.T. took her own temperature last night. It was 101! ailinon! ailinon! [...] Yesterday I worshipped the Cross in the Druid Stone by two lights! 1st the Moon travelling with her horns upright & both pointing North. 2nd the lamps of the Church coming thro' the Windows. How I have prayed there to that erect Phallic Symbol for 3 years that Lulu might come safe home. No use! no use, no use, no use! so I won't pray to it any more at all!

WEDNESDAY 20 DECEMBER How I did scold, rail abuse

implore beseech abjure conjure back-jure her to REMAIN in bed – & yet when – finding for herself, for nobody else did so, that she had a TEMPERATURE of One Hundred & ONE! – she stayed in Bed of her own volition & really did refuse indignantly to be disturbed either by 'the Mistress' or 'the Man'. Were those persons, in plain words were WE pleased & satisfied? On the Contrary! The Mistress got Frantic & wished she were back in America rather than Helpless to wait on her Daughter next Door – & as for the Man he cut his thumb with his boot-lace, kicked over the hot water, forgot to drink his orange juice, didn't shave, forgot where paper was to tie up parcels & in the end took an Hour cursing with string & brown paper & sealing wax to do up his MS for Mrs Meech.

THURSDAY 21 DECEMBER The T.T. because she has bought boxes & presents & sweets disregards her convalescence completely & goes in & out & in and out like one quite well! [...] Talked to Old & was very gentle & tender to the Poor Old, now out of sight out of sight out of sight like Brother be! Like other Brother be, like Nelly be! [...] Up Mountain choosing my Stones in the Lane as carefully as David chose his from the brook! Of course not only will the Carnedd mean in itself the Massacre of many Fairy Cups but it'll also mean a rational excuse for the Man to tread another path, tramp tramp till bruised stalks yes till bruised stalks become by slow degrees dead stalks having been trampled to death – like the laborers at the Pyramids – to build a Monument to Prince Llewelyn! [...] I went to the Duddon & stood on that plank-bridge in the darkness pondering. Oh how I always do imagine that bridge of a shaky plank along with the mud the dark greenish-black water & its reflections all – I say all – carried up outside space & time where the Nothing of Death turns out to be All there is!

FRIDAY 22 DECEMBER Last night at 7 p.m. I talked with Gertrude at 'Chydyok' over the long distance Telephone. At first Gertrude could not make out who was talking to her – & she was very nervous & kept stammering & stuttering & at one point went away altogether. She must have been cooking over the drawing room fire. She said Katie had gone to Wool to meet Alyse & that they would be home at 7.30 – any minute in fact! She said 'Don't tire yourself dear Jack.' I think she would say that if I were carrying her coffin.

SATURDAY 23 DECEMBER I gave the milk boy his tip & left Billy Beckett & the Postman's for Betty to dole out as she thought. Then up Mountain. The first thing I saw there was or were the Arenigs & these great wild mountains I have never seen more beautiful – black below – with Snow on the ridges and a faint rose-colour on the snow! On I went. Saw that queer Sheep half Black half White – black headed & black tailed watching the landscape on its feet – & a great woolly white one chewing the cud & watching the landscape as it lay among the green reeds & the twisted thorn-bushes & grey rocks. The shed door of the Dead Eben's barn – the red-haired girl gone too – wide open – even the last fowls gone. On I went, past the rock I link with Bendegeitvran! On still past the Homeric Fount. On between the larches – until coming near the Gorge, where the stream is low now from lack of rain, and then looking back to that pale green sky I saw the two peaks of SNOWDON. On I went until I came to Rock on Left. [...] Then at last Carnedd Llewelyn to which I added 2 smooth flat stones from our lane. I put my gloves for my knees & my cap at a little distance for Lulu to sit on. I had no ewe to kill so that he could drink the black blood & recognise me – but I surveyed his corrugated forehead & his well-combed beard as he hugged his shins. As I came back I heard one grouse say Go away Go away & another say Get Where? Get Where? & then I heard a Stone-Chat & a Jenny Wren.

SUNDAY 24 DECEMBER I climb to the top of Mynydd y Gaer to finish my *Owen* there, carrying pen, ink & paper to where I imagine Owen's body burnt. [...] Just as I finished writing with my back to the East – and South – and my face to the North – I felt the wind behind me South-East and suddenly over my shoulder into the stone chamber shot a ray of sunlight from the risen sun & made a piece of white crystal – that quartz – gleam like a diamond.

WEDNESDAY 27 DECEMBER Mr Hughes is ill. [...] Talked to Old & took him his usual walk; wherein, as in a Play, I go thro' the exact details of his last walk and his sudden death. Then I went to post. [...] I did meet Will Goch & of Eben's death we talked & Will's last *esprit de voyage* was that We all have something 'Funny' about us! Something Funny! & Will Goch went away chuckling! [...] I return via Zach's cottage, empty now, & was very very glad to find watching me [...] both the black and

1939 the brown heifer. I have learned the deepest piece of Wisdom possible to learn in these last dark days from heifers – young girl cattle. They were chewing the cud […] & they told me to endure & to enjoy enduring was the secret of planetary life. 'Just go on enjoying enduring' they told me. I walked to the Duddon in the dark & stand on the plank.

SATURDAY 30 DECEMBER Yesterday evening we read Alyse's typed copy of Lulu's Last Words & Message. His words are straight-forward & natural. But this letter of Alyse's, quarrelling with me about Lulu, is of the greatest interest. My Lulu is the humorous poetical earthy stylist & original personality; hers is what her life-illusion loved best (& Lulu was influenced by it) pontifical, grave, ungullible, distinguished. All those old lovely 'I'm such a dizzard's gone! gone! gone! The T.T. & I agree that the 'feminine companion' […] of any & every man hath as her chief role to blow up (like blowing up a pricked 'tire' of a bicycle) her man's life-illusion – & while she does this she influences that life-illusion (turning it subtly towards her own) so that the Lulu with whom John lived – 'the younger Dome' – as we used to say after Mary Gillyflower said his forehead was 'Dome-like' – was an un-blown-up Lulu whose great Cult of The Truth, coeval with the race, – hadn't got under way! But this Lulu – my Lulu – is not less of a personality or less of a true personality – but much more! for as with all the great humorists loved by Lulu – like Chaucer for instance – the power to see yourself […] as no more 'right' or 'grand' or 'truthful' or 'distinguished' than those others – but just yourself, with all your weaknesses – was one of Lulu's most bewitching endearing & in the deepest sense of all, sagacious peculiarities. And this peculiarity, Alyse naturally and inevitably just because she was Lulu's feminine companion set herself to destroy! – so that we have not what Lulu feels & thinks but what 'We feel and think'. This Two in One being so powerful an inner circle that it promotes itself to Infallibility & the T.T. does the same with me. But there was more identity, before we met, between the T.T.'s character & mine & her imagination & mine than between Alyse's nature & Lulu's.

SUNDAY 31 DECEMBER A variegated day – a sort of abashed, shy, & bashful day – a faintly weeping faintly blushing day a day in which all manner of moods flicker & fade again! The Old

Year is in his Second Childhood. [...] Patches of blue sky – showers of soft warm rain – faint gleams of sun on snow-mountains. Melting icicles. [...] It is as if on his death-bed the poor old year – this tragic year – were – like Lulu, in those *logoi* of his, so reverently preserved & typed by Alyse, were recalling yes! – just like Lulu – various vignettes of the Past. [...] Fed Rooks talked to Old & took him for his walk to do his business. Poor Old devil I think I must stop worrying him with these walks. I've gone on now for 9 months the time a human embryo takes to be born! I think in future I'll talk to him but stop bothering him with walks. Let the Old rest in peace if he has not already risen to immortality & intense happiness – far beyond my stupid, gross, earth-ridden view! Betty told me Mr Hughes had Pneumonia so I went over there before starting on my walk. I went bustling in – breezy over-riding patronising condescending noisy blustering boisterous in my grand Harris-Tweed suit & with my gloves & stick – just as if the descendant of John Johnson, Tanner of Dereham, Norfolk, had become a genial sixpence-bestowing *Nouveau Riche*! And I can tell you I soon came out again [...] with DEATH giving me a polite and civil *congé*. [...] I start at 4 & take two stones to Carnedd Llewelyn & return by Five o'clock.

MONDAY 1 JANUARY, 1940

New Year's Day.
Bank Holiday in Scotland.
Dog and Annual Motor Licences renewable.

Aye. The Very Old.

Here also lie Llewelyn
&
Bertie
&
Nelly
&
Father
&
Mother
&
Tom Jones
&
The Catholic
&
Arnold.

'Oh my soul, keep the rest unknown.
It is too like a sound of moan
When the charnel-eyed
Pale Horse has neighed.
Yea none shall gather what I hide!
Why load men's minds with more to bear
That bear already ails to spare?
From now alway
Till my last day
What I discern I will not say.'

Thomas Hardy
['He Resolves to Say No More']

INDEX

[No attempt has been made to index recurring themes (for example, what Powys called 'the three incomprehensibles – sex, nature and religion') or important personality traits of John Cowper and Phyllis Playter, or their convoluted relationship: these are topics which recur on virtually every page. However, the index will assist the reader in recreating the story of 'the two terminals'.]

56 q. 1 - Duncan

60 religion
sex
reality - fantasy

61-2 romantic love
/passion

74 decision to dispose
of Magdalen

78 bowels

84 7 Dec family photos

149 Sadism
family resemblance

163 automatic spirit-
writing

176 personal philosophy
as a defence

198 secret life illusion

217 brain

232 nature &c

257 bodily sensations

258 prayers

261 we are all mad

272 self-soul

285 war news

— that Reverberation of a World ...
"on Golden Bough; she wants ...
was well when I returned
...th I felt impelled to give ...
mother of seven children w...
T.T. was pleased when I ...
was not in the least vex...
I had to deal with a terr...
which took the heart o...
indeed of the day — aye!
Alack the Day! But dear ...
at last and I did emp...
her & she looked very ...
better. I rejoiced at this ...
The T.T. went to ...
lunch. And finally after ...
T. came back & I had ...
then we ...
my Book ...
Cable w...

... talk, ... more inclined to ... watch her form under the bed-clothes & watch the flames of the fire in happy meditation! But making the effort to talk I unluckily made use of my malicious Reservoir of unkind commentary on the belligerency of women. This suddenly to my astonishment completely upset the T.T. & she burst into an eloquent diatribe against the English character whose self-control she said always hid ... a dark cavern of Malice that forever kept seeking out in furtive ways. I ... she said, but ... as any ...

... knew but could not fin...